This volume refracts the light of *agape* through the prism of scholarship, enriching with color an understanding of law that is often all too grey. It will provoke lawyers to pursue their true vocation of building a relational society where our knowledge of love and justice is central to what it means to be human.

—Jonathan Burnside, Professor of Biblical Law, Law School, University of Bristol, UK, and author of *God, Justice and Society: Aspects of Law and Legality in the Bible* (Oxford University Press)

An excellent collection of essays on an issue at least as ancient at the Bible and, perhaps surprisingly to some, as important as any humanity is facing today.

—Miroslav Volf, Professor of Theology at Yale Divinity School and author of *Flourishing: Why We Need Religion in a Globalized World* (Yale University Press)

This magnificent collection of essays arrives precisely when it is most needed – at a time when a nation held together primarily by law is severely fractured along economic, racial, gender, and cultural lines, at a time when empathy and hospitality of neighbor toward neighbor are profoundly lacking. In asking whether law can be reimagined as a manifestation of agape – love of neighbor – the book offers the richness of the Protestant and Catholic intellectual traditions, to provide the reader with a thoughtful and lively exploration of the question. The biblical and ethical tradition has long wrestled with the relationships among law, love, and justice. The essays draw deeply upon this wisdom to grapple with the question in all its complexity and in a wide variety of contexts: criminal and tort law, immigration and elder law, corporate and intellectual property law, international law. This bold project is by no means naively undertaken: agape is not a sentimental feeling but rather a moral imperative that generates a framework for law reform. Indeed, while the essays cohere organically around the agape theme, they speak universally to all reformers committed to the task of making law more humane, more fair, more just – to promote the dignity of the human person and to bind us more closely together.

—Angela Carmella, Professor of Law, Seton Hall University School of Law and co-editor of *Christian Perspectives on Legal Thought* (Yale University Press)

The tension between law and justice is an ancient problem, but it takes new institutional forms in societies structured by modern law. *Agape, Justice, and Law* explores the relevance of Christian love to unresolved problems of punishment, property, immigration, international order, and other questions of justice. The contributors are some of the best thinkers in contemporary law, theology, and philosophy, and their essays will inspire new approaches in readers across a range of disciplines.

—Robin W. Lovin, Cary Maguire University Professor of Ethics *Emeritus*, Southern Methodist University and author of *Christian Realism and the New Realities* (Cambridge University Press)

Agape, Justice, and Law is an important and exciting advance in the ongoing project; its authors share with many others – the critical and constructive analysis of law in the United States from a Christian theological perspective. The genuine theological disagreements that run through American Christianity are reflected in the essays, but as a whole this collection demonstrates both the profound commonalities that its authors share and the power of Christian thought to illuminate and challenge our understanding of the law, its limits, and its potential. The essays are all sophisticated and challenging, and many are startling in their depth and novelty: to mention only two, Lucia Silecchia on subsidiarity as the lens through which we can think about a major social issue (care for the elderly), and Thomas Berg on rethinking intellectual "property" in the light of God's universal gift. This is a book for everyone, whether Christian or not, who understands the inescapable role, for good and ill, that American law plays in the present and the future.

—H. Jefferson Powell, Professor of Law, Duke University and author of *The Moral Tradition of American Constitutionalism: A Theological Interpretation* (Duke University Press)

AGAPE, JUSTICE, AND LAW

How Might Christian Love Shape Law?

In a provocative essay, philosopher Jeffrie Murphy asks: "What would law be like if we organized it around the value of Christian love, and if we thought about and criticized law in terms of that value?" This book brings together leading scholars from a variety of disciplines to address that question. Scholars have given surprisingly little attention to assessing how the central Christian ethical category of love – agape – might impact the way we understand law. This book aims to fill that gap by investigating the relationship between agape, justice, and law in scripture, theology, and jurisprudence, as well as applying these insights to contemporary legal debates in criminal punishment, judging, torts, elder care, immigration, corporations, intellectual property, and international relations. At a time when the discourse between Christian and other world views is more likely to be filled with hate than love, the implications of agape for law are crucial.

Robert F. Cochran, Jr. is Louis D. Brandeis Professor of Law at Pepperdine University and Director of the Herbert and Elinor Nootbaar Institute on Law, Religion, and Ethics.

Zachary R. Calo is Professor of Law at Hamad bin Khalifa University in Doha, Qatar, and Research Scholar in Law and Religion at Valparaiso University.

Law and Christianity

The Law and Christianity series publishes cutting-edge work on Catholic, Protestant, and Orthodox Christian contributions to public, private, penal, and procedural law and legal theory. The series aims to promote deep Christian reflection by leading scholars on the fundamentals of law and politics, to build further ecumenical legal understanding across Christian denominations, and to link and amplify the diverse and sometimes isolated Christian legal voices and visions at work in the academy. Works collected by the series include groundbreaking monographs, historical and thematic anthologies, and translations by leading scholars around the globe.

BOOKS IN THE SERIES:

Agape, Justice, and Law: How Might Christian Love Shape Law?, Robert F. Cochran and Zachary R. Calo

Great Christian Jurists in English History, R.H. Helmholz and Mark Hill QC

Calvin's Political Theology and the Public Engagement of the Church, Matthew J. Tuininga

God and the Secular Legal System, Rafael Domingo

How Marriage Became One of the Sacraments, Philip Reynolds

Christianity and Freedom, edited by Timothy Samuel Shah and Allen D. Hertzke

The Distinctiveness of Religion in American Law, Kathleen A. Brady

Pope Benedict XVI's Legal Thought: A Dialogue on the Foundation of Law, Marta Cartabia and Andrea Simoncini

The Western Case for Monogamy over Polygamy, John Witte

Agape, Justice, and Law

HOW MIGHT CHRISTIAN LOVE SHAPE LAW?

EDITED BY
ROBERT F. COCHRAN, JR.
Pepperdine University, Malibu

ZACHARY R. CALO
Hamad bin Khalifa University, Qatar

CAMBRIDGE
UNIVERSITY PRESS

CAMBRIDGE
UNIVERSITY PRESS

University Printing House, Cambridge CB2 8BS, United Kingdom

One Liberty Plaza, 20th Floor, New York, NY 10006, USA

477 Williamstown Road, Port Melbourne, VIC 3207, Australia

4843/24, 2nd Floor, Ansari Road, Daryaganj, Delhi – 110002, India

79 Anson Road, #06-04/06, Singapore 079906

Cambridge University Press is part of the University of Cambridge.

It furthers the University's mission by disseminating knowledge in the pursuit of education, learning, and research at the highest international levels of excellence.

www.cambridge.org
Information on this title: www.cambridge.org/9781107175280
DOI: 10.1017/9781316796931

First published 2017

A catalogue record for this publication is available from the British Library.

Library of Congress Cataloging-in-Publication Data

Names: Cochran, Robert F., 1951- editor. | Calo, Zachary R., editor.
Title: Agape, justice, and law : how might Christian love shape law? / edited by Robert F. Cochran, Zachary R. Calo.
Description: Cambridge [UK] ; New York : Cambridge University Press, 2017. | Series: Law and Christianity | Includes bibliographical references and index.
Identifiers: LCCN 2017006682 | ISBN 9781107175280 (hardback)
Subjects: LCSH: Christianity and law. | Law—Philosophy. | Law—Moral and ethical aspects. | Agape. | Christian ethics. | Love–Religious aspects–Christianity.
Classification: LCC K460 .A35 2017 | DDC 261.5—dc23 LC record available at https://lccn.loc.gov/2017006682

ISBN 978-1-107-17528-0 Hardback

RFC: To Dallas Willard, who got me thinking seriously about the place of the Kingdom of God in this world.

ZRC: To Cathleen.

Contents

Contributors

Thomas C. Berg is James Oberstar Professor of Law and Public Policy at the University of St. Thomas, Minnesota, and an expert on law and religion, constitutional law, and intellectual property.

Zachary Calo is Professor of Law at Hamad bin Khalifa University in Doha, Qatar, and Research Scholar in Law and Religion at Valparaiso University.

Robert F. Cochran, Jr. is the Brandeis Professor at Pepperdine University. His books include *Christian Perspectives on Legal Thought* (Yale) and *Law and the Bible* (IVP).

Alberto R. Coll is Professor of Law at De Paul University College of Law and author of *The Wisdom of Statecraft: Sir Herbert Butterfield and the Philosophy of International* Politics.

Timothy P. Jackson is Professor of Christian Ethics at The Candler School of Theology at Emory University. He is the author of *Political Agape: Christian Love and Liberal Democracy*.

Lyman Johnson is the Robert O. Bentley Professor of Law at Washington and Lee University School of Law and Professor of Law at the University of St. Thomas School of Law.

Jennifer Lee Koh is Professor of Law at Western State College of Law. She is a graduate of Columbia Law School and Yale University.

Charles Mathewes is Carolyn M. Barbour Professor of Religious Studies at the University of Virginia. He has written several books on Christian theology and politics.

Linda Ross Meyer, JD, PhD, UC Berkeley, is Professor of Law at Quinnipiac University and author of *The Justice of Mercy* (2010).

Michael P. Moreland is Professor of Law at Villanova University School of Law. His scholarly interests focus on law and religion, torts, and bioethics.

Richard J. Mouw was appointed Professor of Faith and Public Life at Fuller Theological Seminary in 2013, after serving twenty years as the school's president.

Jeffrie G. Murphy is Regents' Professor of Law and Philosophy at Arizona State University College of Law. He is author of *Forgiveness and Mercy* (Cambridge) and *Getting Even: Forgiveness and Its Limits* (Oxford).

Lucia A. Silecchia, B.A. Queens College, JD, Yale Law School, is Professor of Law and Vice-Provost for Policy at The Catholic University of America.

Darryl L. Tippens, Provost Emeritus, Pepperdine University, is author of *Shadow and Light: Literature and the Life of Faith*. He is University Distinguished Scholar at Abilene Christian University.

James Boyd White is Professor Emeritus at Michigan. His books include *The Legal Imagination*, *When Words Lose Their Meaning*, *Living Speech*, and *The Gospel as Conversation*.

Nicholas Wolterstorff is Noah Porter Professor of Philosophical Theology, Yale University. His books include *Justice: Rights and Wrongs* (2008) and *Justice in Love* (2011).

David VanDrunen, JD, PhD, is the Robert B. Strimple Professor of Systematic Theology and Christian Ethics at Westminster Seminary California.

Foreword

When I first read the English translation of Anders Nygren's now classic study of the concepts of agape and eros, shortly after it appeared in 1969, it forced me to clarify thoughts I had previously expressed on the relationship of love to issues of public life. Agapic love, Nygren argued, is extended to others without taking into account their desirability, as opposed to erotic love, which we extend to those whom we find desirable in specific ways. God's love for fallen human beings, Nygren insisted, is clearly of the agapic variety. And because believers experience that kind of love because God extends it to them in spite of their sinfulness, they are graciously given the capacity to show this same kind of love to others.[1]

Since my own views on Christian social–political thought had been influenced considerably by the writings of John Calvin, I decided to read him again in the light of Nygren's discussion. While Calvin obviously did not have the benefit of Nygren's extensive treatment of agapic love, his account of the love Jesus was commanding when he set forth the "Love your neighbor as yourself" mandate of the Gospel accounts (see Matt. 22:37–40), closely follows the pattern of agapic love set forth by Nygren. Because we are by nature, Calvin says, "all too much inclined to self-love," we need to concentrate on loving God in a way that places the love of self in the background, thereby cultivating in our relationships with other humans a pattern that "transfers to others the emotion of love that we naturally feel toward ourselves." Furthermore, as Calvin said, the "neighbor" we are commanded to love "includes even the most remote person," extending beyond "the ties of kinship, or acquaintanceship, or of neighborhood." It is a love that should "embrace the whole human race without exception in a single feeling of love," with "no distinction

1 Anders Nygren, *Agape and Eros*, trans. Philip S. Watson (Chicago: Chicago University Press, 1982).

between barbarian and Greek, worthy and unworthy, friend and enemy, since all should be contemplated in God, not in themselves."[2]

The civic arena for Calvin, then, offers a network of relationships in which agapic love should abound. This still leaves the significant question, however, whether that divinely mandated unselfish love is to be embodied in societal laws. Is agapic love to be manifested primarily, even exclusively, in the personal dispositions of Christians in their social relationships, or should civil laws themselves be seen as instruments for actively *promoting* agapic love?

For Calvin, the Law – and he has in mind here specifically the Sinai Decalogue – does have a civic function. It serves as a guide to our collective life beyond the church, informing us of what norms for societal life must be enforced in order to maintain a civic order. Protection of property, regard for life, concern for the elderly, the rhythms of labor and rest – these are important for the basic patterns of societal interaction. Here the Law serves "by fear of punishment to restrain certain men who are untouched by any care for what is just and right unless compelled by hearing the dire threats in the law."[3]

But Calvin also insisted upon a more positive function of Law in public life. He refused to accept any "Law versus love" conception. He argued that Law should serve "to shape our manners in accordance with civil justice, to create concord among us, to maintain and preserve a common peace and tranquility."[4] Calvin's verbs point to something beyond a mere negative policing. God wants civil government "to *shape* our manners," "to *create* concord," and "to *maintain and preserve* a common peace and tranquility." In simple terms, love is what the Law is all about, and Law is what gives substance to the life of love. To make use of a Kantian-type formulation: Law without love is blind, and love without Law is empty. Any claim to be living a life of love while engaging in adultery, murder, covetousness, dishonoring of parents, stealing, and the like, is spurious.

This is not the place for me to offer more detail about Calvin's conception of the relationship between Law and love. Suffice it to say that the issues he pursued, along with many others in the Christian tradition, are still being much discussed in the present-day academy. And the wonderful thing – as

[2] John Calvin, *Institutes of the Christian Religion,* John T. McNeill, ed., Ford Lewis Battles, trans. (Philadelphia: Westminster, 1960), 2:54–5, 8:417–19.

[3] Ibid., 2:10, 7:358.

[4] Ibid., 4.20.2; quoted by Sheldon S. Wolin, *Politics and Vision: Continuity and Innovation in Western Political Thought* (Boston: Little, Brown and Co., 1960), 182; Wolin is using here the 1813 translation by John Allen.

evidenced in this fine book of essays – is that scholars from a variety of disciplines are addressing the issues with care and depth.

The ancient psalmist expressed the hope that the policies of a just and loving government "would be like rain that falls on the mown grass, like showers that water the earth."[5] The stimulating discussions that take place in these pages offer us the reassurance that the psalmist's hope is still very much alive.

Richard J. Mouw

[5] Ps. 72:8, New Revised Standard Version (NRSV).

Acknowledgments

This book would not have been possible had it not been for the encouragement, assistance, and hard work of a lot of people.

We are especially indebted to our editors, John Witte, John Berger, and Becky Jackaman, who guided us each step of the way.

In addition, many thanks:

for diligent library support to Don Buffalo;
for careful research to Brett Stroud, Mark Krause, Hilary Davenport, and Jenna King; and
for vigilant word processing to Candace Warren and Sophia Sipsis.

This project grew out of Pepperdine University's 2014 Nootbaar Institute "Love and Law" conference. The thoughtful comments of all who participated in that conference shaped this book. See: https://law.pepperdine.edu/nootbaar-institute/annual-conference/loveandlaw/. In addition, many at Pepperdine contributed financial support and encouragement toward this project. They include Herbert and Elinor Nootbaar, Provosts Darryl Tippens and Rick Marrs, Dean Deanell Reese Tacha, Vice Dean Shelley Saxer, and Associate Deans for Research and Faculty Development Robert Pushaw and Paul Caron. We are grateful for their generosity.

Our spouses, Denise Cochran and Cathleen Phillips, and our children, Christina Cochran Smith, Robbie Cochran, Kevin Cochran, Cecily Calo, and Agatha Calo, have made many sacrifices over the years that have led to this book. Our thanks to them for those sacrifices and for teaching us the meaning of agape (as well as other forms of love) on a day-by-day basis.

Both of us have been inspired over the decades to think Christianly about the world by teachers and pastors. Among them are Jim Houston, Tom Shaffer,

Skip Ryan, Barb Armacost, Dallas Willard, and N.T. Wright. We thank them for enriching our work and our lives.

Finally, we each have been blest with students in law and theology classes who have raised questions that led to this book. In coming decades, they and others like them will be the ones who can bring the insights of agape and justice to law. Our thanks and prayers go with them.

Introduction

In a provocative essay, philosopher Jeffrie Murphy asks: "What would law be like if we organized it around the value of Christian love [agape], and if we thought about and criticized law in terms of that value?"[1] The idea that law should be a manifestation of love stands in stark contrast to reigning modern legal theories. Liberalism controlled legal discourse through much of the nineteenth and twentieth centuries. Its focus is on protecting individual rights, but liberalism offers few resources for adjudicating competing rights claims.[2] Law and economics judges law based on efficiency, but has shorn law of its moral depth and provided little basis for protecting human dignity (at least for the "have nots"). Critical legal studies (CLS) and its interest group progeny have deconstructed law and highlighted ways in which law masks power, but have failed to provide a basis for reconstructing law so as to protect the common good; if, as CLS asserts, law is merely power, it is likely to merely serve the interests of the powerful.

Though each of these schools of thought has brought insight to law, each is ultimately reductionistic, pointing to only a limited aspect of law's reality. These theories have also divorced law from the deeper sources of moral meaning that informed legal thought in the past. This book offers agape as a resource for critiquing contemporary legal theory and for thinking anew about concrete problems within law. Law grounded in agape offers the possibility of more fully encouraging human flourishing in relationship and community

[1] Jeffrie G. Murphy, "Christian Love and Criminal Punishment," in this volume, 151, reprinted from *Christianity and the Law: An Introduction*, eds. John Witte and Frank S. Alexander (New York: Cambridge University Press, 2008), 219. Murphy's question served as the focus of the "Love and Law" conference at Pepperdine University School of Law, 7–8, February 2014. Many of the essays contained in this volume were presented at that conference and address Murphy's question directly.

[2] Mary Ann Glendon, *Rights Talk: The Impoverishment of Political Discourse* (New York: The Free Press, 1991).

than the theories that have dominated legal discourse in recent decades. Agape, as understood today, has its source in the Christian tradition, but we believe it offers a vision for law that will be of interest to those from other traditions as well, both because they are likely to have analogous sources of value and because agape presents an inherently attractive foundation for law.

In the ancient world, "agape" was a seldom used and colorless word, analogous to the English word "like." According to Josef Pieper, "it was a word begging for meaning and Christianity gave it meaning."[3] Agape became *the* Christian word for love. Forms of it occur 341 times in the New Testament.[4] It was the word the New Testament used to capture the love Jesus commanded for God, neighbors, and enemies. Judaism is also responsible for some of what agape has come to mean. The Jewish translators of the Septuagint chose "agape" as the word for the love of God and neighbor, which Jesus identified as the two most important commands in the Mosaic Law.[5]

Four Forms of Love – Agape's meaning is best understood when compared with other Greek words for love – eros, philia, and storge.[6]

The broad range of meanings for eros illustrates that even four terms for love may not be enough. Eros can be used for three very different forms of love – Platonic contemplation of God, romantic love, and sexual attraction. These forms of eros share an attraction to beauty (whether of God, a wonderful person, or an exotic dancer). Their starting point is the need of the lover and their goal is the satisfaction of that need. Eros's danger is obsession – one in the throes of eros may sacrifice reason, money, family, friends, and everything and everyone else for the beloved.

Philia is friendship, a love of those with whom one enjoys common interests.[7] Friends look at something together, whereas lovers look at one another. Philia can be, as Aristotle taught, a school for virtue. The modern notion of friendship often misses this aspect of philia. In the classic notion, the goodness of a friend is part of the project of friends (a characteristic philia shares with agape). Like eros, philia is exclusive – it selects as its objects particular, attractive individuals.

3 Josef Pieper, *Faith, Hope, Love* (San Francisco: Ignatius Press, 1997), 156.

4 William Klassen, quoted in Timothy P. Jackson, *The Priority of Love: Christian Charity and Social Justice* (Princeton: Princeton University Press, 2003), 21.

5 For an examination of Jesus' development of the Mosaic "love your neighbor" commandment, see Robert F. Cochran, Jr., "Jesus, Agape, and Law," in this volume, 13–37.

6 For a fuller development of each type of love, including a consideration of the implications each might have for law, see: Linda Ross Meyer, "Agape, Humility, and Chaotic Good: The Challenge and Risk of Allowing Agape a Role in the Law," in this volume, 57–74.

7 Gilbert Meilaender, *Friendship: A Study in Theological Ethics* (Notre Dame: Notre Dame Press, 1981).

Storge is natural affection, a love like that felt by parents (or at least most parents) for their children (or at least most of their children). In ancient Greek, it was almost always used to describe relationships within the family. Storge can be generated by regular contact with its object and can be felt toward those who are unattractive. It is characterized by loyalty. It is likely to inspire deep ties to the local community, but weak ties or even hostility toward other communities and the broader community. It, like eros and philia, can generate unfair treatment of those outside one's intimate circle. Jesus implicitly criticized this aspect of storge when he asked, "From whom do kings of the earth take toll or tribute? From their children or from others?"[8]

In contrast to the other forms of love, agape is "other-regarding care,"[9] "unclaiming love,"[10] and "universal benevolence."[11] It is other-directed, offered without regard for the interests of the lover or the attractive qualities of the beloved. Timothy P. Jackson defines agapic love as requiring the unconditional willing of the good for the other, equal regard for the well-being of the other, and passionate service open to self-sacrifice for the sake of the other.[12] Gene Outka characterizes agape as "a regard for the neighbor [that] is for every person qua human existent, to be distinguished from those special traits, actions, etc., which distinguish particular personalities from each other."[13]

C. S. Lewis notes that the forms of love other than agape are "always directed to objects which the lover finds in some way intrinsically loveable." By contrast, agape enables one "to love what is not naturally lovable; lepers, criminals, enemies, morons, the sulky, the superior and the sneering."[14] Agape, in other words, is not based on the merit of the recipient, but an ethical duty grounded in the humanity of the other.[15] Agapic love is both particular and universal. It takes as its object the particular neighbor one confronts – the wounded traveler on the side of the road[16] – yet it emanates from a universal love that does not discriminate. As Kierkegaard writes, "Since one's neighbor is every man, unconditionally every man, all distinctions are indeed removed from the object."[17]

8 Matt. 17:25. All Citations are to New Revised Standard Version.
9 Gene H. Outka, *Agape: An Ethical Analysis* (New Haven: Yale University Press, 1972), 1.
10 Paul Ramsey, *Basic Christian Ethics* (Louisville: Westminster/John Knox Press, 1993), 71.
11 Jackson, *The Priority of Love*, 50.
12 Ibid., 9.
13 Outka, *Agape*, 1.
14 C.S. Lewis, *The Four Loves* (New York: Harcourt, Brace, 1960), 177.
15 Rom. 5:7–8.
16 Luke 10:25–37.
17 Søren Kierkegaard, *Works of Love*, trans. Howard and Edna Hong (New York: Harper-Torchbooks, 1962), 77.

Like friendship, agapic love is aspirational. It wants the good for the beloved, including the moral good. As Augustine says, "Love reprimands, ill will echoes."[18] This aspirational character of agape is captured in a line from the movie *Junebug*. Ashley (played by Amy Adams) says to her sullen, ne'er-do-well husband Johnny, "God loves you just the way you are but he loves you too much to let you stay that way."

Paul offers the classic New Testament account of agape:

> [Agape] is patient; [agape] is kind; [agape] is not envious or boastful or arrogant or rude. It does not insist on its own way; it is not irritable or resentful; it does not rejoice in wrongdoing, but rejoices in the truth. It bears all things, believes all things, hopes all things, endures all things.[19]

Agape and Justice – Amidst a general recognition among scholars of agapic love's centrality to the Gospel message and Christian ethics, the relationship between agape and justice has been a hotly contested issue. This issue is particularly important in determining agape's possible implications for law, politics, and social responsibility.[20] Christian thinkers, however, have achieved little consensus on the question of whether agape stands in tension with justice or is rather its fulfillment. Competing theological understandings of agape continue to inform competing understandings of how Christianity should relate to the late modern liberal order.

Some authors contrast agape and justice. Anders Nygren argues that agape supersedes the order of justice – once one is committed to an agapic regime, there is no need for justice.[21] Reinhold Niebuhr holds love and justice in "constant tension," as individual "ideals of brotherhood" and "the moral ambiguities of communities" collide within moral and social life.[22] David VanDrunen identifies agapic love as the standard to be applied in one's personal life and in the church, and justice (generally retributive justice) as the standard to

[18] Quoted in Josef Pieper, *Faith, Hope, Love* (San Francisco: Ignatius Press, 1997), 187.

[19] 1 Cor. 13:4–7. This passage is often quoted at Christian weddings, where to young people eros might seem to be the order of the day. Their elders, however, realize that agape is likely to be the more important form of marital love in years to come. For a further development of Paul's teaching on agape and its relationship to law, see Darryl Tippens, "'Love Calls Us to the Things of This World': The Pauline Tradition and 'The Law of Christ,'" in this volume, 38–54.

[20] For consideration of whether Jesus intended agape to extend to the law and politics, see Cochran, "Jesus, Agape, and Law," 21–27.

[21] Anders Nygren, *Agape and Eros* (Chicago: University of Chicago Press, 1982), 90.

[22] Reinhold Niebuhr, *The Children of Light and the Children of Darkness* (New York: Scribner's, 1972; originally published 1944), 83–84. See also Reinhold Niebuhr, *Moral Man and Immoral Society* (New York: Scribner's, 1960), throughout but especially 53–82.

be applied by the state.[23] In contrast, Paul Ramsey, Timothy Jackson, and Nicholas Wolterstroff argue that agape demands justice.[24]

Gene Outka notes that different understandings of justice may be at the heart of many of the disagreements about the relationship between agape and justice. He identifies four ways of understanding justice that might relate in different ways to agape: (1) "similar treatment for similar cases," (2) "to each according to his merit or works," (3) "to each the same thing," and (4) "to each according to his needs." Outka identifies the last as closest to agape.[25]

Reconciliation of agape and justice may be in part a matter of understanding both concepts in a biblical sense.[26] On the one hand, biblical justice may look more like love than its modern counterparts. Ramsey argues that agape "elevated [earthly cities] and their justice was infused and transformed by new perspectives, limits, and principles."[27] Biblical justice may include meeting people's needs, a role that most in the modern world consign to charity. Wolterstorff notes that the section of Isaiah with which Jesus defines his ministry[28] describes biblical justice in broader terms than the justice of Enlightenment individualism. Biblical justice is not only a call "to let the oppressed go free" but also "to share your bread with the hungry, and bring the homeless poor into your house [and] cover [the naked]."[29]

Moreover, biblical love – agape – may look more like justice than its modern counterparts. Timothy Jackson notes that, "Punishment is often love's taking justice seriously."[30] Paul Ramsey has argued that just war theory was developed by Christians as an application of agape toward both aggressors and victims. Agape will restrain sin, for the sake of both sinners and victims.[31]

William Temple thoughtfully describes the relationship agape and justice might have to legal institutions: "[justice is] the primary form of love in social organization."[32] Justice is the way agape is manifested by those with

23 David VanDrunen, "Justice Tempered by Forbearance: Why Christian Love Is an Improper Category to Apply to Civil Law," in this volume, 125–47.

24 See sources cited below

25 Outka, *Agape*, 89–91. For further development of Outka's point, see Michael P. Moreland, "Justice, Love, and Duties of Care in Tort Law," in this volume, 203–4.

26 Nicholas Wolterstorff, "Love, Justice, and Law," in this volume, 118–24.

27 Paul Ramsey, *War and the Christian Conscience: How Shall Modern War Be Conducted Justly?* (Durham: Duke University Press, 1961), xxi.

28 Luke 4:17–21.

29 Isa. 58:6–7; Nicholas Wolterstorff, *Justice: Rights and Wrongs* (Princeton: Princeton University Press, 2008), 116–17.

30 Jackson, *The Priority of Love*, 153.

31 Ramsey, *War and the Christian Conscience*, 56.

32 "Christian Love and Criminal Punishment," 151–52, reprinted from *Christianity and the Law*, 219, quoting from Lord Denning, *The Influence of Religion on Law* (Alberta: Canadian Institute for Law, Theology, and Public Policy, 1997), 3.

responsibilities to a group. Those in authority should not show love to privileged individuals only, but to all who might be affected by their actions. We are communal beings and must attend in love to everyone involved. Justice may be the most loving thing one can do for all of the people for whom one is responsible.

Agape and Jurisprudence – While agape has been an important dynamic in Christian thought about political justice, surprisingly little attention has been given in the modern era to its relationship to law and jurisprudence. Neither theologians nor legal scholars have focused on how agape – the central ethical category of Christianity – should inform thinking about legal meaning and order.

This omission of agape from Christian legal thought might be explained by both theological and jurisprudential factors. Many Catholics and Protestants have resisted seeing agape as an apposite category for legal thought. Within each tradition, a different pair of dichotomies has tended to separate law from agape. Among Catholics, that dichotomy is nature and grace. As Michael Moreland notes in his essay herein, "while Protestant theologians . . . explored at great length the distinctiveness of agapic Christian love in ethics and politics, Catholic writers more often made arguments about natural law and practical reason when reflecting on social questions."[33] There has been a tendency within certain strands of Catholic social thought, particularly the Thomistic tradition, to separate nature and grace and, by extension, law and love.[34]

While Protestant social thought has given more sustained attention to agape, much of it is colored by a suspicion that love is counter to the vocation of law and politics. The perceived dichotomy between law and grace has limited the influence agape might have on the civil law. Particularly within main currents of Reformed and Lutheran thought, the coercive work of the state and the redemptive work of the church remain at a vast remove from each other. This impulse is captured in Luther's warning that ruling the world by the Gospel, rather than the "godly estate" of the sword, would loose "the ropes and chains of the savage wild beasts." "Christians, among themselves and by and for themselves," might live according to a love that forgives and

[33] Moreland, "Justice, Love, and Duties of Care in Tort Law," 190.

[34] The Catholic tradition has supported varied understandings of the relationship between nature and grace, but has often emphasized that human nature, although corrupted, can discern truths through unaided reason. New ways of understanding nature and grace have flourished since the mid-twentieth century, particularly as influenced by the *ressourcement* movement. Pope Benedict, perhaps most notably in his encyclical, *Charity in Truth: Caritas in Veritate* (San Francisco: Ignatius Press, 2009), made love a central category within Catholic social thought.

does not seek redress, but this cannot be the basis for a legal order.[35] A ruler might engage in acts of mercy or clemency but agape, in the full sense of its Christian meaning, has little to offer the operation of law. David VanDrunen's essay herein addressing why "Christian Love is an Improper Category to Apply to Civil Law" stands within such a tradition. These disjunctive accounts of the relationship between law and love continue to bind the Catholic and Protestant jurisprudential imaginations.

Modern legal thought poses additional challenges to thinking agapically about law. In the modern era, we seldom think of law having any relationship to theology, much less the theological virtue of love. The tension between law and love is not an entirely modern phenomenon, but something has changed in modernity, particularly with respect to how law is conceptualized in relationship to religion. As Remi Brague argues, "in modern societies, law, far from being conceived of in any relation with the divine, is quite simply the rule that the human community gives itself, considering only ends that it proposes for itself."[36] Law in modernity is thus increasingly defined as a closed system of meaning, subject to its own internal rules, and reduced to an expression of self-interested power. Theology, in turn, is not only irrelevant for understanding law, but is rendered antithetical to the construction of legal meaning.

Given these obstacles, how might agape meaningfully speak to law? The essays in this volume explore this relationship. Possibilities include the following:

A New Framework for Thinking about Law – Though we have noted ways in which there might be both theological and jurisprudential resistance to the idea, agape offers resources for drawing Christian thought into conversation with law. Recent years have seen the development of ever more sophisticated scholarship on the relationship between religion and law, but there have been relatively few efforts to connect theology with fundamental questions of law and legal theory. Agape provides a way to facilitate this connection, while also speaking to the distinctive conditions of legal modernity. An agapic account of law addresses questions of power and mercy, judgment and forgiveness, autonomy and the common good. It offers ways to rethink issues arising in the practice of law[37] and the operation of legal institutions. More generally, it

35 Martin Luther, *Temporal Authority: To What Extent It Can Be Obeyed* (1523). A more comprehensive introduction to Luther's doctrine of the two kingdoms and the two governments can be found, e.g., W.D.J. Cargill Thompson, *The Political Thought of Martin Luther* (Brighton: The Harvester Press, 1984), 36–61.

36 Remi Brague, *The Law of God: The Philosophical History of an Idea* (Chicago: University of Chicago Press, 2007), 1.

37 Robert K. Vischer, *Martin Luther King Jr. and the Morality of Legal Practice: Lessons in Love and Justice* (New York: Cambridge University Press, 2013). Vischer presented his discussion of Dr. King at the Pepperdine University conference that led to the present volume.

provokes reflection about the deeper moral life of law that has eluded modern legal theory.

The questions addressed in this volume stand within the long tradition of Christian political and legal thought. Yet, it is the current state of legal thought that gives urgency and shape to this project. As noted in the beginning of this introduction, modern schools of legal thought have failed to provide a grounding for law that encourages human flourishing. The possibility of agape-grounded law challenges the tendencies of liberalism toward isolationism, of law and economics toward selfishness, and of CLS toward cynicism.

The deconstruction of law, which often has revealed law as mere instrumental power, also may open space for law's reconstruction on theologically informed terms. In our view, agape can both illuminate the modern situation and serve as a constructive alternative. As Oliver O'Donovan writes, "Recovery of theological description enables us to understand not only what the goods of our institutions and traditions are, but why and how those goods are limited and corruptible, and to what corresponding errors they have made us liable."[38] This volume offers agape as a source of theological description for diagnosing both the limits and the possibilities of law in the late-modern age.

Agape and the Substance of Law – As Dallas Willard and Gary Black Jr. have argued:

> [In the] social or governmental setting, [agapic] love does what it can to establish and sustain arrangements and practices that will benefit everyone or as many as possible. . . [Agape compels us] to care deeply for the economic, political, social, familial, and religious circumstances within our communities, because we care for (love) the people interacting and engaging in all these aspects of human life.[39]

Jesus summarized the Mosaic Law as love of God and neighbor. Much of the Mosaic Law, as well as much modern law (from the prohibition of murder to the prohibition of double parking), requires citizens to act agapically toward one another. Law based on love would protect all citizens, especially those who have the greatest need – "the widow, the orphan, and the stranger."

Too many people view law either as (1) merely a means of protecting their interests, or (2) too corrupt and corrupting to be worthy of their involvement. However, agape might lead legislators, judges, lawyers, and voters to adopt laws that treat citizens well. One need only travel to one of the many countries

38 Oliver O'Donovan, *The Ways of Judgment: The Bampton Lectures* (Grand Rapids: William B. Eerdmans Pub. Co., 2008), xv.

39 Dallas Willard and Gary Black, *Divine Conspiracy Continued: Fulfilling God's Kingdom on Earth* (San Francisco: Harper One, 2014), 191.

that do not have functioning legal systems to see the harm citizens suffer. Citizens who do not have access to the rule of law suffer great injustice – sex trafficking, wage slavery, casual rape, and police brutality. These citizens need law. Those motivated by agape will be passionate in protecting victims and enforcing the law. Passing and enforcing just laws is one of the most loving things people can do. Law grounded in agape may be a way of thinking about and developing law that will bring meaning to those involved in creating law and yield human flourishing for those impacted by law.

Agape, Law, and Character – Agapic law would not simply be concerned with making people's lives more pleasant. As Jeffrie Murphy notes, agape is not "cuddly."[40] If agape is the aim, a country will "design legal practices and institutions with a view to the moral and spiritual improvement in virtue of affected citizens."[41] Murphy argues that law organized around the value of agape, from regulations governing pornography to the treatment of those in prison, will be concerned with citizens' character. Law can teach citizens to care for one another. In the Hebrew scripture, love for neighbor manifested itself in a practical outworking in everyday life – placing a retaining wall around the roof to keep people from falling[42] and allowing the poor to glean leftovers from the orchards and fields.[43] Hopefully, citizens who engage in such practices and their modern counterparts will develop the habit – the virtue – of caring for other people in ways not required by law.

There are, however, dangers to grounding law in love. C.S. Lewis expresses it well:

> Of all tyrannies a tyranny sincerely exercised for the good of its victims may be the most oppressive. It may be better to live under robber barons than under omnipotent moral busybodies.[44]

But the risk of the abuse does not necessarily mean that something should be avoided all together. The danger of overreach may merely be a risk citizens should be aware of, as they seek to faithfully ground law in love. Moreover, law truly grounded in love will give citizens a substantial amount of freedom within which to operate, at times to fail, and to grow morally.

40 Jeffrie G. Murphy, "Christian Love and Criminal Punishment," in this volume, 155, reprinted from *Christianity and Law*, 224.

41 Ibid. at 156.

42 Deut. 22:8.

43 Lev. 19:9–12.

44 C.S. Lewis, "The Humanitarian Theory of Punishment," *The Twentieth Century: an Australian Quarterly Review* III, no. 3. Reprinted, C.S. Lewis, *God in the Dock*, ed. Walter Hooper (Grand Rapids: William B. Eerdmans, 1970), 287–94.

Essays herein explore law's relationship to agape as a matter of both theory and practice. Part I traces the development of agape in Jesus and Paul – the two most important biblical contributors to its meaning. Part II explores many of the issues raised in this introduction: the meaning of agape, the challenge of acting with agape in law toward all people, the promises and risks of agapic law, the tensions both between love and justice and between love and law, the danger that law grounded in agapic love will be oppressive, and the danger that law grounded in agapic love will not have the muscle to rule effectively. Part III considers the role agape might have in particular areas of law – criminal punishment, judging, torts, elder law, immigration, corporations, intellectual property, and international relations.

Throughout the history of Christianity, many of the greatest Christian thinkers have explored the meaning of agape. The essays herein explore and build on the insights of many of these, including: Augustine, Thomas Aquinas, Martin Luther, John Calvin, Søren Kierkegaard, Anders Nygren, Gene H. Outka, Paul Ramsey, C.S. Lewis, Martin Luther King, Jr., Reinhold Niebuhr, and Popes Pius, John Paul II, Benedict XVI, and Francis.

This book is designed for Christians who want to think deeply and seriously about the implications of the Christian faith for civil law, as well as for non-Christians who want to understand how Christians might thoughtfully engage this subject. Moreover, we believe that agape is not merely a duty imposed on Christians, but is a compelling vision of human relations that will be attractive to those in other traditions. In this respect, agape offers a new and timely lens through which to think about questions of pressing import within law and politics. Yet agape is not simply another interpretive paradigm or another variant of "law and" scholarship. Rather, agape might be understood as the end of law and as thus containing within it a new jurisprudential logic. If this is the case, agape offers ways to fundamentally reorient our thinking about legal meaning and legal problems.

PART I

BIBLICAL FOUNDATIONS

In Part I, Robert Cochran and Darryl Tippens explore the contributions to agape's meaning by its two main New Testament proponents, Jesus and the Apostle Paul. Cochran examines what Jesus' words and life teach about agape, and considers their implications for both the substance and administration of law. Tippens considers Paul's treatment of agape as law, as epistemology, and as justice, as well as its communal, story-shaped, and liturgical nature. He explores implications for both legal education and law practice.

1

Jesus, Agape, and Law

Robert F. Cochran, Jr.

It may seem strange that I write about Jesus and "agape." He may have never uttered the word,[1] though it is the word for love the Gospel writers generally place on his lips.[2] Nevertheless, early Christians developed agape's meaning as they reflected on his teachings and life.[3] Jesus, as well as the New Testament authors, held Jesus up as the model of the love he advocated, and it came to be known as "agape."[4]

Jesus came preaching that he was inaugurating a new kingdom – a message that troubled Roman and Jewish authorities who exercised power and enjoyed the prerogatives of the existing kingdoms. Among the many challenging questions concerning Jesus' kingdom is its relationship to agape and law. That is the subject of this essay.

In the first part of this essay, I will review Jesus' teaching on agape and identify examples from his life that illustrate this teaching. In the second part, I will discuss how his teaching on agape might apply to law and legal administration.

1 James Barr, "Which Language Did Jesus Speak? Some Remarks of a Semitist." Lecture, *Bulletin of the John Rylands Library* (John Rylands Library, 11 February 1970), 9–29, accessed 8 April 2015, available at www.escholar.manchester.ac.uk/item/?pid=uk-ac-man-scw:1m2973. Jesus probably spoke Aramaic, possibly Hebrew.

2 When Jesus quoted the Old Testament, identifying love of God and neighbor as the greatest commandments, he may have quoted the Septuagint – the Greek Old Testament – which translated love as "agape" in both places. The Gospel writers appear to draw from both the Septuagint and the Hebrew text when they quote the Old Testament. Luke 10:27; Deut. 6:5; Lev. 19:18. Consider, Timothy M. Law, *When God Spoke Greek: The Septuagint and the Making of the Christian Bible* (Oxford: Oxford University Press, 2013), 99–105.

3 Paul Ramsey has concluded that "[St. Paul] believed such love as he describes in I Corinthians 13 [the great Christian hymn of agape] would have been unknown except for Jesus Christ and degrees of love in Christians derivative from his as gifts of his Spirit." Paul Ramsey, *Basic Christian Ethics* (Louisville, KY: Westminster/John Knox Press, 1993), 18.

4 "[L]ove one another as I have loved you" John 15:12; "Let the same mind be in you that was in Christ Jesus. . . ." Phil. 2:5.

1.1 JESUS AND AGAPE

Jesus' teaching about agape was built on a foundation laid in the Hebrew Scriptures. He summarized the Mosaic Law as love of God and neighbor, quoting provisions of the Mosaic Law (Luke 10:27; Deut. 6:5; Lev. 19:18). Nevertheless, when compared with the then-current Jewish teaching, Jesus broadened the identity of those to whom love is owed and deepened the quality of love required.

1.1.1 *To Whom Is Agape Due?*

The Mosaic Law required Jews to "love your neighbor as yourself" (Lev. 19:18[5]). When an expert in the law asked Jesus who qualified as his neighbor (a question modern lawyers would identify as a duty question), Jesus responded with the story of the Good Samaritan. An apparently Jewish traveler is beaten and robbed. A Samaritan stranger takes care of the wounded traveler (Luke 10:25–37), despite existing tensions between Jews and Samaritans (see John 4:42). The Samaritan is the obvious hero of the story. He cares for one who is outside his race and ethnic background. Thus, Jesus' implicit answer to the legal expert's question was that he should emulate the Samaritan – his neighbor includes those he might be inclined to hate. Whereas the most important word for "love" in the Old Testament, "chesed," emphasizes loyalty, the most important word for "love" in Jesus' teaching, "agape," emphasizes inclusiveness.

This love of a broad range of "neighbors" was manifested in Jesus' life. He socialized with, befriended, and went to the aid of people whom many of his fellow Jews would have avoided and hated. One of the most notable, and most criticized, things about Jesus was that he ate and drank with "sinners" (Matt. 9:10–11, 11:19; Luke 5:30, 7:34, 15:1–2). He befriended a Samaritan woman at a well – a person with whom "Jews [did] not associate" (John 4:42). He healed the servant of a Roman military officer (Matt. 8:5–13) and the daughter of a Canaanite woman (Matt. 15:21–28).

Beyond neighbors (lest there was any doubt about the extent of one's duty), Jesus taught his followers to love their enemies. He highlighted the difference between his teaching and the Jewish teaching of the day: "You have heard that it was said, '[y]ou shall love your neighbor and hate your enemy.' But I say to you, love your enemies and pray for those who persecute you . . ." (Matt. 5:43–44a).

Jesus did not leave his call to love enemies as an abstraction. His followers were to love their enemies even in the face of physical attack: "If anyone

[5] All citations to the New Revised Standard Version unless otherwise noted.

strikes you on the cheek, offer the other also" (Luke 6:29a). This teaching, along with his command to "pray for those who persecute you," were both dramatically illustrated by Jesus when he was abused by the Roman soldiers at his crucifixion. He prayed, "Father, forgive them. . ." (Luke 23:34).

This duty included doing more than the law required. "[I]f anyone wants to sue you and take your coat, give your cloak as well" (Matt. 5:40). And in a land that for centuries had been occupied by hated foreign military forces, Jesus taught his followers not merely to submit to a law requiring Jews to carry a Roman soldier's pack one mile, but to "go also the second mile" (Matt. 5:41). This teaching, from one who claimed to have brought in a new Kingdom, would have been astonishing. Of what use was a new Kingdom that merely submits to the existing one? Jesus' followers' duty extended to those who slap, sue, and conscript them.[6]

Jesus' teaching that his followers were to love Samaritans, sinners, assailants, opposing litigants, and Roman soldiers illustrates in striking terms some of the differences between agape and Greek terms for two other forms of love, philia (friendship) and eros (romance). Unlike philia, agape does not require mutuality. Unlike eros, agape is not based on the attractiveness of its object. As biblical scholar Anders Negren has written, "When my neighbor happens to also be my enemy, obviously no reason for my loving him can be found in his character or conduct."[7]

1.1.2 *What Is Agape?*

Jesus not only broadened the people to whom agape was owed, he deepened its meaning. By word and example he taught that agape meant humility, service, sacrifice, forgiving, healing, feeding, teaching, and elevating others.

6 Nicholas Wolterstorff argues that the commands to turn the other cheek when slapped, give up one's coat when sued, and carry a soldier's pack an extra mile are "metaphorical and hyperbolic" repudiations of the reciprocity code (e.g., "an eye for an eye"). Instead, Jesus' followers are "to seek the good even of those who do us evil." Nicholas Wolterstorff, *Justice in Love* (Grand Rapids: Wm. B. Eerdmans Publishing Co., 2011), 124. Wolterstorff argues that rejection of the retribution and the reciprocity code does not mean the rejection of punishment. In Romans 13, Paul (also a champion of agape) commends rulers who punish wrongdoers. "Punishment as a condemnation of the wrongdoer is a good in his life and serves the social good of deterring such wrongdoing." Ibid., 128–29 (citing Lev. 19:17). Punishment teaches society in general and the wrongdoer in particular what activities are wrongful. See ibid., 193–98, citing Joel Feinberg, *Doing and Deserving: Essays in the Theory of Responsibility* (Princeton: Princeton University Press, 1970), 95–118.

7 Anders Nygren, *Agape and Eros: The Christian Idea of Love*, trans. Philip S. Watson (Chicago: University of Chicago Press, 1982), 215.

1.1.2.1 Humility, Sacrifice, and Forgiveness

One of the first things the New Testament writers noted about Jesus was that he put aside his status as God and came as a human to be with humans. His story was the story of the incarnation. Three of the Gospel writers (Matthew, Luke, and John) begin with Jesus' birth. He was born in humble circumstances, a human baby, in a stable (Luke 2:1–8). "[T]he Word became flesh and lived among us" (John 1:14a).

Paul held up Jesus' humility – his giving up his rights as God and becoming a human – as a model of the agape his followers should manifest to one another. Christ's agapic love for them should be a motivation for them to love and look out for the interests of other people.

> If then there is any encouragement in Christ, any consolation from [agape] any sharing in the Spirit, any compassion and sympathy, make my joy complete: be of the same mind, having the same [agape], being in full accord and of one mind. Do nothing from selfish ambition or conceit, but in humility regard others as better than yourselves. Let each of you look not to your own interests, but to the interests of others. Let the same mind be in you that was in Christ Jesus, who, though he was in the form of God, did not regard equality with God as something to be exploited, but emptied himself, taking the form of a slave, being born in human likeness. And being found in human form, he humbled himself and became obedient to the point of death – even death on a cross. (Phil. 2:1–8)

Jesus "emptied himself" of his divine prerogatives. He not only joined humanity and befriended those who were considered on the lower rungs of society, he sacrificed his life for them. Ultimately, Jesus' example taught that agape is a matter of sacrifice – in Jesus' case the greatest sacrifice – "even death on a cross!" (Phil. 2:8). John says, "We know [agape] by this, that he laid down his life for us" (1 John 3:16).

Jesus taught his followers to forgive others. In his model prayer, his followers ask God: "forgive us our debts, as we also have forgiven our debtors" (Matt. 6:12). When one of his disciples asked if he should forgive his brother seven times, Jesus responded that he should forgive him seventy times seven times (Matt. 18:21–22). Jesus also demonstrated forgiveness. As noted previously, at his death Jesus prayed that God would forgive his executioners (Luke 23:34). Jesus' followers believed that his death was the means of *their* forgiveness (Eph. 1:7; Rom. 4:25; 1 Pet. 2: 22–25, quoting Isa. 53:5–7).

1.1.2.2 Meeting People's Needs

In the section from Paul's letter to the Philippians quoted above, Paul called on Christians following Jesus' example not to look "to your own interests but each of you to the interests of the others" (Phil. 2:4). This reflected the teaching of Jesus. In calling his followers to love their enemies, Jesus summarized this love: "Do to others as you would have them do to you" (Luke 6:31).

This is similar to, but different from, Jewish teaching of the same era. When a prospective student asked Hillel if he could state the Mosaic Law while his inquirer stood on one foot, Hillel said: "What is hateful to you, do not do to your neighbor. That is the whole Torah; the rest is the explanation of this – go and study it!"[8] Both Jesus and Hillel made an implicit appeal to what we now might identify as empathy – they called on their hearers to consider things from the perspective of other people. The difference is that Jesus went beyond the requirement to do no harm and imposed what modern lawyers might call an *affirmative* duty to aid other people. Jesus required his disciples to aid those attacked and left on the road (Luke 10:25–37). (Anglo-American civil law is more in line with Hillel's teaching on this matter.[9])

Jesus demonstrated this affirmative care for other people. He met the physical needs of people by healing their diseases and feeding them. The Gospel accounts contain over 30 separate stories of Jesus healing individuals from a wide variety of diseases.

1.1.2.3 Agape Teaches

Jesus demonstrated agapic love, not only by providing for the physical and spiritual needs of people, but also by teaching them. At one point, King Herod sadistically murdered Jesus' cousin John the Baptist, displaying John's severed head on a platter at a raucous banquet (Mark 6:6b–29). Shortly thereafter, Jesus and his disciples were exhausted and sought to escape a crowd to a place of rest. But the crowd saw Jesus leaving on a boat, ran around the lake, and beat Jesus and his disciples to the other side. Mark reports that when Jesus saw the crowd "he had compassion[10] for them, because they were like sheep without a shepherd. So he began teaching them many things" (Mark 6:34). Jesus was in need of rest and they were in need of teaching. In an exercise of agapic love, Jesus taught them rather than addressing his own needs.

8 *Babylonian Talmud: Shabbat* 31a, quoted in Shoshannah Brombacher, "On One Foot," available at www.chabad.org/library/article_cdo/aid/689306/jewish/On-One-Foot.htm.

9 Mary Ann Glendon, *Rights Talk: The Impoverishment of Political Discourse* (New York: The Free Press, 1991), 81.

10 The Greek word here is *esplanchnisthe* (a form of the verb *splanchnizomai*, which means to have compassion), rather than agape. *Splanchnizomai* emphasizes the emotion Jesus felt. It is the same word used for the emotion the Good Samaritan felt for the wounded traveler (Luke 10:33). Jesus' and the Samaritan's response – caring for the needs of others – was very much an agapic response. As Nicholas Wolterstorff noted to me in a conversation about this passage, agape may be motivated by a variety of things – including compassion or a sense of duty.

Mark's statement that Jesus "had compassion on them, because they were like sheep without a shepherd" (Mark 6:34) harkened back to numerous images and statements in the Old Testament. Israel had always looked to its king as its shepherd and source of wise leadership. Its two greatest leaders – Moses and David – had been shepherds.[11] Old Testament authors used shepherd imagery of Israel's leaders to lament their loss (Moses; Num. 27:17), moral failure (Ahab, 1 Kings 22:17), and incompetence (Ezek. 34). The prophet Ezekiel provided an extended meditation on the bad shepherd, arguing that as a result of Israel's weak leadership, Jerusalem had fallen, the temple was destroyed, and Israel's leading citizens had been taken into Babylonian exile. In Ezekiel's (and Jesus') day, Israel was without a shepherd and in danger from conquering wolves. As Ezekiel argued of Israel's leaders (presaging Herod in Jesus' day), the "shepherds of Israel" had "eat[en] the fat," had failed to feed the sheep, and the sheep were scattered (Ezek. 34:2–6). In Ezekiel, God made the astonishing (incarnational!) promise that he would rescue the sheep:

> I myself will search for my sheep, and will seek them out . . . I will feed them with good pasture, and the mountain heights of Israel shall be their pasture; there they shall lie down in good grazing land, and they shall feed on rich pasture on the mountains of Israel. (Ezek. 34:11, 14)

Jesus taught the people by the lakeside and then fed them all with five loaves and two fish (Mark 6:35–44). He demonstrated agape by both teaching and feeding them and later identified himself as "the good shepherd" (John 10:11, 14).

Jesus' compassion led him to teach. He saw teaching as a response to the lack of leadership. Sheep without a shepherd are likely to wander off into all sorts of dangers. And Jesus taught people how to deal with many things – murder, anger, adultery, lust, divorce, money, and prejudice. He taught them how they should respond to soldiers, litigants, and enemies. Ultimately he taught them how to find God (John 3–4). His teaching enabled people to lead moral and safe lives. Good teachers – good shepherds – teach moral truth. They teach people how to thrive. Teaching is an act of love.

1.1.2.4 Agape Elevates

The New Testament writers present Jesus as one who elevated the people he encountered. This also was an act of agape. As noted in the first part of this section, agapic love as modeled by Jesus reached out to all, including those people

[11] Kenneth Bailey, *The Good Shepherd: A Thousand-Year Journey from Psalm 23 to the New Testament* (Downers Grove: InterVarsity Press, 2014), 166.

society looked down on. Jesus emptied himself of his divine prerogatives, came to earth, and associated with prostitutes, Samaritans, women, sinners, and tax collectors. His mere association with people gave them dignity. Jesus said that in his kingdom "all who exalt themselves will be humbled, and those who humble themselves will be exalted" (Luke 14:11). In his kingdom, the poor, the hungry, the meek, those who weep, the poor in spirit, and those who mourn were blessed (Luke 6:20–21; Matt. 5:2–5). It is the "upside down kingdom."[12]

Jesus called his disciples from the ordinary ranks, including fishermen and tax collectors. Moreover, he did not leave them as mere followers. He trained them for important responsibilities in his kingdom. In Jesus' final discourse with his disciples he says:

> This is my commandment, that you love one another as I have loved [ēgapēsa] you. No one has greater love than this, to lay down one's life for one's friends. You are my friends if you do what I command you. I do not call you servants any longer, because the servant does not know what the master is doing; but I have called you friends [philous], because I have made known to you everything that I have heard from my Father. (John 15:12–15)

Jesus did not stop with agapic love toward his disciples. Agape led to philia. After their period of discipleship Jesus called his disciples friends.

Whereas the notion of agape had not been developed prior to the Christian era, the notion of friendship (philia) was well established in the ancient world. It was generally a relationship among equals sharing common interests, projects, and responsibilities. For Jesus to call his disciples "friends" was to elevate them and their status. This must have come as a shock to the disciples. Just at the point where they began to see him as "the messiah," "the son of God," and "the Lord," he called them "friends." The disciples had grown morally and spiritually to the point where he could treat them as partners rather than mere servants. Jesus raised his disciples by *teaching* them "everything that [he had] heard from [his] Father." They would "know [his] business" and be prepared to take responsibility and engage in projects on his behalf. Note that a relationship can include both agape and philia. One can selflessly work for the good of the other (agape) and share responsibilities, projects, and interests (friendship).

In what I have said prior to this section, it might be assumed that agape was superior to friendship and the other natural loves. In some respects that is true. As C. S. Lewis notes, without agape all of the natural loves risk becoming vices.

[12] Donald B. Kraybill, *The Upside-Down Kingdom*, 25th ed. (Scottdale, PA: Herald Press, 2003), 3.

Eros can lead people to kill, wound, and maim for the sake of the beloved (including killing, wounding, or maiming the beloved). Left to themselves, philia, and storge[13] can lead one to become indifferent to the outside world.[14] This can happen even within churches as they become self-absorbed and lose sight of the needs of the people around them. But that would be contrary to agape. The natural loves need to be transformed by agape.[15]

But agape can also benefit from the natural loves. A marriage, a friendship, or a family controlled by agape will reach beyond itself and bless other people – it will be a vehicle for agape. Moreover, these other loves can offer the beloved things that agape alone does not provide. Agape is unselfish. It can want the beloved to develop beyond being an object of agape to being a partner. Jesus' desire that his disciples become his friends was itself an expression of agape – a willing the best for the other; it was a desire that they develop to the point that they could share in a mutual relationship with him.

In calling his disciples friends, Jesus raised them. As he said, they were no longer merely servants; they were partners in his enterprise. His goal was that they would not merely be the passive objects of his love, or merely be his servants, but that they would become his philous – that they would collaborate with him, be an active part of his projects, and eventually reign with him (Matt. 19:28). As Amy Sherman has argued, sharing power with other people gives them dignity. Jesus did not hang on to power, he shared it.[16] In this way, Jesus showed agapic leadership.

In summary, Jesus by word and example called his followers to love broadly; they were to love neighbors, Samaritans, and enemies. Agape is to extend to a broad range of situations, including conflict – when Jesus' followers were slapped, taken to court, and ordered about, they were to love their enemies. He also taught his disciples to love deeply. Like him, they were to humble themselves and to serve, forgive, teach, and elevate other people. They were called to seek the good of the other.

1.2 JESUS, AGAPE, AND LAW

In the remainder of this essay, I consider how Jesus' teaching about agape might affect those who influence law, whether as voters, lawyers, judges, legislators, or administrators.

13 That is "affection," most commonly within the family.
14 C.S. Lewis, *The Four Loves* (New York: Harcourt Brace, 1960), 115–22.
15 Ibid., 103, 163.
16 Amy Sherman, *Kingdom Calling: Vocational Stewardship for the Common Good* (Downers Grove: InterVarsity Press, 2011), 136–40.

One of Jesus' main concerns was justice. The Old Testament prophets anticipated a messiah who would inaugurate a reign of justice. The Gospel writers, as well as Jesus himself, identified Jesus as that messiah. For example, Matthew identified Jesus as the messiah promised by God in Isaiah's prophesy:

> Here is my servant, whom I have chosen, my beloved, with whom my soul is well pleased. I will put my Spirit upon him, and he will proclaim justice to the Gentiles. He will not wrangle or cry aloud, nor will anyone hear his voice in the streets. He will not break a bruised reed or quench a smoldering wick until he brings justice to victory. And in his name [Israel will put its[17]] hope. (Matt. 12:18–21 quoting Isa. 42:1–4)

In his first reported sermon, Jesus, also quoting Isaiah, identified himself as the one anointed "to bring good news to the poor," "to proclaim release of the captives," "[t]o let the oppressed go free, [and] to proclaim the year of the Lord's favor" (Luke 4:17–21, quoting Isa. 61:1–2).

On another occasion, Jesus exclaimed, "[W]ill not God grant justice to his chosen ones who cry to him day and night? Will he delay long in helping them? I tell you, he will quickly grant justice to them" (Luke 18:7–8). Jesus called for both agape and justice, suggesting that the two are not inconsistent.[18]

It might appear from some of Jesus' teaching that agape concerns Jesus' followers in their private lives only, and not their social responsibility or the content of law. Jesus' examples of agape arise in one-on-one encounters (with the victim you find injured on the side of the road (Luke 10:25–37), the enemy who strikes or sues you, or the soldier who demands that you carry his pack (Matt. 5:39–43)) and in relations among Jesus' followers ("Love one another as I have loved you" (John 13:34)). Yet several things suggest that agape should also be the standard by which Jesus' followers should judge law.

First, Jesus spoke to people in their situations. He gave examples that shepherds and fishermen could understand, but his followers today rightly draw implications from such examples for their own lives. At the time when Jesus spoke, his followers were powerless and did not have the opportunity to use law to benefit people. This has been the situation of his followers in many eras, as it is today in many parts of the world. But at other times and places, Christians have been able to influence law as voters, lawyers, judges, and executives. Should positions of power be an agape-free zone?

[17] Literally, "in which the Islands will put their hope." In the view of many scholars, "islands" here would have been understood to include the coastal regions, including Israel.

[18] For discussion of the relationship and possible conflicts between agape and justice, see the introduction to this volume, 4–6.

Jesus did not place limits on the situations in which his followers were to love their neighbors. Law, government, and politics are means by which people's lives can be improved (as well as means by which people's lives can be greatly harmed). One need only look around the world at people who have suffered under oppressive governments and at people who have not had functioning governments to see the importance of good government in people's lives. It may be irresponsible to not bring agapic love to them. Agapic love implicates not only the relationship between self and the other, but the place of the church in society, and the moral aims of politics in the earthly city.

In this section, I will suggest that Jesus intended some of his followers to assume positions of power and that agape should be the standard they apply in such positions. I will suggest that government, law, and politics are important arenas for the exercise of agape, but also that agapic leadership is much different from what generally exists in the world around us. This section will consider agape's relationship to justice, legal substance, and legal administration. At the end, I will consider ways in which government, law, and politics might be a means of showing agapic love to people.

1.2.1 *Agape and the Substance of Law: Law Was Made for Humans, Not Humans for Law*

Jesus suggested that agape is the standard by which law should be judged. Most often, he addressed the Mosaic Law, but in this section I will argue that his teaching has implications for all law.

For Jesus, love of God and neighbor were the most important provisions of the Mosaic Law and the framework on which the law, as well as the prophets, depended. When an expert in the law asked him: "Teacher, which is the greatest commandment in the Law?" Jesus replied:

> "You shall love the Lord your God with all your heart, and with all your soul, and with all your mind." This is the greatest and first commandment. And a second is like it: "You shall love your neighbor as yourself." On these two commandments hang all the law and the prophets. (Matt. 22:37–40, quoting Deut. 6:5 and Lev. 19:18; see also Mark 12:28–31 and Luke 10:25–28)

Moreover, when Jesus commanded his followers to love their enemies, he summarized the law in a way that could be a definition of agape: "do to others as you would have them do to you" (Matt. 7:12).

For Jesus, agape was not only the substance of the Mosaic Law, it was the standard by which it should be interpreted. He taught that there were priorities among laws, criticizing the teachers of the Mosaic Law for tithing their spices, while neglecting "the weightier matters of the law – justice, mercy and faith" (Matt. 23:23–24). These "weightier matters of the law" are all means of showing agape to people – they aim at human flourishing.

Although in cases of extreme need, Jewish commentators recognized exceptions to the Mosaic code, Jesus started with meeting human need as the primary standard.[19] When some Jewish legal officials criticized his disciples for picking grain on the Sabbath, Jesus said: "The Sabbath was made for humankind, and not humankind for the Sabbath" (Mark 2:23–28). Jesus here applied love of neighbor as the standard by which to judge the law. Law has instrumental value; it is not the ultimate value.

Note that here Jesus did not critique a minor part of the Mosaic Law. Sabbath observance was rooted in both creation – "God blessed the seventh day and hallowed it, because on it God rested from all the work that he had done in creation" (Gen. 2:3) – and the Ten Commandments – "remember the Sabbath day, and keep it holy" (Gen. 20:8). A very large portion of the Mosaic Law regulated activity on the Sabbath. Some Sabbath violations merited the death penalty (Exod. 31:14; Num. 15:32–36). The underlying purposes of Sabbath regulations were broad, including love of God, love of humans – including slaves, and even love of animals (Deut. 5:14). The sabbatical year, when debts were forgiven and slaves released (Deut. 15), and the jubilee year – the year following "seven times seven years" – when land was returned to families and fields lay fallow (Lev. 25:8–50) were calculated based on the Sabbath. Jonathan Burnside refers to the sabbatical year as "the Sabbath plus" and to the jubilee year as "the Sabbath squared."[20] The intensity with which the Pharisees challenged Jesus regarding the Sabbath indicated both their devotion to it and possibly their belief that the people would turn against Jesus if they perceived that he denigrated it. When Jesus identified a standard by which Sabbath regulations were to be judged, it is reasonable to conclude that he was laying down a standard that had broad implications. Jesus evaluated the Mosaic Law based on its impact on human lives. Indeed, the second part of Jesus' summary of the Mosaic Law ("love your neighbor") might be captured in a variation on Jesus' Sabbath teaching – *law* was made for humans, not humans for law.

Judging All Civil Law as Jesus Judged the Mosaic Law – John Calvin argued that the civil law of all nations should be judged by the standard of agape. Like

[19] Ramsey, *Basic Christian Ethics*, 56.

[20] Jonathan Burnside, *God, Justice, and Society: Aspects of Law and Legality in the Bible* (New York: Oxford University Press, 2011), 201–7.

Aquinas, he divided the Mosaic Law into ceremonial, moral, and civil parts.[21] Calvin argued that the purpose of the Mosaic civil law was

> to preserve that very love which is enjoined by God's eternal law. And as that exercise in ceremonies [the ceremonial law] properly pertained to the doctrine of piety, inasmuch as it kept the Jewish Church in the worship and religion of God, yet was still distinguishable from piety itself, so the judicial form [the civil law], though it looked only to the best method of preserving that charity which is enjoined by the eternal law of God, was still something distinct from the precept of love itself.[22]

Calvin here drew an analogy between the ceremonial law and its relationship to piety on the one hand and the civil law and its relationship to agape (charity) on the other. Just as the ceremonial aspects of the law were enacted to preserve piety, so the civil (or judicial) aspects were enacted to preserve agape; and just as piety was required outside the context of Jewish ceremonial law, so also law grounded in agape was required outside the Jewish civil law. Calvin went on to say:

> Therefore, as ceremonies might be abrogated without at all interfering with piety, so, also, when these [Mosaic] judicial arrangements are removed, the duties and precepts of charity [agape] can still remain perpetual. But if it is true that each nation has been left at liberty to enact the laws which it judges to be beneficial, still these are always to be tested by the rule of charity, so that while they vary in form, they must proceed on the same principle.[23]

Calvin argued that just as Jesus judged the Mosaic Law based on agape, all nations' laws should be judged based on agape. In the following, I will try to flesh out the arguments for this claim. The arguments are based on the nature of agape, on the analogy between the Mosaic Law and law generally, and on Jesus' appeal to creation.

A first argument for extending Jesus' agapic critique of the Mosaic Law to law generally is the nature of agape. One of the primary characteristics of agape, rooted in Jesus' story of the Good Samaritan, is that agape is owed to people of all cultures. In that story, Jesus interprets the neighbor to whom agape is due under the Mosaic Law to everyone, irrespective of race, religion,

[21] See, e.g., John Calvin, *Institutes of the Christian Religion*, IV, XX, 14, trans. Henry Beveridge (Grand Rapids: Wm. B. Eerdmans Publishing Co., 1989), 663; Thomas Aquinas, *Summa Theologica*, 2a, Question 99, Article 4, available at www.newadvent.org/summa/2099.htm. Though this is a helpful means of analyzing the Mosaic Law, there is no such division in the Mosaic Law itself.

[22] Calvin, *Institutes of the Christian Religion*, IV, XX, 14, trans. Henry Beveridge, 664.

[23] Ibid.

or national origin. The laws of the nations of any of these people have the potential to be a blessing or a curse. The Good Samaritan story's extension of the duty of Jews to care for those outside the Jewish race is implicit – the Good Samaritan who cares for the wounded traveler is obviously the hero of the story. He is held up as the role model that Jews are to emulate. Not only is agape due to all, but the fact that the hero of the story is not a Jew suggests that all are called to show agape. One way of showing agape to people in any nation is to see that they have laws that serve them. Agape is a matter of helping other people to flourish, and law can be a source of that help. It can also be a source of great harm. Agapic law is among the most important means of showing agape to people in any country.

A second argument for judging all law by agape as Jesus judged the Mosaic Law is based on an analogy between the Mosaic civil law and the law of other nations. This type of argument is familiar to lawyers. A legal standard in one jurisdiction may serve as influential authority in another. It is worthy of consideration, and possibly of emulation. The field of comparative law notes analogies between legal systems and considers the possibility that the law in one jurisdiction should influence the law in another. Jewish Law commentators have suggested that Jewish Law might have such an influence on the law of other nations.[24] Jesus does not say that other legal systems are bound by his analysis of the Mosaic system, but his treatment provides a pattern that might be persuasive.

In order for the analogy between Jesus' critique of the Mosaic Law and other legal systems to carry weight, the Mosaic legal system – the law that is the object of Jesus' critique – must be similar in important ways to other legal systems. Obviously, legal systems address greatly different cultures, with greatly different practices, and the Mosaic system is quite different in many respects from that of most modern legal systems. But the role and the dangerous tendencies of law in almost any legal system are sufficiently similar to the Mosaic Law that many of Jesus' comments about the Mosaic system apply to them. Law's purposes are to organize society, to restrain evil, and, in some societies, to encourage the good. Agapic love would suggest that all of these functions should be carried out with human well-being in mind. All legal systems carry with them risks of the abuses Jesus confronted – of legal authorities focusing on the details of the legal system and losing sight of the people it serves; of law

[24] Samuel J. Levine, "Applying Jewish Legal Theory in the Context of American Law and Legal Scholarship: A Methodological Analysis," *Seton Hall Law Review* 933, no. 40 (2010): 947, citing to Arnold N. Enker, "Aspects of Interaction between the Torah Law, the King's Law, and the Noahide Law in Jewish Criminal Law," *Cardozo Law Review* 12 (1991): 1137.

being interpreted narrowly to serve only the privileged; of law being implemented harshly and hypocritically; and of authorities using law for their own and their social class's benefit at the expense of other people. The abuses of the Mosaic Law that Jesus addressed have enough in common with practices in other legal systems that his critique might be applied helpfully to them. Jesus' claim that law should serve people might be applied to any legal system.

A third argument for extending Jesus' agapic critique of the Mosaic Law to all civil law is that in making his argument, Jesus appealed to a higher authority (another practice familiar to lawyers). Jesus critiqued the Mosaic Law based on creation.[25] Whereas Jesus' identification of agape as the standard by which to judge the Mosaic Law suggested merely by analogy that agape should judge the law of other nations, Jesus' creation-based arguments apply directly to all humans and therefore to all human law – in the Christian understanding, all people are a product of God's creation (cf. Acts 8:26). In the following, I consider two cases, the Sabbath and marriage, where Jesus pointed to Genesis' creation narrative for the standard by which to judge the Mosaic Law. In both cases, the underlying standard he applied was agape.

Jesus grounded in creation his argument against the legalism with which the Pharisees applied the Sabbath regulations – the Sabbath "*was made* for humankind." He identified a standard that was prior to and went beyond the Mosaic Law. The fact that Jesus' critique was grounded in creation suggests that it applied to all of Adam's and Eve's descendants. In contrast to the dominant rabbinic teaching that the Sabbath was made for the Jews, Jesus taught that the Sabbath was made *for all of humanity*.[26] Jesus applied an agapic critique to the Sabbath – its regulations were to be judged based on its impact on human lives.

[25] Calvin also argued that agape is the higher standard that should judge the civil law. He framed it in traditional natural law terminology as "eternal law." The Mosaic civil law looked (and ultimately all civil law should look) "only to the best method of preserving that charity which is enjoined by the eternal law of God." Calvin, *Institutes of the Christian Religion*, IV, XX, 14, trans. Henry Beveridge, 664. Calvin's argument was based on the natural law notion that there is a divine moral law ("God's eternal law") that should be the basis of human civil law and that the love that is enjoined by God's eternal law should be reflected in the civil law. For discussion of Calvin's views of natural law, see Paul Helm, "Calvin and Natural Law," *Scottish Bulletin of Evangelical Theology* 2 (1984): 5–22; David VanDrunen, "Reforming Natural Law and the Two Kingdoms: John Calvin and His Contemporaries," in *Natural Law and the Two Kingdoms: A Study in the Development of Reformed Social Thought* (Grand Rapids: Wm. B. Eerdmans Publishing Co., 2010); Stephen J. Grabill, "John Calvin and the Natural Knowledge of God the Creator," in *Rediscovering the Natural Law in Reformed Theological Ethics* (Grand Rapids: Wm. B. Eerdmans Publishing Co., 2006).

[26] See John P. Meier, *A Marginal Jew: Rethinking the Historical Jesus: The Roots of the Problem and the Person*, Vol. 1 (New York: Doubleday, 1991), 281–83.

Jesus also grounded his arguments regarding marriage, divorce, and the Mosaic Law in the creation narrative. The Mosaic Law did not explicitly approve of divorce, but it mentioned and did not criticize a husband's divorce if his wife "has become displeasing to him because he finds something indecent about her, and he writes her a certificate of divorce" (Deut. 24:1–4). When some Pharisees asked Jesus, "Is it lawful for a man to divorce his wife for any cause?" Jesus pushed them beyond the controversy over divorce, back to God's original design for marriage:

> Have you not read [suggesting that it should have been obvious] that the one who made them at the beginning "made them male and female," and said, "For this reason a man shall leave his father and mother and be joined to his wife, and the two shall become one flesh"? So they are no longer two, but one flesh. Therefore what God has joined together, let no one separate. (Matt. 19:3–6, quoting Gen. 1:27, 2:24)

Jesus argued, based on the creation narrative that marriage was for life. As Paul Ramsey argues, it is best "to regard [Jesus'] strenuous views on marriage and divorce as another manifestation of unclaiming love [Ramsey's phrase for 'agape'] transcending enactment into statute."[27] "Unclaiming love will hardly find any cause for divorce, least of all will it fasten first upon what is the chief reason for divorce in the attitude of a person mainly concerned to claim his own rights."[28] The moral law, rooted in the creation narrative, called on the parties to a marriage to show self-giving, unclaiming, agapic love and to work through the problems in their marriage.

In these two examples, the Sabbath and marriage, Jesus applies an agapic standard, rooted in the creation account, to judge the Mosaic Law. Note that each example illustrates a different way in which agape might impact law. In the case of the Sabbath, Jesus suggested that the law should be loving toward people – law was made for people and should work for their benefit. In the case of marriage, Jesus' agapic critique suggests that law should teach people to act lovingly toward one another –married couples should show agapic love toward one another.

Agape, the Moral Law, and the Civil Law – If we are to look to creation and to agape for the standard by which to judge the positive law, what does that mean for the content of the civil law? Will the civil law always reflect the content of the moral law? Here again, Jesus' teaching on marriage and divorce is instructive.

27 Ramsey, *Basic Christian Ethics*, 71.

28 Ibid., 72.

Following the section quoted above, in which Jesus argued from the creation account that marriage is permanent, he noted that "[i]t was because you were so hard-hearted that Moses allowed you to divorce your wives" (Matt. 19:8). Jesus appears to have approved of an aspect of the Mosaic civil law that permitted and even identified the procedures for a deviation from God's moral law.[29] It is likely that Jesus, as well as Moses, envisioned the harmful consequences that would have arisen if divorce was not allowed: some husbands would abandon or even kill their wives and take other women without benefit of divorce; husbands would father illegitimate children; it would be unclear whether abandoned women were free to remarry; abandoned wives and children would be destitute; inheritance rights would be unclear and would generate conflict. Law that yielded such consequences would be the opposite of agapic love. Though God's marriage ideal called on both parties to a marriage to show agapic love and to remain together, agape as expressed in the Mosaic civil law, in light of the hardness of human hearts, allowed something short of that ideal. The Mosaic Law was a prudential and agapic response to the situation of the time, though in a different situation law might more closely approach God's creation ideal. As Calvin argued, "every nation is left free to make such laws as it foresees to be profitable to itself. Yet these must be in conformity to that perpetual rule of love."[30]

Jesus' comments on the Mosaic divorce law suggest an enormous opportunity (and responsibility) for judges and legislators who seek to apply agapic love to their work. They will prudently and creatively craft laws that reflect agape with eyes firmly fixed on practical reality. Viewed in this way, agape can pull law in two directions. God's moral law calls people to the full challenge of agapic love, but agapic love also imposes limits on the level to which it might be incorporated in the civil law. The lawmaker must exercise pragmatic, wise, agapic judgment in light of the hardness of human hearts.

1.2.2 *Agapic Governance: Reigning, Judging, and Serving on Earth*

It is one thing for a country to have wise, just, even loving laws; it is another for people to benefit from those laws. Just laws do not yield just rule. The Roman and Jewish laws of Jesus' day were among the best ever crafted, but Caesar and

[29] Ramsey argues that "Jesus's judgment upon the law of Moses that he permitted divorce only on account of the hardness of men's hearts remains an essential part of a Christian theory of law." Ibid., 72. Jesus' standards on divorce "constitute an ethic of perfection which transcends any possible legal formulation." Ibid., 73.

[30] Calvin, *Institutes of the Christian Religion*, IV, XX, 14, trans. Henry Beveridge 663.

Herod were unjust rulers and the people of Israel suffered injustice. For many citizens today, the administration of justice is not any better. As Gary Haugen and Victor Boutros have noted, most of the greatest injustices in the world today are not a result of the content of laws.[31] Laws in almost all countries prohibit slavery, extortion, land grabbing, human trafficking, child labor, and prostitution, but in many countries no one enforces these laws. The law on the books is different from the law on the street. Police, prosecutors, court personnel, and judges – those who are supposed to protect people – take advantage of them. Justice requires not only just laws, but just administration of laws. In the face of the common tendency of leaders in all ages to take advantage of their power, Jesus advocated and modeled leadership as servanthood in his kingdom – a form of leadership that has been and is seldom seen.

Jesus came at a time of political foment. In the prior 600 years, Israel had been subject to one foreign ruler after another – Babylonians, Greeks, Egyptians, Syrians, and in Jesus' day Romans.[32] Jesus followed a series of Jewish revolutionaries.[33] Many of his followers expected him to be such a revolutionary. It is important to see Jesus' teaching and the reaction to him in that light.

I have already noted that justice was a substantial theme in Jesus' teaching. "I tell you, [God] will quickly grant justice to ['his chosen ones who cry to him day and night']" (Luke 18:7–8). Moreover, Jesus' central message (and that of his forerunner, John the Baptist) was that the kingdom of God had arrived in Jesus' ministry (Matt. 4:23, 11:12; Mark 1:15; Luke 4:43, 17:20–21), and that it would be more dramatically manifested in the future. Jesus taught his disciples to pray that God's kingdom would come, that his will would be done on earth (Matt. 6:10; cf. Luke 11:2). He taught his followers that they would be leaders in this new kingdom, and that his disciples would sit on twelve thrones and judge the twelve tribes of Israel (Matt. 19:28; Luke 22:30).

This picture of God and his followers ruling is prominent in the Christian scriptures, from creation to consummation. In the creation narrative, Adam and Eve, as those created "in the image of God,"[34] were to "exercise dominion" (Gen. 1:28). "Dominion" in the Old Testament is often a legal word, used

31 Gary Haugen and Victor Boutros, "And Justice for All: Enforcing Human Rights for the World's Poor," *Foreign Affairs* 89 (May/June 2010).

32 For a chart showing the rulers in this period, see N. T. Wright, *Simply Jesus: A New Vision of Who He Was, What He Did, and Why He Matters* (New York: HarperOne, 2011), 62.

33 Ibid., 106–16.

34 Randy Beck and David VanDrunen, "The Biblical Foundations of Law: Creation, Fall and the Patriarchs," in *Law and the Bible: Justice, Mercy and Legal Institutions*, eds. Robert F. Cochran, Jr. and David VanDrunen (Downers Grove: InterVarsity Press, 2013), 27–31.

to indicate the responsibility of rulers and their administrators (Lev. 25:43, 46, 53, 26:17; Ps. 110:2; Ezek. 34:4).

Centuries of Jewish prophesies had taught that God would be their king (Pss. 10:16–18, 96:10–13) and that he would rule through his appointed, earthly king (Ps. 2:1–9).[35] Daniel prophesied that one would come like a "son of man," to whom God would give everlasting "dominion and glory and kingship, that all peoples, nations, and languages should serve him" (Dan. 7:14). "The son of man" would not rule alone.

The kingship and dominion and the greatness of the kingdoms under the whole heaven shall be given to the people of the holy ones of the Most High: "their kingdom shall be an everlasting kingdom, and all dominions shall serve and obey them" (Dan. 7:27).

When both John the Baptist and Jesus announced that God's kingdom had come and Jesus referred to himself as the "son of man" (Mark 2:10), it is not surprising that people thought of the prophesied kingdom and of Jesus as the king.

Many of Jesus' actions, as well as his teaching, raised hopes that he would be a political messiah. On one occasion, he made a dramatic entry into Jerusalem on a donkey, drawing a large crowd (Matt. 21:1–9, Mark 11:1–10; Luke 19:29–38; John 12:12–19). The people would have readily identified Jesus' entry in this manner (as Matthew does identify it) as a fulfillment of messianic prophesy: "Tell the daughter of Zion, Look, your king is coming to you, humble, and mounted on a donkey, and on a colt, the foal of a donkey." (Matt. 21:5, quoting Zech. 9:9)

As Jesus entered Jerusalem, "[a] very large crowd spread their cloaks on the road, and others cut branches from the trees and spread them on the road" (Matt. 21:8). They shouted: "Hosanna to the Son of David!" (Matt. 21:9), harkening back to Old Testament promises that from the line of David would come a king whose throne would be established forever (2 Sam. 7:12–14).

This understanding that Jesus and his followers would reign over the earth continued after Jesus' death and resurrection. At his ascension, Jesus claimed "all authority in heaven and on earth" (Matt. 28:18). Paul told the Corinthians that they would "judge angels" (1 Cor. 6:1–5). The final book of the New Testament, Revelation, reported that in the New Heavens and the New Earth, worshipers would sing to Jesus: "you ransomed for God saints from every tribe and language and people and nation; you have made them to be a kingdom and priests serving our God, and they will reign on earth" (Rev. 5:9–10; cf. Rev. 1:6, 3:21, 5:10, 20:6). The picture of Jesus and his

[35] Wright, *Simply Jesus*, 106–16.

followers reigning in a New Heaven and a New Earth reached far into the past and into the future.

However, in Matthew, Mark, and John, the story of Jesus' triumphal entry into Jerusalem was paired with stories of Jesus teaching a new form of leadership – humility and servanthood – to his disciples. In Matthew and Mark, prior to his entry into Jerusalem, Jesus' disciples and the mother of two of them were verbally jockeying for position in Jesus' future kingdom. They argued over who would sit on his right and left. Given Jesus' proclamation of the kingdom, it is not surprising that his disciples (and their mothers!) were excited about their roles in this new kingdom. Jesus did not deny that they would reign with him, but he gave them a challenging picture of governance.

> You know that the rulers of the Gentiles lord it over them, and their great ones are tyrants over them. It will not be so among you; but whoever wishes to be great among you must be your servant, and whoever wishes to be first among you must be your slave – just as the Son of Man came not to be served, but to serve, and to give his life a ransom for many. (Matt. 20:25–28; Mark 10:35–45; see also Luke 22:24–30)

In a world where Gentiles – presumably the Romans – "lord[ed] it over" their subjects, Jesus' followers' governance was to be marked by service.

This story has often been interpreted as a description of what leadership should be like within the church, but the context of Jesus' teaching is a discussion of Jesus' disciples' leadership within the kingdom of God. Jesus' followers were to reign with him and their conversation is best viewed as a discussion of what that reign should look like.

Jesus criticized a familiar characteristic of political leaders – they "lord it over" the people who are subject to their control – they push them around. Law is, of course, a common means that leaders use to dominate and coerce people. Jesus' implicit criticism of Gentile leaders suggests that leaders should serve people. Legal administrators were made for humankind, not humankind for administrators. Both law and its administration should be a manifestation of agape. Jesus did not deny that his followers would have responsibilities in the new kingdom – some would even be called on to sit on his left and right – but it would be a new type of leadership, one marked by service rather than authoritarianism. Leaders motivated by agape would serve those under their authority.

Here, as elsewhere, Jesus pointed to himself as the model for his disciples – "just as the Son of Man came not to be served, but to serve, and to give his life as a ransom for many." Two aspects of this statement are striking. Jesus referred to himself as the "Son of Man" – the title the Old Testament writer

Daniel used to describe the one to whom God would give everlasting "dominion and glory and kingship, that all peoples, nations, and languages should serve him" (Dan. 7:14). And yet Jesus presented the Son of Man as a servant. He linked dominion, glory, and kingship with servanthood. Second, note the extent of the sacrifice to which Jesus called his leaders – they, like him, were to give their lives for other people.

John does not report Jesus' and his disciples' discussion about leadership, but shortly after John's account of Jesus' entry into Jerusalem, he reports a striking demonstration of the depth of service to which Jesus called leaders in his kingdom. After receiving a tribute reserved for conquering kings at his entry into Jerusalem, Jesus did the most menial task for his disciples.

> [Jesus] got up from the table, took off his outer robe, and tied a towel around himself. Then he poured water into a basin and began to wash the disciples' feet and to wipe them with the towel that was tied around him. (John 13:3–5)

Jesus then urged his disciples to follow his example and to wash one another's feet.

Agape frames the foot-washing story: it is introduced as a story about Jesus' love for his disciples "to the end" (John 13:1). Jesus concluded the dinner, saying: "I give you a new commandment, that you love one another" (John 13:34). Jesus washed his disciples' feet as an act of agape; he taught them to act with agape.

The disciples must have been struck by this chain of events. It is clear from their argument over their thrones that they were thinking about their roles and status within the new kingdom. Jesus disrupted their dispute and identified servanthood with governance. He then entered Jerusalem triumphantly and washed their feet. The juxtaposition of these events – on the one hand, the celebration of Jesus as king; and on the other, his lecture on servanthood and his washing their feet – would have sealed two thoughts in their minds: Jesus was inaugurating a new kingdom in which he would be king, and this new kingdom's form of governance would be servanthood.

As we have seen, Jesus' words and actions led the people of Israel to identify him as the prophesied messiah. This image fits the Jesus of the triumphal entry, the Jesus who would be king. But there was another Old Testament figure, also identified in the New Testament with Jesus, who illustrated Jesus' servant model. He is the "Suffering Servant" in the book of Isaiah. As noted previously, this servant would "bring forth justice to the nations" (Isa. 42:1),[36]

[36] In some places Isaiah identifies the Servant as the nation of Israel (Isa. 41:8–9); in others, as a messianic individual (Isa. 49:5–6).

but he also would sacrifice his life that those who "like sheep ha[d] gone astray" might return to God (Isa. 53:6). In Jesus, these roles were combined to present an agapic model of leadership. He is both the king who is to rule the world and the servant who sacrifices his life for the world. Jesus brought these roles – leadership and sacrifice – together. He called on his followers to do the same.

Jesus also had a message for those who judge. People in almost any leadership position are called on to judge. In the legal sphere,[37] these include judges, police officers, prosecutors, and executives; they also include legislators, as they determine what activities to criminalize, who receives government benefits, and who is to be admitted into a country. Jesus said, "Do not judge so that you will not be judged… [F]irst take the log out of your own eye, and then you will see clearly to take the speck out of your neighbor's eye" (Matt. 7:1, 5). Those who judge should first recognize and deal with their own shortcomings and then judge. Doing so is likely to have a couple of results. Recognizing one's own weaknesses will enable one to empathize with fellow wrongdoers and make wiser judgments. There is not one class of good people and another of bad people. There is good and evil in all of us. In addition, correcting one's own shortcomings will give one greater standing to make a respected judgment.

Jesus' lesson to those who judge is illustrated in the story of the woman caught in adultery (John 8:2–11).[38] A group of law teachers and Pharisees dragged the woman before Jesus and asked if they should stone her pursuant to the Mosaic Law. Jesus responded, "Let anyone among you who is without sin be the first to throw a stone at her." One by one, they all left. Jesus' statement challenged them to examine their own hearts. They may have reflected on their error in dragging the woman before Jesus, for the Mosaic Code required both parties to adultery to be stoned – the men were guilty of unjust prosecutorial discretion. Perhaps they were protecting a friend. Perhaps one of them was the adulterer. Ultimately, Jesus' response was both to show mercy toward the woman *and* to exercise judgment: "[N]either do I condemn you . . . Go your way, and from now on do not sin again" (John 8:2–11).

[37] Various forms of the Greek word for judge (krino) used in the illustrations in the text are used elsewhere in the New Testament of legal judgment (Matt. 5:40; John 7:51, 18:31; Acts 23:3, 25:10, 26:6) as well as judgment within the church (1 Cor. 5:3, 5:12–13, 6:1–3) and divine judgment (Rev. 6:10, 11:18, 18:20, 19:2).

[38] The earliest and most reliable manuscripts of the Gospel of John do not include this story. Nevertheless, "[t]hroughout the history of the church, it has been held that, whoever wrote it, this little story is authentic." Leon Morris, *The Gospel According to John*, Revised, NICNT (Grand Rapids: Wm. B. Eerdmans Publishing Co., 1995).

In isolation, two of Jesus' sayings from above – "Do not judge" and "He who is without sin cast the first stone" – might suggest that Jesus' followers were not to judge at all. If Jesus' statement to the mob was taken literally, no one would be able to judge. However, Jesus' other statements – to judges: "first take the log out of your own eye" and to the judged: "Go and leave your life of sin" – suggest that exercising judgment is a proper calling. It is to be done, however, with careful reflection on one's own character.

Throughout Christian history, Christian attempts to rule often have not gone well. Christian leaders have been guilty of triumphalism, a pragmatic power grab, and violence that was no different from that of others who sought to dominate. However, as N. T. Wright has written, "[God's Kingdom] cannot be established by *force majeure* [today's leaders might say 'shock and awe'], but only by its proper means: suffering, self-giving love."[39]

1.3 CONCLUSION

As noted in the first section of this essay, Jesus taught his followers to respond to injustice by submitting to it – turning the other cheek, walking the second mile, and loving their enemies. But Jesus also spoke forcefully against injustice and called his followers to reign with him in a kingdom where love of God and neighbor – "justice, mercy, and faith" – would be the standards. Jesus put his followers in the challenging role of submitting to injustice, but seeking justice for other people. This is the opposite of the tendency of many leaders, both in Jesus' day and today – they assert their own rights and take unjust advantage of other people. Jesus presented a challenging call: give up your own rights and protect other people's rights. Christians were to seek for others what they would not seek for themselves.[40]

These responsibilities call on Christian leaders to have qualities that are in tension with one another – they must be both humble and forceful. The two responsibilities are reconciled in Jesus' call to love. As Paul Ramsey argues, "The same inner disposition which, so far as one's self is concerned, leads to a

[39] N. T. Wright, *After You Believe: Why Christian Character Matters* (New York: HarperOne, 2010), 113.

[40] My argument here is similar to that of Ambrose and Augustine that Christians should not engage in self-defense, but should fight a just war. See Ramsey, *Basic Christian Ethics*, 171–76 and *War and the Christian Conscience*, 34–39. Ramsey notes that "both the pacifism of early Christians and their shift over to resistance in the light of increasing responsibility were basically grounded in Christian love . . . One should do for others what one may not do for one's self." Ramsey, *Basic Christian Ethics*, 182. "[T]his was a change of tactics only. The basic strategy remained the same: responsible love and service of one's neighbor in the texture of the common life." *War and the Christian Conscience*, xvii.

renunciation of rights may so far as others must be served, lead to utter insistence upon them: in both, 'you govern yourself according to love.'"[41] Both submission to personal injustice and the pursuit of public justice are reflections of agape. Under Jesus' teaching, the mindset is the same in each setting – the Christian should seek the good of other people, both enemies and victims.

My main argument in this essay is that Jesus would have his followers evaluate law and legal administration in terms of agape. Law should be based on its impact on everyone affected. I hesitate to offer specific policy recommendations, for fear that disagreement over them might distract readers from that main point – the framework within which discussions should take place. Nevertheless, I return to the themes from Jesus' teaching on agape at the beginning of this essay, and I point in the general direction each theme might suggest for law today.

1. **Loving Samaritans** – Samaritans are the outsiders in the midst of a country – those of a different race, religion, nation, and cultural background. Followers of Jesus should be the first to protect them and support laws that give them access to basic needs such as work, education, and medical care.[42]
2. **Loving Enemies** – Government leaders are likely to confront public enemies from within and without. In criminal legislation, prosecution, and punishment, Christians should seek "justice tempered with mercy."[43] Justice and mercy appear to be in tension with one another, but it may be that "*Love does not choose between justice and mercy, for these two goods are internally related to agape*."[44] The question facing those in the public square is the good of all those concerned.

   It is difficult to even imagine conducting war with love for the enemy – the general practice of government public relations efforts is to induce hatred for the enemy. War places great challenges on Jesus' followers, for agape calls for both love of the enemy and protection of those at risk. As Paul Ramsey has argued, just war theory was developed

41 Ibid., 187, quoting Martin Luther, "Secular Authority: To What Extent It Should Be Obeyed," *Works*, III (Muhlenberg, 1943), 241–42.

42 Jennifer Lee Koh, "Agape, Grace, and Immigration Law: An Evangelical Perspective," in this volume.

43 Oliver O'Donovan traces this formulation to Ambrose. Oliver O'Donovan, *Desire of the Nations: Rediscovering the Roots of Political Theology* (Cambridge: Cambridge University Press, 1996), 200.

44 Timothy Jackson, *The Priority of Love: Christian Charity and Social Justice* (Princeton: Princeton University Press, 2003), 110 (summarizing the position of Paul Ramsey; italics in original).

by Christians as an application of agape toward both aggressors and victims. Agape will restrain sin, for the sake of both sinners and victims.[45]

3. **Humility, Service, and Sacrifice** – As argued above, Jesus' followers will serve others with humility, not the haughty arrogance that so often characterizes political and legal administration. When given the opportunity, Jesus' followers will be servant leaders.
4. **Meeting Needs** – Jesus identified himself as having come "to bring good news to the poor . . . to proclaim release to the captives and . . . to let the oppressed go free" (Luke 4:17–21). As William Loader has noted, Jesus' "radical concern for people in need" was reflected in his teaching on law.[46] Jesus envisioned law as a means of serving the poor and oppressed. Agapic love will generate sacrifice for the poor and needy by individuals, churches, and private charitable organizations, but it will also support a public social safety net. The challenge is to help those in need in ways that will enable them to flourish and encourage their independence. The concept of subsidiarity – leaving as much responsibility as possible with families and local communities, with government as a back-up – is among the wisest approaches. As Pope John Paul II said, "Needs are best understood and satisfied by people who are closest to them, and who act as neighbors to those in need."[47]
5. **Teaching** – Agape recognizes the importance of teaching and learning. Agapic leadership will support quality education, whether through a public school system, private schools, religious schools, home schooling, or some combination of these.
6. **Agape Elevates** – Agape in the public sphere will seek to elevate citizens to the point where they can share public responsibility. As noted above, people's needs should be met in a way that will not make people dependent, but enable them to care for themselves and ultimately for others. Though democracy is not a panacea, agape would support democratic participation in government. Citizens see the needs of their communities first hand and this should enable them to make wise choices; they

[45] Ramsey, *War and the Christian Conscience*, 56.

[46] William R. G. Loader, *Jesus' Attitude towards the Law: A Study of the Gospels* (Grand Rapids: Wm. B. Eerdmans Publishing Co., 2002), 130 (commenting on Mark's Gospel). Loader also notes that "Much of Jesus' distinctive Torah interpretation in Matthew reflects the value of compassion for the needy." Ibid., 265.

[47] John Paul II, *Centesimus Annus, The Economics of Human Freedom* (1991), available at http://w2.vatican.va/content/john-paul-ii/en/encyclicals/documents/hf_jp-ii_enc_01051991_centesimus-annus.html. See also Lucia A. Silecchia, "The When and the Where of Love: Subsidiarity as a Framework for Care of the Elderly" in this volume.

> should learn to wisely exercise power by exercising it. Citizens should be shepherds, not sheep.

Jesus called on his followers to have a change of heart. They were to love their neighbors as themselves. That change has implications for all of life, at home, church, office, and courtroom. To the extent Jesus' followers can do so consistently with Jesus' teaching, they should manifest agape in the exercise of political and legal power. This is not to say that it will be easy to determine agape's implications for law. The challenge Jesus left with voters, leaders, lawyers, judges, and administrators is to figure out what agape means in such contexts.

2

"Love Calls Us to the Things of This World": The Pauline Tradition and "The Law of Christ"

Darryl L. Tippens

Many students of the law today would be surprised if not baffled by any effort to connect law and love, yet there is a long and rich history of this association within the Western tradition. If the relationship of law and love is not readily apparent, it only suggests how thoroughly Enlightenment assumptions have eclipsed certain classical ways of understanding. Within both Jewish and Christian traditions, for example, there is an express relationship between law, love, and justice. The commandment to love (Hebrew *ahab*) one's "neighbor" and the "stranger" or "alien" (Hebrew *ger*) in one's community is articulated in the Torah (Lev. 19:18, 34).[1] Deuteronomic law carefully weaves together love, justice, and the duty to obey the commandments (Deut. 10:12–19). "Love" (*ahab*) calls the faithful to imitate the character of Yahweh by treating others with extraordinary kindness, mercy, and love. Because the Creator is loving and just – defending orphans and widows, loving the chosen people and the alien alike – the people of God are directed to do the same: to "keep the commandments of the Lord your God" and "[y]ou shall also love the stranger . . ." (Deut. 10:13, 19). The centrality of love of neighbor has been reiterated throughout the later Jewish tradition as well. According to Rabbi Hillel, love of neighbor is the essence of the Torah, "The rest is commentary. Now go study the commentary."[2]

Christianity builds on the venerable Jewish tradition of law, love, and the just treatment of others. In the Gospels, Jesus emphasizes the centrality of

I wish to express special thanks to Professor Christopher R. Hutson, Abilene Christian University, for reading an early draft of this essay and offering helpful suggestions.

[1] Biblical quotations come from the New Revised Standard Version (NRSV).

[2] David L. Lieber, ed. *Etz Hazim: Torah and Commentary* (New York: Jewish Publication Society, 2001), 697. According to some scholars of early Christianity, the central place of love in the new faith may have been influenced by a particular branch of Judaism that championed Hillel's view. See Hans Dieter Betz, *Galatians: A Commentary on Paul's Letter to the Churches in Galatia* (Philadelphia: Fortress, 1979), 276.

love and its connection to law when he declares love of neighbor one of the two greatest commandments. Indeed, "the entire law" and the prophets hang upon love of God and neighbor (Matt. 22:37–40). Jesus then enlarges the scope of the matter by making it clear that one's neighbor is not limited to the narrow precincts of one's own religion, community, or nation. One's neighbor may be found among those who are religiously, ethnically, or politically different (Luke 10:25–37). The capacity to love in this radical way, Jesus asserts, is the hallmark of his followers (John 13:35).

As Christianity spread throughout the Greco-Roman world and embraced large numbers of Gentiles, the relation of love to law remained vital, but the understanding of "law" as Jewish Torah changed. In St. Paul's teaching, the church was the new "Israel of God" with a new law, "the Law of Christ" (Gal. 6:2, 16).[3] Within the new faith the law (*nomos*) came to be identified with the overarching duty to love. This obligation was not one important command among many, as in the Torah. Love was the very expression and embodiment, the summation, the completion, and therefore the *replacement*, of the Torah. The Apostle writes:

> Owe no one anything, except to love one another; for the one who loves another has fulfilled the law. The commandments, "You shall not commit adultery; You shall not murder; You shall not steal; You shall not covet"; and *any other commandment*, are summed up in this word, "Love your neighbor as yourself." . . . therefore, love is the fulfilling of the law [*nomos*]. (Rom. 13:8–10) (emphasis added)

"For the whole law is summed up in a single commandment, 'You shall love your neighbor as yourself'" (Gal. 5:14).[4] Love becomes the ultimate Christian virtue, new Torah in a word.

3 Richard B. Hayes, "Christology and Ethics in Galatians: The Law of Christ," *Catholic Biblical Quarterly* 49, no. 2 (1987): 268–90. Scholars do not agree on which letters in the New Testament were written by Paul and which may have been written by someone in the Pauline school; for the purposes of this essay, I am considering the ideas deriving from the "Pauline tradition," whether or not specifically written by Paul himself.

4 The semantic ambiguity of "law" (*nomos*) must be noted. When Paul uses *nomos* he usually means the Torah, the Mosaic code; but in some contexts *nomos* means custom, rule, norm, or a statutory legal system – not the Torah. Later interpreters sometimes appropriated Paul's teachings on law as a means to critique religious and political systems of their day, with little or no reference to Jewish Scripture. For example, John Milton and other religious and political revolutionaries in the seventeenth century used Paul's words on law to challenge the religious and legal systems of their day. See John S. Coolidge, *The Pauline Renaissance in England: Puritanism and the Bible* (Oxford: Clarendon, 1970); and Christopher Hill, *Milton and the English Revolution* (New York: Viking Press, 1978).

Love as the supreme law proves an enduring theme in Christian theology and ethics.[5] It appears in the writings of Augustine, Aquinas, the Christian mystics, Reformers like Calvin and Luther, and among major Christian thinkers like Kierkegaard. Given the long dialogue of love and law carried out over two millennia, one can only gesture toward the rich possibilities that arise from a focus on these topics. In the pages that follow I summarize some key themes that might further the conversation about law (in the contemporary legal sense) and the Christian, specifically Pauline, understanding of love.

It hardly needs to be said that St. Paul's concerns were considerably different from our own. As a student of the Torah and as a missionary who wrestled with the urgent problems of nascent Christian communities in the ancient Mediterranean world, the Apostle to the Gentiles did not have his eye on political or legal questions that lay twenty centuries beyond his horizon. Even so, current notions of love and justice have deep roots in antiquity. St. Paul's ideas of ethics, law, human dignity, freedom, and the virtues that enable a just and harmonious community – all these concerns from the Apostle's era – resonate with our own.

2.1 LAW, LOVE, AND THE PAULINE TRADITION

A Christian and specifically Pauline understanding of love begins with a word that had rarely appeared in ancient Greek literature – agape.[6] While the early Christians did not invent the word agape (it appears in the Septuagint, the Greek translation of the Old Testament), they appropriated the term to convey a particular theological and ethical ideal. Because St. Paul provides the first written record of agape's centrality to the new faith (even before the Gospels had been composed), his use of the term is important to understanding how love was understood in early Christian communities. In the Christian lexicon agape means warm regard, esteem, affection, and self-sacrificing care for others, even to the point of extreme personal cost. As St. Paul shows in his hymn to agape in 1 Corinthians 13, love is an attitude, yes, but even more it is *an act of the will*, a disposition that prompts certain behaviors: "Love is patient; love

[5] Victor P. Furnish, *The Love Command in the New Testament* (Nashville: Abingdon Press, 1972).

[6] The Greeks commonly employed three words for love: storge (parental love of children, warm feelings for one's friends and fellow citizens); eros (sexual passion); and philia (friendship, goodwill). The noun form agape was rarely used in ancient Greek writings before the composition of the New Testament. See Ceslas Spicq, *Theological Lexicon of the New Testament*, trans. and ed. James D. Ernest (Peabody: Hendrickson, 1994), 1:8–22.

is kind; love is not envious or boastful or arrogant or rude. It does not insist on its way." Agape is something one *practices*. According to Ceslas Spicq,

> it is essential to charity to manifest itself, to demonstrate itself, to provide proofs, to put itself on display; so much so that in the NT it would almost always be necessary to translate agape as "demonstration of love."[7]

These "demonstrations of love" were exceptional by ancient standards. Acts of love in the Greco-Roman world were based essentially upon rules of reciprocity applicable within defined communities and practiced among social equals (in a *quid pro quo* arrangement). Christian agape radically challenges the social order, for it is a "disinterested and generous love" that unites people from different social, ethnic, and racial conditions.[8] In fact, agape is to be practiced precisely in places where custom and long habit forbade it (toward the weak, the enslaved, the poor, etc.). For this reason, wherever agape is taken seriously, the grounds for a just community become enlarged. It is not too much to say that because agape envisions a radically different way of relating to people across racial, ethnic, and religious boundaries, it serves justice implicitly, if not explicitly. It is this sense of the matter that motivated the ministry and work of Martin Luther King, Jr., who routinely linked the call to racial justice and the claims of agape.

In this essay I will consider five features of Pauline agape that have relevance to a discussion of love's relation to law and justice: (1) agape as Torah; (2) agape as epistemology; (3) agape as justice in action; (4) agape as defined by community and its narratives; and (5) agape acquired through habits and practices ("liturgies").[9]

2.1.1 *Agape as Torah*

Facing extraordinary challenges in young, culturally diverse churches in the Greco-Roman world, far removed from the Jewish homeland where Jesus had lived and taught, St. Paul found new things to say about the law. Jewish and Gentile

[7] Spicq, *Theological Lexicon*, 1:12. See also *A Greek–English Lexicon of the New Testament and Other Early Christian Literature*, eds. William Arndt and Frederick W. Danker (Chicago: University of Chicago Press, 2000): I: 5–7. It is worth recalling that Paul penned the earliest books of the New Testament and is therefore the first Christian writer to use the term agape. Chronologically speaking, agape is therefore particularly "Pauline." Since Jesus spoke Aramaic, agape is the Gospel writers' Greek equivalent for Jesus' Aramaic term.

[8] Spicq, *Theological Lexicon*, 1:13.

[9] Given the rich diversity of discussion concerning Paul's teaching on love over twenty centuries, it is impossible to reduce this voluminous discourse to a brief statement. For a comprehensive analysis of Paul on many of the topics discussed in this essay, consult N. T. Wright's magisterial, two-volume study: *Paul and the Faithfulness of God* (Minneapolis: Fortress Press, 2013).

Christians were at loggerheads over questions of Torah observance. They asked in particular whether the Torah was binding on Gentile converts. Addressing these divided and confused converts, St. Paul offered an alternate way to be faithful to Torah. According to St. Paul, one does not so much love Torah as one comes to see that love, properly construed, is *virtually identical* to the law. Love is the fulfillment, "the end," or *telos* of the law (Rom. 13:8–10). Whereas Jews were obliged to "do" the Torah, observing kosher rules and holy days, according to St. Paul's way of thinking the faithful "fulfill" the Torah through acts of agape, for "in loving, the Torah is always fulfilled."[10] Radical though this move may seem, it did not lead to a break with the ethical principles of the Torah for several reasons (not least because the commandments of the Torah, especially those of the Decalogue, exemplify love). Yet the *motivation* for this conduct changed. Actions are now prompted by a compelling love story, the supreme example of Christ's self-sacrifice. This story of radical, self-giving love is a "world plot," the "cosmic paradigm," that should be endlessly replicated by the followers of Jesus.[11] If agape is defined by the Christ narrative, ethical and just practices will necessarily ensue. This becomes a familiar theme throughout the Christian tradition. St. Augustine, following St. Paul, maintains that "[a]ll the divine precepts are, therefore, referred back to *love*, of which the apostle says, 'Now the end of the commandment is love, out of a pure heart, and a good conscience and a faith unfeigned.' Thus every commandment harks back to love."[12] Hannah Arendt summarizes this Pauline/Augustinian view: "*Caritas* fulfills the law, because to *caritas* the law is no longer a command; it is grace itself."[13]

[10] Betz, *Galatians*, 275.

[11] Hayes, *The Law of Christ*, 280–81.

[12] *Augustine: Confessions and Enchiridion*, ed. and trans. Albert C. Outler (London: SCM Press, 1955), xxxii: 121 (411). Augustine also writes that we should love one another "because *the object of the commandment* (1 Tim. 1:5) and *the fullness of the law is love* (Rom. 13:10). . . . [The end of learning is] constituted by love, and whatever we are doing or saying, our eyes should never be turned away from this goal." *Instructing Beginners in Faith*, trans. Raymond Channing (Hyde Park: New City Press, 2006), 67, 76 (emphasis added). One must take care to avoid conflating Pauline and Augustinian views of law and love, yet the Bishop of Hippo echoes Paul's themes so frequently that contemporary reading of Paul on law and love will to some degree be mediated by the Augustinian tradition.

[13] Hannah Arendt, *Love and Saint Augustine*, eds. Joanna V. Scott and Judith C. Stark (Chicago: University of Chicago Press, 1996), 91. *Caritas* is the Latin Bible's word for agape. According to the *Oxford English Dictionary*, *caritas* was introduced into the English language around AD 1175, morphing into the English word *charite* in Wycliffe's translation of 1382. Subsequent sixteenth-century translations by Tyndale and others render agape as either "love" or "charity," treating the two English words as virtual synonyms. The profoundly influential Authorized Version of 1611 most often translates agape as "love," but employs "charity" in such key texts as Paul's hymn to agape: "And now abideth faith, hope, charitie, these three; but the greatest of these is charitie" (1 Cor. 13:13). Only later did *charity* develop the pejorative sense of perfunctory, unfeeling alms-giving.

2.1.2 *Agape as Epistemology*

If St. Paul's view of Torah is remarkable, equally surprising is his view of love as a new epistemology. Ordinary, discursive knowledge has limits, but agape as understood by St. Paul opens up a superior way of understanding, according to N. T. Wright, "because it is love that, while completely engaging with reality other than itself, affirms and celebrates that other-than-itself reality."[14] Once "the lover affirms the reality and the otherness of the beloved," once one exercises "the readiness to let the other *be* the other," and once one exercises "patient listening," then one is opened up to see more deeply and truly.[15] This is the fundamental insight of Pauline agape: those who love can see in ways others cannot:

> There is, then, an *epistemological* revolution at the heart of St. Paul's worldview and theology. It isn't just that he now knows things he did not before; it is, rather that *the act of knowing* has itself been transformed. . . . Ordinary human wisdom, ordinary human knowledge is not just cancelled. It is taken up into something at one level similar and at another level radically different. St. Paul's name for the new "something" is agape, love.[16]

Wright's insight is not new. According to Gregory the Great, love itself is a form of knowledge (*Amor ipse notitia est*).[17] Tolstoy states it eloquently in *War and Peace*: "Every single thing I understand, I understand only because I love."[18] If love has this heuristic power, it raises important questions about pedagogy and the law – both its study and practice: what if a complex legal matter is more fully grasped through the prism of agape? What if justice is dependent upon a deep commitment to and immersion in the love of one's neighbor? What if agape is a professional virtue, not merely a private one?

2.1.3 *Agape as Justice in Action ("Setting the World to Rights"[19])*

Another feature of Pauline agape is its power to motivate individuals and communities to act with integrity and fairness. According to St. Paul, love

[14] N. T. Wright, *Surprised by Scripture: Engaging Contemporary Issues* (New York: HarperCollins, 2014).

[15] N. T. Wright, *The New Testament and the People of God* (Minneapolis: Fortress Press, 1992), 64. See also N. T. Wright, *Surprised by Hope: Rethinking Heaven, the Resurrection, and the Mission of the Church* (New York: HarperOne, 2008), 72–73.

[16] Wright, *Paul and the Faithfulness of God*, 1355–56. See also Wright, *New Testament and the People of God*, 62–64.

[17] Robert Louis Wilken, *The Spirit of Early Christian Thought: Seeking the Face of God* (New Haven: Yale University Press, 2003), 312.

[18] Leo Tolstoy, *War and Peace*, trans. Anthony Briggs (New York: Penguin, 2000), 1093.

[19] N. T. Wright, *Simply Christian: Why Christianity Makes Sense* (New York: HarperCollins, 2006).

is not only the goal; it is the means to the goal, the engine of the moral life, which "compels" individuals to act boldly on behalf of others' needs: "the love of Christ urges us on" (2 Cor. 5:14). Love motivates (Greek *synechō*: "urges, impels, exercises a constraining influence on") one to act justly. While we have seen that agape constitutes a higher epistemology, enabling deeper insights, one should note that for St. Paul knowledge is not itself the goal; rather, it is a renewed and just world.[20] As Wright points out, the singular Protestant emphasis on the "salvation" of individual souls has unfortunately obscured the vital theme that the advent of God's kingdom is designed to renew relationships and heal communities – to effect a changed world, not merely prepare the faithful for heaven. Jesus prayed that God's will would be done "on earth" as it is in heaven. Indeed, the goal of Pauline "redemption" has a this-world orientation – a restored cosmos, a new heaven and a new earth, with the Creator putting everything back in its proper order. God acts "in the way a human judge acts when re-establishing 'justice' in a community. . . . This particular God has a responsibility to sort out the mess in his creation, to call it to account, to set everything right."[21] Thus, love serves justice in multiple ways: it effects personal renewal (the restoration of the divine–human relationship), and it aims to correct whatever is amiss in the cosmos. This renewal is both present and future, as broken communities and dysfunctional relationships are brought into harmony.

Agape is central to the restoration of all things – first through the preemptive, self-initiated, and unmerited love of God toward his fallen creation, but secondarily through the actions of those who imitate this self-giving love. There is specific content to this love. It entails pouring out one's very self through acts of generosity: extending hospitality to strangers; showing humble deference to others; practicing patience and forbearance; caring for the poor; bearing one another's burdens; and exercising kindness, humility, and meekness. While St. Paul's lists of specific Christ-like actions and attitudes are copious, there is no doubt about the supreme virtue. It is agape "above all," he says; so "clothe yourselves with love, which binds everything together in perfect harmony" (Col. 3:12–14; cf. Rom. 12:9–21).

From St. Paul's perspective, justice apart from agape, or agape apart from justice, is inconceivable since God is love, and he is just. "Love does no wrong to a neighbor" (Rom. 13:10). The understanding that love always leads to neighborly goodwill explains why Augustine could say brashly, "Love, and do what you want," and Simone Weil could write that justice

[20] Wright, *Surprised by Hope*, 215–16, 280.

[21] Wright, *Paul and the Faithfulness of God*, 934.

and love are one.[22] This kind of love naturally tends toward egalitarianism, eliminating barriers between races and genders (Gal. 3:27). Nor is it abstract, esoteric, or particularly otherworldly. Agape is the antithesis of Manichean world-flight. It does not take one out of this world, but draws one more fully into it. Richard Wilbur, paraphrasing Augustine, says it succinctly in the title of his poem (adopted as the subtitle of this essay): "Love Calls Us to the Things of This World."[23]

2.1.4 *Agape Defined by the Community and Its Stories*

Love is a notoriously slippery term, and not just in English. St. Paul, perhaps fathoming the ambiguity, provides helpful strategies to guard against potential semantic slippage. He does this in part by linking love to other closely related virtues, such as peace, patience, kindness, generosity, gentleness, and self-control (Gal. 5:22). He also names specific practices that flow from agape; and, crucially, he shows that love is vibrantly concrete because it is ruled and schooled by a particular, compelling narrative – the life of Jesus. "Paul's ethical directives . . . presuppose a particular understanding of Jesus Christ as a *paradigm* for the life of the Christian believer and . . . for the life of the *community* in Christ."[24] When St. Paul wishes to call his audience to conduct themselves in a loving manner, he resorts to Christ's example of suffering, which is the template for believers' actions. St. Paul maintains that it is possible to have "the mind of Christ" and replicate his love, however imperfectly, by showing compassion and humility, and by preferring others' interests to one's own (Phil. 2:1–5). Love is less vulnerable to idiosyncratic or ideological hijacking when defined by a supremely kenotic love story, the story of a God who empties himself, which is further linked to a long tradition containing an almost infinite variety of narratives concerning those who have radically imitated Christ.

Cognitive science is demonstrating what the ancients have known for centuries – that human consciousness is "storied and relational."[25] Stories

22 Augustine, *Homilies on the First Epistle of John (Tractatus in Epistolam Joannis ad Parthos)*, ed. Boniface Ramsey et al. (Hyde Park: New City Press, 2008), 110. Simone Weil writes: "The Gospel makes no distinction between the love of neighbor and justice. . . . We have invented the distinction between love and justice." *Waiting for God* (New York: Harper and Row, 1951), 139.

23 Richard Wilbur, *New and Collected Poems* (San Diego: Harcourt Brace, 1988), 233–34.

24 Hayes, *The Law of Christ*, 273.

25 Wright, *New Testament and the People of God*, 61; James K. A. Smith, *Imagining the Kingdom: How Worship Works* (Grand Rapids: Baker Academic, 2013), 130. Note, in particular, Smith's Chapter 3: "We Tell Our Stories in Order to Live." Smith, *Imagining the Kingdom*, 103–50.

make sense of the world. Accounts of reality are "narrative-dependent."[26] When Percy Shelley, the English Romantic poet, proclaimed that "poets are the unacknowledged legislators of the world," he was saying that storytellers and artists are vital because they fund the imagination and give birth to alternative ways of seeing things. In doing this they make sense of the world and shape communities in powerful ways. If we would improve our schools, transform our students, and improve our communities, we will give considerable thought to the stories that circulate among us; and we will appreciate all the more why great teachers are typically extraordinary storytellers. Every generation needs its exemplary narratives (whether expressed through film, literature, music, or the visual arts) that embody the ideal of agape. One of the functions of biblical narratives and saints' legend has been to ground the idea of biblical love, to make the abstract concrete, and to inspire imitation. St. Paul's counsel to learn the stories of exemplary believers and then to model one's actions after them makes perfect sense if human beings are hard-wired for stories: "Brothers and sisters, join in imitating me, and observe those who live according to the example you have in us" (Phil. 3:17).

Just as narratives define love and motivate ethical behavior, they do something else important: they explain, clarify, and fill in gaps that no list of rules, legal system, or set of stipulations can satisfy. This insight has immediate relevance to the study and practice of the law, as shown by Samuel Levine and other legal scholars, who observe that within the Jewish tradition valuable guidance to the community comes through the surrounding narratives of which the Law is part and parcel. The Torah's 613 commandments are not sufficient to guide conduct, for no single code can contain every law that will address every situation. The community needs narratives that illuminate new contexts and provide solutions to unforeseen ethical dilemmas. Through these surrounding narratives the community discerns *implied* laws – "unenumerated obligations and prohibitions." Surrounding narratives can convey ethical insights no law system can fully comprehend.[27]

Of course, not just any story will do. Walter Brueggemann argues that we face the task of restoring human imagination through "counterstories,"

[26] Fritz Oehlschlaeger, *Love and Good Reasons: Postliberal Approaches to Christian Ethics and Literature* (Durham: Duke University Press, 2003), 47.

[27] Samuel J. Levine, "Unenumerated Constitutional Rights and Unenumerated Biblical Obligations: A Preliminary Study in Comparative Hermeneutics," *Constitutional Commentary* 15.3 (1998): 511–27. Building on the extensive work of Robert M. Cover and others, Professor Levine demonstrates how literature, particularly biblical literature, provides context and meaning to laws and legal institutions: "Halacha and Aggada: Translating Robert Cover's Nomos and Narrative," *Utah Law Review* 4 (1998): 465–504.

particular narratives that challenge the toxic plots (often narratives of greed and revenge) of contemporary culture. We need "a network of stories, sacraments, and signs that give a certain nuance, shape, and possibility to human interaction." These stories, sacraments, and signs are "more pervasive and elemental than a belief system or a moral code," according to Brueggemann.[28] Helpful narratives might be found many places – in Scripture, in literature, and even in case law. British novelist Ian McEwan describes being deeply affected while reading legal cases. He explains what led to his writing *The Children Act*, the account of a boy dying of leukemia, but whose parents refuse a blood transfusion on religious grounds:

> I just happened to have found myself reading some [court decisions] and thinking, "Well, this is a very interesting sort of subgenre of literature." *The best ones . . . are amazing documents of compassion and rationality and historical and philosophical sense.* Out of that – and again, I had no sense that this was research for a novel – but out of that slowly, a year or two later, came a novel.[29]

If it is true that "[e]very social ethic requires a narrative,"[30] might this also be true of legal studies and law practice? If we hope for a better law school, a better society, a better self, or a better way of life, we will think deeply about the narratives that capture our attention, and those we employ in our teaching and daily discourse. Stories of agape may be conducive to a just and peaceful society. Such stories can be found in classic biblical narratives (Jacob and Esau, Joseph and his brothers, Jesus and Peter, the Parable of the Prodigal Son) and in great secular literature (Victor Hugo's *Les Misérables*, Dostoevsky's *Brothers Karamazov*, and numerous Shakespearean tragedies and comedies). These themes are powerfully demonstrated all around us today – in the stories coming from South Africa's Truth and Reconciliation Commission, in Archbishop Desmond Tutu's "Forgiveness Project," and in the labors of lawyers and law professors working for social justice.[31] Books and articles on the healing power of forgiveness abound in the popular press. For example, Malcolm Gladwell,

[28] Walter Brueggemann, *Texts under Negotiation: The Bible and Postmodern Imagination* (Minneapolis: Fortress Press, 1993), 26–39.

[29] Brenda Cronin, "Science and Religion Clash in Ian McEwan's New Novel," *Wall Street Journal* (3 September 2014), (emphasis added).

[30] Stanley Hauerwas, *A Community of Character: Toward a Constructive Christian Social Ethic* (Notre Dame: University of Notre Dame Press, 1981), 9.

[31] Consider the examples of Gary Haugen, founder and CEO of International Justice Mission; Bob Goff, founder of Love Does, an international NGO devoted to freedom and human rights; and James Allan (Jim) Gash, Professor of Law and Director of the Global Justice Program, Pepperdine University.

the best-selling *New York Times* writer, describes how he was changed when he encountered a dramatic story of forgiveness motivated by agape as expressed through the life of Wilma Derksen, a mother whose teenage daughter Candace was brutally murdered. Mrs. Derksen embraced the Mennonite philosophy that one must "forgive and move on." Gladwell writes:

> something happened to me when I sat in Wilma Derksen's garden. It is one thing to read in a history book about people empowered by their faith. But it is quite another to meet an otherwise very ordinary person, in the backyard of a very ordinary house, who has managed to do something utterly extraordinary. Their daughter was murdered. And the first thing the Derksens did was to stand up at the press conference and talk about the path to forgiveness. "We would like to know who the person or persons are so we could share, hopefully, a love that seems to be missing in these people's lives."[32]

By Gladwell's own admission, this story of love and forgiveness changed his life. Such stories continue to exert mysterious, transformative power in our world.

2.1.5 *Agape Instilled through Communal Practices ("Liturgies")*

Narratives of the right sort are necessary, but not sufficient. Agape also requires "liturgy." While one usually thinks of liturgy as formal rites of worship, James K. A. Smith offers another way of understanding liturgy: as various communal practices, shared habits, and dispositions, which are not always religious in nature. "Liturgy" in Smith's lexicon refers to the panoply of concrete, embodied practices that shape, not just our thinking, but also our feelings, our perceptions, our desires, and our way of being-in-the-world. These communal habits and dispositions form us and make us "the kind of people we are." Over time they define "the good life" and determine "what we ultimately love."[33]

Liturgies of practice are potent because they transcend the merely cognitive and cerebral. They are at once imaginative, kinesthetic, and communal. Through them one experiences a "bodily knowing," a "take on the world that resides in our bones, as if imagination is 'closer' than our gut," Smith proposes. When we *experience* things, the *whole person*, not just the intellect, perceives and interprets the world.[34] We "know" things through our bodies, viscerally, even when we may not consciously know that we know them. For this reason

[32] Malcolm Gladwell, "How I Rediscovered Faith," *Relevant Magazine* 67 (14 November 2014), available at www.relevantmagazine.com/culture/books/how-i-rediscovered-faith.

[33] James K. A. Smith, *Desiring the Kingdom: Worship, Worldview, and Cultural Formation* (Grand Rapids: Baker Academic, 2009): 26–7. See also Smith, *Imagining the Kingdom*.

[34] Smith, *Imagining the Kingdom*, 31–33, 38; Smith, *Desiring the Kingdom*, 40.

they contain critical moral force. Smith argues that the right kinds of practices "seep into our bones and become the background for our perceptions, the baseline for our dispositions, and the basis for our (often unthought) action in the world."[35]

The relevance of all this to learning is considerable, for, as Smith notes, an education "is a constellation of practices, rituals, and routines that inculcates a particular vision of the good life by inscribing or infusing that vision into the heart (the gut) by means of material, embodied practices."[36] It seems proper to ask: what are the specific habits that shape lawyers to love justice? Do you want a student to be a good scientist? Induct her as quickly and thoroughly as possible into a living laboratory. Do you want students to develop a larger view of the world and transcend their native parochialism? Encourage their immersion in a foreign culture. Do you want law students to become wise, effective lawyers? Get them into the right internships, externships, and clerkships. Praxis makes all the difference. In higher education circles, there is mounting evidence that so-called "high-impact practices," such as undergraduate research, faculty mentoring, and study abroad, transform students in ways that traditional classroom instruction does not. A truly excellent legal education will take seriously the role of "high-impact" practices (i.e. "secular liturgies"), which aim to do more than transmit information or teach students how to "think like lawyers," but to form mature persons with a deep understanding of those things that encourage human flourishing.

We return to another feature of an agape-informed educational model, mentioned earlier in this essay. This reframed reality must be "learned" from other people in a vibrant social setting, for love is acquired through a set of habits practiced *in community*. In the succinct words of human rights attorney Bob Goff, *love does.*[37] Goff demonstrates the corollary truth through his own life of service: love does what it does best *in community*. If someone is truly to reframe her thinking to become a just and loving practitioner of the law, she should be exposed to care for the poor *in action*, honesty *in action*, respect for the elderly *in action*, justice *in action*. As poet Gerard Manley Hopkins exclaims, "The just man *justices*":

I say more: the just man justices;
Keeps grace: that keeps all his goings graces;
Acts in God's eye what in God's eye he is –

[35] Smith, *Imagining the Kingdom*, 40.

[36] Ibid.

[37] Bob Goff, *Love Does: Discover a Secretly Incredible Life in an Ordinary World* (Nashville: Thomas Nelson, 2012).

Christ. For Christ plays in ten thousand places,
Lovely in limbs, and lovely in eyes not his
To the Father through the features of men's faces.[38]

Timothy P. Jackson reminds us that according to certain traditions of Christianity, "justice" is a person, best conveyed through narrative, rather than a concept: "given that God is the source and object of this righteousness, the primary question is, '*Who* is justice?' rather than '*What* is justice?' The former query invites a story rather than a definition, poetry rather than theory, and finally imitation rather than contemplation."[39] The same can be said of agape. It is best understood through story, and it is best acquired in communities that engage in shared "liturgies."

Given the generally secular and utilitarian framework of legal education today, how might one bring the ideals of agape into the "real" world of education and the daily life of an academic/legal community? And how might this be done without turning the curriculum into something that is piously abstract, potentially undermining the "hard" subjects of legal studies? Jackson, building on insights from Nicholas Wolterstorff, imagines that justice and love could learn from each other, with love transforming one's understanding of justice; and with justice "checking and transforming" love – preventing it from slipping into a patronizing form of charity.[40] As we reflect on the contentious critique of legal education and the practice of law today, one might consider whether Jackson is right: agape might enrich our understanding of law and appeal to those who long for a soul-satisfying, service-oriented practice of law.

2.2 LAW AND THE LITURGY OF LOVE: AN EXAMPLE

If narratives of agapic love are able to shape whole communities and encourage people to act lovingly and justly as I have maintained, if the love imperative is best understood as a story rather than as an abstract principle, and if justice "has the narrative unity and pathos of a loving personality," as Jackson suggests, then an illustration is in order. The remarkable events that transpired in the village of Le Chambon-sur-Lignon during World War II provide a

[38] Gerard Manley Hopkins, *As Kingfishers Catch Fire*, ed. Catherine Phillips (New York: Oxford University Press, 1986), 129.

[39] Timothy P. Jackson, *The Priority of Love: Christian Charity and Social Justice* (Princeton: Princeton University Press, 2003), 31. Jackson observes that in the Pauline/Reformed strand of Christianity, it is understood that people learn from people – people imitate stories, not definitions. Justice is "not first an abstract entity but a person. . . ."

[40] Jackson, *The Priority of Love*, 33–34.

fitting example. Situated in the mountains of southern France, Le Chambon was populated by seemingly ordinary citizens who proved to be extraordinary in their bold resistance to fascist terror. Defying the Nazi decrees, members of the village, led by Huguenot pastor André Trocmé and his wife Magda, saved hundreds of Jewish children and adults. Philosopher Philip Hallie, who interviewed many of its citizens, muses: "This much is certain: in the course of the first two years of the Occupation, Le Chambon became the safest place for Jews in Europe. How did a life-and-death ethic become incarnate across the whole commune of Le Chambon?"[41] While the answers to Hallie's question are complex, the most concise reply is that the people of the village had been thoroughly schooled in agape. They were so accustomed to hearing love preached by Pastor Trocmé and seeing it modeled in their community that for them loving one's neighbor was more than an abstract principle, dogma, or duty; it was a way of life rooted in a set of particular narratives that formed them into a community of agape.[42]

Magda Trocmé exhibited a mindset that characterizes agape in the Pauline sense: it was costly, risky, and boldly assertive. Love is just what you do. "It amuses me to help somebody, no matter what the cost," she said.[43] Consistent with biblical agape, her love was not particularly sentimental. She did not feel great "overflowing emotion" or "romantic yearning." Her feeling was "practical and abrupt."[44] Pastor Trocmé was driven by a feeling of deep gratitude, believing that he himself had been rescued by Christ. His "ethic drew its power from the life and death of Jesus," Hallie notes. The motivation was not legal: "it was more like the obedience of lover to his beloved," an attitude that the pastor transmitted to his congregants.[45] Having been immersed in a narrative of agape for generations, the Chambonnais took action reflexively, saving perhaps 2,500 Jews, though no one knows for sure as the villagers did

[41] Philip Hallie, *Lest Innocent Blood Be Shed: The Story of the Village of Le Chambon and How Goodness Happened There* (New York: Harper Torchbooks, 1979), 129. Malcolm Gladwell asks a similar question: "Where did the people of Le Chambon find the strength to defy the Nazis?" Gladwell, "How I Rediscovered Faith" (January/February 2014).

[42] A subsequent study of the events in Le Chambon asserts that the heroism was even more extensive than Philip Hallie suggested. Caroline Moorehead reports that "half a dozen" other villages participated in the rescue, "as well as many outlying hamlets." Nor was Pastor Trocmé the sole leader of the resistance – 24 other Protestant ministers as well as a number of Catholic leaders defied the Gestapo and the Vichy government. See *Village of Secrets: Defying the Nazis in Vichy France* (New York: HarperCollins, 2014), 10.

[43] Hallie, *Lest Innocent Blood Be Shed*, 155.

[44] Ibid., 153.

[45] Ibid., 85, 161.

not keep records.[46] The story of Le Chambon is an example of what happens when a whole community takes agape seriously. The just person – the just *community* – justices. Regarding the remarkable witness of these humble villagers, Hallie concludes: "Ethics is not only private; it can be communal. There are ethical communities. . . . Ethical communities are as real as legal institutions."[47]

One may wonder: what if university classrooms were to become ethical communities analogous to Le Chambon? What if legal studies inducted students into a special kind of community that embraced justice and love on the grounds that they are not only compatible virtues, but also intrinsically related ones? What if justice and love were best understood through story and parable since these forms reach beyond the rational, touching hearts and moving people to act justly and lovingly? What if love and justice were best comprehended through narratives centered on exemplars – personae of "righteousness"?[48]

2.3 CONCLUSION

It bears repeating: St. Paul's first-century milieu and pastoral and theological concerns are far removed from our own circumstances; yet by extrapolating from St. Paul's principles and those of his subsequent interpreters we might creatively appropriate what they say about justice, love, and learning. St. Paul and his interpreters taught that love is the way to bring the world around to renewal. There is "a law of love," and it is expressed through care for others (Gal. 6:2). To appreciate fully the relationship of love to law and justice, we must see that Pauline agape is not just an ideal, but a concrete way of life ("a more excellent way" – 1 Cor. 12:31) that must be exhibited beyond the confines of home and houses of worship. Love finds life in social praxis, not in private, romantic sentiment. It is expressed through well-established public practices

[46] The story of Le Chambon illustrates the claims of Robert Cover and Samuel Levine that distinct, often insular, communities, "create law" and "give meaning to law" in the light of their own distinct communal narratives. The historical narrative of the Huguenot community of Le Chambon – one long marginalized and once persecuted by the dominant culture – provided a rationale to its citizens to act courageously and lovingly toward the persecuted in their midst. In this respect, they bear similarities to the Mennonites and Old Order Amish discussed by Levine. See Levine, "Halacha and Aggada," 464–75.

[47] Hallie, *Lest Innocent Blood Be Shed*, 271–72.

[48] Jackson observes: "It is possible to a degree to formulate abstract principles of 'justice,' but the persona of righteousness is only conveyed via stories, poems, and parables." *The Priority of Love*, 34. Levine summarizes the burgeoning scholarship on "legal storytelling" or "legal narrative." Levine, "Halacha and Aggada," 467.

that derive from a long Judeo-Christian tradition that includes "support for the poor (Lev. 19:9–10); honesty in measurements and in social interactions (v. 11); prompt payment to laborers; just law courts that favor neither rich nor poor; respect for the elderly (vv. 13, 15, 32)," and so forth.[49]

Because agape entails a concrete way of life consisting of habits and practices, it seems right to at least consider how it might be taught in the academy. To segregate justice from love is artificial and arbitrary, and to the Christian, incoherent and hollow. In the Pauline–Augustinian tradition love is both medium and message, pedagogical strategy and the ultimate goal of learning: "The aim of instruction is love that comes from a pure heart, a good conscience, and sincere faith" (1 Tim. 1:5). In the learning environment, love flows in a virtuous circle, informing the life and practice of the teacher, transforming the student, and serving as the meta-subject governing everything to be learned. In *Instructing Beginners in Faith*, Augustine called for a pedagogy of love, with the teacher exercising a kind of familial generosity of spirit, which arouses a mutual empathy between teacher and student, and between learners and the subject matter, so that teacher, student, and subject matter are simultaneously transformed: "when our listeners are touched by us as we speak and we are touched by them as they learn, each of us comes to dwell in the other, and so they as it were speak in us what they hear, while we in some way learn in them what we teach."[50]

One might speculate how legal education would be transformed if a pedagogy of love were applied to contemporary courses of study. If, as James K. A. Smith maintains, "We are what we love, and our love is shaped, primed, and aimed by liturgical practices that take hold of our gut and aim our heart to certain ends," then what should the "liturgies" of legal education be?[51] If "justice" is a person as much as it is abstract rules, where and how should students encounter human embodiments of love and justice? In the final analysis, what is the end (the *telos*) of legal education: the production of competent professionals or something more ambitious, perhaps the formation of mature persons committed to an agape-directed way of life?

[49] "Love," *Oxford Companion to the Bible*, eds. Bruce M. Metzger and Michael D. Coogan (New York: Oxford University Press, 1993), 467–69. Metzger and Coogan call love "the theological lodestone of nascent Christianity." *Oxford Companion*, 468.

[50] Augustine goes on to say: "And this we experience the more intensely, the closer our friendship with one another is, for the more the bond of love allows us to be present in others, the more what has grown old becomes new again in our own eyes as well." *Instructing Beginners in Faith*, 97–98.

[51] Smith, *Desiring the Kingdom*, 40.

While such questions may seem strange in a secular milieu, an understanding of agape could lead to some constructive reflection, particularly in light of the litany of complaints about the way the law is taught and practiced today. It is provocative to consider what kinds of graduates our universities would produce and what sort of society we would foster if professors in every discipline took seriously St. Paul's injunction to: *Let all that you do be done in love* (1 Cor. 16:14), or if every professor, student, or practitioner of the law heeded St. Augustine's timeless counsel: "Keeping this love before you then as a goal to which you direct all that you say, recount every event . . . in such a way that your listener by hearing it may believe, by believing may hope, and by hoping may love."[52]

[52] Augustine, *Instructing Beginners in Faith*, 72.

PART II

MODERN PERSPECTIVES ON AGAPE, JUSTICE, AND LAW

Part II presents normative and theological essays on the relationship between agape, justice, and law. Both Linda Ross Meyer and Timothy Jackson identify dangers that can arise when mixing love and law. Meyer argues that the "chaotic good" of a loving humility may be an antidote to a sometimes-evil lawfulness, as well as a sometimes-ravening love. Jackson calls on love to place limits on law, and law to place limits on love.

Like many of the authors in this volume, Nicholas Wolterstorff and David VanDrunen explore the relationship between agape and justice. Wolterstorff argues that there is no conflict between them, either in their motivation or in their direction. He also criticizes the notion of retributive justice and argues that the New Testament supports a "reprobative" account of punishment. In contrast, VanDrunen argues that there is tension between justice and Christian love; that God has ordained the state to enact retributive justice (tempered by forbearance); and that Christian love finds its full and proper expression in the life of the church, not in the government.

3

Agape, Humility, and Chaotic Good: The Challenge and Risk of Allowing Agape a Role in the Law

Linda Ross Meyer

In the old role-play game of Dungeons and Dragons, one rolls the dice to determine the character traits of one's game avatar. One of the character trait rolls determines whether the avatar is Lawful (in the sense of rule-bound, consistent, and predictable) or Chaotic (in the sense of unruly, unpredictable, or inconsistent). A separate roll determines whether the avatar is Good, Evil, or Neutral. Thus, in the game, characters not only can be "lawful and good," or "chaotic and evil," but also "lawful and evil" or "chaotic and good."

From the usual jurisprudential standpoint, both the "lawful evil" and the "chaotic good" seem oxymoronic. We usually think that consistency and goodness go together. As Lon Fuller put it, "I shall have to rest on the assertion of a belief that may seem naïve, namely, that coherence and goodness have more affinity than coherence and evil."[1] From Kant's universal principles of reason, to John Rawls' operationalizing of Kant in his theory of the "original position," which "generalizes and carries to a higher level of abstraction the familiar theory of the social contract,"[2] to Ronald Dworkin's "law as integrity" thesis that prefers the coherent interpretation to the incoherent[3] – main-line legal theorists agree that good government ought to be coherent (lawful) and should not make ungeneralizable, un-rule-bound (chaotic) exceptions. In short, lawfulness is at least an aspect of good; unruliness is at least an aspect of evil.

With many thanks to Bob Cochran and Zachary Calo for their insight and editing, and Pepperdine Law School for sponsoring these conversations. I would also like to thank Quinnipiac Law School, and the many colleagues who helped to shape these thoughts, especially Neal Feigenson, Trisha Olson, Steve Gilles, Jennifer Brown, Jennifer Herbst, Charlie Pillsbury, Sarah Russell, Kevin Barry, Marilyn Ford, and Jamie Wilcox.

1 Lon L. Fuller, "Positivism and Fidelity to Law: A Reply to Professor Hart," *Harvard Law Review* 71, no. 4 (1958): 636.

2 John Rawls, *A Theory of Justice* (Cambridge: Harvard University Press, 1971), 11.

3 Ronald Dworkin, *Law's Empire* (Cambridge: Harvard University Press, 1986), Chapter 7, 225–75.

Political theorists have made similar points. Hannah Arendt and Lon Fuller point to Nazi Germany's lawless use of retroactive legislation and its chaotic, opaque, and unpredictable lines of authority as essential means by which Hitler fostered fear and maintained personal control.[4]

On the other hand, the Dungeons and Dragons categories suggest that the association of lawfulness with goodness is not a logical necessity. Dolores Umbridge, Darth Vader, General Zod, and the Mayor of Pleasantville are among the classic "lawful evil" characters; Hans Solo, Captain Kirk, Robin Hood, and Mary Poppins are among the classic "chaotic good" characters.

And of course, there is love – often considered good, but certainly not predictable, consistent, or orderly. C. S. Lewis, in his Narnia series, portrays a God-figure with a similarly discomfiting disjunction of order and goodness. As Lewis says throughout the series, Aslan is "not a tame lion."[5]

Lawfulness requires, we say, treating like cases alike. Love, by contrast, requires treating each individual as infinitely important.[6] Lawfulness is required. Love is supererogatory. Law is reason. Love is emotion. Law gives us justice. Love gives us mercy. Law gives each their due. Love gives what is not deserved. Law is impersonal and general. Love is personal and particular.

Is love, then, a chaotic good? Can the absence of love be a lawful evil?

3.1 "LAWFUL EVIL"

The possibility or impossibility of "lawful evil" was at the heart of the famous debate between H. L. A. Hart and Lon Fuller over the moral authority of law. For Fuller, lawfulness (mere order, not necessarily "good order") inherently guaranteed to law at least some measure of moral goodness and moral authority. Fuller argued that even the most selfish Rex could not expect to satisfy his whims without his subjects' obedience and therefore needed to make his demands known with a measure of consistency and transparency.[7] This consistency, in turn, enabled the subjects to live lives of some stability and (at least interstitial) autonomy. Consistency and transparency, according to Fuller, would naturally mature into a rudimentary forum for discussion of the coherence or incoherence of a proposed action with Rex's past commands, and, through interpretation, promote reasonable goals for the future. He further

4 Fuller, "Fidelity to Law," 636; Hannah Arendt, *Origins of Totalitarianism* (New York: Harcourt, Brace & World, 1966).

5 C. S. Lewis, *The Lion, the Witch, and the Wardrobe* (New York: HarperCollins, 2000), 180.

6 See Emmanuel Levinas, *Totality and Infinity: An Essay on Exteriority* (Pittsburgh: Duquesne University Press, 1969).

7 Fuller, "Fidelity to Law," 644–45.

clarifies that "when men are compelled to explain and justify their decisions, the effect will generally be to pull those decisions toward goodness, by whatever standards of ultimate goodness there are."[8] The very interpretation of rules, in Fuller's view, required a sense of their "purpose" or "what they are for," which would soon insinuate even more substantive good into Rex's legal system, as interpreters imputed reasonable purposes to the tyrant. Thus, Fuller concludes that the orderliness of law is and produces moral good, thereby granting some level of moral authority to law as a set of coherent rules.

H. L. A. Hart's response to Fuller was to note, "[I]f this [formal legality] is what the necessary connexion of law and morality means, we may accept it. It is unfortunately compatible with very great iniquity."[9] Hart, instead, always insisted on facing up to the idea that moral choices could be chaotic and tragic and that coherence was no guarantee of goodness. He called the view "that all the values we cherish ultimately will fit into a single system," a "romantic optimism," and he insisted that "like nettles, the occasions when life forces us to choose between the lesser of two evils must be grasped with the consciousness that they are what they are. The vice of this use of the principle that, at certain limiting points, what is utterly immoral cannot be law or lawful is that it will serve to cloak the true nature of the problems with which we are faced."[10]

Hannah Arendt's reflections on Adolf Eichmann's "lawful" adherence to the "duties" of his office provide perhaps the iconic modern example of the numbing of one's moral sense by orderliness and coherence. The orderliness of Eichmann's obligations to his Nazi superiors served as moral blinders, blinding him to the horrors he was perpetrating:

> [A]s the months and the years went by, he lost the need to feel anything at all. This was the way things were, this was the new law of the land, based on the Führer's order; whatever he did he did, as far as he could see, as a law-abiding citizen. He did his *duty*, as he told the police and the court over and over again; he not only obeyed *orders*, he also obeyed the *law*. . . .
>
> Whatever Kant's role in the formation of "the little man's" mentality in Germany may have been, there is not the slightest doubt that in one respect Eichmann did indeed follow Kant's precepts: a law was a law, there could be no exceptions. In Jerusalem, he admitted [making] only two exceptions [for personal Jewish friends to the "rule" that all Jews should die]. This inconsistency still made him feel somewhat uncomfortable, and when

8 Fuller, "Fidelity to Law," 636.

9 H. L. A. Hart, *The Concept of Law* (Oxford: Clarendon Press, 1961), 202.

10 H. L. A. Hart, "Positivism and the Separation of Law and Morals," *Harvard Law Review* 71, no. 4 (1958): 620.

he was questioned about it during cross-examination, he became openly apologetic: he had 'confessed his sins' to his superiors.[11]

But we needn't invoke Nazis to find examples of lawful evil. We know only too well the Catch-22s resulting from legal complexity, the word-twisting pettifoggery of clever lawyers, and the procrustean rule-worship of power-proud bureaucrats, all of which infect every legal and bureaucratic system: an immigration judge decides to give asylum to only one of two twin brothers facing the identical danger of being drafted into a terrorist war at home, because the lawyer for one of them failed to file the asylum application on time.[12] The Supreme Court grants review of a death penalty case, while at the same time denying a stay of execution.[13] A judge refuses to keep the courthouse open an extra 20 minutes in order to receive a request for a stay of execution in a capital case based on a new Supreme Court development.[14] A president's lawyers cynically cite to a definition in a hospital medical reimbursement statute in order to "coherently" define the crime of torture as narrowly as possible.[15]

The problem of "lawful evil" is no doubt part of what fuels anger over big government, though any set of rules big or small may be applied in a hellishly persnickety or cramped fashion. As contract high priest Grant Gilmore famously quipped, "The worse the society, the more law there will be. In Hell there will be nothing but law, and due process will be meticulously observed."[16] Similarly, C. S. Lewis, in his short-story parable, *The Great Divorce*, depicts

[11] Hannah Arendt, *Eichmann in Jerusalem: A Report on the Banality of Evil* (New York: Penguin Books, 1994), 135, 137.

[12] 1988 asylum appeal in federal district court before Judge Charles Legge, Northern District of California.

[13] *Herrera* v. *Collins*, 502 U.S. 1085 (1992). The Texas courts later granted a stay of execution, and the case was decided against Herrera, who had claimed he was innocent. He was executed in 1993, protesting his innocence with his last words. More recently, Charles Warner was denied a stay and was executed before the Supreme Court could decide his case. Warren Richey, "Supreme Court Halts Oklahoma Executions Pending Lethal Injection Case," *Christian Science Monitor*, 28 January 2015.

[14] Ralph Blumenthal, "Texas Judge Draws Outcry for Allowing Execution," *New York Times*, 25 October 2007, available at www.nytimes.com/2007/10/25/us/25execute.html?_r=0. For other examples, see James Nye, "Killer Was Executed Four Minutes Before His Final Appeal Was Denied After Guards Hauled Him Away from Phone Call with Lawyer," *Daily Mail* (2 February 2014), available at www.dailymail.co.uk/news/article-2550506/Killer-dragged-phone-call-lawyer-executed-four-minutes-BEFORE-final-appeal-denied.html.

[15] Jay S. Bybee, *Memorandum for Alberto R. Gonzales, Counsel to the President: Re: Standards of Conduct for Interrogation under 18 U.S.C. §§ 2340–2340A* (1 August 2002), 5, available at www2.gwu.edu/~nsarchiv/NSAEBB/NSAEBB127/02.08.01.pdf.

[16] Grant Gilmore, *The Ages of American Law* (New Haven: Yale University Press, 1977), 99.

those who want "only their due" going straight to hell and spurning the "free bus" to heaven.

3.2 CHAOTIC GOOD

If lawful evil is a real danger, then can a chaotic goodness, like agape, alleviate this danger? The answer is not a simple one. While many legal scholars focus attention on the ways in which a universal *law* is incompatible with human finitude and moral experience, a strong strand of discourse in theology focuses attention on the ways in which universal *love* is incompatible with human finitude.

One Augustinian/Niebuhrian position, like that of Justice Oliver Wendell Holmes or Justice Antonin Scalia, is that we need imperfect rules of coercion to constrain the "bad man" in this fallen world, perhaps for his own good, but certainly for the flourishing of the rest. On this view, harsh but clear rules may do "lawful evil," but they are better at giving notice to rule-breakers, and safer than an inevitably naive judicial discretion or loving mercy.

A second, slightly different set of concerns emphasizes the inadequacies of discretionary, potentially discriminatory, love: love does not give people their "due," love doesn't treat like cases alike, love doesn't accord rights, etc.[17] Love is too likely to compromise on social equality and too likely to retreat into quietism. As Eric Gregory writes:

> On the one hand, a prideful Augustinianism is content to repeat its mantras about sin and the realistic limits of politics and virtue. This appeal to the limits of politics often travels with a stern appeal to a politics of necessity that can justify all manner of injustice in the name of two kingdoms, regretful responsibility, and "dirty hands." Lutheran streams of Augustinian politics are particularly vulnerable to this temptation, evidenced most recently in the theological justification of the use of torture to combat terrorism. On the other hand, an equally prideful Augustinianism celebrates its retreat into a postliberal withdrawal from political life altogether.[18]

A third approach is to render love orderly and compatible with law. One might, for example, contain the unruliness of love by allowing it to provide only the *ground* of rights, while seeing that the rights themselves are applied

[17] See Gene Outka, *Agape: An Ethical Analysis* (New Haven: Yale University Press, 1972), 81–4; Reinhold Niebuhr, *Moral Man and Immoral Society: A Study in Ethics and Politics* (New York: Scribner, 1955).

[18] Eric Gregory, *Politics and the Order of Love: An Augustinian Ethic of Democratic Citizenship* (Chicago: University of Chicago Press, 2008), at 28.

in a classically orderly Kantian fashion. Love becomes the unmoved mover of justice, mostly irrelevant in the *application* of law.[19] This move to reinterpret love as a rational, orderly, and more perfect justice is similar to legal scholars' treatment of mercy, often reimagined as a form of equity.[20]

A fourth approach underscores the fundamental impossibility of a *universalized* love. Emmanuel Levinas makes the point that as soon as a third person enters a dialogue of self and other, the self must trade one neighbor's need off against another's need, and the ethical injunction of infinite love cannot be met without compromise. Love, then, becomes the constant critique of law, not its easy partner. As one interpreter puts it, "The dialogue that institutes society is also a standard of permanent critique. Levinas lays a foundation – and at the same time some dynamite – under institutions."[21]

Paul Kahn eloquently summarizes the conflicting, embroiled traditions of law and love that in America seem to sanctify and desanctify law almost simultaneously:

> Americans, perhaps more than any other modern people, think of themselves as a community under law. American citizenship is not a matter of ethnic identity but of belief in a legal order – that created by the Constitution. . . . This myth of law's foundation, however, is only half of our imaginative conception of law. There remains within our culture a competing understanding of law. . . . Law's rule is the state peculiar to fallen man; it is of the flesh, not the spirit. The highest truth, and true freedom, exists beyond law. . . . Beyond law are love, grace, and mercy. If we could realize these elements of our nature, we would not need law. Conversely, just to the degree that we need law we confirm our fallen state.[22]

[19] Nicholas Wolterstorff's work often strikes me this way, for example, except perhaps for his rejection of *lex talionis* – though even this move is very similar to conclusions reached by other legal theorists who adopt expressive theories of punishment. See his *Justice: Rights and Wrongs* (Princeton: Princeton University Press, 2008) and *Justice in Love* (Grand Rapids: Wm. B. Eerdmans Publishing Co., 2010). In short, a lot of work is done by ideals of justice, human rights, and equal treatment, but not much is left for love to do.

[20] See Linda Ross Meyer, *Law, Meaning, and Violence: The Justice of Mercy* (Ann Arbor: University of Michigan Press, 2010), 48–49.

[21] Theodore de Boer, "An Ethical Transcendental Philosophy," in *Face to Face with Levinas*, ed. Richard A. Cohen (Albany: SUNY Press, 1986), 103. See also, Jill Stauffer, "Productive Ambivalence: Levinasian Subjectivity, Justice, and the Rule of Law," in *Essays on Levinas and Law: A Mosaic*, ed. Desmond Manderson (New York: Palgrave, 2009), 80–81. Other political theorists face the same conundrum, as James R. Martel illustrates in his wonderful book, *Love Is a Sweet Chain: Desire, Autonomy and Friendship in Liberal Political Theory* (New York: Routledge, 2001); or as Paul Kahn explains in his classic, *Law and Love: The Trials of King Lear* (New Haven: Yale University Press, 2000). The personal connection and demands of love cannot be expanded to embrace an entire world.

[22] Kahn, *Law and Love*, xii–xiii.

So, let me start over on the other end of the tension, not with the limitations of human law, but with the limitations of human love. C. S. Lewis's lay classic, *The Four Loves*, suggests that human love, while pointing us in the direction of perfect love, is not capable of the universal regard and care that would ground a perfectly loving community, any more than human law is capable of the coherent and universal wisdom and foresight that would ground an absolutely just community.

Though Lewis speaks of the specific defects of his four categories of human love in the personal context, it is illuminating to extrapolate his critique to the legal and political.

Storge, or the love of family, Lewis says, is a human love with the virtue of loving the unlovely, as one loves crazy Uncle Alfred. It is accepting of imperfections and loyal and steady through time. However, love of family also has its human defect. It is tribal and aims at no improvement, stuck in the comfort of a familiar past. Translated to the political, storge extols tradition for the sake of tradition, and while potentially generating long-term loyalty and a localized sit-comesque community-of-quirky-characters, it can be xenophobic toward strangers and stultifying toward its own. Love of one's hometown will not invite outsiders in, but can ignore or demonize immigrants, relish anti-intellectualism, deride change or demean improvement in its members, glorify and whitewash the past, and, at its most virulent, create the conditions for reactionary, tribalistic hate.

Philia, or the love of friends, Lewis says, is a human love that counters some of the defects of Storge. Philia has the virtues of seeking mutual improvement and binding together strangers in a common venture: the more, the merrier. Built around a common activity or vision, this love accepts anyone who shares the activity or vision, and through the relationship, the friends seek to better themselves and each other. The defects of friendship, however, are arrogance and exclusivity, as groups of friends often come to think themselves better or more knowing than others who do not share their common ground or ideals of excellence. Shifting to the political, philia presents the danger of partisanship and the arrogance of perfectionism. An occupational hazard of academics in particular, philia is the sometimes elitist and rigid thinking that presumes outsiders are ignorant and *prescribes* to others before it *understands* them. At its very worst, philia promotes eugenics, discrimination, radical forms of rehabilitation or reformation, ethnic cleansing, proselytizing, and aristocracy, all in the name of the betterment of society.

Eros, or romantic love, Lewis says, is the human love that most closely approaches unconditional love: unconcerned about the imperfections, creed, or provenance of the beloved. Unlike philia, it is not self-aggrandizing or arrogant, but profoundly humble and self-sacrificing. Eros wraps the beloved in an embrace of acceptance and appreciation of the whole person in integrity, not just those aspects that are familiar (storge) or excellent (philia). Eros seeks the good of the other person even at the expense of self. The downside of eros, however, is exclusivity, obsession, and jealousy, and the danger that one will lose all perspective in pursuit of the beloved, sacrificing all others, and even one's own character, for love. Politically, the patriotic hero who gives his life for his country is the positive side of eros, but eros also comprehends the dangers of fanaticism and extremism, illustrated by the suicide bomber, the ideologue, the torturer, or the assassin.

After Lewis's critique, we see the political possibilities love offers for law:

(1) Storge: fosters *deep and enduring community ties* and decentralized forms of mutual aid, instead of a shifting assortment of virtual strangers who interact only through sterile, arms'-length transactions.
(2) Philia: fosters *benevolent perfectionism* that seeks to improve the moral welfare of people throughout the world through teaching, universal aid, and discerning judgment, instead of hands-off libertarianism or social Darwinism.
(3) Eros: fosters dedication and *self-sacrifice* in citizens, and generosity and forgiveness in government, instead of a narrow rights and due process orientation that considers only what is due.

But we also see the dangers of these loves:

(1) Storge: inspires factionalism and cronyism.
(2) Philia: inspires arrogance and totalitarianism.
(3) Eros: inspires fanaticism.

In Lewis's book, of course, agape is the divine love that perfects human love through God, so as to avoid the defects of the forms of human love and enable their excellences. Agape is constant and loves the ugly (like storge), delights in every aspect of the unique person and is self-sacrificing (like eros), and strives to perfect and support all people on their path to the good (like philia).

Is such agape possible for human institutions? The theological answers to this question are better catalogued by others in this volume. But the range is wide, from Augustine's reluctant allowances for just wars and his lament for the inevitably tragic position of a secular judge doomed to act unjustly,[23] to the seemingly sanguine assurance in the 1689 Baptist Confession of Faith that

[23] Saint Augustine, *City of God*, trans. Marcus Dods (New York: Random House Publishing, 2000), 681–82: "What shall I say of these judgments which men pronounce on men and which are necessary in communities, whatever outward peace they enjoy? Melancholy and lamentable judgments they are, since the judges are men who cannot discern the consciences of those at their bar. . . . But though we therefore acquit the judge of malice, we must none the less condemn human life as miserable."

magistrates can plot a course to justice and peace, and even wage just war, without apparent tragic conflict.[24]

In my view, a healthy suspicion of agapic utopian visions is justified. History has too many examples of humans who have imagined, with the best of intentions and even the certitude of divine inspiration, that they could embody agape in politics, only to pave a new hell on earth with a "holocaust of generosity,"[25] with, for example, loving torture,[26] loving castration,[27] loving lobotomies,[28] and loving solitary confinement.[29]

Nonetheless, perhaps law may be able to acknowledge an aspect of agape to this extent: as an immanent loving humility.

Agape in its pre-New Testament usage as a welcome or greeting[30] suggests already a connotation of receptiveness, hospitality, or embrace.[31] The motif of

[24] 689 London Baptist Confession of Faith, Chapter 24.

[25] The phrase is quoted in Gregory, *Politics and the Order of Love*, 27.

[26] Jennifer Diane LaVanchy, "A History of Persecution: Examining and Comparing the Converso Experience in the Spanish and Mexican Inquisitions," Masters Thesis, University of Wyoming (2009): "the primary goal [of inquisition] is reconciliation . . . It seems that voluntary confession is preferred; however, if this cannot be achieved then the inquisitors will then reach their goals by force"; Ana Benito, "Inquisition and the Creation of the Other," in *Marginal Voices: Studies in Converso Literature in Medieval and Golden Age Spain*, eds. Amy Aronson-Friedman and Gregory B. Kaplan (Boston: Brill, 2012), 54: relating the story of Maria Lopez, whose refusal to confess to "judaizing practices" of kosher-style eating and whose continued insistence upon her faithful Christianity under severe torture resulted in her being burned at the stake in 1518.

[27] Madison Park, "Using Chemical Castration to Punish Child Sex Crimes," *CNN* (25 September 2012), available at www.cnn.com/2012/09/05/health/chemical-castration-science; see Louis Le Maire, "Danish Experiences Regarding the Castration of Sexual Offenders," *The Journal of Criminal Law, Criminology, and Police Science* 47, no. 3 (1956): 298: "De-sexing was the main effect [of castration of prisoners] in a positive direction. Seen from a social point of view it is the real purpose of castration and from a sensible consideration of the personal interests of the individual in question, it is likewise a benefit to himself"; Ayaan Hirsi Ali, *Infidel: My Life* (New York: Free Press, 2007): recounting harrowing experience of female genital castration intended to preserve religious duties of obedience and chastity and relating how "loving" her grandmother was in caring for her afterwards.

[28] Egas Moniz received the Nobel Prize in Medicine in 1949 in part for his discovery of the "prefrontal leucotomy," or lobotomy. "Egas Moniz – Biographical" *NobelPrize.org* (2 June 2016), available at www.nobelprize.org/nobel_prizes/medicine/laureates/1949/moniz-bio.html.

[29] Brooke Shelby Biggs, "Solitary Confinement: A Brief History," *Mother Jones* (2 March 2009), available at www.motherjones.com/politics/2009/03/solitary-confinement-brief-natural-history: "Ironically, solitary confinement had been conceived by the Quakers and Anglicans as humane reform of a penal system with overcrowded jails, squalid conditions, brutal labor chain gangs, stockades, public humiliation, and systemic hopelessness. Instead it drove many men mad."

[30] William Barclay, *New Testament Words* (Westminster: John Knox Press, 1974), 19.

[31] The imagery embedded in the word agape may suggest that agape was associated with earth metaphors – perhaps the receptive embrace, hospitality, and drawing-in gravity of Gaia, though I have found no evidence that agape is related to older IE roots of AG or GA, rather than HAB.

welcome, hospitality, and non-reciprocal giving also fits with the willed rather than emotion-based connotations of ancient uses of agape.[32] Its rather generic application (in ancient and Hellenic Greek) to many situations, things, and to persons across social hierarchies also suggests a love open to all, rather than one specifically aimed at family, friends, or lovers.

According to Paul, agape is to be free from envy (non-reciprocal), "suffer long," be "kind," and "bear all things."[33] It is also regenerative: it does not return injury for injury, but turns evil to good.[34] Again, these passages on agape fit with the older sense of welcome, as well as with the ideas of humility and receptivity. Like the gravity of an all-embracing earth, agape is a love that turns the violence of plowing and sowing into the abundance of harvest, a love that takes in and takes on. In New Testament usage, the receptive, suffering, bearing, and grounding images describe God's "descending"[35] unconditional love for all and Christ's earthly incarnation and sacrifice.

Eric Gregory, among others, also sees receptivity as central to agapic politics: "Loving the neighbor involves the virtues of active receptivity and vulnerable responsibility that I have suggested are central to an Augustinian ethic of caritas and moral psychology of enjoyment."[36]

So insofar as agape is possible for human institutions, it is perhaps possible as a form of receptivity and humility. If human law is aware of its own limitations, and if human love is aware of its own liabilities, then perhaps we can avoid the alienated and bureaucratic hell of lawfulness as well as the closed-mindedness of storge, the arrogance of philia, and the fanaticism of eros, through the humility of agape.

Let me suggest some aspects of this humble love of "receptivity" in law:

(1) Openness to other narratives: careful attention to others requires the selflessness of love rather than the self-assurance of law. As many others have pointed out, listening carefully is an essential characteristic of a judge, lawyer, and neighbor.[37] One must listen with full attention,

32 Ibid.

33 1 Cor. 13:4–7 (New King James Version).

34 1 Peter 3:9 (NKJV). See 1 Peter 3:8, admonishing readers to have a tender heart and a humble mind.

35 See Pope Benedict XVI, "Deus Caritas Est: *De Christiano Amore*," *Encyclical Letter* (25 December 2005).

36 Gregory, *Politics and the Order of Love*, 379.

37 Martha Nussbaum repeatedly stresses this point, as well as the importance of compassion and attention to individual circumstances. See Dan M. Kahan and Martha C. Nussbaum, "Two Conceptions of Emotion in Criminal Law," *Columbia Law Review* 96, no. 2 (1996): 269; Martha C. Nussbaum, *Political Emotions: Why Love Matters for Justice* (Cambridge: Harvard

without preconceptions, stock interpretations, judgment, suspicion, or fear. In this way, agape "bears all things, believes all things."[38] Only after a full and fair hearing can one have even a human hope of doing even human justice.[39]

(2) Openness to the possibility of mistake: convictions of the innocent, intelligence that is wrong, prosecutors who believe the wrong cooperator, faulty memories and mistaken eye-witnesses, poor investigations, poorly drafted contracts, baseless law suits, precipitous legislation, and lazy judging are just a few of the many human failings that litter the law. Allowing the opportunity to reevaluate our decisions, and instituting procedures that open us to opposing views, are and should be, key features of human law. Our processes of ongoing legislation, adversarial evidence-gathering and argument, notice and comment on administrative regulations, and multiple layers of appeals are a few of the many legal practices that allow for (sometimes chaotic) revision of imperfect human law.

(3) Openness to the possibility of being wrong: we must also be open to the possibility of being not just mistaken, but wrong in deeper senses. Lawyers and theologians in just the past two centuries found a natural law basis, and even a biblical basis, for slavery,[40] apartheid,[41] eugenics,[42] sexism,[43] and a host of other laws and rulings we now find plainly wrong. There is little doubt that we one day will learn the error of *our* ways as well. The philia that often generates benevolent plans of perfecting others should be tempered by the agape that counsels

---

University Press, 2013). Jill Stauffer's tour de force, *Ethical Loneliness: The Injustice of Not Being Heard* (New York: Columbia University Press, 2015), suggests that careful and attentive hearing, especially of suffering, is essential to rebuilding communities after violence.

38 1 Cor. 13:7 (NKJV).

39 See Jennifer Gerarda Brown, "'For You Also Were Strangers in the Land of Egypt': How Procedural Law and Non-Law Enable Love for 'Strangers' and 'Enemies,'" *Quinnipiac Law Review* 28, no. 3 (2010): 677; Sue Bryant and Jean Koh Peters, "Five Habits for Cross-Cultural Lawyering," in *Race, Culture, Psychology & Law*, eds. Kimberly Holt Barrett and William H. George (Thousand Oaks: Sage Publications, 2005), 58: "the lawyer should engage in 'deep listening' to the client's story and voice. . . . Questions that get the client in narrative mode are usually the most helpful"; Mark Weisberg and Jean Koh Peters, "Experiments in Listening," *Journal of Legal Education* 57, no. 3 (2007): 427.

40 Larry R. Morrison, "The Religious Defense of American Slavery before 1830," *Journal of Religious Thought* 37, no. 2 (1980): 16.

41 Irving Hexham, "Christianity and Apartheid: An Introductory Bibliography," *Journal of Theology for Southern Africa* 32 (1980).

42 Christine Rosen, *Preaching Eugenics: Religious Leaders and the American Eugenics Movement* (New York: Oxford University Press, 2004).

43 *In re Goodell*, 39 Wis. 232 (1875).

awe before the other and humility in knowing what is best. Practices of investigative journalism and free public debate and disagreement allow for challenge to our principles. A humility even about our deepest national commitments is, as C. S. Lewis said, the most important defense against totalitarianism: "If our country's cause is the cause of God, wars must be wars of annihilation. A false transcendence is given to things which are very much of this world."[44]

(4) Openness to the subjectivity and finitude of the person affected by law: law, in its pursuit of the "general case," runs roughshod over the particular. But love looks to the individual other rather than the general or universal. This perspective of the particular, unique person operates as a check on law's tendency to over-generalize. Human law should be a constant dialogue between the framing of rules and their effects on real people. The humility of agape reminds us to pay attention to the sacrificial victim of a generally good policy. When, for example, a prisoner-shackling regulation designed to prevent dangerous escapes is applied to a petite, nonviolent, frightened undocumented immigrant woman who is at a hospital in labor,[45] or when a law designed to protect children from sex offenders results in the permanent social exile and stigmatization of a 17-year-old Romeo for loving a 14-year-old Juliet, or when a felony murder law designed to punish murderers puts a 14-year-old girl in jail for life without parole for helping her boyfriend commit a burglary, or when we discover that ignoring family circumstances in sentencing decisions means that 1.7 million children now suffer economic and emotional instability because they have incarcerated parents,[46] we have to pay attention and not merely accept these harms as justified collateral damage.

(5) Openness to the reality of risk and the certainty of failure: law seeks regularity and security. The openness of agape reminds us that we cannot avoid being vulnerable and finite in this life.[47] No criminal justice

[44] C. S. Lewis, *The Four Loves* (New York: Mariner Books, 1971), 28. Or, to quote Learned Hand, "The spirit of liberty is the spirit that is not too sure that it is right." *The Spirit of Liberty* (New York: Knopf, 1952), 190.

[45] *Villegas* v. *Nashville*, 709 F.3d 563 (6th Cir. 2013).

[46] The Sentencing Project, *Incarcerated Parents and Their Children: Trends 2001–2007* (2009), available at www.sentencingproject.org/doc/publications/publications/inc_incarceratedparents.pdf.

[47] Perhaps this is like the "need love," described by Lewis: "Thus one Need-love . . . makes a main ingredient in man's highest, healthiest, and most realistic spiritual condition. A very strange corollary follows. Man approaches God most nearly when he is in one sense least like God. For what can be more unlike than fullness and need, sovereignty and humility, righteousness and penitence, limitless power and a cry for help?" *The Four Loves*, 4.

system can protect us from all crime. No contract can protect us from the vicissitudes of the future. No tort law can compensate us for all our losses. And agape reminds us that we don't want law to eliminate risk, because a perfectly secure, pain-free life is one in which there is no room for change, redemption, communion with others, parenthood, surprise, grace, or love.

(6) Openness to a recognition that there are limits to law, even within law: agape reminds us that a perfect law is for eternal robots, not finite humans. Agape opens us to the possibility of the inarticulable and un-rulebound "beyond-law." For example, it is difficult to find a reasonable within-law explanation of why we give special constitutional consideration to religion (as opposed to, say, freedom of conscience more generally). Though controversial, it is possible to understand the protections accorded to religion in our Constitution as an acknowledgment of a beyond-law that is not within the jurisdiction of law.[48] Law, in other words, is counseled to tread carefully at its own borders and act with a certain degree of reticence and understatement.

The same humility of law can be seen in other areas of legal doctrine that exclude rules and create pockets of, what Austin Sarat describes as, "lawful lawlessness": the discretion inherent in the executive clemency power, or the leeway and discretion accorded to prosecutors and sentencing judges, or the immunities given to policymakers and lawyers in making legal arguments and in negotiating settlements, or the freedom to speak about ideas without fear of prosecution. Like legal doctrine, legal practice is also already shot through with a recognition of the limits of law: ninety-five to ninety-seven percent of criminal and civil cases settle, sometimes because the categories of the law are inadequate, and those are just the disputes that enter court. Few of us enforce

[48] And hence beyond the formulation of rules, principles, and legal formulae. See Stephen D. Smith, *Foreordained to Failure: The Quest for a Constitutional Principle of Religious Freedom* (New York: Oxford University Press, 1999). The idea that the interpretation of the religion clauses ought to be based on a religiously inspired deference to "higher law" is contrary to the dominant legal theoretical view that the religion clauses ensure only equality of religious opportunity or equal freedom of conscience. See Christopher L. Eisgruber and Lawrence G. Sager, *Religious Freedom and the Constitution* (Cambridge: Harvard University Press, 2007). For an excellent discussion of these points, see Chad Flanders, "The Possibility of a Secular First Amendment," *Quinnipiac Law Review* 26 (2008): 257. Congress, in passing RFRA and RLUIPA in order to protect religious expression in cases where other kinds of meaningful conduct would not be protected, disagreed with the "equal treatment" view of the Free Exercise Clause and arguably enacted a zone of jurisdictional humility.

our legal rights against each other, except in the most extraordinary cases. Usually we settle, we compromise, we get along. While Niebuhr reminds us that these compromises are shot through with power inequalities,[49] so is law itself; and sometimes compromise supports a better-tailored and kinder justice.

Whether human religious institutions can or should also be humble in declaring their doctrines, rules, and laws, is a theological question. But pragmatically, the absolute demands of incompatible religious hierarchies overwhelm us with war, as we have seen so many times in the course of human history and witness daily. If human religious institutions are not also humble in pronouncing their law and in acknowledging the imperfection of all human institutions, including their own, then a holocaust of loving war is and will continue to be religion's legacy.[50]

(7) Openness to the preconditions of law itself: the basis of a social contract is a mutual commitment through time. The commitment to keep one's commitments comes before the first contract, as a given. This "promise to keep promises" is itself a requirement of consistency, of abiding by one's words, of following an articulated rule. Following a rule, in turn, requires being consistent, or, in Kant's vocabulary, reasonable. The basis of reason is in turn an ability to recognize likeness and treat like as like. Hence, at the root of both law as contract and law as reason, there is a primary ability to see likeness, to be open and receptive to what is common, to see the not-me as like-me, and to commit one's future to an other. That perception of likeness cannot itself be rule-bound, but is a gift or grace, already there for us to see. To have law, therefore, is to have already a bond with others – already an ability to see the not-me as like-me and to commit oneself to an other. A commitment to a not-me whom I see as like-me resembles love. So law itself, we might say, is based on the chaotic ability to love, itself a given.

[49] Niebuhr, *Moral Man and Immoral Society*, 129: "No society has ever achieved peace without incorporating injustice into its harmony."

[50] If there is not some doctrinal humility in human religious organizations, the prevailing interpretation of the Constitution's religion clauses as requiring only "equal treatment" for religious practices under "laws of general application" has much to recommend it, merely so as to avoid religious war. See also, Lewis, *The Four Loves*, 30: "Here it will be enough to say that the Heavenly Society is also an earthly society. Our (merely natural) patriotism toward the latter can very easily borrow the transcendent claims of the former and use them to justify the most abominable actions."

3.3 CHAOTIC GOOD IN SENTENCING

So far this description of agape-in-law as "immanent humility" is very abstract, and I'd like to give some sense of how it might apply to a particular area of law: criminal sentencing. I would argue, on grounds of love and humility, that human sentencing law *can* never and *should* never aspire to perfect retributive lawfulness, but should be understood instead as an imperfect settlement.

I start with the point above that humans come into a world that is already given – both the natural world and the political world. We are not self-created beings. We come into a world that is already meaningful and already connected, and we leave it before our projects are finished. We have no "right" to our world or our community; both are a grace and a gift. In this sense, love – a gift of connection – and not justice or right, is at the heart of being human.

In light of our given-ness and in-time-ness, we humans cannot judge or act with perfect justice because: (1) our knowledge both of people and facts is always imperfect in the past, present, and in the future, and time changes knowledge even as we discover it, (2) our ability to formulate rules is imperfect, both because we cannot foresee the future application of our rule, and because we must express our rule in the abstract and sometimes clumsy ways of human language, and (3) no one can see the world clearly on one's own – we see better, though still imperfectly, with the insight and perspectives of others, the blind leading the blind.

Even if we *could* aspire to perfect lawfulness, we *should* not, for we would thereby overlook the "love" (charisma, authority, personal attachment, respect, faith, loyalty) that makes any commitment, including that to law, possible. As Reinhold Niebuhr says: "If reverence for the law is the essence of the moral sense, as Kant maintained, it must be observed that reason may provide the law but does not, of itself, furnish the reverence."[51]

In my work on criminal sentencing, I have tried to advocate a vision of a humbler, more merciful way of criminal sentencing that would work within these human limitations by (1) acknowledging that anyone's future character may never be perfectly known by human means, and therefore there should always be a sense of awe before the mystery of another person that tempers sentencing, (2) acknowledging that we live short lives constantly in progress, and that finitude itself should matter in sentencing, both in limiting sentences and in allowing them to be meaningful, (3) acknowledging that the character of a past crime does not remain static as its reverberations are lived and its context is illuminated, and (4) acknowledging that human selves are interpenetrated

[51] Niebuhr, *Moral Man and Immoral Society*, 37.

by community, profoundly unable to be monadic "individuals," or, to borrow a phrase from Caleb Smith,[52] "cellular souls." The wrong of crime must be understood in part as rupture with others, which is always self-disintegrating for offender and victim, as well as their families and communities. This can be healed only through an ongoing process of settlement and reunification that restores both meaning and relationship.

The first acknowledgment of the unknowability of a person's future character, in practice, means that punishments should not destroy. Criminal sentencing should never presume to reach perfect calibrations of "just deserts." Irreversible and completely destructive decisions like capital sentences, life without parole, life-long mandatory collateral consequences, and absolute limitations on appeals while punishment is still ongoing,[53] ignore both the human limitations on future knowledge and the human potential for growth, healing, and change. The reformed murderer may one day save more lives than he took.[54]

But this is not a scientific claim about the uncertainties of prediction; it is an ethical imperative. We must stand in awe of each other as part of the humility of agape.[55] It is in this sense that we cannot judge, for judging the "whole" of another person "for all time" is a kind of ethical murder and a false claim of superior and eternal knowledge. No one may claim to know me completely, or own me completely, except God.

Second, punishment must allow for human action and meaning. Meaning is constituted, for humans, in temporal terms, as we understand a future on the basis of a past, or understand the world and our lives through actions and narratives that are acted through and structure time. Part of what is ruptured in crime is expectation and trust – the solidity of reliability over time. Victims experience crime as a breach of trust and a violent intrusion of meaninglessness – why did this happen and how can I trust anyone again? And, as anyone who has worked in prison knows, every day of prison time is

[52] Caleb Smith, *The Prison and the American Imagination* (New Haven: Yale University Press, 2009), 109.

[53] See Sarah Russell, "Reluctance to Resentence: Courts, Congress, and Collateral Review," *North Carolina Law Review* 91 (2012): 79.

[54] See Durrie Bouscaren, "After 40 Years, Iowa Inmate Granted Parole to an Assisted Living Facility," Iowa Public Radio (16 April 2014). Raspberry Williams was convicted of first-degree murder after he shot his neighbor outside a pool hall (he claimed self-defense). He was a model prisoner for 38 years, and he saved the lives of two guards during a hostage situation in 1979. He passed away 2 years after his release, 14 November 2016 (*Daily Gate City*, 16 November 2016).

[55] H. Richard Niebuhr, *The Purpose of the Church and Its Ministry: Reflections on the Aims of Theological Education* (New York: Harper & Brothers, 1956), 35: love is reverence and "keeps its distance even as it draws near." I draw here also on the work of Levinas, *Totality and Infinity*.

also a struggle for meaning. Suffering is intimately bound up with meaninglessness.[56] Hence, a humble but loving punishment must be one that allows for meaningful action, but does not dictate or impose it.

People do indeed repent, change, and try to atone; they try to answer the why of evil and to work toward a happier ending to their life narrative. But retributive theories of punishment "eternalize" time: one must serve the sentence required by one's moral desert at the time of the crime. Post-crime conduct or other non-desert-based factors are irrelevant to the idea that retributive punishment must be based solely on desert. Strict retributivists thus freeze the crime in an eternal present and freeze the character/desert of the offender in the moment of the crime, treating time itself as a fungible "timeless" measure of value (like money) – allow no change or action during imprisonment to matter or "mean" something. The sentence becomes the mere persistence of a human body for an arbitrary collection of empty identical moments that have no connection with each other and no trajectory, instead of being a set of human actions that aim to restore meaning to broken lives and restore trust to a community.

For finite and situated humans, age, individual circumstances, particular relationships, and actions *should* matter in sentencing, and efforts to change and atone should be part of what punishment *means*. A "just deserts" model of paying for culpability with mere persistence over time ignores that time is a frame of meaning-making, because trajectory and narrative are temporal ideas.

Third, punishment must acknowledge that lived events and relationships before prosecution, in pre-trial, in post-trial, and during the sentence, may change the appropriate sentence. A sentence focused on working one's way back to community with others should take into account post-offense acts of reform and sacrifice, as well as new criminal conduct.

Fourth, punishment must be about concrete relationships, not abstractions. The needs of neighbors, the victim, and the offender's family members should matter in crafting responses to crime; and those responses can be flexible – chaotic – and do not have to entail imprisonment-as-payment. The categories of victim and offender themselves must not be reified, as offender and victim are often the same person at different times.[57] The overall movement of sentencing should be toward reunification and restoration of relationships

[56] Meyer, *Justice of Mercy*.

[57] Brandon O'Flaherty and Rajiv Sethi explain the prevalence of young non-white men among both homicide victims and perpetrators: "[P]eople sometimes kill simply to avoid being killed. As a result, disputes can escalate dramatically in environments (endogenously) perceived to be dangerous, resulting in self-fulfilling expectations of violence ... and significant racial disparities in rates of murder and victimization." "Homicide in Black and White," *Journal of Urban Economics* 68, no. 3 (2010): 215.

whenever possible, not the orderly but abstract false equivalence of a commodified time with a crime.

Restorative justice options – like victim/offender dialogue, efforts to apologize, and efforts to pay forward in meaningful, committed, and dedicated community service – seem humbler and more appropriate to the relational and temporal nature of being human than desert cashed out as meaningless years in prison.[58] Sentencing should also not, at the other extreme, be understood as an effort to "rehabilitate" or scientifically "fix" the offender's "asocial tendencies," for that, too, presupposes a complete knowledge of and superiority over the offender that is incompatible with humility in sentencing.[59] The specter of a "holocaust of generosity" in sentencing should set outside limits to the state's control over a prisoner, as well as prohibitions on treating prisoners as "patients" rather than brothers, sisters, and parents.

Punishment should provide meaningful ways to respond to wrongful acts and pathways to come home, but should never subvert autonomy or avert respect. Human criminal justice, I conclude, must be humble and relational, not absolute and conceptual. Chaotic good can be part of sentencing as an imperfect, ongoing settlement, provisional and humble, with all the stakeholders at the table. Existing practices of plea bargaining, which resolve ninety-five percent of all criminal cases, often try to function in just this way, and sometimes succeed, at least when adequate resources are available to structure re-entry safely and provide opportunities for apology and service. The chaotic "exception" to the rule of sentencing, therefore, can sometimes be a better form of justice *with* love.

3.4 CONCLUSION

Lawful good for finite humans must co-exist with a humble chaotic good. Otherwise, we lose sight of law's need for defeasibility, particularity, and personal interaction, and we fail to notice law's underlying commitment to see "others" as "like" and to abide with them through time. We may also lose something rarer and more precious: if we banish chaotic love from law, we lose the liminal place at the boundaries of law from which we might catch a glimpse of the graceful wild lion.

58 This argument is elaborated in Meyer, *Justice of Mercy*.

59 See C. S. Lewis, "A Humanitarian Theory of Punishment," *AMCAP Journal* 13, no. 1 (1987): 147 (reprinted).

4

Javert and *Jihad*: Why Law Cannot Survive Without Love, and Vice Versa

Timothy P. Jackson

Sometimes love does what justice requires and assumes its rules and norms, sometimes love does more than justice requires but never less, and sometimes love acts in a quite different way from what justice alone can enable us to discern to be right.

– Paul Ramsey[1]

I start not from the United States Constitution but from the Ten Commandments, with their implicit assertions that all human law is founded ultimately on divine law and that the ultimate purpose of human law is to create conditions in which love of God and love of neighbor may flourish.

– Harold J. Berman[2]

4.1 INTRODUCTION

If asked to name the most heinously immoral act in recorded history, I suspect that most contemporary Americans would pick either the Roman crucifixion of Jesus, the Nazi Holocaust, or perhaps the jihadist terrorism of 9/11. As obscene as these are, however, equally significant (if not equally culpable) is what lies at the root of all three: an anti-Judaism that pits law against gospel and justice against love. Indeed, Western theology and jurisprudence have often been warped by this same basic error. Several New Testament authors put law at odds with gospel, thus alienating Judaism from Christianity very near the inception of the latter. A related invidious distinction with "biblical" warrant is that between "the damned," who lack faith and thus are consigned to hell by the rigors of the law, and "the elect," who believe in the good news of Jesus and thus are redeemed for heaven by grace. More recently, many political theorists have privatized love and defined legal justice in terms of

[1] Paul Ramsey, *War and the Christian Conscience* (Durham: Duke University Press, 1961), 178.
[2] Harold J. Berman, "Law and Logos," *DePaul Law Review* 44, no. 143 (1994): 143.

competing interests in the public sphere, thus alienating individuals from groups. A related false dichotomy with "liberal" warrant is that between "traditional virtue," which assumes real values and a shared human nature, and "democratic praxis," which is strictly a matter of pragmatic convention. Neither biblical faith nor liberal politics will realize its full potential until these false contrasts are overcome. More pointedly, the cross, Auschwitz, and the World Trade Center will be but three icons of endless murder unless law and love can be reconciled. Or so I argue in this essay.

What follows is an analysis of two defects of ethical vision. I begin with love as neglected and/or ghettoized, with Victor Hugo's Inspector Javert and John Rawls as the chief exemplars. For Rawls, love is an important virtue but too demanding and/or dangerous to be included in political reflection. It must be limited to the "background culture" of society, with a metaphysically neutral[3] and tolerant justice as the arbiter of the public sphere. Rawls's severe earnestness reminds one, uncannily, of Javert in *Les Misérables*. Javert's hounding of the increasingly agapic Jean Valjean, together with Javert's self-criticism and eventual suicide, are symbolic of the fact that a modern procedural justice divorced politically from love proves both self-destructive and other-denying. This is the case no matter how well-intentioned the separation. Call this "moral myopia or near-sightedness": one focuses on fine details close to hand, but one misses the larger context, the comprehensive picture, and distorts persons and objects further off.

In the second form of axiological ametropia, law is abused and/or ignored, with Saints Luke and John as the principal heavies. Largely through their influence, many Christians hold that Jesus' crucifixion was carried out by Pharisaic legalism and accepted by non-resisting charity. This is palpably untrue. As gruesome as was the Roman execution of the Christ, the more regrettable murder of the Word, to repeat, is the opposing of law and love, Judaism and Jesus, the damned and the saved. The Book of Revelation is a case in point. It is so full of resentment and revenge fantasies against non-believers that it calls up the controversial word *jihad*. *Jihad* is the Arabic term for "struggle" and my emblematic term for love-unconstrained-by-law. Jihadists "love" God so much and fight so fiercely for their conception of Him that they are anarchic: blind or hostile to finite creatures and temporal obligations.[4] Saint John was an early

3 In *Political Liberalism* (New York: Columbia University Press, 1996), Rawls uses the word "neutral" only reluctantly, but he writes that justice as fairness "hopes to satisfy neutrality of aim in the sense that basic institutions and public policy are not to be designed to favor any particular comprehensive doctrine." Ibid., 194.

4 Lenn Goodman has observed, in e-mail conversation, that "jihadists are *takfiris*, that is, they hold anyone, even Muslims, who countenances a non-Islamic government to be a *kafir*, that is, an infidel. That's how they justify killing other Muslims, including those who died on 9/11."

jihadist, if only ideationally . . . capable of metaphysical speculations of exquisite beauty and power, but also overflowing with cruel and spiteful velleities. Call this "moral hyperopia or far-sightedness": one clearly sees a distant and massive *Imago*, but one cannot discern the concrete individuals immediately affected by one's words and deeds.

Although I do not discuss their work here, my pages are inspired by Paul Ramsey's and Harold J. Berman's life-long efforts to ground justice and law in love. In these pages, "justice" will mean rewarding merit (distribution), punishing demerit (retribution), and/or keeping contracts (fair procedure). "Love" will mean an agape/charity that attends to the needs and potentials of others, beyond what strict merit, demerit, and/or contract require. More specifically, interpersonal agape involves (1) unconditional willing of the good for the other, (2) equal regard for the well-being of the other, and (3) passionate service, open to self-sacrifice, for the sake of the other.[5] My main thesis is that justice without forgiveness and the honoring of sanctity is self- and other-consuming, but love without truthfulness and respect for dignity is equally homicidal. Javert and *jihad* are two sides of the same coin, or, rather, of a slug that passes for "legal tender" but is neither licit nor compassionate.

4.2 MORAL MYOPIA: JUSTICE WITHOUT OR AGAINST LOVE IN HUGO AND RAWLS

4.2.1 *Hugo*

Victor Hugo's *Les Misérables* tracks the career of Jean Valjean who, having stolen bread to feed his starving sister's family and having been sent to prison in the galleys for 19 years, is released to a hostile world. My main focus, however, is on two compelling scenes revolving around Javert. In Volume One, Valjean is on the run for yet another robbery. Javert, a police inspector, thinks that he has falsely accused Mayor Madeleine, in public, of being the thief, Valjean. Javert has been told and quite reasonably believes that another man who has been arrested is Valjean. On that presumption, Javert insists to Madeleine that he, Javert, be removed from office. The cool instrument of justice cannot accept his own fallibility and so would absent himself from social service. Here is the relevant dialogue, beginning with Javert:

> "Monsieur Mayor, there is one thing more to which I desire to call your attention."
>
> "What is it?"
>
> "It is that I ought to be dismissed."

[5] See Timothy P. Jackson, *The Priority of Love: Christian Charity and Social Justice* (Princeton: Princeton University Press, 2003).

Monsieur Madeleine arose.

"Javert, you are a man of honour and I esteem you. You exaggerate your fault. Besides, this is an offence which concerns me. You are worthy of promotion rather than disgrace. I desire you to keep your place."

Javert looked at Monsieur Madeleine with his calm eyes, in whose depths it seemed that one beheld his conscience, unenlightened, but stern and pure, and said in a tranquil voice:

"Monsieur Mayor, I cannot agree to that."
"I repeat," said Monsieur Madeleine, "that this matter concerns me."

But Javert, with his one idea, continued:

As to exaggerating, I do not exaggerate. This is the way I reason. I have unjustly suspected you. That is nothing. It is our province to suspect, although it may be an abuse of our right to suspect our superiors. But without proofs and in a fit of anger, with revenge as my aim, I denounced you as a convict – you, a respectable man, a mayor, and a magistrate. This is a serious matter, very serious. I have committed an offence against authority in your person, I, who am the agent of authority. If one of my subordinates had done what I have, I would have pronounced him unworthy of the service, and sent him away. Well, listen a moment, Monsieur Mayor; I have often been severe in my life towards others. It was just. I did right. Now if I were not severe towards myself, all I have justly done would become injustice. Should I spare myself more than others? No. What! if I should be prompt only to punish others and not myself, I should be a wretch indeed![6]

The Mayor refuses to sack Inspector Javert. In fact, however, Madeleine *is* Valjean. Valjean has reformed and under an assumed name has become a leader and benefactor of his town, M____ -sur- M__, but he now realizes that he must disclose his real identity in order to save the innocent man mistaken for him. He proceeds to do so, and is promptly arrested by Javert.

In Volume Five, anti-Orleanist students apprehend Javert for spying on them and sentence him to death. Valjean, who has escaped Javert and stands with the revolutionaries, manages to save the policeman's life by pretending to execute him but secretly letting him go. Valjean is subsequently arrested yet again by Javert, but when it comes time to turn Valjean over to the authorities, Javert cannot do it. He has unmasked Valjean and captured him on multiple occasions, yet each time the condemned man eludes him psychologically.

6 Victor Hugo, *Les Misérables*, trans. Charles E. Wilbour (New York: The Modern Library, n.d.), 176–77.

Javert simply cannot grasp Valjean. Javert is now bent low with anxiety, riven between his sense of duty to the letter of the law and his feelings of gratitude for Valjean's mercy to him. Here is Hugo's chilling description of Javert's suffering:

> For some hours Javert had ceased to be natural. He was troubled; this brain, so limpid in its blindness, had lost its transparency; there was a cloud in this crystal. Javert felt that duty was growing weaker in his conscience, and he could not hide it from himself. . . . He saw before him two roads, both equally straight; but he saw two; and that terrified him – him, who had never in his life known but one straight line. And, bitter anguish, these two roads were contradictory. . . . What should he do now? Give up Jean Valjean, that was wrong; leave Jean Valjean free, that was wrong. In the first case, the man of authority would fall lower than the man of the galley; in the second, a convict rose higher than the law and set his foot upon it. In both cases, dishonor to him, Javert.[7]

Javert cannot comprehend himself either. He will not accept that Valjean's former poverty may mitigate his crimes, but neither can he accept that he, Javert, should continue to live having set him free. Unable to reconcile justice and charity, he intentionally plunges into the Seine and drowns.

Jean Valjean and Inspector Javert undoubtedly represent contrasting moral poles, but we must take care not to oversimplify them. We tend to romanticize Valjean, seeing him as noble in character from beginning to end, even if forced by circumstances to do wrong, legally understood. Hugo's truth is very different. He gives us a Valjean who is initially quite corrupt and untrustworthy. Valjean has been conditioned by dire straits, including years in prison, and Hugo wants to call critical attention to the squalor and unfairness of French social conditions. But the evil of these conditions is precisely that they have helped make Valjean (and many others) deeply and genuinely unjust. The man we first meet is acquisitive, dishonest, and bitter. It is only with time, effort, and the aid of a saintly bishop that these vices are overcome, and then only partially.

Correlatively, we often too easily vilify Javert, judging him and his "one idea" to be merely obsessed and vindictive. We fail to appreciate that he is, in many ways, upright and true – "a man of honour," as Valjean says. If Valjean's identity challenges Javert, the reverse also holds. Javert worries about "ill-judged kindness" that "disorganizes society,"[8] and so should we. Javert exclaims, "Good God, it is easy to be kind, the difficulty is to be just,"[9] and,

7 Ibid., 1105–6.

8 Ibid., 177.

9 Ibid.

in spite of the overstatement, we know what he means. It is not always easy to be kind, but sometimes apparent benevolence represents either paternalism or an abrogation of responsibility. Javert, then, is more a tragic hero undone by a fatal flaw (*hamartia*), than a villain intent on harming others. Contingency and company unfold his too-severe conscience, and that conscience ultimately destroys him. But this is neither an indictment of justice and law as such, nor a *carte blanche* for the laxity of mere good intentions. It is a cautionary tale of how justice and law go to smash if not leavened with love, yet it is also a saga of the perils of unwise love itself.

A central reason Javert cannot see a way out of his conundrum is that he so dwells on the *ancien régime* values of class and honor that he lacks a sense of solidarity with others. He too much respects temporal power and authority. When he finally begins to perceive the ubiquity of human sinfulness, including his own and the state's, he refuses to receive forgiveness. The drama of *Les Misérables* is in watching Valjean evolve from desperate injustice (theft) to sublime charity (self-sacrifice), even as Javert devolves from confident justice (retribution) to pathetic lovelessness (self-destruction). Yet Valjean's progress from taking to giving involves several misperceptions of what is loveable and is largely sparked by Bishop Myriel's forgiving assistance. Similarly, Javert's regress from self-assertion to self-immolation is more folly than malevolence and is in spite of Valjean's sparing him. Hugo's novel allows, even induces, us to imagine our own lives going in either direction, depending on whether we are offered clemency and how we appropriate it if given.

The paradigm shift that would triangulate Javert's two "contradictory" roads is, as Hugo intimates, something super-natural. A love that falls below giving what is due is unjust, but a love that rises above simple justice to give more is divine. (Think of the parable of the vineyard in Matthew 20:1–16.) I am not saying that Hugo himself was a Jew or a Christian – I take it that, though raised Catholic, he died a Rationalist and Freethinker – but I am maintaining that, in Hugo's story, Valjean needs Myriel, Javert needs Valjean, and all depend upon a grace that outstrips any positive law or historical institution. As James 1:17 puts it, "Every generous act of giving, with every perfect gift, is from above."

4.2.2 *Rawls*

Now let us shift from the moral emotions of a novelist to the ethical cogitations of a philosopher. Consider John Rawls's famous thought experiment, designed to reanimate social contract theory. In *A Theory of Justice*, he imagines persons behind a "veil of ignorance," trying to decide on the principles that will govern the community into which they are about to enter. The veil precludes persons from knowing the particulars of their identity and their specific place in society: race, class, sex, intelligence, vocation, party, creed, etc. The deliberating parties possess only the two broad "moral powers" of a sense of justice and a thin conception of the human good. Under these original conditions, Rawls theorizes that the first tenet of justice selected would be:

> Each person is to have an equal right to the most extensive basic liberty compatible with a similar liberty for others.[10]

Because those in "the original position" do not know of which class they will be a member, Rawls believes they would be convinced that a second principle is a reasonable restriction on *in*equality:

> Social and economic inequalities are to be arranged so that they are both (a) to the greatest benefit of the least advantaged and (b) attached to offices and positions open to all under conditions of fair equality of opportunity.[11]

Some commentators have interpreted this second tenet – especially the first half, "the difference principle" or so-called "maximin rule" – as more akin to charity than to fairness. But charity is precisely the sort of robust, other-regarding virtue that Rawls forbids to his social contractors (and to public reason generally). His contractors are to be thought of as "rational and mutually disinterested," as "not taking an interest in one another's interests."[12] How then does maximizing the minimum fall out as singularly justified?

Let me probe Rawls's position by imagining that the society he contemplates is extremely simple, with only three classes: the most well off, the middle class, and the least well off. How is one to apply the second principle of justice to concrete cases? Even if an inequality were "open to all under conditions of fair equality of opportunity," one might still be uncertain as to what the second condition (maximin) requires. Suppose, for instance, that the benefits of an open inequality might be structured in one of four possible ways:

10 Rawls, *A Theory of Justice* (Cambridge: Harvard University Press, 1971), 60. Rawls gives a more elaborate formulation of this principle in *Political Liberalism*, 5: each person has an equal claim to a fully adequate scheme of equal basic rights and liberties, which scheme is compatible with the same scheme for all; and in this scheme the equal political liberties, and only those liberties, are to be guaranteed their fair value.

11 Rawls, *A Theory of Justice*, 83. A slightly different wording of this principle appears in Rawls, *Political Liberalism*, 6: social and economic inequalities are to satisfy two conditions: first, they are to be attached to positions and offices open to all under conditions of fair equality of opportunity; and second, they are to be to the greatest benefit of the least advantaged members of society.

12 Rawls, *A Theory of Justice*, 13.

SCENARIO #1:

40 benefits to the most well off
40 benefits to the middle class
40 benefits to the least well off
120 = Total

SCENARIO #2:

150 benefits to the most well off
100 benefits to the middle class
55 benefits to the least well off
305 = Total

SCENARIO #3:

30 benefits to the most well off
40 benefits to the middle class
60 benefits to the least well off
130 = Total

SCENARIO #4:

85 benefits to the most well off
75 benefits to the middle class
65 benefits to the least well off
225 = Total

Which of these four scenarios is mandated by the difference principle? Scenario #1 might be called "Strict Egalitarianism," since all three classes receive exactly the same amount of benefits. Scenario #2 represents "Maximal Utility," since the total benefits are here greater than in any other possibility. Scenario #3 is plausibly labeled "Envy Canonized," because it means that the least advantaged settle for less than they might otherwise receive in order to get the most within their own society. Some early commentators on Rawls thought that he was militating for #3, but this is a misunderstanding. It would indeed amount to a kind of irrational jealousy. Scenario #4 is, in fact, Rawls's "Justice as Fairness," because "the greatest benefit of the least advantaged" is to be calculated *across* alternatives, *not within* each alternative. Or so I now think. In #4, the least well off receive 65 benefits, as opposed to 60 in #3, 55 in #2, and 40 in #1. This satisfies the maximin rule, even though the uppermost and middle classes within #4 both get more benefits than the lowest.

Now, what would move persons in the original position to embrace a principle that entailed Scenario #4? Rawls wants the relevant persons to be conceived of as rational, but would such individuals necessarily forgo Scenario #2, with its higher overall utility and greater benefits to the uppermost and middle classes? Many have argued that it would not be irrational to "gamble" that one would be in the upper two classes, especially if the potential reward is significant and the potential risk insignificant.[13] Might one not decide to hope for 150 or 100 benefits, over against 85 or 75, knowing that in the worst-case scenario one would receive 55 rather than 65? Such a calculated risk does not seem insane or imprudent, nor is it manifestly unfair to others. Rawls merely defines the original posits as risk averse.

I do not see how rational self-interest alone can move one to dismiss Scenario #2 and affirm Scenario #4. Further, possessing the sense of justice and a thin conception of the good allowed by Rawls does not seem sufficient to rule out the gambling described above. If one opts for #4, one's motive must be something closer to charity than to prudence or even fairness. Rawls's difference principle is really a function of not wanting *anyone* to have less than he or she might have, regardless of the impact this might have on oneself. If I forgo the chance for great riches in order to secure a higher floor for the least advantaged, my action is more altruistic than self-concerned. The paradox is that Rawls himself banishes such an ethical inspiration from law and politics; it is too overweening and "perfectionist." In his account, one refuses egregious inequalities *a priori* because one fears that one will get the short end of the stick, not because one feels for the possible plight of others as such.

Rawls is no cynic, dismissing care for others as humanly impossible or unnecessary. Nor does he think that rational agents *per se* are "solely self-interested."[14] He acknowledges "our need for love and sympathy,"[15] and he makes it very plain that "we should not expect justice as fairness, or any account of justice, to cover all cases of right and wrong. Political justice needs always to be complemented by other virtues."[16] Nonetheless, Rawls holds that, *for fundamental political purposes*, we can bracket robust fellow-feeling and rely on a sense of justice and a thin conception of the

[13] See, *inter alia*, Brian Barry, "John Rawls and the Priority of Liberty," in *Philosophy and Public Affairs* 2 (Spring 1973): 274–90; John C. Harsanyi, "Can the Maximin Principle Serve as a Basis of Morality? A Critique of John Rawls's Theory," in *American Political Science Review* 69, no. 2 (June 1975): 594–606.

[14] Rawls, *Political Liberalism*, 51.

[15] Ibid., 105.

[16] Ibid., 21.

good to generate fair social cooperation. I believe this "moral" basis, which Rawls calls "reciprocity,"[17] amounts to a questionable form of individual pragmatism. More pointedly, however, if, *pace* Rawls, love of neighbor, rather than pragmatism, is required for the validation of Rawls's own second principle of justice, then his claim to detach "public reason" from the metaphysics of morals and to relegate agapic love to the "background culture" is exploded. Like Hugo's Javert, Rawls ends in self-contradiction. He is not literally suicidal, of course, but in undermining his own theory he enacts the death of the lamb – the end of what I have called "liberalism as morally basic."[18] Instead of showing how liberal political theory can get along with minimal justice alone, Rawls actually demonstrates the poverty of fairness without sympathy.

Rawls's argument for excluding substantive philosophy from public decision-making about basic matters of justice sounds hauntingly like Javert's brief for his being dismissed from office for being haughty and fallible. "Political liberalism applies the principle of toleration to philosophy itself,"[19] and so becomes self-muzzling. For Javert, "honour" dictates that he not challenge governmental authority, even as, for Rawls, "civility" and "the burdens of judgment" demand that we not contest "public reason" or a liberal "overlapping consensus."[20] Thus both men too completely bind conscience to the *Zeitgeist*, however democratic or undemocratic.

To put the point another way, if we limit our political reflection to an abstract procedural fairness, purged of all "comprehensive doctrines" about the intrinsic worth of human beings, we will never reach the virtue of respect for others as free and equal citizens that Rawls evidently cherishes. Abiding by his own "duty of civility,"[21] it would seem that Rawls can only endorse freedom and equality as Western conventions or assumptions of his thought experiment, not as the implications of a shared human nature. According to Rawls, to appeal to human dignity or sanctity, for instance, would be to introduce controversial (and coercive) religious or philosophical beliefs into political discourse. Without such beliefs, however, Rawlsian civility is but a simulacrum of respect. I safeguard others' interests, not because I honor them as fellows, but because I fear myself being victimized by social inequality. Thus is the motive of neighbor love supplanted, politically, by personal prudence or

[17] Ibid., 16 and 50.

[18] See Timothy P. Jackson, "The Return of the Prodigal? Liberal Theory and Religious Pluralism," in *Religion and Contemporary Liberalism*, ed. Paul Weithman (University of Notre Dame Press, 1997).

[19] Rawls, *Political Liberalism*, 10.

[20] Ibid., 55–62, 213–20, and 236.

[21] Ibid., 217.

what Rawls dubs "rational advantage."[22] And thus does justice devolve, Javert-like, into something less than itself.

Rawls protests that "justice as fairness is not procedurally neutral" and that his "principles of justice" and "conceptions of society and person" represented in the original position are "substantive."[23] But this is to want it both ways. If Rawls considers persons as free and equal because they have a sense of justice and can make rational choices between goods,[24] then thick anthropological and sociological theses are built into his reflections *ab initio*. (If we can pack this much into the original position, why even take the veil?) We are back again with Immanuel Kant; despite protests,[25] justice as fairness is not independent of comprehensive truth claims after all. If, in contrast, persons are merely "regarded"[26] as free and equal because this is the "common" or "politically constructed" or "freestanding" way of the West – i.e. not a matter of truth but consensus[27] – then Rawlsian justice has insufficient body to constitute virtue, even political virtue. We have indeed gone pragmatic, and Richard Rorty's conventionalism is the order of the day; we "honor" persons not because they inherently deserve it, but because this keeps the peace or otherwise gets us what we want.[28] Once more like Javert, Rawls has placed before himself two roads that are contradictory, and he is fatally unable to pick one.

4.3 MORAL HYPEROPIA: GOSPEL WITHOUT OR AGAINST LAW IN "THE NEW TESTAMENT"

4.3.1 *The Christian Gospels*

From literature to philosophy, and now to scripture. All four canonical gospels offer affirmative accounts of Jesus and his teaching, of course, but all four also show palpable signs of anti-Jewish sentiments. (Matthew, for instance,

22 Ibid., 179–80. See also Timothy P. Jackson, "Liberal Integrity: Lenn Goodman's Case for Democratic Virtue," part of a roundtable discussion of *Religious Pluralism and Values in the Public Sphere*, in *Political Theology*, 16.6 (November 2015).

23 Rawls, *Political Liberalism*, 192.

24 Ibid., 18–19.

25 See ibid., 203.

26 Cf. ibid., 20.

27 "Within itself the political conception does without the concept of truth. . . ." Ibid., 94.

28 Rawls insists that his scheme is not a mere *modus vivendi* (e.g., ibid., 147), but he sure sounds like Thomas Hobbes at times. Like Hobbes, Rawls is deeply troubled by the European creedal wars of the sixteenth and seventeenth centuries (ibid., xxiv–xxvi). He is so fearful of religious and philosophical truth claims becoming overbearing and violent – so afraid of *jihad*, if you will – that he places peace and fair cooperation above truth and open contestation. Only now, in place of Leviathan, the sovereign king, we have Behemoth, the sovereign public.

is notoriously ambivalent about Judaism: appreciating the Torah but condemning the Jewish leaders.) There is no unmediated access to "the historical Jesus," and there is no ordered development of his image(s) across Mark, Matthew, Luke, and John.[29] It is generally accepted, however, that the later the gospel the more aggressively it is detached from its Jewish/Torah background. As Paula Fredriksen says, "The more the tradition evolves, the worse the Jews become."[30] Mark is commonly judged to be the earliest canonical gospel (probably composed in the 60s CE), with Matthew the closest to it chronologically (likely written in the late 70s or early 80s CE) and the most "Jewish." By the time of John (ca. 90 CE), "the Jews" and "the law" have virtually become dirty words. They are what "we Christians" oppose, our enemies.[31]

The most striking feature of Jesus in Mark and Matthew is his profound sense of the nearness and goodness of God. Yahweh is a loving and forgiving Father, rather than an abusive and vengeful tyrant. The holiness of the Creator is fearful in its majesty, and it represents a demanding claim on the life of creatures, but it is fundamentally *for* us instead of *against* us. So intimate and benevolent is God that the hairs on our heads are numbered (Matt. 10:30). Indeed, the Father sent His beloved Son to suffer for the redemption of the whole world. These facts are both comforting and unsettling. A proper understanding of the divine character elicits gratitude, but it also means surrendering (even reversing) worldly wisdom. Jesus' God prefers universal love over burnt offerings (Mark 12:28–33); in fact, all neighbors are to be perfectly cherished and served, including enemies (Matt. 5:43–48). Divine power is self-emptying – "made perfect in weakness," to borrow St. Paul's phrase (2 Cor. 12:9) – and what makes Jesus the Messiah is his willingness to turn away from earthly glory, to obey God, and to serve others even unto death. We too are to display such kenotic virtue, to deny ourselves and follow Jesus to the cross (Matt. 16:24).

This vision of Deity and humanity is entirely Judaic in style and content. One need only recall five salient "Old Testament" passages:

> So God created humankind in his image, in the image of God he created them; male and female he created them. God blessed them, and God said to them, "Be fruitful and multiply, and fill the earth and subdue it." (Gen. 1:27–28)

[29] See Paula Fredriksen, *From Jesus to Christ: The Origins of the New Testament Images of Jesus*, 2nd ed. (New Haven: Yale University Press, 2000), 19.

[30] Ibid., 121.

[31] See "Introduction to the Gospels" and notes to "The Gospel According to Matthew," *The New Oxford Annotated Bible (NRSV)*, 4th ed. (Oxford and New York: Oxford University Press, 2010), 1743–47.

> The LORD passed before [Moses], and proclaimed, "The LORD, the LORD, a God merciful and gracious, slow to anger, and abounding in steadfast love and faithfulness, keeping steadfast love for the thousandth generation, forgiving iniquity and transgression and sin, yet by no means clearing the guilty." (Exodus 34:6–7)
>
> The LORD your God is God of gods and Lord of lords, the great God, mighty and awesome, who is not partial and takes no bribe, who executes justice for the orphan and the widow, and who loves the strangers, providing them with food and clothing. You shall also love the stranger, for you were strangers in the land of Egypt. (Deut. 10:17–19)
>
> I hate, I despise your festivals, and I take no delight in your solemn assemblies. Even though you offer me your burnt-offerings and grain-offerings, I will not accept them; and the offerings of well-being of your fatted animals I will not look upon. Take away from me the noise of your songs; I will not listen to the melody of your harps. But let justice roll down like waters, and righteousness like an ever-flowing stream. (Amos 5:21–24)
>
> But this is the covenant that I will make with the house of Israel after those days, says the LORD: I will put my law within them, and I will write it on their hearts; and I will be their God, and they shall be my people (Jer. 31:33).

Jesus was a Jew, and his message of a gracious God, upholding heartfelt love and justice over empty rituals, is manifestly Jewish. So how did it get translated into its opposite? How, in the very name of God, did key authors of the New Testament turn the Prince of Peace into an occasion for ethnic strife? Why, quite generally, have the Jews been persecuted by Christians for centuries, even millennia? For my purposes, there are five related (putative) justifications, which I trace back mainly to Luke and John and analyze critically below:

*(1) **The Jews perversely refuse to recognize Jesus as the Messiah.***

> For this reason the Jews were seeking all the more to kill him, because he was not only breaking the sabbath, but was also calling God his own Father, thereby making himself equal to God. (John 5:18)

Here "the Jews" are made out as murderous because they fail to affirm the unique divinity of Jesus. This reflects a concern to celebrate Jesus as creative and authoritative, but it takes on an increasingly hostile tone. Even John grants that "salvation is from the Jews" (John 4:22), but for him "the Jews" typically means those who vilify the Christ and reject his message:

> The Jews said to him, "Now we know that you have a demon. Abraham died, and so did the prophets; yet you say, 'Whoever keeps my word will never taste death.'" (John 8:52)

The redactive nature of John's animosity is made obvious in 9:22–23. "The Jews" summon the parents of the man born blind and healed by Jesus, but they decline to say how or by whom their son has been made to see. John comments:

> His parents said this because they were afraid of the Jews; for the Jews had already agreed that anyone who confessed Jesus to be the Messiah would be put out of the synagogue. Therefore his parents said, "He is of age; ask him."

Most scholars surmise that the Gospel of John was written about 90 CE,[32] some 55 years after the death of Jesus and some 20 years after the destruction of the Temple in 70. It was only after the destruction of the Temple, however, that Rabbinic Judaism based in synagogues began to emerge. John is here projecting back into the time of Christ a gripe that festered over half a century later. By the writing of John, that is, "the Jews" had become "them," standing over against and victimizing "us Christians."

To be sure, John's immediate targets were the priestly leadership who opposed Jesus and were putting Christians out of the synagogues, but his rhetorical excesses invited the blanket condemnation of "the Jews" that later led to violent anti-Semitism. Is John himself anti-Semitic? It is a fine point, but I think it is too easy to say that the problem is simply one of later interpreters' failing to appreciate the original polemical context. When John has Jesus say to "the Jews," "You are from your father the devil, and you choose to do your father's desires. He was a murderer from the beginning and does not stand in the truth, because there is no truth in him" (8:44), John is like a parent leaving a loaded gun in a house full of children. The parent did not intend for the children to shoot each other, but when they do, the parent is culpable.

Luke and Acts also emphasize the singularity of Christ and the blindness of "the Jews":

> Saul became increasingly more powerful and confounded the Jews who lived in Damascus by proving that Jesus was the Messiah. (Acts 9:22)

The Gospel of John seems particularly embarrassed that the Messiah should have once been a disciple of John the Baptist, so His dependence on the Baptist is played down and His superiority over him is played up. If pushed, however, this high Christological line replaces the faith *of* Christ with faith *in* Christ, as Friedrich Nietzsche observed.[33] Jesus is metaphysically matchless and does it all; he is a law unto himself, and we need not share his costly

[32] *The New Oxford Annotated Bible*, 1879.

[33] Friedrich Nietzsche, "The Antichrist," in *The Portable Nietzsche*, trans. Walter Kaufmann (New York: The Viking Press, 1954), § 39, 612–13.

obedience to God and service of the neighbor. Thus agape becomes something already fully accomplished, and we are let off the moral hook.

The "good news" preached by Jesus is that "the kingdom of heaven has come near" (Matt. 10:7). The kingdom is the initiative of God (Matt. 25:34), and it means both spiritual and physical healing: the forgiveness of sins (Matt. 6:12, 18:21–22, 26:28) and the curing of disease and infirmity (Matt. 4:23, 11:5, 14:35–36). Indeed, in the case of the bed-ridden paralytic, the two forms of healing are so closely related as to seem interchangeable (Matt. 9:2–7). The proper human reaction is a thankful repentance and faith (Mark 1:15). The extent to which Jesus thought of himself as uniquely divine – his Messianic self-consciousness – is highly debatable and debated. Sometimes he emphasizes his consanguinity with God (Mark 14:61–62); sometimes he accents his difference from God (Matt. 24:36); and sometimes he is evasive (Matt. 26:63–64). Particularly striking is Mark 10:17–22:

> As he [Jesus] was setting out on a journey, a man ran up and knelt before him, and asked him, "Good Teacher, what must I do to inherit eternal life?" Jesus said to him, "Why do you call me good? No one is good but God alone. You know the commandments: 'You shall not murder; You shall not commit adultery; You shall not steal; You shall not bear false witness; You shall not defraud; Honour your father and mother.'" He said to him, "Teacher, I have kept all these since my youth." Jesus, looking at him, loved him and said, "You lack one thing; go, sell what you own, and give the money to the poor, and you will have treasure in heaven; then come, follow me." When he heard this, he was shocked and went away grieving, for he had many possessions.

These lines are remarkable for two main reasons. First, they involve an explicit denial by Jesus of his identity with God: "Why do you call me good? No one is good but God alone." Second, they reference the Ten Commandments of Exodus and Deuteronomy as the keys to eternal life. Jesus also stipulates dispossession and discipleship, but these injunctions seem to follow from or consummate the traditional ten, rather than to add something new and different.

In any case, human conscience as to Jesus' status cannot be compelled. And why should a theoretical affirmation of the metaphysical significance of Jesus be more important than a practical following in his ethical footsteps? Even if one thinks, as I do, that Jesus is profoundly one with the Father and an indispensable source of divine grace, the key question is to whom this grace is available. If Christ came to save only "the elect," and "the reprobate" in turn are forever consigned to retributive flames – so-called "limited Atonement" – then the Christian "gospel" cannot help but sow distrust and discord. It will inevitably encourage invidious contrasts between "us-who-are-beloved-of-God" and "them-poor-bastards-lost-in-the-law." This is especially true if salvation and damnation are deemed irresistible, since one can then do absolutely nothing about one's lot. Thus does the New Testament *euangelion* become a *malangelion* for many, especially the Jews.

(2) The Jews were responsible for the crucifixion of Jesus, God's Son.

> Then Pilate entered the headquarters again, summoned Jesus, and asked him, "Are you the King of the Jews?" Jesus answered, "Do you ask this on your own, or did others tell you about me?" Pilate replied, "I am not a Jew, am I? Your own nation and the chief priests have handed you over to me. What have you done?" Jesus answered, "My kingdom is not from this world. If my kingdom were from this world, my followers would be fighting to keep me from being handed over to the Jews. But as it is, my kingdom is not from here." (John 18:33–36)

John's normative sympathies are clear: he would blame the Jews and exonerate Pilate for the killing of Christ:

> [Pilate] went out to the Jews again and told them, "I find no case against him. But you have a custom that I release someone for you at the Passover. Do you want me to release for you the King of the Jews?" They shouted in reply, "Not this man, but Barabbas!" (John 18:38–40)
>
> [Pilate] said to the Jews, "Here is your King!" They cried out, "Away with him! Away with him! Crucify him!" Pilate asked them, "Shall I crucify your King?" The chief priests answered, "We have no king but the emperor." Then he handed him over to them to be crucified. (John 19:14–16)

Luke/Acts is not as anti-Jewish as John, but he is moving in that direction. As Fredriksen observes,

> Luke's concept of Christianity's relationship to Judaism, and consequently his presentation of Jesus' relationship to Judaism, are complicated. On the one hand, the two religions are viewed as continuous: Jesus fulfills the promise of salvation made to Israel long ago. . . . Yet with a clumsy foreshadowing that borders on anachronism, Luke works into his narrative the later tensions between Christianity and its parent religion. . . . Jesus warns his disciples that the Jews will drag them "before the synagogues and rulers and authorities," as they are about to do to Jesus (12:11). . . . Finally, once Jesus stands before Pilate, "the people," who only a chapter before were a serious impediment to the chief priests' plots, suddenly demand that Barabbas be released and Christ be crucified. A reluctant Pilate delivers Jesus up "to *their* will" – one has the impression that the Jews, not the Romans, performed the execution. (23:1–25)[34]

[34] Fredriksen, *From Jesus to Christ*, 33–34.

The problem for both John and Luke is that there is no historical record of a custom of Passover prisoner release,[35] and crucifixion is a Roman punishment for sedition, not a Jewish punishment for blasphemy. John seems at least partly motivated by a resentment of the Jews for not acknowledging their "King" and a prudent desire to mollify the Romans and to keep Emperor Domitian from further persecuting Christians.[36]

Matthew also exculpates Pilate and contains the chilling attribution of blood guilt:

> So when Pilate saw that he could do nothing, but rather that a riot was beginning, he took some water and washed his hands before the crowd, saying, "I am innocent of this man's blood; see to it yourselves." Then the people as a whole answered, "His blood be on us and on our children!" So he released Barabbas for them; and after flogging Jesus, he handed him over to be crucified. (Matt. 27:24–26)

But Matthew speaks of "the people," rather than of "the Jews." Matthew still sees the Jews as essentially "us." With Luke (likely written a bit later, between 85 and 95 CE), the political and ideological fissure has widened; with Acts (written sometime after that),[37] the gulf is almost complete:

> The chief priests and the scribes stood by, vehemently accusing [Jesus]. Even Herod with his soldiers treated him with contempt and mocked him; then he put an elegant robe on him, and sent him back to Pilate. That same day Herod and Pilate became friends with each other; before this they had been enemies. (Luke 23:10–12)
>
> But the residents of the city were divided; some sided with the Jews, and some with the apostles. (Acts 14:4)

According to Acts, "the Jews" also conspired against Paul the way they had against Jesus:

> In the morning the Jews joined in a conspiracy and bound themselves by an oath neither to eat nor drink until they had killed Paul. (Acts 23:12)

To summarize, the references to "the Jews" in Luke/Acts and John are a manifestation of the growing alienation between early converts to Christianity and their native faith communities. They mark the increasing enmity toward Jewish officials who were putting new Christians out of the synagogues.

[35] See Raymond E. Brown, *The Death of the Messiah* (New York: Doubleday, 1994), 818–20.

[36] Domitian was Roman Emperor from AD 81 to 96. Eusebius and Tertullian affirm that both Nero and Domitian persecuted Christians, though to different degrees; see Eusebius, *Church History*, Book III, Chapter XVII, and Tertullian, *Apology*, Chapter V.

[37] *The New Oxford Annotated Bible*, 1919–20.

They were also an effort on the part of those Christians to curry favor with the Romans. What more expedient way to assert their emerging identity and to avoid additional imperial belligerence than to vilify Herod Antipas and to rehabilitate Pontius Pilate? Nevertheless, it was Pilate and the Romans who executed Jesus, not Herod and the Jews.

Herod the Great and Herod Antipas were more or less imposed as puppet rulers on the orthodox Jews of Judea, first by Marc Antony then by Augustus, and it was the Romans who could not abide a competitor with Caesar. Some Jews were opportunistic collaborators with the Empire, and one rightly finds fault with this. In cleansing the Temple, Jesus certainly challenged the religious authorities of Jerusalem. But corrupt Jewish authorities are not synonymous with Judaism. Moreover, to blame Herod or the Sanhedrin for the murder of Jesus is like blaming the *Judenräte* for the Nazi Holocaust. In Christ's Passion, Herod Antipas was a Roman patsy.

*(3) **The Jews are legalistic and without grace or mercy.***

> The law indeed was given through Moses; grace and truth came through Jesus Christ. (John 1:17)

Moses and Hebrew Scripture generally insist on external obedience to restrictive rules, while Jesus preaches a spontaneous and inner love. Moses imposes legal burden and judgment; Jesus brings the good news of salvation and forgiveness. Or so the all-too-familiar story goes. This is a grave misunderstanding of Moses and Torah, however, as well as of Jesus and the Gospel. The first five books of Hebrew Scripture may be chiefly designed to curtail sin, but Torah itself is a much higher and wider reality. It is God's positive ordering of creation, so there would have been Law even without the Fall. In addition, Jesus overtly validates Moses at Matthew 23:1–3: "Then Jesus said to the crowds and to his disciples, "The scribes and the Pharisees sit on Moses' seat; therefore, do whatever they teach you and follow it."' Jesus goes on to say "but do not do as they do, for they do not practice what they teach," yet this is a criticism of hypocrisy not of *halakha*. Jesus explicitly says in Matthew 5:17: "Do not think that I have come to abolish the law or the prophets; I have come not to abolish but to fulfill."

Admittedly, Matthew depicts Jesus as a new Moses offering a new covenant on a new mountain, but this is far from being anti-Torah. Imitation is the sincerest form of flattery. Torah is grace, God for us, and Jesus teaches a rigorous form of Torah-piety. As noted, Jesus refers to the Ten Commandments as the keys to eternal life (Mark 10:17–20), and the love commandments of Matthew 22 are his summary of the law and the prophets, not his abrogation of them. Further, again as Fredriksen points out, "everything we know about

Jesus' original disciples indicates that they kept the Law."[38] Any stark Law vs. Gospel antithesis is evidently a departure from Jesus' own teaching; for him, Gospel and Torah are one.

It is instructive to compare Jesus' two commandments of love with Rawls's two principles of justice, quoted above. Rather than elevating maximal liberty and individual self-interest, Jesus first echoes the Shema's insistence on unstinting devotion to God and then correlates this piety with service to the other, the neighbor:

> He said to [the lawyer], "'You shall love the Lord your God with all your heart, and with all your soul, and with all your mind.' This is the greatest and first commandment. And a second is like it: 'You shall love your neighbor as yourself.' On these two commandments hang all the law and the prophets." (Matt. 22:37–40)

In the beginning as at the end, "the weightier matters of the law" are for Jesus what they were for Moses: "justice and mercy and faith" (Matt. 23:23).

(4) The Jews pridefully rely on works rather than faith.

> Then they said to him, "What must we do to perform the works of God?" Jesus answered them, "This is the work of God, that you believe in him whom he has sent." (John 6:28–29)
>
> At that time they made a calf, offered a sacrifice to the idol, and reveled in the works of their hands. (Acts 7:41)

Luke and especially John extol "works" over and over again, but the primary "work" of God is to send the Son, and the primary "work" of human beings is to confess that Son. The emerging subtext is that belief is to supplant works, that any other activity besides faith in Christ is idolatrous. Here again we see the active faith *of* Christ being replaced by a passive faith *in* Christ. Even if one accepts the Pauline idea that justification – i.e. restoration of right relation with God – is by faith alone, sanctification still comes through works in much of scripture. More bluntly, as James drives home, "faith by itself, if it has no works, is dead" (James 2:17). To set works and faith at odds is as misguided and hazardous as pitting law against love or Judaism against Christianity. One immediate danger is quietism.

Embracing a literal reading of Matthew 5:39 – "Do not resist an evildoer" – some biblical commentators equate both Jesus' faith and faith in Jesus with a passive acceptance of injustice.[39] On this view, Christ-like love

[38] Fredriksen, *From Jesus to Christ*, 146.

[39] In *The Peaceable Kingdom* (Notre Dame: University of Notre Dame Press, 1983), 87, Stanley Hauerwas declares that Christians are "no longer driven by the assumption that we must be in control of history, that it is up to us to make things come out right." This statement seems to

is not only non-violent, it is inactive; it does not strive to redress wrongs or otherwise "make history come out right," but rather leaves everything to God.[40] To the extent that Jews (or others) endorse just war or political protest, say, they are lapsing into works righteousness. The rub is that this interpretation of scripture makes hash out of Jesus' actual ministry. Jesus' trust in God is radical, but he repeatedly challenges hubris, heals infirmity, and combats unrighteousness. We can debate whether his "cleansing of the Temple" is violent or non-violent, but it is clearly not non-resisting.[41] Jesus cares too much about real people and real evils to withdraw into the purity of the sectarian. We ought not to be *conformed* to evil, but if obliviousness to it is a decree, then Jesus is markedly inconsistent.

Nobody favors arrogance, but charging others with "works righteousness" is frequently a smokescreen for jealousy over their accomplishments. One covertly wants to be like the adept rival or the joyful stranger, but one falls bitterly short. The opposite of jealousy, but no less ignoble, is *Schadenfreude*: one overtly celebrates not being like the hapless rival or the unfortunate stranger, even though one has done nothing to deserve one's deliverance. One takes such pleasure at others' misery, in fact, that often one is moved to compound their affliction by fate with calculated harshness of one's own. Both jealousy and *Schadenfreude* are unjust, a refusal to admit what is due or undue; both have been at work in the Christian (and pagan) persecution of the Jews, as the Nazis made obvious.

(5) The Jews are culturally and politically unassimilated and thus poor citizens, subversive of temporal law.

> Their laws are different from those of every other people, and they do not keep the king's laws, so that it is not appropriate for the king to tolerate them. (Haman to King Ahasuerus in Esther 3:8)

---

flirt with nonresistance to evil, but I believe that Hauerwas's considered position is nonviolent resistance. I discuss these issues in *Political Agape: Christian Love and Liberal Democracy* (Grand Rapids: Wm. B. Eerdmans Publishing Co., 2015), Chapter 8. A notable Christian thinker who does embrace nonresistance to evil and thereby eschews concern for social justice is Jacques Ellul. See his *The Subversion of Christianity*, trans. Geoffrey W. Bromiley (Grand Rapids: Wm. B. Eerdmans Publishing Co., 1986), and *The Ethics of Freedom*, trans. Geoffrey W. Bromiley (Grand Rapids: Wm. B. Eerdmans Publishing Co., 1976).

40 In *What about Hitler?* (Grand Rapids: Brazos Press, 2006), 117, Robert W. Brimlow summarizes (and evidently agrees with) a central tenet of Dietrich Bonhoeffer's *The Cost of Discipleship*: "The right way to requite evil, according to Jesus, is not to resist it." Brimlow goes on to disagree with Bonhoeffer's later willingness to participate in the plot to assassinate Hitler, writing: "It is not clear to me that God has laid responsibility on us for the course that history will take." Ibid., 124.

41 Paul Ramsey makes this point in *Speak Up for Just War or Pacifism* (University Park and London: Pennsylvania State University Press, 1988), 115–23.

It is not only Christians, early and late, who victimize Jews. The latter's ethnic and juridical differences were perceived as threats in ancient Persia and still are today in modern Russia and elsewhere. True pluralism lets a thousand flowers bloom, so long as none strangles the others, but such liberality is hard to come by. It requires a sense of the variability and peccability of peoples, laws, and nations, including one's own. Lack of that sense Judaism faults as idolatry. It is precisely the Jews' unconditional love of God and God's Torah that is perceived as threatening to earthly legal agendas. When King Ahasuerus promoted Haman above all his other court officials, "all the king's servants who were at the king's gate bowed down and did obeisance to Haman; for the king had so commanded concerning him. But Mordecai did not bow down or do obeisance" (Esther 3:2). Jews as such are not civic anarchists, any more than Christians; they are not, as a rule, bad citizens. On the contrary, some of the world's greatest public servants have been Jewish. But the Jews are conspicuously loyal to a Law higher than temporal laws and a Lord higher than temporal lords. Such relativizing of worldly powers tends, if anything, to make them good citizens in a just state. This, then, is a fundamental reason why Jews are perpetually ill-treated: Mordecai won't bow down. To take offense at, or to give offense to, such monotheism is what I call "anti-Judaism."[42]

4.3.2 A *Brief Word on Revelation*

If you want a clue to the mindset of a present-day, Middle-Eastern terrorist, read The Book of Revelation, standardly attributed to John. There you will find extraordinarily violent images of eschatological vengeance against infidels:

> Then another angel, a third, followed them, crying with a loud voice, "Those who worship the beast and its image, and receive a mark on their foreheads or on their hands, they will also drink the wine of God's wrath, poured unmixed into the cup of his anger, and they will be tormented with fire and sulphur

[42] Paula Fredriksen distinguishes between anti-Judaism, anti-Semitism, and anti-Zionism, with the first being "a theological position," the second "a racist one," and the third a "political one." See her "The Birth of Christianity and the Origins of Christian Anti-Judaism," in *Jesus, Judaism & Christian Anti-Judaism: Reading the New Testament after the Holocaust*, ed. Paula Fredriksen and Adele Reinhartz (Louisville: Westminster John Knox Press, 2002), 28. Susannah Heschel, on the other hand, finds the anti-Judaism versus anti-Semitism contrast porous and hard to defend historically. In practice, the Nazi theological critique of Judaism often went hand-in-glove with a racist critique of Jewishness, for example. See her "Historiography of Antisemitism versus Anti-Judaism: A Response to Robert Morgan," in *Journal for the Study of the New Testament* 33, no. 3 (March 2011): 257–79. See also Heschel, "When Jesus Was an Aryan: The Protestant Church and Antisemitic Propaganda," in *Betrayal: German Churches and the Holocaust*, ed. Ropert P. Ericksen and Susannah Heschel (Minneapolis: Fortress Press, 1999).

> in the presence of the holy angels and in the presence of the Lamb. And the smoke of their torment goes up for ever and ever." (Rev. 14:9–11)
>
> Then another angel came out from the altar, the angel who has authority over fire, and he called with a loud voice to him who had the sharp sickle, "Use your sharp sickle and gather the clusters of the vine of the earth, for its grapes are ripe." So the angel swung his sickle over the earth and gathered the vintage of the earth, and he threw it into the great wine press of the wrath of God. And the wine press was trodden outside the city, and blood flowed from the wine press, as high as a horse's bridle, for a distance of about two hundred miles. (Rev. 14:18–20)

Revelation 21:1–5 is quite touching:

> Then I saw a new heaven and a new earth; for the first heaven and the first earth had passed away, and the sea was no more. And I saw the holy city, the new Jerusalem, coming down out of heaven from God, prepared as a bride adorned for her husband. And I heard a loud voice from the throne saying, "See, the home of God is among mortals. He will dwell with them as their God; they will be his peoples, and God himself will be with them; he will wipe every tear from their eyes. Death will be no more; mourning and crying and pain will be no more, for the first things have passed away." And the one who was seated on the throne said, "See, I am making all things new."

Revelation 22:11 even achieves a kind of *amor fati*: "Let the evildoer still do evil, and the filthy still be filthy, and the righteous still do right, and the holy still be holy." But "the great wine press of the wrath of God" (14:19) is usually our own prejudice – a phenomenon alive and well in the Holy Land today, and everywhere else. The grapes of that wrath are what inebriate jihadists, yesterday and today. Far from being cowardly, they are rash;[43] far from being bound by law – Torah, Sharia, or otherwise – they are drunk with a piety that is beyond measure or restraint. They cannot see the human faces right in front of them. Theologically put, they so disconnect supposed love of God from actual love of neighbor that their behavior is unjust to both Creator and creature.

4.3.3 *Can Biblical Agape Be Murderous?*

The meaning of agape is complicated by the fact that there are two objects of agapic love in the New Testament: God and the neighbor. St. Paul occasionally talks about "agape" for God, but he typically limits his use of the word to human-to-human interactions, since "agape" usually connotes the bestowal of worth, something we cannot do with or for God. Yet the two great love

[43] Jeffrey Stout made this point, in conversation, about the terrorists of 9/11.

commands of Matthew 22 – requiring love of God and love of neighbor – both use a form of agape (*agapao*). And there's the rub.

Some Christian ethicists have argued that there can be a hard contradiction between love of God and love of neighbor, such that the former may require us to surrender or even sin against the latter. Philip Quinn argued this way, and some see Søren Kierkegaard (or at least his pseudonym, Johannes de Silentio) as doing so as well.[44] Both Quinn and de Silentio analyze the Abraham and Isaac story of Genesis 22, for instance, as mandating murder in the name of obedience to/faith in God. The willingness to make a burnt offering of an innocent child is the sort of zeal that I associate with *jihad*. One might argue, of course, that this is a false or skewed version of agape, but it remains what some see as ardent love of the Deity.

A murderous agape is profoundly mistaken, but it is too quick just to say it is not really agape. The concrete task is to explain what has gone wrong. My main contention here is that slaughter in the name of God only appears theologically plausible if we arbitrarily separate the two love commands or put them at odds. In contrast to Quinn and de Silentio, but in line with most of the Christian tradition, I see the two great commands as consistent – indeed, as deeply related. The first calls for our utmost dedication in relation to God and is not simply reducible to the second, but the second is "like unto it." Put another way, love of God must be compatible with, even at times constrained by, justice to the neighbor.

Is perverse love of the Deity still love? Ask jihadists, and then ask their innocent victims or their survivors. Is perverse justice for humanity still justice? Ask Javert, and then ask his guilty benefactor, Valjean. Both jihadists and Javert are murderous to others and themselves. In contrast and *pace* John, the Lamb absorbs hatred and injury rather than fomenting them. In place of vendetta, he preaches forgiveness (Matt. 6:12, Mark 11:25, etc.). Jesus cried out from the cross, "*Eli, Eli, lema sabachthani*?": "My God, my God, why have you forsaken me?" (Matt. 27:46). The one who lived with a constant sense of the presence and guidance of the Father died obedient to Him unto death but feeling abandoned. This is practically a job description for being a Jew in a Gentile land. It will remain so until Torah and Gospel are recognized as one

[44] See Philip L. Quinn, "Agamemnon and Abraham: The Tragic Dilemma of Kierkegaard's Knight of Faith," *Journal of Literature and Theology* 4, no. 2 (1990); and "Moral Obligation, Religious Demand, and Practical Conflict," in *Rationality, Religious Belief, and Moral Commitment*, ed. William Wainwright and Robert Audi (Ithaca: Cornell University Press, 1986). See also Søren Kierkegaard (Johannes de Silentio), *Fear and Trembling*, trans. Howard V. Hong and Edna H. Hong (Princeton: Princeton University Press, 1983).

and until the Christ is offered as a healing word rather than a vengeful sword. Until then, our moral vision will be strabismic and our daily lives tragic.

4.4 CONCLUSION

Fear of *jihad* can make a reasonable person a Javert, but dismissal of Javert can make a faithful person a jihadist. Both phenomena are symptoms of distorted vision, and if three people tell you that you look sick, or sickly look, sit down. If Victor Hugo, John Rawls, and the Holy Bible show us, directly or indirectly, that law cannot survive without love, and vice versa, then stand up for their integration. Such integration I call "political agape." Political agape rejects the assumption that Javert and *jihad* represent an either/or; it dictates, among other things, militating for same-sex marriage, adoption rights, and the right to life, and against the death penalty, racism, and all forms of terrorism (Eastern and Western). Or so this theologian has argued.[45]

4.5 POSTSCRIPT

In his contribution to this volume, "Love, Justice, and Law," Nicholas Wolterstorff vigorously criticizes my conception of love/sanctity and justice/dignity. He repeatedly quotes from my *The Priority of Love* or "The Image of God and the Soul of Humanity," and then faults me for not elaborating a key idea more fully. I can only protest that Professor Wolterstorff focuses exclusively on one book and one essay on agape and related themes, when I have written three books and over a dozen articles on same, and I have edited and contributed to two relevant collections. (Wolterstorff does refer in a footnote to my latest book, but he initially got the title wrong.) In reality, I have said a good deal about what he suggests I pass over in silence. For more on equal regard, for instance, see my chapters on Abraham Lincoln and the morality of adoption in *Political* Agape, as well as that text's conclusion on Martin Luther King, Jr.

Space constraints do not permit a fuller response here, but consider just one concrete example of a false or misleading reading by Wolterstorff. On pages 11–12 of his manuscript, he writes:

> First, at a number of places in "The Image of God and the Soul of Humanity" he [Jackson] attributes to Kant the view that dignity is "achieved merit based on personal performance" (101, 110, and *passim*). That was not Kant's view. Kant understood human dignity as grounded in the *capacity* for rational and moral action, not in the meritorious exercise of that capacity.

45 See Jackson, *Political Agape* and *The Priority of Love*.

> On Kant's view, the lazy moral scoundrel who is seriously deficient in achieved merit nonetheless has the same dignity as every other person, namely, that which supervenes on possessing the capacity for rational or moral agency. By contrast, on Jackson's account, the lazy moral scoundrel who has little achieved merit to his credit has little dignity.

If Wolterstorff had considered my other writings, he would have found this passage in "A House Divided, Again":

> On one common reading, "dignity" refers to a basic faculty; it denotes the bare capacity for intelligent free choice possessed by all nondamaged persons. One's rational freedom may be misused, but the simple possession of it is the ground of respect. Kant, for instance, held that all persons are to be treated as ends, and not as means only, because they are capable of acting autonomously – i.e., according to imperatives they willingly give to themselves out of respect for the moral law. On another reading, in contrast, "dignity" is explicitly a term of achievement; it requires that actual choices be meritorious or at least responsible. Here respect awaits some historical performance that claims our special acknowledgement; only a limited number of individuals (e.g., the noble) possess personal dignity and the rights that go along with it. An ethic emphasizing dignity as something common to rational agents will tend, naturally, to equality (among persons); one in which dignity is something achieved, to hierarchy (even between persons).
>
> Both of these senses of "dignity" are at work in liberal political contexts, and it is important to appreciate the differences between them. For present purposes, however, a fundamental similarity is most germane. On both readings, dignity is a function of the freedom of self-conscious agents, their ability to choose intentionally or their having chosen rightly or virtuously. Indeed, even if dignity is taken to stem from simple rational agency, rather than actual excellent choices, it still requires that a threshold of cognitive maturation be reached. Even the first sense of "dignity" demands, after all, a kind of achievement – namely, that one have passed one's spiritual nonage and acquired a fairly robust self-awareness. Only the subject who is aware of herself as an abiding rational agent is a "person," properly so-called, on this view.[46]

Here I describe the very contrast that my critic accuses me of confusing or misattributing – between having a capability for autonomy and a specific exercising of it – and I say explicitly that Kant grounds respect in the capability. In "The Image of God and the Soul of Humanity," I do describe "Kantian

[46] Timothy P. Jackson, "A House Divided, Again: Sanctity vs. Dignity in the Induced Death Debates," in *In Defense of Human Dignity*, ed. Robert P. Kraynak and Glenn Tinder (Notre Dame: University of Notre Dame Press, 2003), 143. (This essay is Chapter 5 of *Political Agape*; the quotation comes there on pages 191–93.)

dignity" as "an achievement from within, something active,"[47] but in this I am again alluding to growth into rational agency. (The key point is that a two-week-old baby has not "achieved" such agency, hence its dignity must be suspect for Kant.) Kantians do often base merit on the exercise of autonomy, and, *on my view*, one can lose dignity by behaving immorally. But I make it clear in several contexts, including in the two works Wolterstorff addresses, that *for Kant himself* it is the capacity for free choice, not the exercise of that capacity, that is the foundation of dignity. In *The Priority of Love*, for instance, I distinguish my position from Kant's by writing:

> The Greek basis of ethics is a dignity grounded in teleological rationality (realized intellect), while the Kantian basis is a dignity found in personal autonomy (good will). The Biblical basis of sanctity, in contrast, is the passive potential for charity (the ability to give and/or receive love). This potential constitutes the Image of God, and though it is in no way antithetical to the dignity associated with contemplation and choice, it precedes these as their necessary condition.[48]

It is dismaying to see a colleague treat one's words unjustly, but we are all fallible, and faith in the Christian Word that Professor Wolterstorff and I share calls us both to patience and forgiveness. (It should not be necessary, but it helps that Nick is also a friend.) In any case, I close with a famed quotation from Saint Augustine: "Let those who think I have said too little, or those who think I have said too much, forgive me; and let those who think I have said just enough give thanks, not to me, but rather join me in giving thanks to God."[49]

47 Timothy P. Jackson, "The Image of God and the Soul of Humanity: Reflections on Dignity, Sanctity, and Democracy," in *Religion in the Liberal Polity*, ed. Terence Cuneo (Notre Dame: University of Notre Dame Press, 2005), 55. (This essay is Chapter 2 of *Political Agape*; the quotation comes there on page 101.)

48 Jackson, *The Priority of Love*, 67.

49 Augustine, The City of God, trans. M. Dods, G. Wilson, and J. J. Smith, in *Basic Writings of Saint Augustine*, vol. 2 (New York: Random House, 1948), Book XXII, Chapter XXX, 663.

5

Love, Justice, and Law

Nicholas Wolterstorff

My main project in this essay is to bring to light the harmony that exists among love, justice, and law. In previous writings I have discussed aspects of the relation between love and justice,[1] aspects of the relation between justice and law,[2] and aspects of the relation between love and law.[3] In this present essay I will bring these scattered discussions together. In doing so I will, in good measure, be repeating points made previously. But the way a point is formulated will sometimes be different, and some of the connections that previously were only implicit will now be made explicit. I will also be asking whether the thesis of harmony between love and justice that I defend could be defended as well by a different line of thought from that which I employ.

The connections a writer claims to hold among love, justice, and law depend, obviously, on the concepts of love and justice the writer employs and on what he or she regards as the purpose and function of law. On none of these points is there agreement. Later I will explain how I think of justice and law. The concept of love I have employed in my writing is that which Jesus employed when he said we are to love God above all and our neighbors as ourselves. The Greek verb the gospel writers used to report what Jesus said was *agapaô* (noun: agape). So I, along with many others, call the love Jesus had in mind, agapic *love*. That is only to give it a name, of course; the issue of substance is just what sort of love Jesus had in mind.

[1] Nicholas Wolterstorff, *Justice in Love* (Grand Rapids: Wm. B. Eerdmans Publishing Co., 2011); and *Journey toward Justice* (Grand Rapids: Baker Academic, 2013).

[2] Nicholas Wolterstorff, *The Mighty and the Almighty* (Cambridge: Cambridge University Press, 2012).

[3] Nicholas Wolterstorff, "Does Forgiveness Violate Justice?," Chapter 17 in Justice in Love; and in "Is It Possible and Sometimes Desirable for States to Forgive?," *Journal of Religious Ethics* 41, no. 3 (September 2013): 417–34.

A prominent theme in traditional discussions of the relation between love and justice has been the theme of tension. It has commonly been held that there is what one might call *motivational* tension between the two: in acting out of love, one is not doing what one does because justice requires it; and conversely, in doing what one does because justice requires it, one is not acting out of love. (This leaves open the possibility of performing one and the same action both out of love and because justice requires it.) Some writers have held that there is also what one might call *directional* tension between love and justice: acting out of love may direct one to do something that justice directs one not to do, and conversely. Justice, for example, may require paying everybody the same wage, whereas love directs one to give more to those who need it more.[4]

The main thesis of my *Justice in Love* was that, between agapic love rightly understood and justice rightly understood, there is no tension, neither motivational nor directional. Well-formed agapic love, so I argued, will often seek to promote the flourishing of the one loved beyond what justice requires; but it will never do less than justice requires.[5] Later in this essay I will explain how I defended this thesis.

A common theme in traditional discussions of the relation between love and law has likewise been the theme of tension: witness the gospel/law dichotomy that has shaped much of Protestant theology and New Testament interpretation. Here too it is useful to distinguish between motivational and directional tension. It has commonly been held that in acting out of love, one is not doing what one does because the law requires it, be it God's law or human law; and conversely, in doing what one does because the law requires it, be it God's law or human law, one is not acting out of agapic love. And some writers have held that cases arise in which acting out of love directs one to do something the law directs one not to do, even if the law is a just law. The thought is not merely that mercy sometimes calls for tempering justice, that is, sometimes calls for rendering to some malefactor less by way of reactive or corrective justice than the law permits. The thought is that love and legal justice sometimes conflict.

A thesis implicit in a good deal of what I have written about love and law is that between agapic love, rightly understood, and a just system of laws justly administered, there is no tension, neither motivational nor directional.[6] This present essay provides the occasion for making explicit what was previously implicit.

4 I am indebted to Paul Weithman for the very useful terms "motivational tension" and "directional tension." See his review of *Justice in Love* in *Faith and Philosophy* 30, no. 2 (April 2013): 213–21.

5 I explain my use of the term "flourishing," and my use of the terms "life-goods" and "well-being," in *Justice in Love*, 15.

6 On this point I have no doubt been shaped by my rootage in the Calvinist tradition, which rejects the dichotomy of God's grace vs. God's law. God's law for human beings is a manifestation of God's grace.

5.1 TYPES OF AGAPISM

I understand agapism to be that long tradition of ethical reflection which takes its bearings from what Jesus is reported by the gospel writers as having said about agapic love and from what the letter writers of the New Testament said about such love. I stand in that tradition. I am an agapist.

In the twentieth century there emerged, within contemporary agapism in general, a movement that articulated more sharply than ever before a certain understanding of the love for the neighbor that Jesus enjoined, namely, love understood as gratuitous benevolence, and that developed in greater depth than ever before the theme of tension between love, so understood, and justice, both motivational and directional.

Not all agapists of the contemporary period agreed that the love for the neighbor Jesus enjoined is to be understood as gratuitous benevolence. In *Justice in Love* I quoted the prominent ethicist, Paul Ramsey, as saying that, among his fellow Christian ethicists, a prominent alternative to the gratuitous benevolence interpretation was the *mutual love* interpretation – mutual love being love that both loves and seeks to be loved. After taking note of this alternative, Ramsey brusquely dismissed it in favor of the benevolence interpretation. "Surely," he says, the benevolence interpretation "is the more correct reading of Biblical and New Testament texts . . . When the scripture enjoins: "Let love be among you," it does not mean, "Let 'among-you-ness' be among you." It is one thing to say, "Let mutual love be mutual," and quite another to say in the New Testament meaning of the word, "Let *love* be mutual." For the love in question takes its measure from Christ's love for the church when he "gave himself up for her."[7]

Just as not all agapists of the contemporary period agreed that the love for the neighbor Jesus enjoined is to be understood as gratuitous benevolence, so too not all agreed that there is tension between love and justice. Among those who did not understand agapic love as gratuitous benevolence, some understood it in such a way that there is neither motivational nor directional tension between love and justice. And among those who did interpret agapic love in such a way that there is motivational tension between love and justice, a good many held that there is no directional tension between them. Paul Ramsey was a prominent representative of this latter position. Ramsey writes,

> Sometimes love does what justice requires and assumes its rules as norms, sometimes love does more than justice requires but never less, and sometimes love acts in a quite different way from what justice alone can enable us to discern to be right.[8]

7 Wolterstoff, *Justice in Love*, 24 (quoting Ramsey).

8 Paul Ramsey, *War and the Christian Conscience: How Shall Modern War Be Conducted Justly?* (Durham: Duke University Press, 1961), 178.

In general, the rejection of directional tension has been much more common than the rejection of motivational tension.

I called the movement within contemporary agapism I had in mind in *Justice in Love*, "modern day agapism." I know of one reviewer who interpreted me as meaning to refer to contemporary agapism in general with the term, "modern day agapism," and who forcefully insisted that there were many contemporary agapists who did not hold the views he took me to be attributing to all of them. As I indicated above, he is right on this latter point. There may well be readers in addition to this reviewer who also misinterpreted me in this way and who have similarly bridled at the inaccuracy of what they took me to be claiming about contemporary agapism in general.

I now judge that I should have forestalled this misunderstanding by using a different term for the movement I had in mind than "modern day agapism," and that I should have explained more clearly and emphatically than I did that it was only a *movement within* contemporary agapism I had in mind, not contemporary agapism in general.[9]

When I was writing the book, I worked for some time with the term "nygrenist agapism." Eventually I rejected it because it seemed to me to suggest that members of the movement were all followers of Nygren. Though Nygren was certainly one of the most influential members of the movement, the other members were not all his followers. In the book I now and then called the movement *benevolence-agapism*, as in the title of Part One of my book. This term highlights the fact that at the core of the movement was the claim that what Jesus meant by agape was gratuitous benevolence. But at the core of the movement was another claim as well: namely, that between gratuitous benevolence and justice there is not only motivational but also directional tension. The term "conflict-benevolence agapism" highlights both theses. It is a clunky term! But for the sake of forestalling further misunderstanding I will, in the remainder of this essay, sacrifice aesthetics and will call the movement in question, *conflict-benevolence agapism*.

I repeat: what previously I called "modern day agapism," and will now call "conflict-benevolence agapism," has two main theses: the thesis that the love

[9] Part One of the book is titled "Benevolence-Agapism." It opened with this sentence: "In the twentieth century there emerged, among Christian (especially Protestant) ethicists and theologians, a highly articulate and provocative version of agapism." In the next two sentences I spoke of what emerged as a "movement." In a good many other passages I used the same terms. To my mind, speaking of what I was referring to as a *version* of agapism and as a *movement within* agapism indicated quite clearly that it was not contemporary agapism in general that I was referring to. Wolterstorff, *Justice in Love*, 21–74.

for the neighbor Jesus enjoined is to be understood as gratuitous benevolence, and the thesis that between gratuitous benevolence and justice there is both motivational and directional tension.

When composing *Justice in Love* I decided that, rather than plunging straight ahead to develop my thesis that there is neither motivational nor directional tension between the love for the neighbor Jesus enjoined, rightly understood, and justice, rightly understood, I would first look with some care into the writings of those members of the movement of conflict-benevolence agapism who had most powerfully stated the position that there is both motivational and directional tension. I judged these to be Anders Nygren and Reinhold Niebuhr. Accordingly, I devoted several chapters to discussing their views, supplementing my discussion of their views with a discussion of Kierkegaard's *Works of Love*.[10]

After discussing Nygren, Niebuhr, and Kierkegaard, I immediately struck out on my own, arguing that there is no directional tension because there is no motivational tension. I did not inquire whether there were others who had defended the thesis of no directional tension in the same way. Nor did I look at that considerable number of contemporary agapists who have affirmed motivational tension but denied directional tension, to find out whether among these there are some who have not just declared that there is no directional tension but have gone on to show why there is not. In short, I did not ask whether the thesis of no directional tension could be defended along a very different line from that which I followed. I propose doing that in this essay.

Of all the contemporary agapists who have affirmed motivational but denied directional tension between agapic love and justice, it is Timothy Jackson who, to my knowledge, has developed his views on the relation between agapic love and justice most thoroughly. If there are contemporary agapists who have not just declared that there is no directional tension but have explained why that is, Jackson is likely to be among them.[11] So let's look to see. An ancillary benefit of my presentation of Jackson's line of thought will be that it will bring into sharper relief certain aspects of my own way of thinking about the relation between agapic love and justice. I will base my analysis of Jackson's views

[10] I called Niebuhr a "non-classical representative of the movement," on the ground that, unlike most other representatives of the movement, he was willing to say that in cases of directional conflict between love and justice, one should choose justice. Given his prominence within the movement and his influence, it was perhaps ill-advised to call his position "non-classical."

[11] Jackson is a fellow contributor to this present volume. See Timothy P. Jackson, "Javert and *Jihad*: Why Law Cannot Survive Without Love and Vice Versa," 75–100.

on his book, *The Priority of Love: Christian Charity and Social Justice*,[12] and on his essay, "The Image of God and the Soul of Humanity: Reflections on Dignity, Sanctity, and Democracy."[13]

5.2 JACKSON'S ACCOUNT OF THE RELATION BETWEEN LOVE AND JUSTICE

Many times over, in formulations that are identical or differ only slightly, Jackson affirms the thesis of no directional tension. "Love transcends and transforms justice, but it never embodies injustice."[14] "I do not directly equate justice and love, . . . but neither do I set them at one another's throats . . . Love without justice or a love that lapses into injustice is less than loving."[15] How does Jackson develop and defend this thesis?

Let's begin with his understanding of agapic love.[16] His official explanation, repeated a number of times, goes as follows: agapic love "involves three basic features: (1) unconditional willing of the good for the other, (2) equal regard for the well-being of the other, and (3) passionate service open to self-sacrifice for the sake of the other."[17] Rather often, Jackson uses the terms "benevolence" and "charity" for agapic love as he understands it,[18] and in at least one place he calls it "universal benevolence."[19]

As to the second of the three features of agapic love in Jackson's listing, I noticed no passage, either in the book or in the essay, in which he explains what he means by "equal regard." But since nothing in what I have to say by way of critique hangs on what he does mean, let's set this point aside. As to the third feature, Jackson notes that contemporary agapists have rather often described agapic love as *self-sacrificial*. His own view is that agapic love is *open* to self-sacrifice but

[12] Timothy Jackson, *The Priority of Love: Christian Charity and Social Justice* (Princeton: Princeton University Press, 2003).

[13] Timothy Jackson, "The Image of God and the Soul of Humanity: Reflections on Dignity, Sanctity, and Democracy," in *Political Agape: Christian Love and Liberal Democracy* (Grand Rapids: Wm. B. Eerdmans Publishing Co., 2015), 84–115.

[14] Jackson, *Priority of Love*, 156.

[15] Ibid., 38.

[16] In a footnote he remarks, "My debt to Anders Nygren is considerable." Ibid., 8.

[17] Ibid., 10.

[18] Ibid., 2, 15.

[19] Ibid., 50; Jackson writes, "I interpret benevolence . . . as consistently willing another's good, whatever that entails. . . . Thus I associate it with agapic love." Ibid., 2. "Christian charity" and "love" are used as synonyms in the title and subtitle of the book.

that self-sacrifice is not definitive of agapic love.[20] I share this view. It is on the first of the three features Jackson mentions that I will focus my attention.

Jackson's phrase, "for the other," is misleading. Interpreting the love Jesus enjoined as gratuitous benevolence, Nygren concluded that we are enjoined by Jesus to extirpate all self-love. Jackson demurs; "I part company with Nygren" on this point, he says.[21] "Self-love is compatible with or even part of agape, broadly construed, but proper self-love comes only through self-transcendence."[22] I share Jackson's view that it is not just others who are the object of well-formed agapic love, but oneself as well.

I noticed no passage in which Jackson explains what he has in mind with the term "unconditional." Clearly part of what he means, however, if not the whole, is "willing the good for someone independently of merit."[23]

My main question is what Jackson has in mind by "the good for" someone. Rather often he speaks of the good for someone as his or her *well-being*; he does so in his statement of the second feature of agape. But he offers no explanation of how he understands "well-being;" and in the absence of an explanation, to call the good for someone "well-being" doesn't help much. To explain what I think Jackson has in mind by *the good for* someone, when he says that agape is willing the good for someone, we have to take a roundabout course and bring a number of other aspects of his thought into the picture.

A central component in Jackson's thought is his distinction between what he calls *dignity* and what he calls *sanctity*. He defines "dignity" as "achieved merit based on personal performance. Dignity is won by individuals in self-consciously embodying the good, freely choosing the right, and effectively maximizing social utility. . . . Dignity is accomplished in time and inspires or ought to inspire respect and admiration in others."[24]

After thus defining "dignity," Jackson goes on to say that "dignity is closely allied with social justice, construed as giving persons what they merit. A dignified party is given her due when she is respected."[25]

Before we move on to what Jackson says about sanctity, let me pause to make some comments about his understanding of justice and dignity. Jackson offers what seems, on first reading, to be a bewildering variety of explanations of how he understands justice. He speaks of "the reciprocity characteristic of justice."[26]

20 Ibid., 55, 143.
21 Ibid., 11.
22 Ibid.
23 Jackson, *Image of God*, 90.
24 Ibid., 89–90.
25 Ibid., 90.
26 Jackson, *Priority of Love*, 7.

He says that doing justice involves "our adult capacity for balancing competing interests and for keeping valid contracts."[27] He says that justice can be "defined as *suum cuique*."[28] Expressing the same idea in English, he says that justice is rendering to each what is due him or her.[29] He describes a just society as a "procedurally fair" society.[30] He says, "justice is largely concerned to distribute preexisting goods between persons."[31] He says, "A 'duty of justice' is a matter of rewarding achieved merit, punishing demerit, or keeping promises or contracts."[32] He says "social justice" consists of "giving persons what they merit."[33]

I interpret these diverse formulations as different ways of saying that justice consists of distributing benefits and burdens in accord with what "has been earned or contracted for."[34] "Justice distributes a range of goods (food, money, honor) according to various objective criteria (contract, merit)."[35] Though he happens not to mention it in this last sentence, Jackson sees justice as also involved in distributing burdens, especially punishments, according to objective criteria. Justice consists of "keeping contracts [and promises] or rewarding merit [and demerit]."[36] This, he says, is its "preeminently modern connotation."[37]

The idea, in my own words, is that justice consists of distributing benefits and burdens in accord with what is due persons on account of achieved merit or demerit or on account of contracts and promises they have freely made. A person's dignity is grounded in her achieved merit. What is due someone on account of her dignity is respect. Thus, justice consists, in part, of treating persons with due respect for their dignity. Additionally, it consists of keeping contracts and promises. And reactive or corrective justice consists of rendering to a wrongdoer the harm or burden that is due him on account of achieved demerit. That, as I understand him, is how Jackson thinks of justice.

Jackson notes, correctly, that when justice is so understood, those individuals who "are not self-aware agents capable of independent thought and action" fall outside the purview of justice.[38] This is a matter of concern for him. It is for me as well.

[27] Ibid.
[28] Ibid., 13.
[29] Jackson, *Image of God*, 89, 90; Jackson, *Priority of Love*, 63, 80.
[30] Jackson, *Priority of Love*, 62.
[31] Ibid., 178.
[32] Jackson, *Image of God*, 87.
[33] Ibid., 90.
[34] Jackson, *Priority of Love*, 19.
[35] Ibid., 28.
[36] Ibid., 37.
[37] Ibid.
[38] Jackson, *Image of God*, 94.

In an important passage, Jackson explains why he has chosen to employ this particular concept of justice:

> The more one identifies "justice" with biblical "righteousness" – with a prophetic *tsedaqah* that cares unselfishly for widows and orphans or a Pauline *dikaiosune* that accepts martyrdom – the more "love" and "justice" will tend to coalesce without remainder. A return to etymological origins can sometimes be illuminating, but in this instance it risks blinding us to our current condition. The danger is that such an extreme reformation of our moral vocabulary will seem merely to change the subject. It is better, I think, to note how the word "justice" is now standardly used to contrast it with the more ancient and more comprehensive ideals of faith, hope, and especially love.[39]

I find this a strange decision on Jackson's part, to employ what he understands to be the modern concept of justice. I do not agree that "in the New Testament, love and justice coalesce sufficiently that no simple contrast between them is tenable."[40] Be that as it may, however, when the topic is how love should be understood, Jackson has no hesitation in rejecting the way it is commonly understood and employing instead his understanding of what Jesus meant by agape. Why not do the same for how justice is commonly understood? Why not work to reform the common understanding of justice? After noting that justice as commonly understood is not how Scripture understands justice and that the common understanding leaves "non-persons"[41] outside the scope of justice, why decide, nonetheless, to employ this ordinary concept of justice when articulating and defending the claim that agapic love transcends, but never violates justice? If love is understood as the agapic love of Scripture, while justice is understood in what Jackson takes to be the ordinary modern way, as "keeping contracts or rewarding merit," should we not expect that agapic love will, on occasion, violate justice? Why would it not?

Let me make two additional brief comments about Jackson's understanding of justice. First, he attributes to Kant the view that dignity is "achieved merit based on personal performance."[42] That was not Kant's view. Kant understood human dignity as grounded in the *capacity* for rational and moral action, not in the meritorious exercise of that capacity. On Kant's view, the lazy moral scoundrel who is seriously deficient in achieved merit nonetheless has the same dignity as every other person, namely, that which supervenes on possessing the

39 Jackson, *Priority of Love*, 37–38.
40 Ibid., 36.
41 Jackson, *Image of God*, 94.
42 Jackson, *Image of God*, 101, 110.

capacity for rational or moral agency. By contrast, on Jackson's account, the lazy moral scoundrel who has little achieved merit to his credit has little dignity.

Second, if we connect justice with rights, as Jackson and I do along with many others,[43] I think we have to conclude that his explanation of our common concept of justice is not accurate. Distinguish between explanations of the concepts of *justice* and *rights* given by theorists, and the concepts themselves. Jackson's account of these concepts is that the dignity that grounds an individual's rights supervenes on his or her achieved merit (and on freely entered contracts and promises). I judge the Kantian account to be much more common than Jackson's account: the dignity that grounds an individual's rights supervenes on his or her capacity for rational or moral agency – or, as it is often put, on his or her capacity for autonomy. But neither account seems to me an accurate characterization of the full range of rights that we do in fact commonly recognize; in mischaracterizing the rights we commonly recognize, these two accounts also mischaracterize our common understanding of the contours of justice. Let me confine myself to two examples.

I judge that almost everyone would agree that one has been wronged when one's privacy has been invaded for prurient reasons, even if the voyeurist does nothing with what he discovers other than gloat over it when alone at home. One has a right not to be so treated; this is an infraction of justice. But it is not a case of failing to pay due respect to one's achieved merit, nor does it in any way restrict one's rational or moral agency – one's autonomy.

Rape is another example of the point. Everyone agrees that rape wrongs the victim; she has a right not to be raped. Rape is a serious infraction of justice. But in what way has the rapist failed to pay due regard to his victim for her achieved merit? As to autonomy, the rapist has indeed restricted her autonomy. But I find it grotesque to suggest that what's wrong about rape is that the victim's autonomy has been restricted. The rapist has *violated* her; that's what wrong about it.[44]

In my book, *Justice: Rights and Wrongs*,[45] I argued against the ways in which theorists commonly think about justice, rights, and wrongs, and argued for a better understanding. Mainly I did so by employing the counter-example strategy of first taking note of what most of us recognize to be rights and wrongs, and then pointing out that the generalizations commonly offered by theorists do not fit the cases. Jackson declines to "reform" what he takes to be the

[43] Shortly we will see that he does not connect justice with rights in general but with what he calls "dignity" rights in distinction from what he calls "sanctity" rights.

[44] I give additional examples of the point in my essay, "Grounding the Rights We Have as Human Persons," included in my *Understanding Liberal Democracy: Essays in Political Philosophy* (Oxford: Oxford University Press, 2012).

[45] Nicholas Wolterstorff, *Justice: Rights and Wrongs* (Princeton: Princeton University Press, 2008).

common use of the terms "justice" and "rights." I attempt to reform what Jackson and other theorists *take to be* our common use.

Of course we have our disagreements over whether someone does or does not have a certain right. If the issue is important, we do our best to come to agreement. When employing the counter-example strategy, one gives priority to cases on which there is little or no disagreement. Some people refuse to employ the concept of a right and its correlative concept of being wronged; they don't enter the "calculus." Of those who do employ these concepts, I judge that very few would disagree with me that to have one's privacy invaded for prurient reasons is to be wronged; I judge that none of them would disagree with me that to be raped is to be wronged.

It's time to move on to Jackson's explanation of what he means by "sanctity." He writes:

> Sanctity inheres in the species by virtue of its typical needs and given potentials: the basic need for food, drink, company, clothing, health, and companionship, for example, together with the passive potential for rational thought, bodily growth, emotional pleasure, and religious faith. . . . Sanctity presupposes no particular action in time and induces or ought to induce awe and wonder in others. As such, sanctity is closely allied with agapic love construed as willing the good for someone independently of merit. A sanctified party is not approached from within economies of exchange, but rather is treated with awe precisely to indicate that he is beyond price. More broadly, sanctity underlies the extension of compassion and self-sacrifice.[46]

Jackson ascribes sanctity to the soul and dignity to the self:

> If "dignity" is identified with the achieved merit of mature selves, then "sanctity" refers to a gratuitous legacy owned equally by all souls. Selves are to desert and prudence as souls are to grace and providence. . . . All human selves have souls, but not all human souls have selves. . . . All human persons (you and I) have souls, but so do prepersons (fetuses and babies), postpersons (the senile and the aenile), and nonpersons (the mentally retarded and even, in a sense, future generations).[47]

And:

> If intellect and will are the primary seats of the self and its dignity, then emotion and the body are the primary seats of the soul and of its sanctity. Rather than associating the soul with some rational and immaterial part of the person, I associate it with the passionate and material flesh.[48]

46 Jackson, *Image of God*, 90.
47 Ibid., 97.
48 Ibid.

Jackson often abbreviates his explanation of what grounds our sanctity by saying that our sanctity is grounded in our "neediness."[49]

Let me observe, parenthetically, that Jackson's disconnecting of neediness from justice results in a strikingly non-biblical way of thinking of justice. It is especially the fate of "the needy and vulnerable"[50] that Scripture connects with justice. When the prophets cry out for justice, it is the fate of the widows, the orphans, the aliens, the impoverished, and the oppressed that are at the center of their attention. In his self-identification in the synagogue in Nazareth,[51] Jesus quoted a passage from Isaiah in which the prophet explicitly connects justice to the fate of the needy and the oppressed.[52] Jackson's decision to employ what he understands to be our common modern way of thinking of the contours of justice, rather than the biblical way of thinking of those contours, has the consequence that the pervasive connection in Scripture of justice with the fate of the needy and the vulnerable is completely lost from view. As noted earlier, Jackson often speaks of agapic love as *charity*. As Jackson sees it, neediness and vulnerability call for charity, not for justice. It is achieved merit and contracts that call for justice. That is not how the biblical writers speak!

Another implication worth noting of Jackson's definition of "sanctity" is that God lacks sanctity. God has no body, no "basic need" for food, drink, clothing, and the like, no "passive potential" for bodily growth, religious faith, and the like. And given that God lacks sanctity, Jackson's declaration that agapic love is aimed at honoring the sanctity of individuals rather than their dignity implies that God cannot be the object of agapic love. The love for God that Jesus enjoined has to be something very different from the love of neighbor Jesus enjoined, this in spite of the fact that the same term agape is used in both cases.

Jackson is aware of this implication of his line of thought. He says that "uniform translation [of agape is] difficult."[53] Nygren was of the same view. Jesus, said Nygren, must be understood as having spoken loosely when he said that we are to love God. What he must have meant, speaking strictly, is that we are to have faith in God. In my own approach to interpreting the New Testament concept of agape, I have taken it as a desideratum that agapic love for one's neighbor is understood as essentially the same as agapic love for God. I take that to be implied by Jesus' declaration that the second love command is like

[49] Jackson, *Priority of Love*, 172.

[50] Jackson, *Image of God*, 87.

[51] Luke 4:17–21.

[52] I develop this point about the contours of biblical justice in chapters 3, 4, and 5 of *Justice: Rights and Wrongs*.

[53] Jackson, *Priority of Love*, 120.

the first.[54] Though God is not needy, God is like us in that God is vulnerable to being wronged. Hence it is that we pray, "Hallowed be your name."[55]

Jackson observes, "In many circumstances, the need for agapic love constitutes the right to receive it; even as, in many circumstances, the capacity for agapic love constitutes the duty to give it."[56] Agapic love is sometimes required of one. This leads Jackson to speak of *sanctity rights* in distinction from *dignity rights*: "rights that depend on achieved merit I call 'dignity rights,' while rights that presuppose only shared need or potential for care I call 'sanctity rights.'"[57]

Nygren argued at length for the position that whereas justice *requires* of us that we act in certain ways, agapic love pays no attention whatsoever to requirements; agapic love is always an act of gratuitous spontaneity. Jackson's alternative way of thinking is that agapic love may indeed be required, and that one may offer it *because* it is required.[58] But if one does offer it because it is required, one does so because it is required by the individual's sanctity, not because it is required by the person's dignity.

It follows from this way of thinking that individuals may be wronged even though there is no infraction of justice; this would be the case if their sanctity rights were violated but not their dignity rights. In my own way of thinking about these matters, I preserve the traditional connection between justice and rights: to treat someone as they have a right to be treated is to treat them as justice requires, and conversely.

One more expository point must be made concerning Jackson's understanding of agapic love and sanctity. The *imago dei* consists, says Jackson, in the capacity and need to receive and/or the capacity to give agapic love.[59] "The young and the old, the masculine and the feminine, the weak and the wicked all need agapic love and can receive it with profit . . . hence they must be

[54] Matt. 22:39.

[55] I develop the point that agapic love, rightly understood, can have God as its object, in *Justice in Love*, 105–7.

[56] Jackson, *Image of God*, 86–87.

[57] Jackson, *Image of God*, 110. "A 'duty of justice' is a matter of rewarding achieved merit, punishing demerit, or keeping promises or contracts, while a 'duty of charity' is a matter of responding to God's call or to the claim that another creature has on one simply by virtue of sharing the image of God." Ibid., 87.

[58] Jackson is not explicit on the second point; I am guessing that this is his view. He gives the example of a woman who makes a promise to her friend not to abandon her "*out of love and for the friend's sake*, and thus [becomes] genuinely duty-bound." Jackson, *Priority of Love*, 79. I interpret Jackson as meaning that, having made the promise, the woman is now duty-bound to extend agapic love to her friend. But the passage could instead be interpreted as saying that the woman now has two distinct motivations for the same action: the motivation of extending agapic love, and the distinct motivation of doing what duty requires.

[59] Jackson, *Image of God*, 102.

counted as bearers of God's image."[60] The *imago dei* is thus connected with sanctity rather than dignity. "The need to receive love or the potential to give it I equate with the core of human sanctity."[61]

Jackson considers the objection that his definition of the *imago dei* is too expansive. "If the *imago Dei* is minimally a function of the need to receive or ability to give agapic love, does this not mean that plants and animals also bear the divine image? . . . And, if so, aren't they all made in the image of God and possessed of sanctity rights?"[62] His response is that, though plants and animals can often benefit from human care, they do not *need* human care. Human beings need it. He concedes that some domesticated plants and animals may actually need human care. His response to this point is that their need for human care is a need they have acquired by being domesticated; it is not "part of their intrinsic natures."[63]

This response seems to me inadequate. Whatever may be true of some species as such, very often domesticated varieties of the species do need human care; those varieties of the species could not survive without human care. Given Jackson's understanding of the *imago dei*, those *varieties* of the species bear the *imago dei*, and thus have sanctity.

My main problem with Jackson's understanding of the *imago dei* is not that, however. Given Jackson's concept of agapic love, God neither needs agapic love nor is capable of receiving it. It follows that there is nothing at all in God that is imaged by our human need for agapic love and by our capacity to receive it. Our capacity to *offer* agapic love to our fellows images God's capacity to offer agapic love; likewise our *actual offer* of agapic love to our fellows images God's actual offer of agapic love. But our need for agapic love and our capacity to receive it images nothing in God.

It follows that, on Jackson's way of thinking of the *imago dei*, those who can and do offer agapic love to their fellows image God, whereas those who cannot offer it but do need it and can receive it, do not image God. This is a most ironic outcome, given Jackson's resolute opposition to those who locate the *imago dei* in the capacity for rational and moral agency.

Whereas we do not image God with respect to our need for agapic love and our capacity to receive it, we do indeed image God with respect to our capacity for extending agapic love to our fellows. But our imaging God in that respect cannot be what accounts for the fact that every human being has

[60] Ibid., 104.
[61] Ibid.
[62] Ibid., 107.
[63] Ibid., 108.

rights, including those who cannot function as persons, since some human beings do not have that capacity and hence do not image God in that respect.

My own view is that it is not our imaging God with respect to agapic love that accounts for the fact that every human being is a rights-bearer, but the worth or dignity possessed by every human being on account of God's actual love for each and every human being – God's love being understood here as desire for fellowship. And as for the *imago dei*, that, so I argue, should be understood not as imaging God with respect to one's possession of certain capacities but as imaging God with respect to one's nature, that is, with respect to human nature. To every creature who possesses the *imago dei* so understood, God offers fellowship; and with every such creature, God desires fellowship. That's what accounts for the dignity borne by each and every human being.[64]

I join with Jackson in regarding justice as grounded in the dignity or worth of persons and human beings; to treat someone as justice requires is to treat them in a way that befits their dignity or worth. An adequate account of justice requires a conceptuality that includes not only the concept of life-goods, but also the concept of the worth of those who have lives, the individuals themselves. The basic reason utilitarians cannot offer an adequate account of justice is that the conceptuality they employ includes only the concept of life-goods. Where I depart sharply from Jackson is that I do not regard the worth or dignity of persons as grounded only in achieved merit. In my essay, "Grounding the Rights We Have as Human Persons," I point to a number of other features of persons that ground worth or dignity.[65] And as for human beings in general, both those who can function as persons and those who cannot, their dignity is grounded in their being one of those creatures possessing human nature with each of whom God desires fellowship.

5.3 NO DIRECTIONAL TENSION BETWEEN LOVE AND JUSTICE

Let me bring my exposition of Jackson's version of agapism to a close. In the course of my exposition of Jackson's thought I have expressed my agreement on a good many points and my disagreement on others. What especially interests me, however, is whether he succeeds in defending his claim that there is no directional tension between agapic love and justice.

64 I develop these ideas in chapters 16 and 17 of *Justice: Rights and Wrongs*. In my essay, "On Secular and Theistic Groundings of Human Rights," I present what I judge to be an improved statement. The essay is included in *Understanding Liberal Democracy*.

65 The essay is included in *Understanding Liberal Democracy*.

In *Justice in Love*, the strategy I followed to defend the claim that there is no directional tension between agapic love and justice was to argue for understanding love and justice in such a way that there is no motivational tension between them. Jackson and I agree that agapic love seeks the good of someone as an end in itself. I hold that seeking the good of someone as an end in itself has two dimensions: the dimension of seeking to promote good in her life, and the dimension of paying due respect to her for her worth or dignity. I suggested that our word "care" comes closer than any other in English to capturing both dimensions: when one cares about someone, one both seeks to promote her life-goods and one sees to it that her worth or dignity is duly respected. I further argued that well-formed agapic love for someone – well-formed care – not only sees to it that due respect is paid to the direct recipient of one's care, but also sees to it that no one else's rights are violated.

My claim that agapic love should be understood in such a way that there is no motivational tension, and therefore no directional tension, between agapic love, rightly understood, and justice, might appear to be "cooking the books." To defend myself against that charge, I noted that when Jesus presented the two love commands, he was not just stating the essence of Torah, but was quoting from the Torah. The second love command is a quotation of Leviticus 19:18. When we look at the context within which the command occurs there, we discover that treating the neighbor justly is not pitted against love of neighbor but is cited among examples of loving the neighbor. I further noted that when Jesus enjoined agapic love of the neighbor, he did not enjoin any particular motive. Whether one seeks the good of the neighbor out of gratuitous benevolence, out of empathy, out of attachment, out of duty, because justice requires it, or whatever – it makes no difference: seek the good of the neighbor as an end in itself. If one makes it definitive of agapic love that it cannot be motivated by the desire to do justice, then one has created ineluctable motivational tension between agapic love and justice.

The agapic love of neighbor Scripture enjoins does not exclude seeking justice, but incorporates seeking justice. Seeking justice is motivationally integrated within agapic love. That's why we can be assured that the two will not come into directional tension with each other.[66]

From my presentation of Jackson's thought it is clear that he understands agapic love and justice in such a way that the two are in motivational tension with each other; no need to belabor the point. In acting out of agapic love, one is not doing what one does because justice requires it; and conversely, in doing

[66] I develop these points at length in *Justice in Love*.

what one does because justice requires it, one is not acting out of agapic love.[67] So what is Jackson's reason for insisting that there is, nonetheless, never any directional tension between love and justice? Starting from an understanding of love and of justice such that there is motivational tension between them, how does one arrive at the conclusion that "Love without justice or a love that lapses into justice is less than loving"?[68]

I am not aware of any passage in which Jackson explains why agapic love, as he understands it, never violates justice. Several times over he takes note of the charge that agapic love all too often results in unjust paternalism; each time he emphatically rejects the charge.[69] But I know of no passage in which he explains why the charge does not stick. If some great good can be achieved by forfeiting some lesser good required by justice, does not love direct one to forfeit that lesser good?

To the charge that "agapic love will lead to political despotism," Jackson replies that agape "respects freedom of conscience as an intrinsic rather than merely an instrumental good."[70] The thought is not developed. He declares that agape avoids "the twin vices of injustice and insensitivity. . . . [It is] both self-empowering and self-limiting precisely because it builds personal relations."[71] Again, the thought is not developed. In Jackson's way of thinking there are, so far as I can see, no resources for defending the claim that between agapic love and justice, as he understands them, there will never be directional tension. If there are such resources, he does not employ them.

I now hazard a guess. I guess that, no matter how agapic love and justice are understood, if they are understood in such a way that there is motivational tension between them, one will not be able to defend the claim that there is no directional tension between them. I hazard a stronger guess: not only will one not be able to defend that claim; with just a bit of imagination one will be able to think of cases of conflict. Instances of benevolent paternalism come at once to mind.[72]

67 Jackson, *Priority of Love*, 13, 47, 69 (passages in which the motivational tension comes through with special force).

68 Ibid., 38.

69 Ibid., 34, 52, 61– 62, 64–65, 95.

70 Ibid., 62.

71 Ibid., 52.

72 In *Justice in Love* I discuss this and several other types of conflict between agapic love understood as gratuitous benevolence and justice.

5.4 HARMONY BETWEEN JUSTICE AND LAW

In *Justice in Love* I develop at length the thesis of harmony between love and justice. Readers of this present essay who have not read the book will have caught its line of argument from the contrasts drawn between Jackson's views on the relation between love and justice and my own; and those who have read the book will probably have found that identifying points of contrast and disagreement has made the main points of my argument stand out more clearly. What has not thus far emerged from our discussion is the harmony I see between justice and law and between love and law. So let's turn to those, beginning with the first.

In thinking about law and justice, I again take my bearings from Scripture. Paul's description in Romans 13 of the God-given task of the state is a highly condensed statement of what Scripture in general says on the topic. The passage is well known, but let's have it in front of us:

> Rulers are not a terror [*phobos*] to good conduct, but to bad. Do you wish to have no fear [verbal form of *phobos*] of the authority? Then do what is good, and you will receive its approval; for it is God's servant [*diakonos*] for your good. But if you do what is wrong, you should be afraid, for the authority does not bear the sword in vain! It is the servant [*diakonos*] of God to execute wrath [*orgê*] on the wrongdoer. Therefore one must be subject, not only because of wrath but also because of conscience. For the same reason you also pay taxes, for the authorities are God's servants [*leitourgoi*] busy with this very thing.[73]

Government is a servant of God assigned the task of exercising governance over the public for the purpose of executing wrath on wrongdoers, thereby at the same time indicating its approval of those who do good.

From the benefits Paul cites of government carrying out its assignment, we can infer that we would interpret him in too pinched and literalistic a fashion if we held that it was only punishment he had in mind. The two main benefits Paul cites are deterring bad conduct and indicating approval of good conduct. Paul's thought, so I suggest, is that God has assigned government the task not just of *punishing* wrongdoing once it has occurred, but also of *deterring* its occurrence and *protecting* the public from its occurrence.

Government does this by publishing a law code which specifies actions that are forbidden and that attaches coercive sanctions to those laws, by establishing a judiciary to determine whether someone has violated the law and to order punishment in case it determines that he has, by setting up a

[73] Rom. 13:3–6.

police force to prevent or deter violations of the law, and by maintaining a militia. It is this fourfold system that brings about the benefits of executing anger on wrongdoers that Paul cites. Paul's words, "execute anger on the wrongdoer," should be understood as a synecdoche for the workings of a comprehensive system of this sort. The God-assigned task of government is to exercise governance over the public for the purpose of *curbing and punishing wrongdoing*.

Obviously government cannot curb and punish all wrongdoing, if for no other reason than that it lacks the resources. To insult someone is to wrong her, but no government has the resources to curb all insults. Government has to set priorities, overlooking minor forms of wrongdoing and focusing on the major.

To wrong someone is to deprive her of something to which she has a legitimate claim, a claim-right. And to deprive her of something to which she has a claim-right is to treat her unjustly. So instead of saying that it is the God-assigned task of government to curb and punish wrongdoing, we could say that it is the God-assigned task of government to *curb and punish injustice* – or, to put it positively rather than negatively, to *secure justice*. Paul does not say that government is permitted to do no more than this; I would be surprised were I to learn that it was his view that the Roman government was acting impermissibly when it went beyond securing justice to enhancing the common good with its astonishing infrastructure of roads and aqueducts. What we can infer is that when government does promote the common good in ways that go beyond what justice requires, it must do so in such a way that it does not itself wrong members of the public.

This understanding of the teaching of Scripture in general, and of Paul in particular, concerning the function of law and civil government, namely, that the primary function of civil law is to secure justice in society, is different from what almost all Christian thinkers, until roughly the mid-seventeenth century, took to be the function of law. The common traditional view was that civil law is not only to secure justice, but is to cultivate virtue and piety in the citizenry. Law's function is not just protectionist, but perfectionist. Calvin's statement is representative of the main tradition:

> [Civil government] does not merely see to it . . . that men breathe, eat, drink, and are kept warm, even though it surely embraces all these activities when it provides for their living together. It does not, I repeat, look to this only, but also prevents idolatry, sacrilege against God's name, blasphemies against his truth, and other public offenses against religion from arising and spreading among the people; it prevents the public peace from being disturbed; it provides that each man may keep his property safe and sound; that men

> may carry on blameless intercourse among themselves; that honesty and modesty may be preserved among men. In short, it provides that a public manifestation of religion may exist among Christians, and that humanity may be maintained among men.[74]

I share the view of many that it was the emergence of intense religious conflict within Western Christendom in the sixteenth and seventeenth centuries that forced Christians to rethink their traditional interpretation of the task of government.

5.5 HARMONY BETWEEN LOVE AND LAW

What remains to consider is the harmony between love and civil law. It was Aristotle's view that justice is to be located in the way benefits and burdens are distributed: justice consists of equitable distributions. The main alternative way of thinking of justice is that justice (*justitia*) consists, as the ancient Roman jurist Ulpian put it, in rendering to each his or her *ius* – that is, his or her right or due. To put the same idea in other words: justice consists in rendering to each what he or she has a legitimate claim to. In my thinking about justice, I stand in the Ulpian tradition.[75]

That to which one has a right is always a state or event in one's life.[76] More specifically, it is a state or event that would be a good in one's life, a life-good; one never has a right to something that would be an evil in one's life. More specifically yet, the life-goods to which one has a right are always *ways of being treated*. Normally it is to the good of being treated a certain way by others. In the limiting case it is to the good of being treated a certain way by oneself. We can wrong ourselves; we do so, for example, if we allow ourselves to become drug addicts.

Our use of rights-language often conceals from us the fact that claim-rights are to the good of being treated a certain way. We say that someone has a right to a seat on the plane; a seat on the plane is not a way of being treated. Closer analysis of the situation reveals, however, that a more explicit description of

[74] *Institutes of the Christian Religion*, trans. Ford Lewis Battles (Philadelphia: Westminster Press, 1950), IV.xx.3, 1488.

[75] Jackson stands in this tradition as well. Where we differ is that, going along with what he takes to be the modern concept of justice, he limits what is due persons to what is due them on account of achieved merit or demerit or on account of contracts and promises they have made. I do not limit what is due them in that way. In *Justice: Rights and Wrongs* I explain why I regard the Aristotelian approach as inadequate.

[76] This is true for claim-rights; permission-rights are rights to do something. When I use the term "rights" without qualification, it will always be claim-rights that I have in mind.

the right in question is that it is to the good of being given a seat on the plane by an airline employee; and that is a way of being treated.

Though a right is also a way of being treated that would be a good in one's life, the converse is not the case; there are ways of being treated that would be a good in one's life to which one does not have a right. The main challenge facing anyone who wants to construct a theory of rights is to explain why it is that one has a right to certain ways of being treated that would be a good in one's life and not to others. In *Justice: Rights and Wrongs*, I discuss the matter at length. To put my view epigrammatically: one has a right to the good of being treated a certain way just in case, if one were not treated that way, one would not be treated in a way that befits one's worth or dignity.

To extend agapic love to someone is to seek to promote her good as an end in itself, no matter what the motive. To treat her as justice requires is to treat her in a way that would be a good in her life to which she has a right. It follows that to treat her as justice requires is perforce an exercise of agapic love. It is perforce to care about her. And given that the main function of civil law is to secure justice, supporting a just system of laws justly enforced is an exercise of agapic love for one's fellow citizens.

This is true for primary justice: a just system of laws justly enforced aims at securing primary justice for the citizens. Is it also true for reactive or corrective justice – the justice that consists of doing to those who have wronged someone what is permissible to be done to them and of offering recompense to the victim if that is possible? Punishment of those whose wronging of someone is a violation of the law is an essential aspect of civil law.

Is punishing wrongdoers or supporting their punishment an exercise of agapic love? How could it be? Is not punishment payback, retribution, paying back harm with harm? That is the traditional view of punishment, both among Christians and others. By virtue of creating an imbalance of benefits and burdens, wrongdoing is a breach of the moral order. This breach has to be repaired by rectifying the imbalance. Justice requires that the imbalance be rectified. Punishment rectifies the imbalance by imposing on the malefactor a harm roughly equivalent to the harm he imposed on his victim. Punishment repairs the breach in the moral order by paying back harm with harm, evening things up. Seeking the good of the wrongdoer as an end in itself is nowhere in view.

This is the classic retributive understanding of punishment. But is it acceptable? Is this how punishment should be understood? Those of us who take our bearings from Scripture should have our doubts.

In Matthew's report of the Sermon on the Mount Jesus says, "You have heard that it was said, 'You shall love your neighbor and hate your enemy.' But

I say to you, Love your enemies and pray for those who persecute you."[77] In Luke's report of the sermon Jesus says, "Love your enemies, do good to those who hate you, bless those who curse you, pray for those who abuse you."[78] This theme, of answering harm with good rather than harm, is picked up in chapter 12 of Paul's letter to the Romans: "Repay no one evil for evil. . . . Never avenge [*ekdikêo*] yourselves, but leave room for the wrath [*orgê*] of God; for it is written, 'Vengeance [*ekdikêsis*] is mine, I will repay, says the Lord.' . . . Do not be overcome by evil, but overcome evil with good."[79] These passages would seem to rule out punishment as retribution. Traditionally they have not been so interpreted, however. Let's see why.

When one has been wronged, one is permitted, in reaction, to treat the person who wronged one in ways that previously were impermissible – to be angry at him, for example. To be wronged is to acquire various permission-rights. Call them *reactive* rights. Reactive justice is present in society insofar as persons and institutions do not treat wrongdoers in ways that violate reactive rights.

Among the reactive rights acquired by being wronged is the right to punish the wrongdoer or to support his being punished, with this qualification: only those who possess authority of some sort over the wrongdoer can inflict punishment – governmental authority, parental authority, ecclesiastical authority, the authority that comes with being the head of some educational institution, and so forth. Others can, of course, inflict hard treatment on the wrongdoer; often they do. But hard treatment inflicted by those who have no authority over the wrongdoer does not constitute punishment.

In Romans 13, Paul says it is the God-given task of governmental authorities to punish wrongdoers – in his words, "to execute wrath on the wrongdoer."[80] But in the preceding chapter he said to his readers that they were never to avenge themselves, never to repay harm with harm; vengeance is God's business.[81] The traditional way of fitting these declarations together is the following: those who exercise authority, especially those who exercise civil governmental authority, act not in their own capacity, but on behalf of God. In particular, when punishing wrongdoers they exercise vengeance on behalf of God. No one is permitted, when acting in his own capacity, to exercise vengeance; when acting in one's own capacity, one is never to repay harm

77 Matt. 5:43–4.
78 Luke 6:27–8.
79 Rom. 12:17–21; see also 1 Thess. 5:13–16.
80 Rom. 13.
81 Rom. 12.

with harm, one is always to seek the good of the other as an end in itself. But when acting on God's behalf in some position of authority one is permitted, often indeed required, to exercise vengeance on the wrongdoer. This is the traditional view.

I hold that this is not what Paul was saying. *Ekdikêsis* is the Greek word Paul uses in chapter 12 that gets translated in our English Bibles as "vengeance." If there is to be *ekdikêsis*, Paul says, leave it to God; it is not our business. Paul connects *ekdikêsis* with repaying.

The word *ekdikêsis* does not occur in chapter 13. In 13:4 Paul says the ruler "is a servant of God, an *ekdikos* who executes wrath on the wrongdoer." My *Greek–English Lexicon of the New Testament* gives, as the meaning of *ekdikos*, "an avenger or one who punishes." The former of these two possibilities would be compelling as the translation if Paul connected being an *ekdikos* with repaying. But nowhere in chapter 13 does he use the language of "repaying." He does not say that it is the business of government to repay evil with evil. What he says is that rulers are a "terror" to bad conduct and that they are to "execute . . . wrath on the wrongdoer." Neither does he anywhere say that rulers act *on behalf of* God. He describes them as *servants* and *ministers* of God, not as deputies of God. I submit that the traditional interpretation is a misinterpretation. The ruler is not an avenger who acts on behalf of God but one who serves God by punishing wrongdoers.

But is punishment in the nature of the case retribution, payback, getting even? It is not. Unless the relation between parent and child is profoundly disordered, a parent does not think of herself as paying back when she punishes the child. She thinks of herself as forcefully reproving the child, doing so for the good of the child, and for the good of others as well. I call this understanding of punishment the *reprobative* understanding, from the English word "reprove."[82] In Leviticus we read, "You shall reprove your neighbor, or you will incur guilt yourself. . . . You shall love your neighbor as yourself."[83]

It appears to me that most people in the United States, including most Christians, work with a retributive rather than a reprobative understanding of punishment. When punishment is understood as retribution, there is sharp conflict between agapic love and justice. Jesus and Paul, and the New Testament writers generally, teach us that we are to reject the retributive understanding of punishment and are instead to understand and practice punishment as reprobative in function. So understood and practiced, punishment is an exercise of agapic love.

[82] I discuss this understanding of punishment in *Justice in Love*, 193–8.

[83] Lev. 19:17–18, NRSV.

And what if the wrongdoer is repentant? Has punishment then lost its point? We are to forgive the repentant wrongdoer, says Jesus, no longer holding against him what he did to us. But suppose one is responsible for administering a system of laws. Does one pardon the penitent lawbreakers? Nor necessarily, I argue in *Justice in Love*. Deterrence may require that punishment be imposed even on repentant wrongdoers.[84]

A pervasive claim or assumption in discussions about love and justice is the theme of tension or conflict. I have argued, in the first part of this essay, that when agapic love and justice are rightly understood, there is neither motivational nor directional tension between them. Similarly, a pervasive theme in discussions about the relation between love and law is the theme of conflict. In the second part of the essay I have argued that the fundamental purpose of law is to secure justice, and that when law does in fact secure justice, there is no tension between law and agapic love.

[84] I devote chapters 15 and 17 of my *Justice in Love* to analyzing the complicated interplay among forgiveness, law, and justice.

6

Justice Tempered by Forbearance: Why Christian Love Is an Improper Category to Apply to Civil Law

David VanDrunen

Jeffrie Murphy has posed the question: "What would law be like if we organized it around the value of Christian love and thought about and criticized law in terms of that value?"[1] I present a contrarian perspective in comparison to most other contributors to this book. I suggest that civil law should not be organized around Christian love. Instead, justice tempered by forbearance is the proper foundation for civil law.

A number of clarifications are in order from the outset. Most obviously, the terms "Christian love" and "justice" have no universally accepted definitions. While Scripture and all of the main Christian traditions view love and justice positively, understandings of what each term means and how each relates to the other vary significantly. Thus, an important goal of this essay is to explain how I understand "justice" and "Christian love" (at least as they relate to civil law) and to defend this understanding as a biblical and theological matter. The final product, as a matter of substance, may not be as different as one might suspect from many studies that defend and develop the idea that civil law should be evaluated by means of Christian love. The substantive conclusions are ultimately the important thing, but the terms we use can affect the degree of success with which those conclusions are communicated.

Another point of clarification is that I present a Christian theological argument against organizing and evaluating civil law through the value of Christian love, not a secular argument. Christian moral and legal conceptions of love and justice are intimately related to theological convictions about God's nature, sin, atonement, and salvation, and thus I will consider several of these issues in developing my case. My contribution comes specifically from a classic Reformed theological perspective, although other Reformed thinkers may not

[1] Jeffrie G. Murphy, *Christian Love and Criminal Punishment*, 151–65.

agree with my conclusions.[2] The Reformed accent of this essay will be evident in its attention to the biblical covenants as well as in its conceptions of divine justice, common grace, the atonement, and soteriology. Nevertheless, at every step I will try to demonstrate how my conclusions are grounded in biblical exegesis, and thus worthy of consideration by Christians of various traditions.

In this essay I argue that the main purpose of civil law is to enforce justice according to the terms of the covenant with Noah (Gen. 8:21–9:17) and Romans 13:1–7, and should be organized and evaluated according to this end. More specifically, *retributive* justice (tempered by forbearance) should be the central concern of civil law, although it need not be its exclusive concern. This justice is indeed an expression of love in several important respects. But I also argue that there is something distinctive about *Christian* love, as grounded in the new covenant in Christ. A distinctively Christian love refuses to pursue retribution, but freely forgives instead – not because it ignores the claims of retributive justice but because it recognizes the satisfaction of retribution's claims in the cross of Christ. Therefore, since God has commissioned civil law to enforce retributive justice and has ordained Christian love to forgo retribution, Christian love is not the proper category by which to organize and evaluate civil law.

To make this argument, I first defend the idea that God has commissioned civil law and government to enforce justice, of which retributive justice is an essential component. Then I explain in what respects this commission to pursue justice is an expression of love. Following this, I identify what makes Christian love unique and discuss why this makes it an inappropriate category for evaluating civil law. Finally, I address a few plausible objections to my thesis, which will offer an opportunity to clarify several important issues.

6.1 CIVIL LAW AND GOVERNMENT: DIVINELY COMMISSIONED TO ENFORCE (RETRIBUTIVE) JUSTICE

In this opening section I defend the basic claim that God has commissioned civil law and government to enforce justice,[3] of which retributive justice is

[2] By "Reformed" I refer to the Protestant tradition whose early theologians included Martin Bucer, John Calvin, and Heinrich Bullinger, whose convictions have been summarized in documents such as the Heidelberg Catechism and the Westminster Confession of Faith, and whose churches have often been called "Reformed" or "Presbyterian."

[3] In this essay I usually speak of *enforcing* justice (rather than simply *doing* justice) since I refer primarily to retributive justice, which is a form of *rectifying* justice rather than *primary* justice. Primary justice refers to the obligation to treat people justly by giving them their due (e.g., paying for a product rather than stealing it), while rectifying justice refers to the just remedy

an essential component. Few readers are likely to disagree that civil law and government ought to enforce justice, but my claim that they should enforce *retributive* justice will be controversial. In this section, therefore, I interact with Nicholas Wolterstorff's claim that God has commissioned civil law and government to enforce justice, but not retributive justice.

6.1.1 *Romans 13:1–7: Civil Magistrates Called to Pursue Justice*

A predictable place to begin a biblical-theological consideration of this topic is Romans 13:1–7. In this text Paul states that God has "instituted" and "appointed" civil authorities (13:1–2), and thus they are God's "servant[s]" (13:4, 6). Paul identifies two specific responsibilities God has assigned them: they are to praise those who do good (13:3) and to be avengers who bring God's wrath against evildoers, for which task they bear the sword (13:4). It is not clear what Paul had in mind by saying that magistrates praise those doing good, although the most thorough study I am aware of argues that it refers to the public honor Roman officials accorded to wealthy benefactors.[4] The other magisterial task seems straightforward: civil authorities are to punish wrongdoers. Whatever the precise nature of the punishment or the wrong contemplated, Paul indicates that magistrates are to enforce justice in response to wrongdoing. As Wolterstorff puts it in a discussion of this text, "we could say that it is the God-assigned task of government to *curb injustice*. Or we could say that it is the God-assigned task of government *to protect the rights* of the public. God has assigned government the task of being a *rights-protecting* institution."[5] I agree. Paul makes clear that promoting justice is a central responsibility of civil law and government.

But what kind of justice does Paul refer to? According to Wolterstorff, Paul promotes an expressive theory of punishment, such that God authorizes the state to reprove evildoers, but God does *not* authorize retributive justice in Romans 13.[6] I believe this is incorrect. Before I argue why this misinterprets

---

for a violation of primary justice. On this terminology, see Nicholas Wolterstorff, *Justice: Rights and Wrongs* (Princeton: Princeton University Press, 2008), ix–x. The two biblical texts I chiefly consider, Genesis 9:5–6 and Romans 13:1–7, speak of the authority to render rectifying justice, not the general obligation to pursue primary justice.

4 Bruce W. Winter, "The Public Honouring of Christian Benefactors: Romans 13.3–4 and 1 Peter 2.14–15," *Journal for the Study of the New Testament* 34 (1988): 87–103.

5 Nicholas Wolterstorff, *The Mighty and the Almighty: An Essay in Political Theology* (Cambridge: Cambridge University Press, 2012), 90 (emphasis added).

6 Ibid., 85–87; and Nicholas Wolterstorff, *Justice in Love* (Grand Rapids: Wm. B. Eerdmans Publishing Co., 2011), 198.

Romans 13:1–7, I turn back in Scripture to the Old Testament to explore the roots of this text and the idea of retributive justice.

6.1.2 *The Noahic Covenant as Background for Romans 13:1–7*

Probably no Old Testament text is more foundational for understanding Romans 13:1–7 than the account of the Noahic covenant in Genesis 8:21–9:17.[7] In part this is because God, in this covenant, delegates authority to human beings to enforce justice, the very same dynamic as in Romans 13:4. First, God claims such authority for himself: "For your own lifeblood I will surely require a reckoning: from every animal I will require it and from human beings" (9:5). Then God delegates this authority to human beings to secure justice within their own communities: "From human beings, each one for the blood of another, I will require a reckoning for human life. Whoever sheds the blood of a human, by a human shall that person's blood be shed; for in his own image God made humankind" (9:5–6).[8] The idea that God delegates judicial authority to human beings, so crucial for Paul in Romans 13:1–7, appears for the first time explicitly in Scripture in the Noahic covenant. If we read the Christian Scriptures as a unified canon, we thus have an important initial reason to see the Noahic covenant as crucial background for interpreting Romans 13.

Three characteristics of the Noahic covenant further demonstrate why it provides this interpretive background. First, God puts the Noahic covenant in place "as long as the earth endures" (Gen. 8:22). In other words, God established this covenant until the consummation of the present world at the final judgment and revelation of the new creation (to put it in New Testament terms). Thus the Noahic covenant remained in effect when Paul wrote Romans and remains in effect today. Therefore, since the Noahic covenant

7 For a more thorough defense of this claim than I am able to present here, see David VanDrunen, "Power to the People: Revisiting Civil Resistance in Romans 13:1–7 in Light of the Noahic Covenant," *Journal of Law and Religion* 31.1 (March 2016): 4–18. In what follows I take the covenant with Noah after the great flood to be a covenant distinct from God's covenant with Noah before the flood (see Gen 6:18); these two covenants have different participants and purposes. For defense of this, see, e.g., Steven D. Mason, "Another Flood? Genesis 9 and Isaiah's Broken Eternal Covenant," *Journal for the Study of the Old Testament* 32.2 (December 2007): 48–66; Jeong Koo Jeon, "The Noahic Covenants and the Kingdom of God," *Mid-America Journal of Theology* 24 (2013): 179–209; and David VanDrunen, *Divine Covenants and Moral Order: A Biblical Theology of Natural Law* (Grand Rapids: Wm. B. Eerdmans Publishing Co., 2014), 108–11.

8 With most ancient and modern commentators I take this to be prescriptive and not simply descriptive. For an interesting defense of this from within my own Reformed tradition, by someone who interprets the Noahic covenant generally in ways very similar to my approach, see Abraham Kuyper, *Common Grace*, vol. 1.1 (Grand Rapids: Christian's Library Press, 2013), 74–79.

divinely authorizes human judicial authority for as long as the earth endures, the human judicial authority Paul describes in Romans 13 must be a manifestation of God's governance under the Noahic covenant.

Second, the Noahic covenant is universal in scope. According to the text, God entered the covenant with every human being from that time until the end of history: "Then God said to Noah and to his sons with him, 'As for me, I am establishing my covenant with you and your descendants after you'" (Gen. 9:8–9). God also entered the covenant with the entire animal kingdom, with "every living creature that is with you, for all future generations" (9:12). The covenant also includes the natural cosmic order, for God promises never again to destroy the earth with a flood (8:21; 9:11, 15) and to sustain the cycles of "seedtime and harvest, cold and heat, summer and winter, day and night" (8:22). To put it negatively, the Noahic covenant did not encompass only a part of the human race – as did the Abrahamic and Sinaitic covenants later in the Old Testament – but the entire human race, together with the rest of the created order. This has an intriguing parallel in Romans 13:1–7. The very first words in the Greek text are "every person" [pasa yuxh], as in, "Let *every person* be subject to the governing authorities." Immediately thereafter Paul states: "there is *no authority* except from God." Thus, these instructions are not limited to Christian believers or Christian magistrates, but apply to all those under civil authority and to all civil officials. The universal horizon of Romans 13:1–7 corresponds to the universal scope of the Noahic covenant.[9]

Third, the purpose of the Noahic covenant is preservative. Through it God promises to sustain the present world, and human society within it. He pledges to keep the floodwaters from destroying the earth again (9:11, 15), to maintain the cycles of the natural order (8:22), and to keep animals from overwhelming the human community (9:2). Furthermore, God promotes the

9 At this point it may be worth mentioning briefly the Jewish tradition of the "Noahide laws." According to Jewish theology, God gave seven commandments to the "Noahides" (i.e. the Gentiles) before the covenant with Israel at Sinai, and he continues to hold Gentiles accountable through them. One of these laws, especially relevant for present purposes, is the obligation to uphold justice through courts of law. While my interpretation of the Noahic covenant is not identical to the Jewish Noahide law tradition, there are many intriguing parallels. Seeing the Noahic covenant as an enduring divine bond with the entire human race has ancient precedent. On the Noahide law tradition generally, see especially David Novak, *The Image of the Non-Jew in Judaism: An Historical and Constructive Study of the Noahide Laws* (Lewiston: Edwin Mellen, 1983). On the Noahide tradition and the obligation to uphold justice through courts of law, see especially Nahum Rakover, *Law and the Noahides: Law as a Universal Value* (Jerusalem: Library of Jewish Law, 1998). For further reflections on the similarities and differences between my interpretation of the Noahic covenant and the Jewish Noahide tradition, see VanDrunen, *Divine Covenants and Moral Order*, 543–45.

preservation of human society by giving them food to eat (9:3), a commission to procreate (9:1, 7), and a charge to do justice (9:6). The Noahic covenant, however, does not express any redemptive purpose. Unlike later biblical covenants, this one promises no Messiah, forgiveness of sins, or eschatological new creation. It aims merely to constrain evil for a time, not to conquer it. Romans 13:1–7 mirrors the Noahic covenant on this point as well. In this text Paul mentions nothing about Christ, salvation in him, or the hope of glory – themes that pervade so much of the rest of Romans. Romans 13:1–7 is like an island, set apart in many ways from the texts that immediately surround it, 12:1–21 and 13:8–14, which give rich moral instructions to the "one body in Christ" (12:5) in light of the immanent hope of Christ's return (13:11–12). In contrast, 13:1–7 speaks merely of (pagan) magistrates instituted by God as part of the present order to praise and punish those who do "good" and "bad."[10] Thus, the preservative, non-redemptive purpose of the Noahic covenant corresponds to the preservative, non-redemptive role of civil authorities described in Romans 13:1–7.

To summarize the broader point thus far: several interlocking considerations suggest that the Noahic covenant is crucial background for interpreting Romans 13. God established the Noahic covenant as a charter for his providential government of the entire world for the rest of history, and part of this covenant's purpose is to constrain the effects of evil through delegating authority to human beings to enforce justice. It is compelling to conclude that the work of magistrates Paul describes in Romans 13:1–7 reflects the realities instituted in Genesis 8:21–9:17. Thus, if we wish to understand what sort of justice Paul envisioned magistrates pursuing, we do well to determine first what sort of justice the human community was to pursue under the Noahic covenant.

6.1.3 *Retributive Justice*

In this section I take up that inquiry, and my conclusion is straightforward: in the Noahic covenant God delegates the authority to enforce retributive justice: "Whoever sheds the blood of a human, by a human shall that person's blood be shed" (Gen. 9:6). I understand this not as a narrow statement about murder but as an expression of a broader judicial principle, the *lex talionis*,

[10] Among many scholars commenting on the distinctiveness of the Romans 13:1–7 ethic in comparison with surrounding texts, see Robert H. Stein, "The Argument of Romans 13:1–7," *Novum Testamentum* 31.4 (1989): 326; and Troels Engberg-Pedersen, "Paul's Stoicizing Politics in Romans 12–13: The Role of 13.1–10 in the Argument," *Journal for the Study of the New Testament* 29.2 (2006): 163–72. Among scholars noting the lack of anything distinctively Christian in 13:1–7, see Leander E. Keck, *Romans* (Nashville: Abingdon, 2005), 324; and James D. G. Dunn, *Word Biblical Commentary, vol. 38B, Romans 9–16* (Dallas: Word, 1988), 771.

better known under the formula "eye for an eye, tooth for a tooth."[11] The *lex talionis* represents retributive justice, the idea that a wrongdoer deserves a punishment proportionate to his crime.

The *lex talionis* captures this general notion through the idea that a person who harms another deserves an equivalent harm in return. *Proportionality* is the key idea. Retributive justice, exemplified in the *lex talionis*, does not require punishment to be equivalent in a woodenly literal way, as if physical mutilation is the necessary just response to physical mutilation. Rather, the punishment should be proportionate to the crime. The genius of the *lex talionis*, I take it, is how it captures the principle of proportionality so crisply: what is more closely equivalent to an eye than another eye? As a matter of history, legal systems that enshrined the *lex talionis* as a touchstone for justice usually permitted other punishments for bodily assault as substitute for physical mutilation, so long as they retained the principle of proportionality.[12]

According to the Noahic covenant, God commissions human beings to enforce retributive justice against those who harm other people. This should be a weighty consideration for Christians exploring the purpose of civil law and government. Yet retributive justice is a controversial notion. Before proceeding further, therefore, I briefly defend the soundness of the idea. For the sake of brevity I focus upon a few biblical and theological considerations.

First of all, Scripture often presents God's judgment as retributive in nature. Sinners deserve punishment for their rebellion against God, and God punishes them through penalties proportionate to the wrong they have done. Many Old Testament prophets, for example, foretelling God's temporal judgments against Gentile nations, describe divine judgment in terms of the *lex talionis*, or in terms of poetic justice, in which the punishment perfectly fits the crime in a wonderfully ironic way (e.g., Isa. 14:2, 12, 13–15; 23:1–4, 16; Jer. 49:2; 50:15, 29; Ezek. 25:12–14, 15–17; Joel 3:4–8; Obad. 15; Hab. 2:8, 15–17).[13] The ideas of proportionate punishment and just deserts also pervade many New Testament texts that describe the final judgment. Some of them reflect the *lex talionis* by describing the punishment as equivalent to the wrong. For instance, the

[11] This formula appears several times in the Mosaic law, which in part reflects the Noahic standard of justice; see Exod. 21:23–5; Lev. 24:18–21; and Deut. 19:21. The general applicability of the formula, and the range of circumstances to which these texts apply it, offer support for my interpretation of Genesis 9:6 as a judicial principle rather than as simply about murder.

[12] For helpful discussion of many issues related to this point, including the question of how proportionality is determined, see William Ian Miller, *Eye for an Eye* (Cambridge: Cambridge University Press, 2006). The idea of substituting monetary compensation for physical punishment appears in the Mosaic law, for example, in Exod. 21:29–30.

[13] For discussion of these texts, see VanDrunen, *Divine Covenants and Moral Order*, 183–85.

wicked will "be *destroyed* in their *destruction*, suffering *wrong* as the wage of their *wrongdoing*" (2 Pet. 2:12–13).[14] The Revelation of John offers several poignant examples: the day of God's wrath will be "the time for judging the dead . . . and for *destroying* those who *destroy* the earth" (Rev. 11:18); "You are just, O Holy One, who are and were, for you have judged these things; because they [the wicked] shed the *blood* of saints and prophets, you have given them *blood* to drink. *It is what they deserve*" (Rev. 16:6–7); "*Render to her* [Babylon] as she herself has *rendered*, and *repay her double* for her deeds; *mix* a double draught for her in the cup she *mixed*.[15] As she glorified herself and lived luxuriously, so give her *a like measure* of torment and grief" (Rev. 18:6–7).

Is it problematic to portray God as a judge who claims: "Vengeance is mine, I will repay, says the Lord" (Rom. 12:19; cf. Deut. 32:35)? If so, this problem pervades the Christian Scriptures, Old and New Testaments alike. I am not able in this essay (or perhaps anywhere!) to provide a comprehensive defense of God's retributive justice, but I suggest a few thoughts. Taking offense at such biblical statements may be inevitable for sinners, who have a vested interest in finding God forgetful and indulgent with our faults. But if we take seriously Scripture's portrayal of God as supremely holy, righteous, and good, the profound offence of human wickedness and rebellion against our creator begins to become comprehensible, however sobering. The more penetrating one's view of God's holiness, the more compelling it becomes that sin deserves punishment.[16]

In the case of intra-human wrongs, furthermore, the perpetrator wrongs not only God but also those who bear his image. It may be difficult for people like me and surely many readers of this book – who live in safe neighborhoods, in First World countries, and who have never been raped, been beaten to a pulp, had our homes seized by someone without title, or seen our children killed in warfare – to appreciate just how heinous an offence against a divine image-bearer can be. The idea that people *deserve* punishment for their misdeeds against human beings is probably more comprehensible for the multitudes that have suffered the wrongs mentioned above, often without any redress in human courts. They probably also understand the profundity of forgiveness much better too.

[14] This translation is from The Holy Bible, English Standard Version® (ESV®), copyright 1 2001 by Crossway Bibles, a publishing ministry of Good News Publishers. Used by permission. All rights reserved.

[15] The talionic theme is all the more evident in this verse if "double" is better translated as "equivalent," as argued in Meredith G. Kline, "Double Trouble," *Journal of the Evangelical Theological Society* 32 (June 1989): 177.

[16] See further discussion below on how these remarks about God's justice relate to an understanding of Christ's atonement.

But even if the propriety of God's retributive justice is conceded, is the human exercise of retributive justice problematic? By indicating that human judicial authority is delegated from God, Genesis 9:5–6 and Romans 13:1–7 suggest not. God views intra-human wrongdoing as ultimately an offence against himself; he will hold the perpetrators responsible. Human authorities act first and foremost on God's behalf. In fact, Scripture often directs human justice to reflect divine justice.[17]

I do not imagine that the previous paragraphs will put debates about retributive justice to rest, but I draw a basic conclusion from this section: in the Noahic covenant God commissions human beings to enforce retributive justice, a justice that reflects God's own. I now return to Romans 13:1–7.

6.1.4 *Romans 13:1–7 and Retributive Justice*

I initially argued that Romans 13:1–7 presents the enforcement of justice as at least one important task of civil law and government. In itself that is not a controversial conclusion. But I then asked what kind of justice Paul had in mind, and noted Wolterstorff's claim that the state, in Romans 13:1–7, is to enforce justice, but not retributive justice. My subsequent argument from the Noahic covenant offered a reason to question Wolterstorff's claim. I argued that the Noahic covenant is crucial background for interpreting Romans 13:1–7, and that the role Paul ascribes to magistrates in Romans 13 reflects God's general delegation of judicial authority to enforce retributive justice to the human community in Genesis 9:5–6. What evidence does Wolterstorff have that this is not the case?

An important element of Wolterstorff's view is that Jesus thoroughly rejected the *lex talionis*, in his Sermon on the Mount especially but also elsewhere. To be more precise, Wolterstorff argues that Jesus and the New Testament epistles reject the "reciprocity code" as a whole, of which the *lex talionis* was a key aspect.[18] And rejection of the *lex talionis* "implies the rejection of retribution."[19] Furthermore, Wolterstorff claims, Jesus did not mean to command only Christians to shun the reciprocity code, for the Sermon on the Mount was "an ethic for everybody."[20] If correct, Wolterstorff has understandable reason to suspect, even before reading Romans 13:1–7, that it will not promote

[17] An interesting text that exemplifies these themes is Exod. 23:7: "Keep far from a false charge, and do not kill the innocent and righteous, for I will not acquit the wicked." For further discussion of the propriety of human retributive justice, see VanDrunen, *Divine Covenants and Moral Order*, 503–4.

[18] Wolterstorff, *Justice in Love*, 120–26.

[19] Ibid., 128.

[20] Ibid., 127.

retributive justice. Otherwise Paul would be in direct conflict with Jesus, and also in conflict with Paul's own rejection of retribution a few verses earlier in Romans 12:17–19.

When Wolterstorff turns to Romans 13:1–7 itself, he writes this: "Nothing is said about retribution, about getting even, about reciprocating evil with evil, about redress, about vengeance." Elsewhere he adds, "Nowhere does he [Paul] suggest that retributive punishment is a legitimate function of government." Paul does teach that government is to punish wrongdoers, Wolterstorff states, but this punishment is reprobative, not retributive, and it functions to deter wrongdoing.[21]

Wolterstorff's makes his case with clarity, and I agree heartily with his general claim that several New Testament epistles reject the *lex talionis*. But I believe his conclusion about Romans 13 and retribution is incorrect. As the Noahic covenant would lead us to predict, Romans 13:1–7 indicates that civil authorities should enforce retributive justice.

Paul describes the magistrate in Romans 13:4: "he is the servant of God, an avenger who carries out God's wrath on the wrongdoer."[22] An initial clue that Paul thinks magistrates should enforce retributive justice is that he calls him an *avenger* [ekdikoj]. If Paul meant to avoid any suggestion of retributive justice, this title is a most curious choice. An avenger seeks vengeance, and securing vengeance is at the heart of retributive justice. Blind or disproportionate vengeance is inconsistent with justice, but the *lex talionis* aims to prescribe a fittingly proportionate penalty as an outlet for vengeance as a valid expression of just outrage. The New Testament and Septuagint (the Greek Old Testament of Paul's day) do not use the word "avenger" [ekdikoj] frequently, but the Septuagint often uses cognate words to describe vengeance,[23] sometimes in explicitly retributive ways. For example, God "will avenge the blood of his children, and take vengeance on his adversaries; he will repay those who hate him" (Deut 32:43); and God commands Jehu to "strike down the house of your master Ahab, so that I may avenge on Jezebel the blood of my servants the prophets, and the blood of all the servants of the Lord" (2 Kings 9:7). This is precisely the kind of thing Wolterstorff claims the New Testament prohibits all people from doing. Yet Paul names the civil magistrate an avenger.

That Paul thinks of the avenging magistrate as pursuing retributive justice is all the more evident when we compare 13:4 with Paul's teaching a few verses earlier, in 12:17, 19. I quote 13:4 again, this time using italics to highlight

[21] Ibid., 128–29, 198.
[22] This translation is from the English Standard Version.
[23] These cognate words include ekdikhsij and ekdikew.

several key words: "he is the servant of God, an *avenger* who carries out God's *wrath* on the *wrong*doer."[24] In comparison, Paul wrote this just earlier: "Do not repay anyone evil for evil [i.e. *wrong* for *wrong*]. . . . Beloved, never *avenge* yourselves, but leave room for the *wrath* of God; for it is written, '*Vengeance* is mine, I will repay, says the Lord'" (12:17, 19). The matching vocabulary is easy to see in English, and is even more evident in the original Greek.[25] It cannot have been coincidental. Paul's point in Romans 13:4 is that God commissions the civil magistrate to do the very things that he prohibits his Christian readers from doing a few verses earlier. In chapter 12 Paul instructs Christians not to follow the *lex talionis*, repaying evil for evil; they are not to avenge themselves but leave it to the wrath of God. This task is God's, but he has also appointed civil authorities to do such work on his behalf. What the Noahic covenant would lead us to expect is exactly what we find.

I have now completed the argument for my first main point: one important purpose of civil law and government is to enforce retributive justice. I have not considered what other purposes they may legitimately have, but have focused simply on showing that retributive justice is one of them. For a Christian understanding of law and government this is a significant conclusion in its own right, but it is also foundational for thinking through the relationship of law and love.

6.2 THE PLACE OF LOVE IN CIVIL LAW AND GOVERNMENT

Thus far this essay has focused upon God's call for civil law and government to enforce justice, and specifically retributive justice. What place, if any, does this leave for love in the operation of law and government? In this section I argue, again from a Christian perspective, that there is indeed an important place for love in the justice-enforcing work of the state. I highlight two matters: first, the enforcement of retributive justice is itself an expression of love and, second, love ought to temper the enforcement of retributive justice. Only in the next section will I broaden the inquiry and ask whether speaking of *Christian* love changes the terms of discussion.

First, then, the enforcement of retributive justice is itself an act of love. Above all, when civil authorities enforce retributive justice they show love for God. To obey God's commands – at least when done with proper motives and

[24] This translation is from the English Standard Version.

[25] Christians are not to return kakon for kakou (Rom. 12:17), while magistrates are to punish those who do to kakon (13:4). Christians are not to avenge (ekdikountej) themselves, for vengeance (ekdikhsij) is the Lord's (12:19), while the magistrate, as servant of God, is to be an avenger (ekdikoj) (13:4). Christians are to leave place for God's wrath (orgh) (12:19), while the magistrate, again as God's servant, is to be an avenger unto wrath (orghn) (13:4).

for proper goals – is to honor him and to love him. Thus, if God has commissioned civil authorities to enforce retributive justice, as argued above, their obedience constitutes an act of love.

Enforcing retributive justice is also an act of love toward the victims of injustice and toward the community as a whole. Pursuing retributive justice loves victims by recognizing the serious nature of the harm done to them as dignified divine image-bearers and by accounting for their justified outrage through a lawful and measured punishment of their assailants. If the assailant is punished through exacting compensation, retributive justice also advances the restoration of victims.[26] With respect to the community as a whole, enforcing retributive justice teaches that it is wrong to harm another person and promotes order and safety in general human life, thereby enabling people to collaborate peacefully and to pursue their vocations unmolested. Enforcing retributive justice may even serve as an act of love to wrongdoers, insofar as their punishment – unpleasant as it may be – impresses the gravity of their action upon them and motivates them to reform.

Second, love ought to temper the enforcement of retributive justice. Retributive justice is severe, and the relentless pursuit of proportionate punishment in response to every intra-human wrongdoing seems simultaneously horrifying and impossible. It is hardly conceivable that a society filled with sinners could seek proportionate retribution for every last wrong without consuming itself. Is there dissonance, therefore, between practical exigencies and the Noahic covenant's call for retributive justice? I do not believe so, for the Noahic covenant itself provides reason to think that the pursuit of retributive justice should be restrained by a measure of forbearance. The Noahic covenant, I argued, grounds the human responsibility to enforce justice on God's behalf. But the Noahic covenant also manifests the forbearance of God. Interpreting this covenant in canonical context demonstrates how it does so. Genesis 6–7 describes the great flood, which God sent because of human wickedness (6:5) and violence (6:11). The external wickedness and violence had an internal source: God saw "that every inclination of the thoughts of their hearts was only evil continually" (6:5). After the flood God entered a covenant with Noah and the entire creation with him. On the surface there seemed to be a fatal problem: human nature had not changed. As God noted at the outset of the covenant account, "the inclination of the human heart is evil from youth" (8:21). But in fact this is precisely why God established this covenant. To use popular Reformed language, the Noahic covenant is a covenant

[26] On how the *lex talionis* principle can promote restorative as well as retributive justice, see VanDrunen, *Divine Covenants and Moral Order*, 504–5.

of *common grace*.[27] God extends gracious blessings to all his creatures, and especially to sinful human beings. In particular, God pledges to withhold his hand from bringing another great flood on the earth – not because humanity is so wonderful, but in spite of its wickedness. The Noahic covenant manifests God's love for human beings in preserving a good and orderly world for them.

But what sort of love is this, precisely? I call it a love of *forbearance*. In the Noahic covenant God does not promise to forgive sins and to save people from his judgment altogether. This covenant does not cancel the final judgment, but postpones it.[28] Many subsequent biblical texts speak of a final judgment yet to come, a final judgment that will resemble the great flood in its suddenness and severity (e.g., Isa. 24:18; 26:20; Luke 17:26–27; 2 Pet. 3:5–7). God will never again destroy the earth with a flood, but he will send judgment by fire. What the Noahic covenant does is postpone that judgment so that history can unfold and God's manifold purposes for this world be fulfilled. Through this covenant God forbears with much human wrongdoing, for the time being.

This has implications for the question at hand. As already argued, God has supreme authority to enforce justice, and human beings have authority to do so only because God delegates it to them. In the Noahic covenant God delegates his own authority, and thus human justice should reflect divine justice. Therefore, if God tempers his retributive justice with forbearance, human authorities properly temper their retributive justice with forbearance. This claim undoubtedly raises many questions concerning how, when, and under what circumstances legislatures and courts ought to show forbearance toward wrongdoers. I do not have space to explore these questions here, and in any case I do not think the Noahic covenant – or anywhere else in Scripture – provides

[27] Here I follow the line of Reformed thinking that understands the Noahic covenant as a covenant of common grace distinct from the later biblical covenants organically unified as administrations of the "covenant of grace." Among defenses of this perspective, see Herman Witsius, *The Economy of the Covenants between God and Man: Comprehending a Complete Body of Divinity*, 2 vols, trans. William Crookshank (1822; reprint, Phillipsburg: Presbyterian and Reformed, 1990), 2.239; Wilhelmus à Brakel, *The Christian's Reasonable Service*, 4 vols., trans. Bartel Elshout (Ligonier: Soli Deo Gloria, 1992–95), 4.384; Kuyper, *Common Grace*, 1.1, 15–17; Herman Bavinck, *Reformed Dogmatics, vol. 3, Sin and Salvation in Christ*, trans. John Vriend (Grand Rapids: Baker, 2006), 218–19; Geerhardus Vos, *Biblical Theology: Old and New Testaments* (Grand Rapids: Wm. B. Eerdmans Publishing Co., 1949), 56, 62–3; Meredith G. Kline, *Kingdom Prologue: Genesis Foundations for a Covenantal Worldview* (Overland Park: Two Age Press, 2000), 164, 244–62; Michael Horton, *God of Promise* (Grand Rapids: Baker, 2006), chap. 6; and VanDrunen, *Divine Covenants and Moral Order*, chap. 2.

[28] I believe the term "mercy" also could appropriately describe God's love in the Noahic covenant. I prefer "forbearance" because I judge that forbearance is clearly distinct from forgiveness, while mercy can imply forgiveness.

detailed guidance. Undoubtedly much must be left to political and judicial wisdom, exercised in the interests of the common good.

Properly interpreting the appeal to the image of God in Genesis 9:6 further strengthens the case for justice-with-forbearance. The appeal to the image in Genesis 9:6 – "Whoever sheds the blood of a human, by a human shall that person's blood be shed; for in his own image God made humankind" – could explain either why the punishment is so severe (i.e. because the slain human being bore God's image) or why a fellow human being has the authority to mete out the punishment (i.e. because bearing God's image entails authority to do justice). Both views have theological plausibility. Although I cannot make a full argument here, the close association between bearing God's image and exercising royal rule on earth in Scripture's first reference to the image (Gen. 1:26) ultimately makes the latter view compelling.[29] Human beings enforce justice as those reflecting God's image, and thus they should temper justice with forbearance as God does.

In this section I have argued that love does in fact have an important place in the divine commission of civil law and government to enforce retributive justice. The enforcement of retributive justice expresses love to God, the victim, the community, and perhaps even the wrongdoer. And love – in the form of forbearance – ought to temper the enforcement of retributive justice. But the central issue of this essay, and the book as a whole, concerns *Christian* love. If we ask whether there is a place for *Christian* love in the work of enforcing retributive justice, is there anything more to say?

6.3 CIVIL LAW AND CHRISTIAN LOVE

I suggest that there is indeed more to say. In response to Murphy's question that opened this essay, I argue in this section that Christian love – insofar as it is distinctively Christian – should not play a role in the organization and evaluation of civil law. This claim depends upon a distinction between more general forms of love and a distinctively Christian form. I will defend the existence of such a distinction and conclude that what is truly distinctive about Christian love is the call to forgo retribution and to forgive freely. The commission of civil law and government is to enforce retributive justice, while the call of Christian love is to forgo it. Thus the work of civil law and government cannot be an expression of love in its distinctively Christian form.

29 For defense of this view, see, e.g., Mason, "Another Flood?" 192–93; W. Randall Garr, *In His Own Image and Likeness: Humanity, Divinity, and Monotheism* (Leiden: Brill, 2003), 163; Kline, *Kingdom Prologue*, 252–53; and VanDrunen, *Divine Covenants and Moral Order*, 116–17.

I wish to clarify one point before proceeding. I do not deny that Christians are obligated to practice the general forms of love discussed in the previous section, that is, the love that enforces and tempers retributive justice. Indeed, love in its general forms obligates all human beings. Christians, I believe, have an additional obligation of love, which is to forgive freely through forgoing retribution. Thus, God calls Christians both to support the work of civil law and government and to practice love in a distinctive form.[30] One might object that this creates mutually contradictory aspects in the Christian's obligation to love. I respond to this concern in the argument that follows.

To begin, I wish to defend the distinction between general forms of love that obligate all people and a distinctive form of love that obligates Christians. I could approach this issue from different paths, but since I have already discussed the Noahic covenant at some length, I will continue to reason in covenantal terms. Specifically, I argue that the distinction between general forms of love and a distinctively Christian form of love is rooted in two divine covenants. The general forms of love are rooted in the Noahic covenant, which binds all human beings, while the distinctively Christian form of love is rooted in the new covenant, which binds those united to Christ by faith.

The Noahic covenant reveals God as the creator of the world who now preserves that world although it is fallen. As noted above, this covenant binds the entire human race, and thus binds every individual, whether he or she has ever heard of the triune God, the God of Abraham, Isaac, and Jacob. This is fitting: God's work of providence encompasses all people universally, and hence the covenant that reveals his providential work extends to and obligates all people universally. As also considered above, in this covenant God treats human beings as those who bear his image. In Genesis 9, as elsewhere in Scripture, the image of God is a morally freighted reality. To be the image of God entails moral responsibilities before God in this world. More specifically, being the image of God entails a commission to carry out God's work in a God-like way. Genesis 1:26 (in the creation story) presented this in terms of exercising benevolent dominion, and Genesis 9:5–6 in terms of administering

30 Some readers may wonder why I have not referred to "agape," a term often employed in discussions of Christian love. I do not see any advantage in using this term. Agape was one of several words for "love" in the Greek language of New Testament days. The New Testament often uses the term and cognates when exhorting Christians to love. But the New Testament also uses other terms for love, such as filoj and cognates, and it often uses these various terms in ways indistinguishable from each other. John 21:15–17 provides a straightforward example. Therefore it seems to me that labeling a specific form of love "agape" may misleadingly suggest that the term "agape" in the New Testament carries a technical meaning that clearly distinguishes it from other Greek words for love. Thus, I prefer not to use "agape" but simply to describe carefully the nature of love as prescribed in various places in Scripture.

justice. God exercised supreme dominion in creating the world, and his image-bearers should exercise a lesser dominion in his service; God holds all people ultimately responsible for their acts of injustice, and his image-bearers should hold their fellow humans penultimately responsible for their acts of injustice. In short, image-bearers are called to image God in their moral lives. And they can only image the God they know, that is, God as he reveals himself to them.

How does this analysis apply to love? It suggests that we should ask what sort of divine love the Noahic covenant reveals, and understand that sort of love as a model of love for the human race generally. The Noahic covenant does in fact reveal God's love, for God shows himself to be benevolent, kind, and generous. Immediately prior to this covenant he has reshaped the earth devastated by flood (Gen. 8:1–19). In the covenant he grants human beings and animals life in the world, and provides good things for people to eat (9:3–4). He also displays forbearance in promising not to send another flood, despite human wickedness (9:11, 15). The loving God of the Noahic covenant seeks and promotes the well-being of his creation in all sorts of ways. Those bearing his image, living under this covenant, ought to pursue an analogous love.

In discussing these matters I assume that the divine moral character revealed in the Noahic covenant is internally harmonious. One aspect does not contradict another. Thus, the love of God revealed in the Noahic covenant is compatible with the revelation of his retributive justice. God enforces retributive justice as creator and sustainer, as Genesis has already revealed (e.g., 2:17; 6:5–7, 11–13) and which later biblical texts repeatedly affirm. There is no conceptual difficulty in understanding the harmony between God's retributive justice and God's love revealed in the Noahic covenant. Benevolence, kindness, generosity, and forbearance are consistent with retributive justice and, as I noted previously, enforcing retributive justice is in fact a manifestation of love toward those who are injured, toward the broader community, and even toward perpetrators of harm. But one sort of love does not seem consistent with retributive justice, and that is forgiveness. Retributive justice holds a person liable for his or her wrong and administers a punishment proportionate to that wrong; in contrast, forgiveness releases a person from liability and does not press punishment. This insight fits the larger theological context. God's work of creation and preservation *per se* does not reveal divine forgiveness. The Noahic covenant never mentions it.

Hence I suggest an initial conclusion. Under the Noahic covenant, God commissions image-bearing human beings to pursue love with justice, or justice in love. But an aspect of this justice is retributive, and thus the love prescribed in the Noahic covenant should only be exercised in a way consistent with enforcing retributive justice. Therefore, the human race under the Noahic covenant ought to abound in benevolence, kindness, generosity, and forbearance, but ought not to forgive when retributive justice demands punishment.

I now turn to the other covenant mentioned above: the new covenant. This covenant does not concern God's work of creation and preservation, but redemption.[31] The new covenant is sealed in Christ's blood (Matt. 26:28; Mark 14:24; Luke 22:20). Not all human beings participate in this covenant, for participation involves baptism, faith, and other things pertaining to the life of the Christian church (see, e.g., Gal. 3:25–29; Heb. 8–11). Christians bound to God under the new covenant are called to lives of love. That is abundantly clear from the New Testament, but in itself that does not make Christians distinctive, since God calls all people to lives of love under the Noahic covenant. But there is something distinctive about Christian love, and this distinctive thing entails a transformed relationship to retributive justice. Under the new covenant, Christian love bestows forgiveness, and it refuses to press the claims of retributive justice insofar as it forgives.

In the preceding discussion, I pointed to the importance of the image-of-God theme for understanding moral obligation under the Noahic covenant. This theme is crucial for moral obligation under the new covenant too. The new covenant promises restoration in the image (rather than creation or preservation in the image), and such restoration entails appropriate moral behavior (e.g., Eph. 4:21–25; Col. 3:8–10). Thus, we would expect new covenant love to reflect the love of God as revealed in the new covenant. This is precisely how the New Testament presents matters. The New Testament calls for Christian love to be analogous to God's love displayed in the death of Christ. Paul puts it this way: "Be kind to one another, tenderhearted, forgiving one another, as God in Christ has forgiven you . . . Live in love, as Christ loved us and gave himself up for us, a fragrant offering and sacrifice to God" (Eph. 4:32; 5:2). The First Epistle of John is similar: "We know love by this, that he laid down his life for us – and we ought to lay down our lives for one another" (3:16); and again shortly thereafter: "In this is love, not that we have loved God but that he

[31] Although I focus here on the new covenant in order to be focused and concrete, I do not mean to imply that the Old Testament never revealed God's redemptive work, for it clearly did. I regard the Abrahamic and Mosaic covenants, for example, as lying in organic continuity with the new covenant and as anticipating the full revelation of God's redemption in Christ, along the lines explained in the Westminster Confession of Faith (7.5–6). In fact, God's redemptive promises appear already in Genesis 3:16 following the account of the fall into sin. Thus, under both Old and New Testaments God has revealed himself as both preserver and redeemer, although different covenants reveal different aspects of God's character and distinct ways he relates to his world in different contexts.

loved us and sent his Son to be the propitiation for our sins. Beloved, if God so loved us, we also ought to love one another" (4:10–11).[32] These texts highlight the self-giving character of this new covenant divine love, and Ephesians 4–5 links it especially to the idea of forgiveness. The New Testament often teaches that divine forgiveness comes through the death of Christ (e.g., Eph. 1:7; Heb. 9:26), and thus it is fitting that Christian love under the new covenant, imaging God's new covenant love at the cross, ought to bestow forgiveness.

The Noahic covenant does not reveal the forgiving love of God, at the cross or otherwise, and hence it does not obligate human beings to forgive. The new covenant reveals the forgiving love of God in the cross of Christ, and hence it obligates Christians to forgive.

But if Christian love is a forgiving love, we would expect it to contrast with retribution. Again, the New Testament meets our expectations. It prohibits Christians from seeking retribution, on several occasions doing so explicitly with reference to the *lex talionis*: "You have heard that it was said, 'An eye for an eye and a tooth for a tooth.' But I say to you, Do not resist an evildoer. But if anyone strikes you on the right cheek, turn the other also" (Matt. 5:38–39); "Do not repay anyone evil for evil. . . . Beloved, never avenge yourselves" (Rom. 12:17, 19); and "Do not repay evil for evil or abuse for abuse; but, on the contrary, repay with a blessing. It is for this that you were called" (1 Pet. 3:9). What the Noahic covenant commands, the new covenant prohibits. A distinctively Christian love is to forgive, and forgiving is to shun retribution.

This Christian love, furthermore, finds institutional embodiment in the life of the church, the community of new covenant participants. In the descriptions of church discipline in Matthew 18:15–20 and 1 Corinthians 5, retributive justice plays absolutely no role in the process. Instead, the purpose of church discipline is to bring wrongdoers to repentance and to restore them to the fellowship of believers. The church should embody corporately the Christian love that forsakes retribution for the sake of forgiveness.

With this, we have come full circle. Something about new covenant Christian love distinguishes it from the general forms of love obliging all human beings. That distinctive element (or at least the only one considered here) is forgiveness, which entails forgoing retribution. The church, which finds its basis in the new covenant, embodies this forgiveness-seeking, retribution-spurning love in its discipline. The state, on the other hand, finds its moral basis in the Noahic covenant, not the new covenant, and thus rightly enforces retributive justice. Therefore, since a distinctively Christian love

[32] This latter translation is from the English Standard Version.

forgoes retribution through forgiveness, and since civil law and government ought to enforce retributive justice, Christian love cannot be the basis for civil law and government. Thus, in response to Murphy's query, law should not be organized or critiqued in terms of Christian love.

6.4 OBJECTIONS AND CLARIFICATIONS

I have now completed the main outline of my argument. But I recognize that readers may wish to raise several significant objections. This final section of the essay attempts to respond to four possible objections that I regard as serious and important. Indeed, I am happy to respond to them, since they provide a good opportunity to elaborate and clarify certain points that I believe will strengthen my overall case.

First, someone might understandably object that my argument seems to imply that Christian love requires people to be unjust. After all, if retributive justice is a valid form of justice, rooted in God's own character and action, and forgiveness entails forgoing retributive justice, then justice and Christian love seem to be at irreconcilable odds.

Since I have presented God as the archetype for both retributive justice and forgiveness, I begin my response by defending the ultimate harmony of divine forgiveness and retributive justice. I suggest that God's forgiveness is not inconsistent with his justice because he forgives through the cross of Christ. Whatever retributive penalty my sins deserved, Christ bore on my behalf (e.g., Isa. 53:5–6; Heb. 9:28; 1 Pet. 2:24). Whatever divine wrath and vengeance stood against me because of my sin, Christ endured when he drank the cup (e.g., Matt. 26:39; Mark 14:36; Luke 22:42; cf. Isa. 51:17; Jer. 25:15). When God forgave me in Christ, he did not ignore his retributive justice but acknowledged that the demands of his retributive justice are satisfied in full.[33] Some have argued that there cannot be both vicarious punishment and forgiveness; if God accepts the punishment of one on behalf of another, he has not really forgiven the other.[34] This has a certain logical attraction, but I fear it imposes

[33] These claims reflect a theology of Christ's atonement often called the "penal substitutionary" view. It is not the only theory of the atonement. I have no space to defend a penal substitutionary view here, but I believe Scripture teaches it as an aspect of its broader presentation of the work of Christ. Among representative Reformed treatments, see John Calvin, *Institutes of the Christian Religion*, vol. 1, ed. John T. McNeill, trans. Ford Lewis Battles (Philadelphia: Westminster Press, 1960), 503–34; and Francis Turretin, *Institutes of Elenctic Theology*, vol. 2, trans. George Musgrave Giger, ed. James T. Dennison, Jr. (Phillipsburg: P&R, 1994), 417–55.

[34] See, e.g., John Miley, *Systematic Theology*, vol. 2 (New York: Eaton & Mains, 1894), 95–6, 310–12; and more recently see Wolterstorff, *Justice in Love*, 192.

upon theology a preconceived notion of what forgiveness must be rather than allowing Scripture to define for theology what God's forgiveness entails. If God declares my sins forgiven through Jesus' bearing their penalty, it is still the case that God forgives *me*. And it is not as though God were simply extracting my penalty from another person; *God himself* bore my penalty. If I deserve a penalty before God the just judge, and God on his own initiative graciously bears the penalty himself, I dare not suggest that God thereby transacts a cold piece of accounting. Whatever cost there is of forgiving me, God assumes it entirely.

This points the way to an initial response to the concern that Christian love (as I have described it) requires Christians to act unjustly. Christians forgive because God has forgiven in Christ. Thus, from one perspective, Christians can forgive others because they believe God has already accounted for the claims of justice in Christ's cross, having reconciled the claims of justice and grace. From another perspective, Christians can forgive others because in doing so they are living parables of God's own forgiving work in Christ. Their acts of forgiveness are not mere ethereal changes of attitude toward those wronging them. They should actually be willing to bear the penalty their wrongdoer deserves. Christians are not simply to forgive the person who slaps them on the cheek; they are to bear a second slap (Matt. 5:39) – the one their assaulter deserved as penalty. They are to restore the person caught in transgression, not by a bare act of pardon but by bearing that person's burdens (Gal. 6:1–2). Distinctively Christian love is a burden-bearing love, a living display of God's new covenant love for sinners in Christ.

Thus, in response to the first objection, Christian love does not require injustice. When Christians forgo retributive justice they do so only in response and in testimony to the satisfaction of the claims of retributive justice in Christ's cross. Another part of my response to this first objection could be this: Christian love does not set Christians in opposition to justice because Christians should support the work of retributive justice carried out by civil law and government. But I think it will be most helpful to address this issue as a separate objection, and I proceed to do so now.

This second possible objection is that my claims are self-contradictory, because I assert that Christians participate in both the Noahic covenant and the new covenant, and thus are required both to promote retributive justice and to reject retribution through forgiving love. Or, to put it another way, I imply that Christians both may share in the work of civil law and government and must shun the enforcement of the justice God calls law and government to pursue. In response, I wish to be clear that I do indeed believe that Christians should be supportive of the work of law and government, and may hold civil office. The fact that Christians remain under the Noahic covenant is good reason to affirm this. In addition, the New Testament identifies a number of converts to the faith who held civil appointments, even some who literally bore the sword. In no case does Scripture give any intimation that they should have abandoned their posts (Matt. 8:5–13; Luke 7:1–10; Acts 10:24–48). This need not create any contradiction in the Christian life. Christians may hold civil office and serve God and neighbor nobly in this capacity, but should not use their civil appointments to carry out their call to forgive. Christians can serve God in many legitimate vocations and through many legitimate institutions, but each vocation and institution has its own purposes and limitations. The task of Christians *as civil officials* is to carry out the state's work of justice, not their call to forgive.

A third objection may flow from the preceding: my claims seem to imply that Christians are only to exhibit their distinctive love of forgiveness within the walls of the church, while New Testament evidence points strongly against this. My proposal may seem to create an untenable dualistic bifurcation between a distinctively Christian life within the Christian community and a non-recognizably Christian life elsewhere.

I begin my response by noting what I said above about Christian love and the church. The church is the *institutional embodiment* of a distinctively Christian love. This is not the same thing as saying that Christians may only display their distinctively Christian love when dealing with other believers in ecclesiastical life. As God established the new covenant in the work of Christ, Christ only established one institution: "on this rock I will build my church, and the gates of Hades will not prevail against it" (Matt. 16:18). Many other human institutions are legitimate and important, but only the church has sprouted from new covenant soil. Thus, the church's institutional life should – to apply Murphy's language in a different context – be organized and criticized by means of a distinctively Christian love. But the New Testament also intimates that Christians should seek to extend their distinctively Christian love beyond their intra-ecclesiastical relationships. Jesus' commands to turn the other cheek and to go the second mile (Matt. 5:39, 41) surely do not envision the experience of a Christian worship service. Paul writes: "whenever we have an opportunity, let us work for the good of all, and especially for those of the family of faith" (Gal. 6:10). Christians indeed have many opportunities to show Christian love, to a variety of people in a variety of settings, and ought to take advantage of them. Carrying out the work of a civil office that exists to enforce retributive justice, however, is not such an opportunity. Maintaining distinctions among vocations and institutions is not dualistic or bifurcating; it is simply, I believe, a result of careful thinking for the sake of serving God and neighbor faithfully.

Fourth and finally, one might object that my conclusions do not correspond with New Testament statements that love is the summary of the law (e.g., Rom. 12:9). Such statements, I note first, refer to the Mosaic law, so it is appropriate to ask: in what sense does love summarize the law given at Sinai? The Mosaic law comprises complex collections of rules meant to govern the life of Israel, God's old covenant people. In many respects it reflected the obligations of love flowing from the Noahic covenant, as discussed earlier. The Mosaic law in various ways commends benevolence, kindness, and generosity. It also contains several stark exhortations to administer the *lex talionis* (Exod. 21:23–25; Lev 24:18–21; Deut. 19:21). But love in the form of forgiveness also appears in the Mosaic law, at least in rules pertaining to the sacrificial system (e.g., Lev. 4:20, 26, 31, 35; 5:18; 6:7). Many sacrifices provided expiation for the guilt of sin, which the New Testament interprets as anticipating the perfect and final sacrifice of Christ (e.g., Heb. 9–10). In light of these various elements of the Mosaic law – both reflecting the Noahic covenant and anticipating the new covenant – it seems entirely appropriate to call love its summary.

Even more interesting to my mind are New Testament texts that speak a bit differently, calling (Christian) love the *fulfillment* of the (Mosaic) law (Rom. 13:8, 10; Gal. 5:14; cf. Matt. 5:17). This seems to be a way of saying that all of God's purposes in giving the law find their completion in new covenant love. This beautiful idea relates to my previous comments about how God's forgiving love in Christ does not cancel out retributive justice but ensures that retributive justice's claims against sinners are fully satisfied *and* that sinners are forgiven and reconciled to God. God's new covenant love in Christ realizes all of the law's purposes – from God's holy judgment against sin to his gracious forgiveness – and Christians individually and the church corporately have the high privilege of displaying this truth in their conduct here and now. And one day the kingdom of righteousness, peace, and joy in the Holy Spirit (Rom. 14:17), foreshadowed now in the church as it loves according to Christ's command, will be revealed in full glory in the new creation.[35]

6.5 CONCLUSION

In this essay I have taken up the old question of the relationship of law and love. I have argued, as a matter of Christian theology, that God has commissioned civil law and government to enforce retributive justice. This commission is rooted in the Noahic covenant and confirmed in Romans 13.

[35] For more detailed exploration of these ideas, see VanDrunen, *Divine Covenants and Moral Order*, 448–69. This includes discussion of the Sermon on the Mount.

A general love of benevolence, kindness, and forbearance – also rooted in the Noahic covenant – is expressed through this justice and properly tempers its strict administration. But a distinctively Christian love, rooted in the new covenant in Christ's blood and requiring forgiveness in place of retribution, has no proper role in the organization and evaluation of civil law. New covenant love is profound, but God simply did not intend it to shape the limited purposes of Noahic law and government. If we are looking for something by which to organize and evaluate civil law, I suggest that the justice of the Noahic covenant is a much better choice than the Christian love of the new covenant.[36]

[36] I have attempted to show what that might look like in a number of essays: "A Natural Law Right to Religious Freedom: A Reformed Perspective," *International Journal for Religious Freedom* 5.2 (2012): 135–46; "The Market Economy and Christian Ethics: Refocusing Debate Through the Two-Kingdoms Doctrine," *Journal of Markets and Morality* 17 (Spring 2014): 11–45; "The Natural Law and Liberal Traditions: Heritage (and Hope?) of Western Civilization," in *The Law of God: Exploring God and Civilization*, ed. Pieter Vos and Onno Zijlstra (Leiden: Brill, 2014), 64–83; "Natural Rights in Noahic Perspective," *Faulkner Law Review* 6.1 (Fall 2014): 103–34; "The Protectionist Purpose of Law: A Moral Case From the Biblical Covenant with Noah," *Journal of the Society of Christian Ethics* 35.2 (Fall/Winter 2015): 101–17; and *Power to the People*, 4–18.

PART III

"WHAT'S LOVE GOT TO DO WITH IT?"[1] APPLICATIONS OF AGAPE TO LAW

Authors in this Part provide assessments of agape's application to particular areas of law. The essays appear roughly in order of the size of the group or entity affected by law, from individual criminal defendants (Jeffrie G. Murphy on punishment and Charles Mathewes on judging) and injured parties (Michael Moreland on torts), through vulnerable groups (Lucia Silecchia on the elderly and Jennifer Lee Koh on immigrants), to commercial institutions and their rights and responsibilities (Thomas C. Berg on intellectual property and Lyman Johnson on corporations), and finally to nations (Alberto Coll on international politics).

These essays bring the promise and challenge of agape to contested questions of contemporary importance. Biblical themes run throughout the analyses: love of enemies and aliens, human judgment, violence and peace, care for the sick and poor, and the responsibilities of wealth and power. In addition, some authors give substantial attention to treatment of agape and law within particular Christian traditions and by some seminal Christian theologians.[2]

1 Song written by Terry Britten and Graham Lyle and recorded by Tina Turner (Capital Records, 1984). Turner's question has been raised as to law in W. Burlette Carter, "What's Love Got to Do with It? Race Relations and the Second Great Commandment," in *Christian Perspectives on Legal Thought*, ed. Michael W. McConnell, Robert F. Cochran, Jr. and Angela C. Carmella (New Haven: Yale University Press, 2001), 133; and Lynn Branham "'What's Love Got to Do With It?' Incarceration in the United States and Conditions of Confinement," presentation at the "Love and Law" Conference, Pepperdine University School of Law, February 7–8, 2014.

2 See discussion in essays by Mathewes (on Augustine), Moreland (on Aquinas, Kant, and Gene Outka), Silecchia (on Catholic Social Thought), Koh (on evangelicalism), and Coll (on Reinhold Niebuhr).

7

Christian Love and Criminal Punishment

Jeffrie G. Murphy

What would law be like if we organized it around the value of Christian love, and if we thought about and criticized law in terms of that value? Christian love, as a divine command, is of course not identical with either philia (friendship love) or eros (erotic love), although it may incorporate elements of both. Christian love is rather that kind of universal (that is, non-particular) love called agape or love of neighbor. American philosopher John Rawls claimed that "justice is the first virtue of social institutions."[1] But what if we considered agape to be the first virtue? What would social institutions – law in particular – be like?

My primary focus in this chapter will be to explore criminal law and the practice of criminal punishment from a perspective of Christian love. Why should anyone really care about such an exploration? Almost everyone would acknowledge that Christianity's emphasis on the moral and spiritual significance of the inner life exercised great influence on the development of a comparable emphasis on this in Western criminal law – for example, the idea that *mens rea* (intent) is generally required for conviction of any serious crime. But this general rejection of strict liability, one might think, has more to do with justice than with love, and this may still leave one with the question of why one should care about the value of love in thinking about criminal law.

One might begin to answer this question by noting that one does not have to choose between love and justice and that, indeed, justice (properly understood) may be entailed by love (properly understood). Former Archbishop of Canterbury William Temple put it this way: "It is axiomatic that love should be the predominant Christian impulse and that justice is the primary form of

A slightly different version of this essay originally appeared in the following book and is reprinted herein with permission: John Witte, Jr. and Frank S. Alexander, eds. *Christianity and Law: An Introduction* (New York: Cambridge University Press, 2008).

1 John Rawls, *A Theory of Justice* (Cambridge: Harvard University Press, 1999), 3.

love in social organization."[2] To say that one is acting in a loving way while subjecting a person to unjust oppression can only be seen as a sick joke.

In addition to welcoming Archbishop Temple's invitation to think of justice as a part of love, I also have some personal reasons for caring about the issue of love and punishment. Because of my upbringing, I have always been someone whose moral sensibilities are grounded – even when in the past I called myself an atheist – in the Christian tradition, a religious tradition that makes love of neighbor central. When a person brought up as a Christian becomes an atheist, he tends to become a Christian atheist. The questions he chooses to make central and many of the answers that tempt him are often framed, even if he does not realize it, by the very set of beliefs he claims to reject. I suspect that this is true for other religions as well. I suspect, for example, that my Protestant upbringing had a great deal to do with the fact that early in my studies I was so drawn to the moral philosophy of German philosopher Immanuel Kant, a philosopher who has been interpreted, with some justice, as seeking a secular and rational defense for what is essentially a Protestant moral vision. The child is father of the man, as Wordsworth reminded us.

Of course, even those outside the Christian tradition generally celebrate some version of the value of love. We know from popular culture and music that "love makes the world go round," that "love conquers all," and that "all we need is love." One might thus find it both interesting and puzzling to consider how, if at all, that value can consistently sit with law – particularly criminal law, which often seems a very harsh and unloving institution.

Finally, there is a great deal of public sermonizing from politicians these days – far too much for my taste – that purports to draw the basic tenets of Christianity into political decision-making. It might be useful to examine what the actual legal consequences of Christianity properly interpreted would be, consequences that could turn out to be quite different from those represented in much current political posturing. As the bloody record of historical Christianity clearly reveals, those in power who speak the language of love do not always act in loving ways but can instead be vessels of intolerance, persecution, hatred, and cruelty.

I realize that I cannot speak for all Christians or survey Christian scholarship in a brief chapter, but I can, at most, give my own "take" on what Christianity has to offer on the topics of crime and punishment. Neither can I explore every aspect of the relationship between criminal law and love. So I shall focus on only one aspect: the nature of *forgiveness* – often seen as a paradigm Christian virtue – and its relation to criminal law and criminal justice. I focus on this aspect because many people seem to think that forgiveness is at odds with

[2] Lord Denning, *The Influence of Religion on Law* (Alberta: Canadian Institute for Law, Theology, and Public Policy, 1997), 3.

criminal punishment, that to the degree we are forgiving then to that degree we will oppose punishment. Indeed, in a recent provocative essay, Notre Dame law professor Thomas Shaffer goes even farther than this. In developing what he calls a "jurisprudence of forgiveness," Shaffer argues that forgiveness is not simply incompatible with criminal punishment but with the very idea of law itself. Speaking of those prisoners securely imprisoned on death row, he writes:

> There is no rational argument any longer to kill them – much less the common good argument Caiaphas had for killing Jesus. Legal power, it seems, has to kill them anyway, if only because it would not be legal power if it didn't. Law here cannot take the risk of forgiveness. Forgiveness would remove the fear, the accountability, and the responsibility that law provides – and this, as law sees it, would invite chaos [because] . . . forgiveness disrupts legal order.[3]

Shaffer's claim strikes me as deeply wrong – confused all the way down, if I may say so. I think that he misunderstands both forgiveness and love, and thus misunderstands the relationship that forgiveness and love bear to law and punishment. I realize that this is a strong claim made against a distinguished academic who has produced much admirable work, and I will have an uphill fight making a case for it. Since many people share some version of this confusion, however, unmasking it is worth a shot.

7.1 THE LOVE COMMANDMENT

Before getting into the details of a law-versus-loving forgiveness debate, however, let me begin with a bit of background, and remind you of the Christian love commandment itself. It occurs most famously in Luke 10:25–37 when a lawyer – yes, a lawyer – interrogates Jesus and asks him how one might gain eternal life. Jesus answers that the lawyer knows the answer to this question already, for it is found in Jewish law: "You shall love the Lord your God with all your heart, and with all your soul, and with all your strength, and with all your mind, and your neighbor as yourself." Continuing his cross-examination, the lawyer then asks: "And who is my neighbor?" Jesus replies not with a definition of "neighbor" but with the parable of the Good Samaritan.[4]

Two things relevant to the present chapter are worth noting about this scriptural passage. First, it must be emphasized that, for the Christian, what happens to the human soul – in this life and the next – is of primary concern. Note that

[3] Thomas L. Shaffer, "The Radical Reformation and the Jurisprudence of Forgiveness," in *Christian Perspectives on Legal Thought*, ed. Michael W. McConnell, Robert F. Cochran, Jr., and Angela C. Carmella (New Haven: Yale University Press, 2001), 325–26.

[4] All references to the Bible are taken from the English Standard Version (ESV), unless otherwise noted.

the love commandment is endorsed by Jesus as the correct answer to the question "What shall I do to inherit eternal life?" Thus a central question for the Christian with respect to punishment must be, not simply what will happen to the body, but what will happen to the soul. (Those who prefer a less metaphysically rich term might here substitute "character" for "soul.") One who is impatient with this concern must necessarily be impatient with Christianity at its core and thus with much of what Christianity will have to say about punishment.

Second, and intimately related to the first point, is the importance of not mistakenly interpreting the role played by the parable of the Good Samaritan in this scriptural passage. If one mistakenly sees this parable as primarily an answer to the question "What is love?" one might be led to see agape as nothing more than what could be called liberal compassion – helping the sick, the despised, and the poor. The love commandment surely involves that, as it involves justice, but I think that it also involves much more. The actual question answered through the parable, however, is not "What is love?" but is rather "Who is my neighbor?" The answer that seems to emerge from the parable is that *all human beings* are to be seen as neighbors. As Danish theologian and philosopher Søren Kierkegaard puts it: "when you open the door that you shut in order to pray to God and go out the very first person you meet is the neighbor whom you *shall* love"[5] – regardless of whether that person is your enemy, a member of some despised group, your king, a criminal, or someone who strikes you as intrinsically and grotesquely unlovable.[6] This is a doctrine of universalism, in contrast to tribalism, with respect to loving concern. Some Christians like to claim that it is unique to the moral outlook of Christianity, but in fact a similar kind of moral universalism can be found in some aspects of Stoicism and Judaism, and I suspect elsewhere as well.[7]

There are, of course, many fascinating questions that could be raised about the love commandment. Does it command love as an emotion or simply that we act in a certain way? Kant, convinced that we can be morally bound only to that which is in our control and believing (hastily in my view) that emotions are not in our control, called emotional love *pathological love* and claimed that it could not be our duty to feel it. What is actually commanded he called *practical love*, which is simply acting morally, as Kant conceived it.[8] In the

5 Søren Kierkegaard, *Works of Love*, ed. and trans. Howard V. Hong and Edna H. Hong (Princeton: Princeton University Press, 1995), 51.

6 Ibid., 17–90.

7 See David Novak, "Law and Religion in Judiasm," and Brian Tierney, "Natural Law and Natural Rights," in *Christianity and the Law: An Introduction*, eds. John Witte, Jr. and Frank S. Alexander (New York: Cambridge University Press, 2008).

8 Immanuel Kant, "Groundwork of the Metaphysics of Morals," trans. Thomas K. Abbott, ed. Lara Dennis (Ontario: Broadview Editions, 2005), 61.

century after Kant, Kierkegaard famously raised a variety of additional puzzles about Christian love of neighbor. He assumed that we would all agree that most human beings seem to be anything but lovable.[9] (If you think it is possible to love everyone, just look around in a supermarket, as Ayn Rand once suggested.) Given the apparent unlovability of those Kierkegaard called "your very unpoetic neighbors," would it be possible to love them absent a divine command to do so? Kierkegaard thought not.[10] And to what degree, if at all, is the command of love of neighbor compatible with the particular love of lovers, spouses, children, parents, friends, and one's own country that Kierkegaard calls "preferential"?[11] Such love seems to many of us among the crowning glories of human life and thus most of us will not look with favor upon Jesus' teaching that "anyone [who] comes to me and does not hate his own father and mother and wife and children and brothers and sisters, yes, and even his own life, . . . cannot be my disciple" (Luke 14:26). Even most devout Christians will seek some way of interpreting this remark to keep it from having the unhappy consequence it seems to have upon first reading.

Given my limited purposes to explore the place of agapic forgiveness in the context of law, particularly criminal punishment, I think that all I will need to say about love here is the following, which I hope most interpreters of Christianity would find non-controversial: agape is not simply a matter of being nice and cuddly – of giving everyone a warm hug, saying "have a nice day," and sending them on their way. In spite of what the secular mind and even some religious believers might wish, the full doctrine of agape is to be found not simply in the social gospel films of Frank Capra, but also in the grim stories of Flannery O'Connor and in the hard and demanding theologies of Augustine and Kierkegaard. "God loves you whether you like it or not," as the bumper sticker says.

One of the things that is manifestly not cuddly about agape, at least as I understand it, perhaps shows the influence of ancient Greek thought on love and friendship (philia). It is this: agapic love is concerned not simply with satisfying preferences, alleviating distress, providing for people's material well-being, and thereby making their lives more pleasant – what I earlier called liberal compassion. It is also centrally concerned with promoting their moral and spiritual good – helping their souls or characters to grow in *virtue*. (Recall Aristotle's discussion of what he calls "the perfect form of friendship."[12]) In this way, a legal order dominated by agape would almost certainly be

9 Kierkegaard, *Works of Love*.

10 Ibid.

11 Ibid.

12 Aristotle, *Nichomachean Ethics* (Indianapolis: Hackett Publishing, 2014), 139–40 (see 136–74).

more paternalistic than would be acceptable to the more value-neutral and libertarian versions of political liberalism of, say, John Rawls or Ronald Dworkin. Those motivated by agape, as a basic principle, will (subject no doubt to some major side-constraints of a prudential nature) seek to design legal practices and institutions with a view to the moral and spiritual improvement in virtue of affected citizens.

In the area of free expression, just to give one example, such persons will probably seek greatly to restrain the corrupt and corrosive availability of pornography – refusing to see its production, distribution, and consumption as an important human liberty. They might very reluctantly allow pornography for practical or instrumental reasons if they think that it is impossible to design a legal prohibition that would not constrain legitimate expression. But they would never seek to protect it in principle under the general heading of a fundamental right of personal autonomy. Rather than seeing basic rights as freedom to exercise unrestrained "do your own thing" autonomy, they would tend to see such rights (as some perfectionist liberals see them) as freedom to choose only among options that could all be part of a good life. Thus they would see conversation about the good life as being central to law and politics, not as a "private" matter that should be left out of the political and legal domains. This suggests that there may be some interesting tensions between some forms of political liberalism and agapic love as I have conceptualized it – tensions that might force some choices that many would find hard and unattractive.

For the law of crime and punishment, those motivated by agape will seek punitive practices that contribute to, or at least do not retard, the moral and spiritual rebirth of criminals. It is perhaps regrettable, but true, that there may be little that the state can do actively to promote virtuous character. This might be because the state is sometimes nothing but a collection of inept apparatchiks who cannot even deliver the mail. Or it could be because, even at its best, the state must be very cautious about using state power to encourage a particular vision of the good life, in an environment of religious pluralism and free exercise of religion. For such a vision may capture the moral view from only one segment of those with deep and serious commitments to seeking what they deem to be the good life. I, for one, am less concerned about those who are indifferent to the good life and who want only to revel under an uncritical "do your own thing" conception of liberty.

But surely, even under these constraints, it ought to be possible to do *something* for prisoners that would be potentially character-building. If Aristotle is right, then virtue is often acquired through a process of *habituation* – becoming by doing – and encouraging certain habits might promote, for example, a virtuous kind of empathetic kindness often absent or greatly limited in criminal wrongdoers. A small start in this direction might involve something as simple as the Prison Dog Project, a program in which prisoners care for dogs and thereby perhaps develop some of the virtues that come from the receiving and giving of love they have been missing in their prior lives. This program is only one small thing, but great things often consist of many small things.

Even those who remain skeptical of all positive programs for character reform, however, should still at the very least seek to create a prison environment where opportunities for positive character development are not radically minimized or even extinguished by unspeakable conditions. For example, those who claim to champion agapic love should be on the forefront of any movement to eliminate those current aspects of criminal punishment and prison life, such as gang rape, that – to put it mildly – are hardly likely to encourage the reflection, repentance, and spiritual rebirth that should be hoped for from those culpable of serious wrongdoing. In this case, religious believers and traditional secular liberals should find, and have found, themselves united. The Prison Rape Elimination Act, for example, enacted by Congress in 2003, was supported by diverse agencies and individuals: Amnesty International, Human Rights Watch, Senator Ted Kennedy, the Southern Baptist Ethics and Religious Liberty Commission, and Charles Colson's Prison Fellowship Ministries.

Of course, none of this is even worth thinking about if Shaffer is correct that (1) the duty to forgive is mandated by the love commandment and (2) forgiveness is incompatible with criminal punishment.[13] I think he is right about (1), but dead wrong about (2), and so I will now move to a discussion of forgiveness, its nature, value, and relation to punishment.

7.2 FORGIVENESS AND PUNISHMENT

What is forgiveness? I think that one of the most insightful discussions of forgiveness ever penned is found in Bishop Joseph Butler's 1726 sermon "Upon Forgiveness of Injuries" and its companion sermon "Upon Resentment."[14] These sermons are long and carefully reasoned philosophical essays on the character of forgiveness, and they must have greatly tried the patience of his congregation. According to Butler, forgiveness is a moral virtue (a virtue of

[13] Shaffer, *Jurisprudence of Forgiveness*, 52.

[14] *Works of Joseph Butler*, ed. W. E. Gladstone, vol. 2, *Sermons* (Oxford: Clarendon Press, 1897), 115–41.

character) that is essentially a matter of the heart, the inner self, and involves a change in inner feeling more than a change in external action.[15] The change in feeling is the overcoming, on moral grounds, of the intensely negative and reactive attitudes that are quite naturally occasioned when one has been wronged by another – the passions of resentment, anger, the desire for revenge, and even hatred. We may call these the vindictive passions. A person who has forgiven has overcome those vindictive passions and has overcome them for a morally creditable motive – for example, being moved by repentance on the part of the person by whom one has been wronged. Of course, such a change in feeling often leads to a change of behavior – reconciliation, for example. But, as our forgiving of the dead illustrates, change in feeling does not always change behavior. Forgiveness, so understood, is often a good thing because it may allow us to reconcile and restore relationships of value, free us from the inner turmoil that may come from harboring grudges, and free us from an overly narcissistic involvement with our own unjust victimizations, for it seems the common human tendency is often to magnify such victimizations out of all reasonable proportion.

None of this shows, however, that forgiveness – particularly hasty and uncritical forgiveness – is *always* a good thing. Sometimes forgiveness mistakenly tempts us into restoring relationships that would be better left permanently ruptured. Also, hastily overcoming anger and resentment through forgiveness may sometimes show insufficient self-respect, since feeling such reactive emotions when wronged is a characteristic sign of self-respect. This is no doubt the point of S. J. Perelman's famous quip: "to err is human; to forgive, supine." The popular self-help literature on forgiveness tends to stress only its benefits, but I think it is important to note at least some of its potential costs.[16]

On my Butler-inspired analysis of forgiveness as a victim's change of heart toward culpable wrongdoing, it is useful initially to distinguish forgiveness from four other responses to wrongdoing with which forgiveness is often confused: justification, excuse, mercy, and reconciliation. Although these concepts are to some degree open-textured and can bleed into each other, clarity is served if one at least starts by attempting to separate them. I discuss each of them briefly.

[15] Ibid.

[16] Butler believed the benefit of forgiveness is a God-given check on the valuable passions of resentment and anger, which are necessary to defend one's own rights, the rights of others, and the moral order itself. For uncannily similar observations, see Reinhold Niebuhr, "Anger and Forgiveness," in *Discerning the Signs of the Times—Sermons for Today and Tomorrow* (London: S.C.M. Press, 1946), 26–39.

Justification. To regard conduct as justified (as in lawful self-defense, for example) is to claim that the conduct, though normally wrongful, was the right thing to do in the given circumstances and all things considered. In such cases, there is nothing legitimately to resent and thus nothing to forgive.

Excuse. To regard conduct as excused (as in the insanity defense, for example) is to admit that the conduct was wrong but to claim that the person who engaged in the conduct was not a fully responsible agent. Responsible agency is, of course, a matter of degree. But to the degree that the person who injures me is not a responsible agent, resentment of that person would make no more sense than resenting the wasp that stings me. Again, there is nothing here to forgive.

Mercy. To accord a wrongdoer mercy is to inflict a less harsh consequence on that person than allowed by institutional (usually legal) rules. Mercy is less personal than forgiveness, since the one granting mercy (a sentencing judge, say) typically will not be a victim of wrongdoing and thus will not have any feelings of resentment to overcome. (There is a sense in which only victims of wrongdoing have what might be called *standing* to forgive.) Mercy also has a public behavioral dimension not necessarily present in forgiveness. I can forgive a person simply in my heart of hearts, but I cannot show mercy simply in my heart of hearts. I can forgive the dead, but I cannot show mercy to the dead.

This distinction between mercy and forgiveness allows us to see why there is no inconsistency in fully forgiving a person for wrongdoing but still advocating that the person suffer the legal consequence of criminal punishment. Here you see one of my primary disagreements with Professor Shaffer. To the degree that criminal punishment is justified in order to secure victim satisfaction, then of course the fact that the victim has forgiven will be a relevant argument for reducing the criminal's sentence and the fact that a victim still resents will be a relevant argument for increasing that sentence. It is highly controversial, of course, that criminal punishment should to *any* degree be harnessed to a victim's desires. Such considerations are generally considered only in assessing damages in a private suit in tort. Even if the criminal punishment is partly calibrated by the victim's desires, however, it must surely be admitted that the practice of punishment serves other values as well, such as crime control and justice. With respect to these values, a victim's forgiveness could hardly be dispositive. In short, it would indeed be inconsistent for a person to claim that he has forgiven the wrongdoer and still advocate punishment for the wrongdoer in order to satisfy his personal vindictive feelings. If he still has those feelings, he has not forgiven the wrong or the wrongdoer. It would not be inconsistent, however, to advocate punishment for other legitimate reasons – for example, crime control and just deserts. Of course, the possibilities for self-deception are enormous here. As Friedrich Nietzsche reminded us, our high-sounding talk about justice and public order is often simply a rationalization for envy, spite, malice, and outright cruelty – the cluster of emotions for which Nietzsche used the loaded French term *ressentiment*.[17]

But what about mercy itself as a virtue independent of forgiveness? Is it not also required, as an aspect of Christian love, to exhibit mercy in dealing with wrongdoers? And would this not involve mercy to criminals? I think that the answer to this question is yes. Yet it is important to see that the requirement to exhibit mercy is best understood not as a requirement never to punish, but rather as a requirement to develop a character that is not hardened and rigidly formalistic – a requirement that leaves room for considering relevant features of a criminal (remorse, repentance, or apology, for example) that might legitimately incline one to favor a reduced sentence for that criminal. This is most appropriately done in an executive clemency decision rather than at the time of sentencing.

Reconciliation. The vindictive passions (those overcome in forgiveness) are often a major barrier to reconciliation. Since forgiveness often leads to reconciliation, it is thus easy to confuse the two concepts. I think, however, it is important to see how they may differ – how there can be forgiveness without reconciliation, and how there can be reconciliation without forgiveness.

For an example of forgiveness without reconciliation, imagine a battered woman who has been repeatedly beaten and raped by her thuggish husband or boyfriend. This woman – after a religious conversion, perhaps – might well come to forgive her batterer (for example, stop being angry with him) without a willingness to resume her relationship with him. "I forgive you and wish you well" can, in my view, sit quite consistently with "I will never allow you in this house again." In short, the fact that one has forgiven does not mean that one must also trust or live again with a person.

For an example of reconciliation without forgiveness, consider the South African Truth and Reconciliation Commission. In order to negotiate a viable

[17] As I have argued in my "Legal Moralism and Retribution Revisited," *Proceedings of the American Philosophical Association* 80, no. 2 (2006): 45–62, one must be careful about how one understands the idea of criminal just desert. This idea legitimately focuses our attention on the criminal's act, the intentionality of that act, and the degree of responsibility for that act. However, if one employs the concept of just desert to target deep character, ultimate evil, or what Kant called "inner viciousness," then one is presuming to judge what no human being should presume to judge. For "thou, [God] thou only, knowest the hearts of all the children of men" (1 Kings 8:39, American Standard Version). It is hard enough for us to discern the shallows of intentions to surmise the utter futility of probing the depths of character – for whether, to use some language from American homicide law, the criminal has "a hardened, abandoned, and malignant heart" or a character that is "cruel, heinous and depraved."

transition from apartheid to democratic government with full black participation, all parties had to agree that there would in most cases be no punishment for evil acts that occurred under the previous government. Politically motivated wrongdoers, by making a full confession and accepting responsibility, would typically be granted amnesty. In this process the wrongdoers would not be required to repent, show remorse, or even apologize. I can clearly see this process as one of reconciliation (although I might prefer the term cooperation) – a process that would allow all to work toward a democratic and just future. I do not so easily see this process as one of forgiveness, however. No change of heart was required or even sought from the victims – no overcoming of such vindictive feelings as anger, resentment, or hatred. All that was hoped of them was a willingness to accept this process as a necessary means to the future good of their society.

It should now be obvious why I reject Shaffer's claim that agapic forgiveness is incompatible with legal punishment. In my view, following Bishop Butler, forgiveness is mainly a matter of a change of heart, not of external practice.

So can forgiveness of a person, thus understood, still be compatible with the continued demand that the person be punished – perhaps even executed? In my view the answer to this question is yes. It all depends on the *motive* or *reason* for the demand. If the motive or reason is to satisfy one's vindictive passions, then of course there is immediate inconsistency. If one still retains those passions, one has not forgiven. Thus an appeal to agapic forgiveness does constitute a powerful attack on legal punishment to the degree that such punishment is driven by vindictive passions, particularly by hatred.

Of course, if one is doing something truly horrendous to another human being, the chance that hatred and cruelty are behind it should not be too quickly dismissed. In fact, many present penal practices in America are, alas, hard to understand on any other terms. To return to my earlier example of prison conditions, Mary Sigler has recently written on such terrible conditions as subjecting inmates to repeated acts of forced sodomy, which prison officials and the public generally tolerate. She notes that the popular media freely makes jokes about this. For example, there was a soft drink commercial in which someone is handing out cans to prison inmates, drops one on the floor, and notes that in this environment it probably would not be a good idea to bend over and pick it up. The commercial closes with a scene in which the soft drink huckster is shown sitting at a table with a large inmate who has an arm around him. The voiceover says that this drink makes friends, the inmate tightens his arm, and the huckster says in dismay "not that kind of friend." What kind of a society is it that knows about forced sodomy in prison and feels comfortable making jokes about it? In trying to answer this question, the words "hatred" and "cruelty" certainly come to my mind.[18]

Callous indifference also deserves a place next to hatred as something that is ruled out by agape – something that should be guarded against in the realm of punishment. Recall the New Testament parable in which a servant, who had his debt forgiven out of compassion from his master, is blind to the suffering of one of his own servants and shows no compassion when that servant cannot pay a debt to him (Matthew 18:23–35). The sin of the forgiven servant inflicting harsh treatment on his own servant was not based on any hatred he felt toward his servant. Rather, it was a radical failure of compassion, a total indifference to the adverse life circumstances that caused the servant to become indebted – the very kind of life circumstances that the master, out of compassion, had taken account of in showing mercy to him. As Raimond Gaita (drawing on Simone Weil) argued, our indifference to the suffering of those whom we regard as outsiders – an indifference that makes them invisible to us – often flows from an incapacity to see anything that could *go deep* in their inner lives, a failure to find it even intelligible that someone could love them. This is at least part of what Simone Weil meant when she said that "love sees what is invisible."[19]

Suppose, however, that the motive or reason for punishment is not grounded in any vindictive passion or in callous indifference of the kind just noted. Suppose, rather, it is grounded in the sincere belief that punishment of the kind prescribed is necessary to control crime and thereby promote the common good. Or suppose punishment is required by justice (what the criminal deserves for his wrongdoing), or that it will be instrumental in the moral and spiritual transformation of the criminal. Then, even if one has doubts about one or more of these justifications, those doubts cannot legitimately be grounded in the claim that they are inconsistent with the demands of Christian love.

The main point, then, is this: agape does not forbid punishment. What it forbids is *punishment out of hatred or other vindictive passions*. What Jesus counseled, it will be recalled, is that we visit and comfort those in prison; he did not counsel the abolition of prisons (Matt. 25:36). To visit and comfort those in prison – even those justly there – is a way of saying that they are still loved and not hated, that their essential humanity is still being acknowledged, and that we have not presumed to banish them from the domain of loving

[18] See Mary Sigler, "By the Light of Virtue: Prison Rape and the Corruption of Character," *Iowa Law Review* 91 (2006): 561–607.

[19] Raimond Gaita, *A Common Humanity: Thinking About Love and Truth and Justice* (London: Routledge, 2000), 84.

concern. Such loving concern is quite consistent, however, with thinking that it is proper that they be in prison – because they deserve it or for the common good.

As stated above, the possibilities of self-deception here are enormous – particularly the possibility that, as Nietzsche warned, we use the rhetoric of justice and the common good in order to hide from ourselves the fact that our actual motives are instances of *ressentiment* – spite, malice, envy, and cruelty. Thus, although I think that Shaffer overreaches when he uses the virtue of forgiveness to condemn all law and punishment, he has offered an important corrective to much of what we are *actually* doing in contrast to what we say and think we are doing. This contrast is dramatically illustrated when we consider the actual conditions present in many of our jails and prisons. For this he deserves our gratitude.

7.3 LOVE AND THE DEATH PENALTY

In closing, let me briefly say something about agape and capital punishment. The death penalty is so extreme that many might think that, even if much punishment is consistent with agape, this punishment cannot be. This was certainly the view of Catholic theologian Bernard Häring. He acknowledged that the Old Testament is filled with what appear to be robust defenses of capital punishment, but then claimed that "it would not be in harmony with the unique fullness of salvation and its loving kindness to apply drastic [Old Testament] directives without any qualification as obligatory in the present order of salvation and grace."[20]

Not all Christians would agree with Häring, of course, and the fact that so many prominent Christian philosophers and theologians have through the ages been supporters of capital punishment should make us pause before hastily assuming that the practice is inconsistent with agape. However, the enthusiasm expressed by these thinkers for capital punishment has often been radically overstated by supporters of the death penalty. The radio show host and newspaper columnist Dennis Prager, for example, has cited Augustine as a Christian authority to support his belief in the legitimacy of capital punishment. He quoted this passage from *The City of God*: "It is in no way contrary to the commandment 'thou shalt not kill' to put criminals to death according to law or the rule of natural justice."[21]

[20] Bernard Häring, *The Law of Christ* (Westminster: Newman Press, 1966), 3:124.

[21] Dennis Prager, "There's A Moral Reason That McVeigh Must Die..." *Los Angeles Times* (8 June 2001).

Augustine did indeed make this claim, but it takes a great deal of creative free association to turn this into a statement of support for the death penalty. And getting Augustine right is a matter of some importance, since, after Jesus and Paul, he has probably done more than anyone else to set what might be called "the moral tone" of Christianity, at least among educated people. I read Augustine – and here I impose on him a modern distinction – as asserting the *right* of the state to execute but also arguing that *it is almost always wrong for the state to exercise that right*. The state may not be denied to have, in the abstract, the right to execute if this promotes the common good, gives the criminal the punishment that he in justice deserves, or promotes the personal repentance and rebirth of the wrongdoer – the only three objectives that could justify it. (And, before you laugh dismissively at the idea of capital punishment as personal reform, recall Samuel Johnson: "Depend upon it, Sir, when a man knows he is to be hanged in a fortnight, it concentrates his mind wonderfully."[22]) One can hold this view of capital punishment's three possible justifications, however – common good, just deserts, and personal rebirth – and also consistently hold that in every particular case that one knows of or can imagine, execution either does not promote these goals or does not promote them any better than less drastic means. Augustine sometimes argues in this way and indeed, for all his reputation to the contrary, offers some of the most eloquent objections to capital punishment ever given in our culture. For example, in a letter to Marcellinus, the special delegate of the Emperor Honorious to settle the dispute between Catholics and Donatists, Augustine is concerned with the capital punishment to be administered for what must have, to him, seemed the most vicious of crimes: the murder of one Catholic priest and the mutilation of another by members of a radical Donatist faction. He wrote:

> I have been a prey to the deepest anxiety for fear your Highness might perhaps decree that they be sentenced [to death]. Therefore, in this letter, I *beg* you by the faith which you have in Christ and by the mercy of the same Lord Christ, not to do this, not to let it be done under any circumstances. ... [W]e yet do not wish that the martyrdom of the servants of God should be avenged by similar suffering, as if by way of retaliation. ... We do not object to wicked men being deprived of their freedom to do wrong, but we wish it to go just that far, so that, without losing their life or being maimed in any

[22] James Boswell, *Boswell's Life of Johnson*, ed. Charles Grosvenor Osgood (New York: Scribner's Sons, 1917), 338–39. Or, as Flannery O'Connor's Misfit said of his victim: "She would of been a good woman if it had been someone there to shoot her every day of her life." Flannery O'Connor, "A Good Man is Hard to Find," in *Collected Works* (New York: Library of America, 1988), 153.

> part of their body, they may be restrained by the law from their mad frenzy, guided into the way of peace and sanity, and assigned some useful work to replace their criminal activities. It is true, this is called a penalty, but who can fail to see that it should be called a benefit rather than a chastisement when violence and cruelty are held in check, but the remedy of repentance is not withheld?[23]

Of course capital punishment is far too complex an issue and too dependent on a variety of contested empirical claims to be settled here. And philosophy, an *a priori* discipline, is certainly in no position simply to pronounce finally on whether the fear of death as a punishment could ever promote the common good or could ever provoke spiritual rebirth on the part of the criminal. So let me close by making a claim that I can in conscience endorse: to the degree that our willingness to support the death penalty is based on the thoughtless cruel hatred or indifference to the humanity of criminals (and I suspect that much of it is), then it manifestly is not consistent with agape, a love that teaches that all human beings, even the worst among us, are precious because created in the image of God. And thus Christians, Jews, those from many other religions, and decent people who are not religious should, I think, be willing to join in endorsing these words of Ezekiel 33:11: "I have no pleasure in the death of the wicked, but that the wicked turn from his way and live."

[23] Donald X. Burt, *Friendship and Society: An Introduction to Augustine's Practical Philosophy* (Grand Rapids: Wm. B. Eerdmans Publishing Co., 1999), 195–96.

8

"Be Instructed, All You Who Judge the Earth": Law, Justice, and Love during the World

Charles Mathewes

8.1 INTRODUCTION

How should Christians think about the possibilities of justice, and the practices meant to secure it, in this dispensation? More specifically, how should Christians reflect on the duties and implications – civic and theological – of judgment, exercised by judges, but perhaps of relevance far beyond the judicial bench? I want to offer one answer to that question in this essay, by discussing the relationship between law and love, during the world, according to Augustine. Ultimately I want to talk about the *dialectic* of law and love, as I understand Augustine to understand it, as both a political and a theological reality. This dialectic is manifest in a distinct way in the act of judgment, an act which, for Augustine, is something of the acme of politics, where "politics" signifies all those human efforts to achieve something like community, and realize something like truth, in this sinful world. If politics is so understood, it is a semi-sacramental reality where love and justice, providence and prudence, the gospel and the world, each transect and transfigure the other. In fact it is the very worldliness of judgment that reveals its inescapable transfiguration as a theologically significant reality, which transfiguration stands also as a judgment upon our prior misapprehension, and over-estimation, of such judgment, and the worldliness of which it partakes. That is to say, to understand the theological significance of this-worldly justice is simultaneously, on Augustine's terms, to apprehend the true, theological, meaning of judgment, and the ultimate relative insignificance of what we typically call politics, and law, and even justice, during the world.

I thank Robert Cochran, Zak Calo, Mark Storslee, and the other participants of the Pepperdine conference for conversation and instruction on these matters. For its faults I have only myself to thank.

I offer this proposal in support of Jeffrie Murphy's eloquent culminating discussion, in his chapter above on "Christian Love and Criminal Punishment," of Augustine as especially important for Christian thinking about justice. I believe Murphy is right that Augustine asserts "the *right* of the state to execute" while also insisting "that *it is almost always wrong for the state to execute that right*."[1] More generally, my argument is meant to support the late William Stuntz's proposals about the relationship between (civic) justice and (cultural and spiritual) mercy, proposals that seem to me rooted in his broadly Augustinian intuition that "[c]onflating God's law and man's law thus does violence to both. It makes far too much of man's law, and far too little of God's."[2] Augustine's well-known programmatic statements are amenable to multiple developments at the level of policy, of course; but we are well advised to attend to his own more concrete and policy-level statements – typically captured in letters and sermons rather than in his treatises – if only to see how *he* sought to develop them.

I also offer it in supportive response to our editors' initiating question of how agape should be manifest in law. I am broadly in that line of Christian realists whose first intuitions, when they think politically, are so often *critical* – suspicious of sentimental misapprehensions and ham-fisted applications of the Gospel and moralist calcifications of it as well. Yet Christian realism also insists that love and justice must be dialectically interrelated. In Reinhold Niebuhr's terms, justice is the self-limitation of love.[3] Love fuels the drive for justice, but justice is a reflexive self-critique of love in an age of always imperfect, flawed love. Love sees and is moved by the other – so much so, indeed, that it knows to mistrust slightly its own vision and operation, as both are insidiously infected with a large (perhaps for some of us, massive) leaven of self-interest, and so love seeks to set up controls and checks against itself, which are relatively autonomous from itself, as a way of policing love's own ardor. This roots justice in love, as a "strange work" of love, fundamentally emerging from it and ultimately returning to it as well; but it gives justice, during the world, a relative independence as a norm, over against the waves of our various loves.

Here I want to try to bring Murphy's and Stuntz's and our editors' prompts together, and explore how Augustine's reflections on judgment offer guidance both for the agape-informed exercise of law, and the agape-fueled executors

1 Jeffrie G. Murphy, *Punishment and the Moral Emotions: Essays in Law, Morality, and Religion* (Oxford: Oxford University Press, 2012), Chapter VI, 43.

2 David A. Skeel and William J. Stuntz, "Christianity and the (Modest) Rule of Law," *University of Pennsylvania Journal of Constitutional Law* 8 (2006), 809–39 (at 839).

3 See, e.g., Reinhold Niebuhr, *Love and Justice: Selections from the Shorter Writings of Reinhold Niebuhr*, ed. D. B. Robertson (Philadelphia: Westminster, 1957).

of it. I do so for reasons both more civic and more theological – though (as should be clear) I do not think the two ought finally to be divvied up that way. Civically, I write out of alarm at the crisis of criminal justice in the United States today, where corporations often have more rights *as persons* than do persons of color, rich or poor; where a police officer in New York City can get away with no criminal charges for slowly strangling a citizen of color, on camera, but where another police officer, in Colorado, gets four years of probation and a $10,000 fine for shooting an elk.[4] In this setting, justice seems to many little more than a cynical joke, and Christians have a civic duty to understand why we ought to make it more than that. I also do so out of concern that, if Christian theological voices do not help catechize Christian believers across their whole lives, we are failing them in profound ways, and we will be held accountable for that lapse; and the exercise of this-worldly political judgment can be – indeed, on my reading, necessarily *is* – a synecdoche of Christian citizens' engagement in civic life more generally. Both for reasons of pressing import for our earthly cities and for our better membership in the heavenly one, then, a theological reading of justice is imperative.

Before getting to the details of this issue, I should say something about what I take to be the theological context in which this issue presses upon those of us who see ourselves as Christians, and so I will start by saying something about this odd phrase "During the World." Then I will introduce why what I call our predicaments regarding the ideas of judgment and authority present us with a distinct form of this challenge, in this time and place. Here I will discuss Richard Posner's challenge, particularly in *Reflections on Judging*, that judges must engage the "complexity" of cases with the tools of judging, in order to work through the complexity of the case and render vivid, to her or his democratic audience, the core of the matter under consideration, and the judge's judgment about that core. Posner's recognition of the need to render judgment visible is democratically admirable, and worth affirming. But his construal of what that judgment entails and how it proceeds is, I propose, too two-dimensional, and reduces the role of the judge to one of an information-processor, and not that distinctive creature, the *judge*, exercising a distinctive virtue, that of juridical *wisdom*. Then, finally, I will turn to Augustine's thoughts on this subject, drawing out several lessons from his work that may I hope be of interest, civically and theologically, to complement and correct Posner's vision.

4 I am informed by my reading of John Hagan, *Who Are the Criminals? The Politics of Crime Policy from the Age of Roosevelt to the Age of Reagan* (Princeton: Princeton University Press, 2010).

8.1.1 *During the World*

The phrase "During the World" may seem an odd neologism, but in fact it's very old. It appeared as long ago as 1435, as a request in a will "that there be said every day, during the Worlde . . . three masses" for the dead man's soul.[5] The idea behind it is older still. The struggle to grasp the idea expressed by that phrase has been one of the primary tasks of Christian thought from its beginnings.

A whole cosmology is packed into those three words, one suggesting that our immurement in the world as we find it is in some way then not the whole story about us, that our current condition in this dispensation is crucially contingent – at least in the sense that our lives' significance is not absolutely determined by the immanent forces that both press upon us and seem to sustain us. We live not simply in the created order, but in the *factitious* order, and we must recognize that there is a difference between the "world" as we now have it and "creation" as God first made it, and the contours of our situation, East of Eden, are contingent. Yet it insists that the right language in which to register that contingency is not most fundamentally *spatial* (as if there were some *other place* to which we could flee) but rather *temporal*. It helps to recall that the Latin word that we transliterate as "secular" is *saeculum*, which we typically understand to mean "world" but actually more properly means "era" or "age." (This sense is still available in the French word *siècle*.) The phrase "During the World" reminds us to see our situation as inhabiting an *era* more relevantly, and more fundamentally, than a *place* – so that we cannot imagine an "elsewhere" to which we may flee in this context where we would not be marked by the most fundamental conditions of this era, this "world."

And in this recognition of the world's temporal structure, we find a wise recommendation that our mode of inhabiting it should be one of *endurance*. We cannot expect our moral and spiritual lives to be ones of accomplishment; rather, we should expect our lives to be marked by various forms of suffering, including, we hope and pray, suffering the mercy of grace. Our agency is primarily responsive, not pro-active, and successful human life is marked more by waiting, watching, and enduring than by accomplishment or *ex nihilo* action. "In this life," Augustine said, "justice . . . consists more in the forgiveness of sins than the perfection of virtue."[6] This is why, to depict the church,

5 From the will of Richard Beauchamp, Earl of Warwick; see George Holmes, *The Later Middle Ages: 1272–1485* (New York: W. W. Norton, 1962), 180. See also Charles Mathewes, *A Theology of Public Life* (Cambridge: Cambridge University Press, 2007).

6 *De civitate Dei* 19.27: *Ipsa nostra justitia, quamvis vera sit propter veri boni fidem ad quem refertur, tamen tanta est in hac vita, ut potius peccatorum remissione constet quam perfectione virtutum.*

Augustine chose the metaphor of the hospital over against the Pelagians' gymnasium, and grace he depicted as *medicine*, opposed, one imagines (perhaps anachronistically) to the Pelagians' temptation to think of grace as a steroid.

Yet this emphasis on endurance should not blind us to the real presence of genuine goods in our world; just as the desert was an arena of holy dramaturgy for the monks of old, Augustine says, *saeculum autem hoc eremus est*, "the world itself can be our desert," the site where we receive, and endure, the strange mercy of God's redemption and sanctification.[7] Thus this is a broadly ascetical approach to life, one that sees life as a matter of becoming shaped by a gracious discipline.

In these ways, the phrase "During the World" encapsulates an attitude that I want to call paradigmatically Augustinian. This is perhaps a "new" Augustine to some, emphasizing more vigorously both sides of the dialectic between sin and grace, not simply sin, and thus splitting the difference between the more establishmentarian and integralist "political Augustinianism" of several generations ago and the more Niebuhrian and apophatic "realist Augustinianism" of the past generation.[8] Furthermore, this Augustinian recommendation of endurance suggests that we inhabit a perennial crisis, not a historically contingent one. Whether we live in modernity, or post-modernity, or late modernity, or some other description of our situation, the crucial part of our address is that it is East of Eden, and has been ever since Adam and Eve. Augustinians are in this way *not* declensionist historicists, suggesting a substantial collapse from an earlier age of virtue.[9] Such an approach is escapist nostalgia, luring us away from seeing clearly our situation.

Nonetheless, the manifestations of our permanent crisis, during the world, will take different forms in different contexts, as different ages, equipped with different material and cultural capacities and habits, will manifest our fundamental pathologies in markedly different configurations. Because of this, we always need some relatively fine-grained language of theo-political social criticism indexed to our particular place and time. We simply don't need that language to go full-apocalyptic, and seduce us into thinking we

7 *Sermo* 4.9.9.

8 For a helpful summary of the history of the reception of Augustine's political thinking, see Michael Bruno, *Political Augustinianism: Modern Interpretations of Augustine's Political Thought* (Minneapolis: Fortress Press, 2014). On my reading, Augustine is a profoundly worldly thinker, yet deeply insistent that the world as we find it is still systematically flawed, a site of real, though always fugitive, "sacramental" goodness, before the eschaton. For more, see Charles Mathewes, "A Worldly Augustinianism," *Augustinian Studies* 41:1 (Fall 2010): 333–48.

9 This is what Augustine tried to do with his critique of the nostalgia of pagan Roman criticisms of the Roman Empire, in favor of a whitewashed vision of the early Roman Republic, throughout the first five books of *City of God*.

stand at Armageddon and we battle for the Lord. So even while we eschew melodramatic Manichean-MacIntyrean or Milbankian or John Pauline and Benedictine jeremiads against an age after virtue, or nihilism, or a culture of death, we will still need something more soberly diagnostic, like Charles Taylor's critique of contemporary liberalism's "ethics of inarticulacy" in order to help us see, and attempt to confront, some of the most obvious manifestations of our problems today.[10]

In our context, it does seem to me that a reading of the signs of the times suggests a particular configuration of our predicament. For our purposes, one crucial facet of our age is what I want to call the "crisis of judgment and authority" that we currently face. I turn to that next.

8.1.2 *The Crisis of Judgment and Authority*

In talking about this crisis of judgment and authority, I could have framed my remarks around William Stuntz's remarkable *The Collapse of American Criminal Justice*, or Oliver O'Donovan's theologically searching *The Ways of Judgment*. But instead I will take a more proximate provocation, Richard Posner's recent, more ephemeral, but still quite clever book *Reflections on Judging*. Posner's full argument is not entirely legible to an outsider to jurisprudence (perhaps ironically, given his professed aim), but it seems clear that he worries about the danger of what he calls "complexity" for the future success of the law. Most basically, he worries that judges increasingly "escape from complexity into complexity," not reducing but further obfuscating what Posner calls the "external complexity" of the enormous technical intricacy of many of the situations or issues under judgment, the increasingly byzantine pandaemonium of the legal precedents that may be relevant to any given situation. Posner worries that judges fail to confront the real task of the judge, which he takes to be the act of reducing the complexity of a situation to an act of actual judgment – one that can be itself understood, and then judged, assessed, by the judge's fellow citizens, so that the juridical task has as its telos democratic transparency. This is a deeply pragmatic and democratic attitude, and in both of these ways, in this context, deeply admirable.[11] He blames the current judicial failure to do this on technical factors related to changes in

[10] See Charles Taylor, *Sources of the Self: The Making of the Modern Identity* (Harvard University Press, 1989), 53–90.

[11] Richard Posner, *Reflections on Judging* (Cambridge, MA: Harvard University Press, 2013), 14. I especially found Posner's satirizing of the "Blue Book" illuminating (if a bit terrifying).

legal and broader social institutions, and in particular law schools, on which he is interesting.

All this is admirable, but notice what it focuses on: the problem of *complexity*. Most generally, Posner argues that the law is becoming ever more complicated, both because of the sheer complexity of the cases under judgment, and because of the increasing complexity of the world out of which those cases come. This complexity is not simply "difficulty," the sheer hard-ness of thinking deep and abstract thoughts; it is due to the complicated interdependence of mutually influencing factors within a whole system. It is complex because of the incredible sensitivity of the outcomes to initial conditions and to the various inputs and influences of multitudinous variables along the way. The phenomena may well be incalculably complex, and hence strictly unpredictable.[12] The vast elaborations of law, especially the regulation of an ever-more complicated and multilayered governmental-regulatory structure – all of this presents itself as urgent and worthy of the judge's serious cogitations.

Posner calls this "external complexity." But note: this complexity is not marked by (deep) profundity, but (superficial) intricacy; the judge's object of study is not (vertically) mysterious – a matter of bottomless motivational mystery – but rather (horizontally) complex – a matter of seeing broadly enough the whole shape of the evidence. The ontological situation the judge faces is one fundamentally of two dimensions, not three.

To face this essentially technical problem, Posner offers a technical solution, urging "greater judicial recognition of the ever-increasing complexity of the factual underpinnings of modern federal litigation." What does this "recognition" of complexity amount to? Fundamentally, it comes down to a matter of clear writing: "judges have to learn to write about complexity in ways that they and their audience . . . can understand."[13] For my money, what is interesting but almost totally obscured in this quote is the idea that in a democracy, the judiciary, and thus the law, gains legitimacy by being understood and at least tacitly affirmed (the philosophical complexities of such a legitimation process need not concern us here) by the people in whose name they purport to judge. But the accessibility of the process, for Posner, seems mostly a matter of superficial intelligibility.

[12] Thus in addressing complexity, we are dealing with "a system not a monad." Ibid., 45–55.

[13] Posner, *Reflections on Judging*, 355. I don't quite understand what that last sentence is gesturing at, but I suspect Posner writes it as an impatient hand-waving figure at those who see him as an anti-humanist. That is not my complaint; my complaint is that he thinks all criticisms of a technique-based solution come down to accusations of "anti-humanism." My accusation is that he fails to recognize the difference between expertise or technique, and authority.

Posner's confidence here seems a matter of people being given the right information in the right way. There is a confidence that understanding, and legitimation, here amounts to providing the audience with sufficient information so that they are able to see the logic of the decision thus made. The legitimation, then, lies in abutting the evidence and the judgment (or judicial decision) in such a way that the evidence mounts inevitably in the judgment. The judges have no special subjective quality, no "judiciousness" *per se*, that would legitimate them having this role and exercising this office. They are effectively experts, bureaucrats, virtuosi of data, managing information flows.

Yet what if there is an important difference between authority and expertise? Consider this proposal: expertise is, in a way, essentially an open status. Anyone can gain it from where they stand, with no change in their existential status required: all they need to do is get the right education, or even more simply, the right *training* or data. Authority is something else. It may be that to become an authority involves some qualitative change in the person, some sort of alteration (however partial, however momentary) of disposition, of character. Now, perhaps this understanding of authority is simply a premodern, pre-democratic mystification of expertise; but for the moment allow that it may not be. Consider the possibility that in fact anyone *can* become an authority, but that in the process of so becoming one, a moral change happens in the subject, so that the data genuinely *looks different* from that place, though in a way that would be apprehensible for anyone who had undergone the same sort of cultivation. In this case it may be that Posner is wrong: that what the judge needs, and is expected to have, is not just intelligence or cleverness, but *wisdom*. This is, in fact, my proposal.[14]

Part of the problem in this case lies in Posner's sheer brainpower. He is such a virtuoso that he may be tone-deaf to the sheer difficulty of some of the challenges ordinary judges face; he may be so allured by the exercise of his intellectual virtues that he does not notice the distinctive *moral* virtues he employs in judging. Just as hard cases make bad law, perhaps supra-genius judges give bad judgmental advice. But more deeply, I think, there is a possible misconstrual of the judicial situation, and the reality of human justice,

[14] I believe there is a difference between authority and authoritarianism, and I take the at least superficial conceptual distinction in our language between the two (with the latter related to tyranny) to reinforce my point; but I recognize that establishing this would be a longer project. For a very thoughtful social constructivist account of authority that fails to recognize this, see Bruce Lincoln, *Authority: Construction and Corrosion* (Chicago: University of Chicago Press, 1994). For an incisive account of expertise, see Stephen Brint, *In an Age of Experts: The Changing Role of Professionals in Politics and Public Life* (Princeton: Princeton University Press, 1996).

altogether. Posner seems, that is, to think the problem faced by judges is one of *technique*, of means and not of ends, and he proposes a technical solution for it. As we will soon see, for Augustine, the issue is not simply a matter of technical complexity; it is a matter of metaphysical profundity – of attempting to express, and perhaps enact, ultimate meanings, in a condition of historical temporality whose conclusion remains apparently, from within the flow of time, still indeterminate.

It is also the case, though Posner does not mention it, that two other factors are worth considering. The first is the question of whether, in our day, the criminal justice system is in any way fair, and thus whether the crisis of judgment has something to do with a larger and more fundamental crisis of civic justice (such is partly the case William Stuntz made in *The Collapse of American Criminal Justice*). The second is the question of whether we as a culture face an even deeper crisis, whether we have confidence in judging at all, or whether we have largely lost the requisite support concepts that would enable us to know what we are doing when we engage in it, and in particular the category of authority (which is largely the case O'Donovan makes, in *The Ways of Judgment* and throughout his corpus). I think these two claims are importantly right, and I would put my formulation of their worries – and thus make a general point of culture-criticism – this way: we live in a culture where justice is increasingly hard to articulate as a moral source independent of aggrieved self-interest, and we face this difficulty because our overall common moral languages offer fewer and fewer ways to acknowledge extra-subjective moral authorities in general; so that, while this conceptual inhospitability to authority is the setting in which our own more specific anxieties about judgment are rooted, we yet live in a culture where reliance on things that look like "authorities" of various sorts is ever-more pressing upon us, as we grow ever more reliant upon others as regards their special forms of expertise over ever-larger dimensions of our lives.

What do I mean by this? Consider, just for a moment, the vast and ever-increasing gap between our everyday habits and behaviors, and the practices that underlie those habits. Ever-increasing specialization in our daily life and work has meant that we become more intensively skilled in one thing, precisely by allowing ourselves to be unskilled in many others. Email, cellphones, air travel; we rely on technologies that we cannot explain, and barely can understand. We do not grow our own food, make our own clothes, heat our own houses. We even have "personal trainers" and "life coaches." (The culture's current fascination with apocalyptic television shows has something to do, I suspect, with a continued anxiety that outside very specific civilizational circumstances we might well not be able to live.) I do not mean to recommend some sort of rejection of or escape from this cultural situation; after all, the division of labor in such ways has allowed many more people to develop particular gifts and skills to a remarkable degree, while we remain deeply dependent upon others for much of the basic conditions of our lives. I simply wish to have us recognize the interesting position that this puts us in vis-à-vis our dominant moral languages, which – whatever else they do – most definitely prioritize autonomy and sovereignty as the inevitable goal of our lives. An ironic situation ensues, one that scholars from Weber to Tocqueville to Elias and Foucault have noted: a situation of inevitably increasing mutual dependency and forms of life disciplined (that is, both constrained and enabled) by multiple interacting forms of expertise, enjambed alongside a moral language that has a harder and harder time finding anything admirable or even unshameful in any forms of subjective submission to extra-subjective structures of competence or anything not autonomous.

Given all these facts, we can see that we face a puzzle: for what are we to do with the growing *facts* of authority (and not just expertise) in our lives, even as the languages we have for describing our lives offer ever more marginalized ways of recognizing and discussing the fact of our need for and submission to such authorities? How, in this setting, are we faithfully to undertake the act of judging?

Judgment is a human practice that partakes of ultimate significances. *Pace* Posner, the issue in judgment is not simply technical complexity; when one confronts a difficult legal case, there are mysteries of human motivation and profundities of human psychology that cannot be rendered thoroughly transparent, that remain blazingly opaque to our inquiries. And in these cases, the judge is called upon to decide how best to render judgment, in frank recognition of those opacities. It seems clear to me that there are not just moral, but even theological dimensions latent in the practice of judging; that judging is a matter of legal ultimacies, and that these ultimacies have something to do with other ultimacies, and so judging is a particularly charged, particularly obvious moment of civil religion; hence we should, and typically do, approach judging – however tacitly, however inarticulately – with a certain civic piety.[15] We recognize the need for sobriety in this act. Yet we seem to lack the ability to do honor to what the act implies, in our vocabulary for talking about

[15] For an opposing view, see Hannah Arendt's essay "What Is Authority?," in *Between Past and Future* (New York: Viking Press, 1961), 91–141, where she argues that this kind of authority, that I am suggesting is still operative in judging today, is defunct; she argues this case in part based on a rather flat-footed secularization theory. Thanks to a forthcoming book by Mara Willard, I have come better to appreciate Arendt's work as such a critical voice in political theology.

it. Ironically, when we take up the question of authority, we typically do so under the very different sociological category of "expertise." Posner is a terrific example of this. He is very clever, but he fails to see something fundamental, the way that complexity is different from not only difficulty but profundity. As deeply alert as he is to complexity, and as comfortable as he is with expertise, he is in a way tone-deaf to authority. And his tone-deafness bespeaks a larger problem, as I have tried to say. How can we best try to confront this problem today, during the world?

8.1.3 *Sermon 13 and the Dialectic of Law and Love for Augustine*

This is where Augustine comes in. What does he have to teach us? Quite a bit, in fact – about the nature and perils of judgment, the moral and theological debts one tacitly incurs whenever one accepts the duty of judgment, and one way to think about how to accept this gracious, but terrible, duty in this life, during the world. He offers a theological gloss on what looks to us, at least initially, like a wholly "secular" and this-worldly civic activity – namely, the activity of judgment. In his reading, a Christian construal of judgment reveals depths that we are well-advised to acknowledge. We can extend that point by arguing that this investigation may be of value, even for non-Christian civic actors. I want to use one relatively unknown sermon on judging that Augustine gave, the one named as Sermon 13 in contemporary scholarship. This sermon speaks of how to be a judge, how to exercise political power, and most generally how to be an authority, in a way that may be of interest today.

8.1.3.1 The Sermon

A bit of background for the sermon may be in order. The sermon was given in a setting that was redolent of authority, triumphant and also complexly compromised. First of all, Augustine gave it, we believe, on AD 27 May 418, in Carthage, at the Basilica of St. Cyprian, built on the site where Cyprian had been martyred in 258 during the Valerian persecution for refusing to sacrifice to the Emperor. The Basilica, raised on the spot where Cyprian had been executed by the worldly authorities, had become a particular locus of spiritual energy.

Now, a century and a half later, as he sat in the shrine's throne before the crowd of (mostly standing) congregants, Augustine was himself an *auctoritas*, an "authority," at the height of his authority in North Africa, for the Christian community and the political order alike. As such, his responsibilities would have included not simply ecclesiastical ones, but even civic juridical ones; Augustine's daily "episcopal audiences" functioned effectively like a small claims court for the town of Hippo. He was a man concerned not just with his congregants' souls, but very much also with their bodies, and their worldly goods.[16] The struggle against the Donatists had propelled him to close contact with the authorities, and they had supported his strategies. Among the populace of Carthage he likely had all the glamour of a great man with none of the over-familiarity of a prophet in his own country; Hippo was close enough for him to have been to Carthage innumerable times for important matters, yet far enough away that he always seemed fresh and new. The sermon is given by a man who is profoundly authoritative, yet suspicious of authority; and not surprisingly, given the speaker and his audience, it concerns most fundamentally what it means to exercise authority, and specifically the authority of judgment.

Indeed, it may well have been that his sermon was preached to some of those *viri illustris* who held the offices once occupied by Cyprian's killers. There were still Caesars, and still an *imperium Romanum*, though now of course Rome was professedly, more or less, Christian. Yet no one in the service of the Emperor, whether sitting in a chair or standing at the front of the congregation, could have missed the complex situation in which representatives of the *imperium* were put, by being in that place.

The structure of the sermon and its explicit argument reinforce each other. First of all, the pattern of biblical texts cited in the sermon is unusual and significant. The text on which Augustine preaches – "Be instructed, all you who judge the earth" (Ps. 2:10) – he uses to explore the relation between law and love, justice and mercy. He spends the first part of the sermon talking about the general story of sin, grace, and redemption, in which all humans should be involved. In this story we are all, at best, co-workers with God in our own journey back to God, and secondary co-workers at that, for God gives us the will to do good, Augustine insists; so we are to work out our redemption, he reminds us in an explicit echo of Paul, in fear and trembling (Ps. 2:11 and Phil. 2:12), working under God's guidance, "that you might find yourself in him, as you have lost yourself in yourself" (*Sermo* 13.3). Hence his first interpretation of the text is to construe it in terms of humanity's common struggle with our inherited sin from Adam.

Then, and only then – fully a third of the way into the sermon – does he turn to what he calls the "everyday understanding" of "judging the earth," namely, the political sense. Certainly such judging, the mark of real political rule, is inevitable, but such judging is immediately fraught, for kings are no closer to God than anyone else: "the earth itself is judging the earth, and when earth judges earth it ought to fear God who is in heaven. It is indeed judging

[16] See Kevin Uhalde, *Expectations of Justice in the Age of Augustine* (Philadelphia: University of Pennsylvania Press, 2007).

its own equal, a human judging a human, a mortal judging a mortal, a sinner judging a sinner" (*Sermo* 13.4).

Why is this so fraught for Augustine? Because, he says, it is both mortally perilous and utterly necessary. Christ tells us that only the sinless should judge. And the one sinless man who could judge, chooses *not* to do so. At a minimum, then, in political action, we should be merciful, as Christ demonstrated in his dealings with the woman caught in adultery. Politics is simply too tempting an arena for humans, with our ever-ready longing for glory, which is inevitably just a polite mask for our desire to dominate one another; we need to be reminded continually of this fact, and checks should be put in place to protect us from our own proclivities.[17]

And yet politics is inevitable and necessary; the point of political judgment is found in its salvific benefits, its ability to serve the redemptive purposes of God.[18] Political authorities are put in their offices (*officium*, "duty" is the revealing root sense of the word Augustine uses) to secure justice and be merciful in their dealings with those who are subject to their authority – as God surely is with them when they do that. But the problem is, from their perspective, they are fallen humans prone to doing injustice themselves. They must remember that *all* will be judged, even those – perhaps especially those – who exercise authority during the world, and all must act in fear and trembling. So now he turns directly to the authorities (one can imagine him literally turning toward them, were they in church that day) and says "judge yourself first" in all things, and understand that such a duty is not to be enjoyed, but something to be endured, to be experienced as being tortured "on the rack of your heart." "If, then, you don't want to exercise your authority unjustly, all you human beings who wish to have authority over human beings, well, *be instructed*, so that you avoid judging corruptly, and perishing in your soul before you manage to destroy anyone else in the flesh." If you seek authority, you must pay bribes, Augustine says – it was a fairly universal, if still formally embarrassing, practice at that time – adding (somewhat impishly) "I'm not criticizing you – yet" (*Sermo* 13.7).

Only after this final, chastising swipe at political rulers, does Augustine turn to the text that had already become one of the most fundamental texts for Christian political understandings, namely, Romans 13 ("let every soul be

[17] As Augustine puts it in *City of God* 19.15, no *dominari* (political lordship) was intended as part of the created order; lordship (and subservience) is one of the consequences of the Fall.

[18] This is how he understands the Caesar's coin story: "just as the image of Caesar on the coin is restored" to Caesar, Augustine says, so we should "restore to God the image of God in the human being" (*Sermo* 13.4).

subject to the higher authorities, for there is no authority except from God," etc.). Yet here again Augustine hedges the approbation of political authorities in interesting ways. For in such offices, sinful humans do not exhibit glory or splendor or authority *in themselves* – such presumptions should be far from the judge's mind. Rather, in fear and trembling they work, in the dark, to serve the inscrutable providence of God. It is almost inadvertently, Augustine seems to imply, that they will fulfill God's plan. They should not feel confident that they are agents of God's governance, in charge of a part of the script, dispensers of God's plan through their righteous intentions and actions; rather they are more akin to *conduits* of God's justice, the channels through which it runs. So they will "praise" those under their authority, in their dealings with them, either by properly honoring those subjects' justice (much of the time, Augustine says, simply by leaving them alone), or by "honoring" those subjects' righteousness with persecution, as the curious honor due to those whom God has marked out for special signification (not significance) through martyrdom (13.8).

This mention of persecution further complicates the authorities' authority by recalling his congregation's attention to where they physically are – "think of the blessed man whose blood was shed on this very spot." In light of this, he urges on his audience a moderation and a mercy in exercising the awesome duty of judgment; he urges them especially to avoid passing judgments that are by nature irrevocable, and so to avoid, whenever and wherever possible capital punishment (13.8), and always in their judgments to look for ways to exhibit, and recursively participate in, the mercy that is a perpetual mark of God's character as revealed in Jesus Christ.

8.1.3.2 The Dialectic of Law and Love

All of this – the locale, the progression of Scriptural passages discussed, and the argument's structure itself – reinforces Augustine's basic message, which is that to exercise authority is a grave, terrible, and always potentially presumptuous thing, to be undertaken only when necessary, and then in fear and trembling, for duties simultaneously political, evangelical, and ascetical.

Yet in no way is he saying we *should not* exercise such judgment when it is necessary. And there are times when it is, he thinks, quite clearly necessary. Human society needs people to decide, to engage in an act of judgment. If this be a frank, even rank, affirmation of paternalism, Augustine did not shy from it. The exercise of warranted authority is a necessary thing, and for one in authority over others, the exercise of discipline is necessary, and ignoring the need of discipline would be *cruel* (13.9). Parents and teachers know this, and both practice in their deeds that they should profess with their words and confess in their hearts. Augustine simply thinks that such functioning relationships of superior and inferior do not stop in the nursery and the classroom; they extend well beyond that, to other realms of human affairs. We may disagree with Augustine about the *extent* of such realms of legitimate authority, but it is hard to deny that it exists.

Nor, Augustine thinks, is such judgment required simply in scenes of explicitly juridical or evaluative action. Juridical judgment is continuous with other forms of judgment, from aesthetic to political, moral, and beyond. More specifically, he did not distinguish between judgment as a political matter and judgment as a judicial matter; but perhaps he was simply acknowledging a mutual contamination of the law and politics – that the law is always a matter of political contestation, and that politics inescapably elicits from us a set of not just legal but moral judgments. In refusing to see a firm distinction there, that is to say, perhaps he is not entirely mistaken. Perhaps the problem even with judicial judgment is precisely that it remains, ultimately, in this dispensation *one* person's judgment – unable to hide behind other methods or algorithms to apply principles, or any form of virtuoso expertise. Perhaps there is something in the idea of imagining the working out of judgment in fear and trembling – precisely because the judgment speaks inextricably of *you*.

In performing judgment, exercising power, and inhabiting authority, Christian judges should understand themselves – and Christian citizens should understand any judge, Christian or not – to engage in a dialectical practice of affirming law and love, justice and mercy. Such an understanding of the practice is useful both as a counterweight against the seductions toward pride that are faced by our own souls when tempted by righteousness (and thus it is an *ascetical* practice), and as a way to teach others about the peculiarly distended way in which God's love, and God's law, are manifest during the world (and thus it is a political and *pedagogical* practice). In both ways, it relies upon the claim that this world is a partial and provisional place, where full justice will not be accomplished, and the realization of what justice there *can* be is always a murky and tragedy-laced endeavor; and yet our longing for justice is real and to be respected, for it speaks of a deeper and higher justice yet to come, a justice that we are promised will be riddled with mercy and forgiveness, on the judgment day (and thus it is finally an *evangelical* practice).

One might imagine that Augustine's proposed practice of judgment, piously and wisely enacted by a judge, would do all these things in several ways. First of all, the very character of the judge should matter. The judge should speak modestly, and minimally, being chaste in his or her words, refusing invitations to speculate or indulge in hypotheticals, a hesitancy in what one says and in the practices of reason-giving – they should work on a case-by-case basis, and not lay down a marker for all eternity in their words. A judge's words matter, and so they should be used sparingly, lest the coin of her or his voice be debased. Furthermore, the judge should be humble, and exhibit that humility – that is, there should be a public display of humility in not offering too determinate and fixed a vision of what is going on, nor in the ultimate metaphysical propriety of their own judgments as replacing God's right to judge. Second, the judge must exhibit a properly courageous, or perhaps faithful, insistence on the necessity of judgment, and a willingness to face the winnowing pressures that must be faced if one is to undertake this particular office. All this is part of the practice of judgment, of meting out judgment, as our common life requires. And yet, third, the judge must be engaged in a relentless, remorseless quest for opportunities for mercy – for opportunities and reasons (I almost say excuses) to exhibit mercy and thus, in a way, *defer* judgment. Whether this is done (as it was urged by Augustine) by a strict avoidance of the death penalty, or by a refusal to engage in certain kinds of prosecutions, such a practice of seeking mercy is, both civically and theologically, a very powerful good that we ought to promote. Because of this, fourth and finally, the fact of the necessity of this practice at all should be lamented, and the need for judging bewailed, as the judge cries out, in another famous Augustine text, "from my necessities deliver me!"[19]

In all of this, there is a certain indirectness to Augustine's concern with the judge and judgment in general. In a way, the aim is not simply to mete out justice, but to announce a new dispensation in which justice is fully done, but done under the sign of mercy. It is not the direct delivery of actual justice that is for Augustine the ultimate aim of the exercise of judgment, but rather the ascetical, pedagogical, and evangelical dimensions of the judge's witness – of the necessity, even urgency, of their role, and the terrible weight and consequences of their role. This was recognized by Augustine's pagan contemporaries; indeed it was part of their larger suspicion that Christians like Augustine never *really* cared about the polis in itself. Augustine's response to that charge was that it was God's providence that cared about the polis directly; the duty of Christians was to try to discern God's providence, and participate in it – a slightly but hugely significantly different proposal. For our purposes, this indirectness is itself perhaps a deeper witness, one that simultaneously affirms and critiques a "liberal" age like our own in ways

[19] Augustine, *City of God*, 19.6.

more complicated than Augustine's pagan contemporaries. I try to say why next, in the Conclusion.

8.2 CONCLUSION

The proposal here detailed, which I take to be Augustine's, teaches us something about the nature and origins of both justice and mercy in this dispensation.[20] The judge's diligent effort to pursue mercy instead of justice is, for Augustine, a sign that mercy is ontologically available, though it may need to be articulated in multiple diverse registers. The search for mercy is always undertaken while recognizing the eschatological proviso that "our" justice is actually *God's* justice, and this means that our justice now should be, as God's ultimately will be, at least leavened with mercy. If we realize this, we know we must simultaneously affirm the moral energies that drive us to seek such justice, while also graciously relativizing whatever justice we manage to achieve. This is important, for it tells us that justice and politics are not all we are: we share in realities that have no native home in the worldview of sheer *quid pro quo* egalitarian justice.

This is especially important in the liberal social orders that we all, in different flavors, inhabit today – for better or worse, perhaps, but till death do us part from them, anyway.[21] Typically we understand the liberal state to be all about de-theologizing, disenchanting the human sphere, or at least the explicitly political mechanisms within human society. This is true, but it needs to be complicated, and Augustine's thoughts about judgment help us complicate it, in two different ways.

First, justice is, I submit, inescapably (though *not* exclusively) about enchantment, about a metaphysical reality. (This is why worries about the use of discretion are often framed as worries about humans "playing god.") Questions about justice are, I think, inevitably if often covertly theological; in particular, the criminal justice system has an ineliminably ritualistic aspect, as regards its *visibly* meting out justice for crime through a broadly public judicial process. As William Stuntz put it, "legal condemnation is a necessary but terrible thing;"[22] the aroma of the apocalypse hangs about the judge as she

[20] Some of the thoughts and words in this conclusion are drawn from my "Response to the Work of Professor Steiker," *Studies in Christian Ethics* 27:3 (August 2014): 334–39.

[21] My understanding of liberalism may be surprisingly un-demonizing to some readers. For more on what I take liberalism to be, see my "Augustinian Christian Republican Citizenship," in Michael Jon Kessler, *Political Theology for a Plural Age* (New York: Oxford University Press, 2013), 218–49.

[22] William J. Stuntz, *The Collapse of American Criminal Justice* (Cambridge: Harvard University Press, 2011), 311.

or he goes about her daily work. Political and legal theorists sometimes try to capture this ritualistic dimension in a sheerly immanentist language of "legitimacy," but it seems to me that in this aspect of human political reality, more than all other aspects, we feel the grip of ultimate matters. Human politics must of necessity court ultimacy, though in a liberal political era such as our own, political institutions, and the humans who enflesh them, often cannot easily be brought to acknowledge this fact, much less think through how that necessary courting ought to inform our understanding of politics and shape our inhabitation of it.

Christians ought not be afraid of recognizing the theological resonances of justice and using those resonances to inform in their political mobilization. Consider again the work of William Stuntz, who may exemplify this in surprising ways. Now, Stuntz was a fierce defender of what he took to be traditional Christian orthodoxy, and he was clear that much of the moral energy behind his legal thinking flowed from what he took to be basically Christian convictions about law, sin, grace, and mercy. No one will confuse him with a secular legal theorist. His magisterial work *The Collapse of American Criminal Justice* is thoroughly a work of legal thought, but clearly informed throughout both by a deep moral and civic sense that something has gone wrong with public justice in the United States, and a deep spiritual sadness that among the casualties of this calamity was any public place for a theological vision of mercy to be active in the legal system, and perhaps across public culture as a whole. He believed that one powerful impetus for our situation was conservative Christian Americans' deeply punitive understanding of the will of God in public culture. He knew that in other contexts this was not the way Christianity had manifested its Gospel publicly – in the cause of Abolitionism, for instance, or in the Civil Rights movement of the 1950s and 1960s, or in British legal reforms that provided "moral comfort" to jurors anxious about their theological presumptuousness as regards judging another's guilt or innocence.[23] As he put it, "[t]he association between Christianity and leniency is not surprising at all: it is historically common and theologically reasonable.

[23] For the British legal reforms, see pages 372–73; for the Civil Rights movement, pages 382–84 in William J. Stuntz, "Law and Grace," *Virginia Law Review* 98, no. 367 (2012): 367–84. For the British legal reforms, he draws upon James Q. Whitman, *The Origins of Reasonable Doubt: Theological Roots of the Criminal Trial* (New Haven: Yale University Press, 2008), but he does not note any scholarship for the Civil Rights movement. That is not entirely surprising; I would suggest his picture of that movement is insufficiently attentive to the use of force and compulsion in dismantling (partially, at least) Jim Crow.

Which means that the association between Christianity and severity that has characterized recent American politics should be very surprising indeed."[24]

A less punitive legal system, Stuntz believed, could well produce a more just social order. (After all, the title of his book was *The Collapse of American Criminal Justice*, not *The Collapse of the American Criminal Justice System*.) One can understand the trajectory of his thought to be presenting a vision of the law as a vehicle not only of distributing a good kind of justice fairly across the land, but also as a site wherein Christians have historically and can again give a kind of witness to their faith that is both pedagogically powerful, evangelically effective, and widely seen to be civically beneficial. Such a vision was argued for by Stuntz with powerful legal scholarship employed in thoroughly publicly accessible ways, with no special pleading or parochial presuppositions; but we would be blind if we denied that there was an organic theological motivation behind the whole project, or that he hoped that such a more merciful, less punitive criminal justice system would not only make the United States a place of greater justice, but also enable it to be a land where it was marginally less difficult to live a properly Christian life.

Second, this use of mercy – informed by Augustine but also inspired, at least in part, by Stuntz – teaches us that this understanding of liberalism – as in some important way "de-theologizing" – may itself spring from properly theological motives, however paradoxical that may sound. Consider: one achievement of the liberal secular state is the prying apart, over several centuries and continuing today, of the theo-ethical horizon from the secular political one; and a second achievement, less frequently understood and less reliably enacted, is the recognition of our continued need to remind the secular state, and its more vigorous, more enthusiastic devotees, of that distinction, as a bit of rain on their Rousseauean parade. It is no small irony that both of these achievements are the realization of aims first put forward by some of the earliest exponents of the political positions that slowly coalesced into what we call "liberalism," and that they proposed these views for properly *theological* reasons, especially related to concerns about the idolatry of this-worldly political forms.[25] In other words, Reinhold Niebuhr was right: the straightforward achievement of full and absolute justice is not a proper ambition of a liberal society, and such achievement cannot be an aim, precisely because

[24] Stuntz, "Law and Grace," 378.

[25] For more on this, see Eric Nelson, *The Hebrew Republic: Jewish Sources and the Transformation of European Political Thought* (Cambridge: Harvard University Press, 2011) and Michael McConnell's essay on liberalism in *Christian Perspectives on Legal Thought* (New Haven: Yale University Press, 2001).

of the moral insight, funded by theological sources, that no society in this dispensation can achieve perfect justice.[26] It is in such ways that we see once again that living in liberal societies, on liberal societies' own terms, is a far from straightforward, indeed fairly complicated, thing to do. Law's asymptotic ambition may be to achieve a one-to-one relation to morality, but speaking in politically realistic and liberal terms we should not, we must not, allow that longing free rein in mobilizing and guiding our legislative energies.

This lesson, like the one about justice above, will be audible to Christians and non-Christians alike, albeit in different ways. Consider, for instance, how a position such as this might speak to Posner. Posner's insistence on judges' clarity seems to me – an amateur – to be deeply wise, puncturing the mystifications that so easily accrete upon the role of the judge: the way they seem to court theurgical rituals, with their austere black robes, sober faces, and bushy eyebrows. (The ghost of Learned Hand still haunts the American juridical imagination.) And yet even in Posner's case, the desire to disenchant judging arises from the deepest theo-political longing that a democratic age can express, the longing for democratic legitimacy. The point of Posner's jeremiad-like pronouncements about judging just is that judges are losing their ability to render justice *legitimately*, because the extreme technical complexity of current jurisprudence makes it opaque to all but the most elevated votaries of the turgid yet hierophanic mysteries of the Blue Book. And yet all he has to say about legitimation seems to be reduced to the need to be clear and intelligible, as if the challenges of Machiavelli and Hobbes could be silenced by a brisk rereading of Strunk and White. We must certainly laud his anxiety about rendering justice as accessible as possible to those who are not experts in our legal system. But we may still ask him whether more will be needed, once legal writing is transparent in the sense that he wants it to be, to authorize (there's that word) a technical expert as one who, in fear and trembling, speaks beyond all intersubjectively verifiable claims, and makes a judgment about the *justice* of a case. For this justice most often cannot be established in dissent-silencing ways in a democracy, given not just the complexity of the issues that concern Posner, but also the inescapable plurality of human opinions and experiences and points of view, as well as the multitudinous historical forces that collectively bring us to the point where a judgment

[26] Note I am not saying Niebuhr was right as a theologian here, but rather as a political thinker, about liberalism. I think especially of his book *The Children of Light and the Children of Darkness: A Vindication of Democracy and a Critique of Its Traditional Defense* (New York: Charles Scribner's Sons, 1944). I think he's right on strictly theological grounds as well, but in this case he is arguing in a way that can be widely apprehended, even by those without Christian commitments, as plausible.

is needed, as well as the manifold implications that follow from it, far into the future, once it is pronounced. And when *that* judgment is enunciated, I suspect that Posner himself would recognize that reasonable people can disagree, and all the judge has to go on is their own best judgment, given in humility and in the recognition that they are making something like ultimate judgments on something else that is clearly less-than-comprehensive and doubt-silencing information; and then the judges have to appeal to something else, something more, something beyond the lucidity of their prose for their decision to be legitimate: a sober and somber humility, to be sure, but also the potentially terrifyingly hubristic claim that they are structurally better positioned, experientially better trained, and temperamentally better suited, to make these claims than anyone else in our polity. And that is not a claim about clarity; quite the opposite. And that is precisely my point.

This brings up a final issue: as I said above, our curious collective anxiety about the use of mercy teaches us about our culture, because it bespeaks the larger and ironic crisis of authority in which we exist today. It is good, in all places and at all times, to not be too confident of our judgments, and to work out what modicum of justice we can achieve in fear and trembling. But today this hesitation has nearly curdled into an indifference, an indifference rooted in a common fear, the fear of judging, the fear of imposing one's subjective reality on others, or trusting others to do that. This is also the fear of authority, and more precisely of humans exercising authority over one another. This anxiety is expressive of an attempt to escape the human situation, in which we have nothing more reliable than our own apprehensions on which to base our efforts.

On the other hand, along with insisting on the possibility of justice, we must never forget that it can be only, at best, imperfect in this dispensation, during the world. We should frankly recognize our desire to make justice impersonal and hence beyond critique, to make it ultimately unquestionably legitimate, and hence insulate its exercise from political contestation. Obviously there is something noble in this longing, an attempt to honor the way justice reaches beyond the grubby transactional wheeling and dealing with which we associate "politics." But this longing is always also, at least in part, a somewhat defensive attempt, in Augustinian terms, to hasten the apocalypse, to insist that complete justice, unstained by self-interest, is available, at least when we are the ones meting it out. This desire manifests itself at least as much in putatively secular forms of political thought as it does in overtly religious ones. Admitting this, and organizing our moral lives so to resist this desire, need not result in a surrender to relativism or an appeal to some sort of pragmatic communitarian solipsism; any sane form of theological or moral realism and certainly the ecclesiology of all the major Christian churches and many other religious bodies frankly recognize the fact that our judgments are *our* judgments, and that we are responsible for them, and will be responsible *to others* for them. But recognizing that it is *we* who are responsible does not entail that we, in making such judgments, are or ought to be trying genuinely to be responsive to the salient realities in the world, as best we may discern them, given the sinful corruptions of our own capacities, as well as the corruption of those we judge. There is a world of difference between acknowledging that the judgment of a moral situation is made by a human, intinctured with the contingencies of a particular history, in a particular place and time, and assuming that this acknowledgment necessarily entails that the human is merely reporting facts derived from those contingencies, rather than the reality that those contingencies, have conspired to shape them to perceive.

This very dialectical approach to justice is perhaps one pungent form of witness that Christian jurists, and all those who engage with the legal world, may provide to that world, and the wider world in which we all live. As Zachary Calo has suggested, we ought to take seriously the theological possibilities of a Christian eschatological standpoint – one that, again, affirms a semi-realized, though always in this life incomplete realization of the kingdom. Such a standpoint can help us to destabilize a too-ossified dualism that sets mercy against justice, private convictions against public propriety; the dialectical vision elucidated above helps in that task. As such, it helps to fracture our received secular "political imaginary," and speaks of a different way of imagining political life, one in which even the most mundane or this-worldly of civic actions – like being a judge in a small claims court – can have distinct theological significances, whether we admit them to ourselves or others or not.

But it is worth reemphasizing, here at the end, that Augustine seems to take the more immediate value of this approach to be what it does to those who profess it, in their vocation as Christian citizens, of both cities. As I read it, while Augustine's proposal supports the project that Calo proposes, it speaks more to the obverse side of that project: namely, how this fugitive eschatological imagination can work on *us*, as subjects, and particularly as agents of the law, who want to find in our daily life and work the clues to a Christian pedagogy, an ascetics of citizenship. And so, as I said at the beginning, the effect of Augustine's vision is not simply to offer us what Posner wants, namely a technique or a technology, a practical trick that solves the problems we bring to his texts; in hearing his proposal, our vision of the overall situation, and our place in it, is transformed, and we are given a new and quite different understanding both of what it is we are doing, when we "judge the earth," and what we might expect to come of such judging.

9

Justice, Love, and Duties of Care in Tort Law

Michael P. Moreland

9.1 INTRODUCTION: JUSTICE IN TORT LAW

In an essay on the unlikely topic of what philosophy might learn from tort law, Bernard Williams wrote that legal reasoning – with its body of "shared interpretations and concepts" – is like a "microwave oven" for testing the deliberations of philosophers.[1] Williams's point is that tort law's demand for an answer to particular cases (Who is responsible? How should we allocate the risk of loss in this instance?) reflects and may help refine philosophical concepts. In this essay, I propose to explore the central problem of Christian legal theory – justice and its relation to love – and use it as a background to help us understand the duties owed in the common law of torts. While much of the essay will be taken up with a discussion of justice and love in representative figures from the Christian tradition, my hope is that it will suggest a way of thinking about tort law and also open up avenues of inquiry for those working in Christian legal theory on issues of private law more generally.

Contemporary tort theory is broadly divided into two basic approaches: economic analysis and corrective justice. The former view has its more libertarian and progressive variations,[2] and corrective justice views developed in conversation with the seeming imperialism of economic analysis and its focus on welfare maximization and efficiency.[3] A more recent and influential view

[1] Bernard Williams, "Afterword: What Has Philosophy to Learn from Tort Law?," in David Owen, ed. *Philosophical Foundations of Tort Law* (Oxford: Clarendon Press, 1995), 493.

[2] See, e.g., Richard A. Posner, "A Theory of Negligence," *Journal of Legal Studies* 1 (1972): 29 and Guido Calabresi, *The Costs of Accidents* (New Haven: Yale University Press, 1970).

[3] See, e.g., Arthur Ripstein, *Equality, Responsibility and the Law* (Cambridge: Cambridge University Press, 1998); Ernest J. Weinrib, *The Idea of Private Law* (Oxford: Oxford University Press, 1995); Jules A. Coleman, *Risks and Wrongs* (Oxford: Oxford University Press, 1992); Stephen R. Perry, "The Moral Foundations of Tort Law," *Iowa Law Review* 77 (1992): 449.

focuses on the "civil recourse" aspect of tort law with a focus on the role of providing a redress for wrongs.[4]

This essay is an effort to take the core insight of corrective justice and civil recourse views – that tort law is irreducibly about *justice* or *redress* – and place it in a wider and more complete context, a context that also takes seriously the philosophically and theologically rich account of justice and its relation to love in the Christian tradition. For while justice-based accounts of tort law are right to avoid the pitfalls of economic analysis and its reductionism, their account of justice is itself inadequate to explain the range of tort doctrines as to, for example, the basis of duties of care. As John Finnis notes:

> Many contemporary legal theorists seem to value only one part of classical legal theory, a part that is among its weakest: Aristotle's account of corrective justice. True, Aristotle is right to say that the restoration of a wrongfully disturbed equality between one person and another is the principle requiring tortfeasors to compensate those whom they have wrongfully subjected to harm or loss and that that principle is an essentially true principle of justice even though its concern to restore equality differs from the concern to maintain equality in disturbing some shared stock of benefits or burden among a set of persons. But he has little or nothing helpful to say by way of response to the decisive and difficult questions: are persons drastically unequal in, say, wealth to be treated as having been *equals* immediately prior to the tort? How is a tortious to be distinguished from an inculpable or non-tortious causing of loss? What measure of compensation restores the hypothesized pre-existing equality when both the fault and (independently) the resources of defendants differ so greatly relative to any scale of loss?[5]

In part, then, this essay will take up Finnis's challenge by placing justice in tort law into a larger conceptual scheme informed by reflections on justice and love and the place of beneficence and equal regard in the moral life. In keeping with the theme of this volume, love – and specifically Christian love (agape) – as a moral and political concept will expand upon the bare duties of justice that have often been the focus of corrective justice theorists in tort law. In particular, I will argue that the longstanding debate[6] in tort theory over

4 John C. P. Goldberg and Benjamin C. Zipursky, "Torts as Wrongs," *Texas Law Review* 88, no. 5 (2010): 920 (arguing that "there is value to having law that defines private wrongs and provides recourse to victims of those wrongs, and that this value does not reduce down to other values such as enhancing safety, compensating persons in need, or achieving justice").

5 John Finnis, "Natural Law: The Classical Tradition," in *The Oxford Handbook of Jurisprudence and Philosophy of Law*, eds. Jules Coleman and Scott Shapiro (Oxford: Oxford University Press, 2002), 45.

6 See John C. P. Goldberg and Benjamin C. Zipursky, "The Moral of MacPherson," *University*

duties of care – to whom they are owed and on what basis – is illuminated by the concepts of justice and love that have been central concerns for Christian ethics. The twin poles of universal and particular concern as developed in the Christian tradition (and that tradition in conversation with secular sources as well) might help inform ongoing debates about duties of care in tort law.

The general themes I will explore that animate the Christian tradition on these matters – justice, beneficence, equal regard, and charity – provide a research agenda for those working in tort law and other fields in which the concerns noted by Finnis hold a central place.

9.2 LOVE AND JUSTICE IN THE CHRISTIAN THEOLOGICAL TRADITION

The dominance for many centuries of natural law accounts in Catholic political thought caused the relation of law and love to be until recently an under-appreciated and under-explored topic in that tradition. Love (or charity, from the rendering of Greek agape in Latin as *caritas*)[7] is not a common theme, for example, in the papal social encyclicals from Pope Leo XIII forward, with the recent and notable exception of Pope Benedict XVI's *Deus Caritas Est* and *Caritas in Veritate*. Also, the Catholic emphasis on the teaching tradition of the Church occasionally led to a marginalization of certain scriptural themes, including love. And so while Protestant theologians such as Anders Nygren explored at great length the distinctiveness of agapic Christian love in ethics and politics, Catholic writers more often made arguments about natural law and practical reason when reflecting on social questions.

In this part of the essay, I will outline the discussion of love and its relation to law and justice in Thomas Aquinas. Throughout the discussion of Aquinas on love, I will compare and contrast Aquinas to representative secular (primarily Kant) and Protestant (primarily Gene Outka) figures, which will highlight congruences and differences among these traditions, as well as distinctive aspects of the Catholic view. I will compare Thomistic charity with Kantian respect for persons as an illustration of two prevailing ways of relating justice and love.

This section will seek to vindicate a set of claims about beneficence and its relation to our duties of care. First, beneficence (that is, simply doing well toward others) is a specific moral obligation under law as informed by love.

---

of Pennsylvania Law Review 146, no. 6 (1998): 1733 for an extended discussion of the modern debate over duties of care.

7 I will generally use the terms "love," "agape," and "charity" interchangeably except where discussing authors for whom one of the terms (charity for Aquinas, agape for Outka) is used in a distinctive manner. For a discussion of the differences between the terms, see page 191–92 below.

Aquinas and Kant bear some resemblance in their respective analyses and in the formulation of moral prescriptions, including a common acknowledgment that much of the material content of beneficence must be left to moral judgment. Insofar as duties of care in the law of torts are meant to reflect something like a concern for beneficence, this exploration of Aquinas and Kant will help us discern ways in which such duties are universal (thereby extending to all) or particular (thereby depending on special relationships). As we will see, the potential scope of beneficent concern is expressly universal in both Aquinas and Kant, though they differ (in emphasis) on the role for special relations within this scope.

I will also compare Aquinas and a leading modern Protestant account of agape, Gene Outka's 1972 book, *Agape: An Ethical Analysis*.[8] In his book, Outka argues for an understanding of Christian love modeled on equal regard. One criticism of Outka's thesis has come from those who offer the alternative account of charity found in Aquinas, beginning with a defense of the moral value of special relations in Christian life. A related line of inquiry begins from the distinction between charity and justice. In this section, I will outline the views of charity and justice as found in Aquinas and the equal regard thesis and its relation to justice described in Outka's work. After examining these two alternatives, the important differences between Aquinas's account of charity and Outka's theory of agape will be apparent even if Thomistic justice will be shown to have a passing resemblance to equal regard. Once again, this will provide a basis for further reflections on duties of care in the law – where and to what extent such duties are grounded in equality and justice.

9.2.1 *Charity and Respect for Persons*

It may be helpful at the outset to define certain terms that are often used interchangeably in much of the current discussion of Christian love. "Agape" is the Greek word in the New Testament translated as love or charity. For example, in the famous concluding line from 1 Corinthians, "These remain: faith, hope, and love, the three of them; and the greatest of them is love" (1 Cor. 13:13), the Greek word used for love is agape. In contemporary ethics, agape generally denotes specifically Christian love: "Agape ... is conspicuously prevalent in the New Testament and in current usage is almost uniformly the referent for any alleged distinctiveness in Christian love."[9]

8 New Haven: Yale University Press.

9 Outka, *Agape: An Ethical Analysis*, 7.

Charity is the English rendering of the Latin word (*caritas*) used by Aquinas to denote a particular type of love (*amor*) and one of the three theological virtues. Aquinas understands charity in a technical sense to mean a movement of the passions in complacency with (receptivity toward) the good (I.II.26–8). In I.II.62.2 ad 3, Aquinas states, "Charity is love, yet love is not always charity." How should we define this broader conception of love in this discussion? To take an example of an attempt to do so, Edward Vacek defines it phenomenologically as "an affective, affirming participation in the goodness of a being (or Being)."[10] In classical authors, love is held to be three-fold: philia (friendship), eros (erotic or romantic love), and agape (neighbor-love).

9.2.1.1 Aquinas on Charity

Aquinas places charity within the context of the theological virtues in the *Secunda secundae* of the *Summa Theologiae*. Although charity is mentioned earlier in the general discussion of the virtues in the *Prima secundae*, it is in the treatise on charity from II.II.23 to 46 that charity is most fully addressed. Before discussing charity as such, it may be helpful to mention Aquinas's treatment of love (*amor*) and some of the distinctions he makes in his discussion of the virtues.

For Aquinas, love is simply "the first movement of the will and of every appetitive faculty."[11] Elsewhere, in the treatise on the passions, he speaks of charity as an inclination toward the good: "Good causes in the appetitive power, a certain inclination, aptitude, or connaturalness in respect of good: and this belongs to the passion of love."[12] This inclination to the good is followed by the movement of desire and reaches its completion in the repose of joy.

Regarding the virtues, it is important to recall Aquinas's distinction between acquired and infused virtue. Acquired virtues are those virtues that a person gains through habitual practice in accord with right reason. A life of the acquired virtues attains for a person the flourishing commensurate with natural human happiness. Infused virtues are those given a person directly by grace from God and orient a person to the supernatural end for human beings. Charity, according to Aquinas, is one such infused virtue: "Charity itself surpasses our natural faculties . . . therefore charity can be in us neither naturally, nor through acquisition by the natural powers, but by the infusion of the Holy Ghost."[13]

[10] Edward Collins Vacek, *Love, Human and Divine: The Heart of Christian Ethics*, (Washington DC: Georgetown University Press, 1994), 34.

[11] I.20.1. All quotations from the *Summa Theologiae* are taken from the English Dominican translation.

[12] II.II.23.3.

[13] II.II.24.2.

Related to this distinction between acquired and infused virtue is the distinction between the moral and theological virtues. Aquinas follows Aristotle in arguing that the four moral (or cardinal) virtues are prudence, justice, temperance, and fortitude. These virtues may be either acquired naturally or infused supernaturally. The theological virtues of Christianity are faith, hope, and charity. Because the theological virtues pertain to a person's supernatural end, they cannot be acquired through natural means. In light of these distinctions, charity is the infused theological virtue whereby a person is oriented toward friendship with God (and, importantly, love to other persons in relation to God). It is an infused virtue because, unlike the acquired virtues of justice, fortitude, prudence, and temperance, it directs a person toward his or her supernatural end, union with God.[14] This is possible only if God infuses this theological virtue by grace.

In the *Prima secundae*, Aquinas introduces the idea that charity is "the mother and root of all the virtues, inasmuch as it is the form of them all."[15] Charity directs the person to the last end by means of love.[16] This last end is God, the object of the theological virtues.[17] After these preliminary remarks, Aquinas leaves a fuller understanding of charity to the *Secunda secundae*.

Aquinas begins the so-called treatise on charity by claiming that charity is a type of friendship. Friendship is understood here in the complex and specifically Aristotelian terms of viewing the other as another self, as found in Books VIII and IX of the *Nicomachean Ethics*. In the case of charity, the object of friendship is God. Of note here is that this form of friendship violates at least one aspect of Aristotle's account: "If friends come to be separated by some wide gap in virtue, vice, wealth, or something else ... then they are friends no more, and do not even expect to be. This is most evident with gods, since they have the greatest superiority in all goods."[18] Friendship between unequals is difficult, for Aristotle, and appears to be impossible with divinity. Nevertheless, "In spite of his strong sense of the infinite gap between creature and creator. . ." Porter notes, "Thomas takes the Aristotelian conception of friendship as the framework for his account of charity."[19]

[14] Aquinas also holds that the cardinal virtues can be infused. For an extended treatment of this distinction between infused and acquired virtues in Aquinas, see Jean Porter, "The Subversion of Virtue: Acquired and Infused Virtues in the Summa Theologiae," *Annual of the Society of Christian Ethics* (Washington DC: Georgetown University Press, 1992), 19–41.

[15] I.II.62.4.

[16] I.II.62.3.

[17] I.II.62.2.

[18] Aristotle, *Nicomachean Ethics*, trans. Terence Irwin (Indianapolis: Hackett, 1985), 1158b35.

[19] Jean Porter, "De Ordine Caritatis: Charity, Friendship, and Justice in Thomas Aquinas' Summa Theologiae," *The Thomist* 53 (April 1989): 197–239.

Closely related to the concept of charity as friendship is the notion of charity as bringing about union, or, more properly, union as an effect of charity. "The key to understanding charity is union," according to James Keenan, "which Thomas uses to distinguish charity from any form of love, including benevolence, because charity is benevolence based on union."[20] The other two theological virtues, faith and hope, are expressive of union not yet attained. Charity, however, effects union with God immediately: "We must assert that to love which is an act of the appetitive power, even in this state of life, tends to God first, and flows on from Him to other things, and in this sense charity loves God immediately, and other things through God."[21]

As his discussion of charity moves forward from establishing it as a virtue that directs the person to God, Aquinas makes the stronger claim that charity makes possible all other true virtue. Aquinas maintains his break from Augustine first made in I.II.55.4 that it is possible to be virtuous apart from the divinely infused virtues. Since it is only through charity, however, that we are directed to our final good, charity enables true or perfect virtue. "We may speak of virtue being where there is no charity, in so far as it is directed to some particular good," Aquinas writes – virtue distinct, that is, from divinely infused charity.[22] If this particular good is a true good, there will be imperfect true virtue. But only by charity can one speak of perfect and true virtue.

9.2.1.2 Aquinas on Justice

Aquinas's treatment of justice is found in II.II.57–122. At the very beginning of the treatise on justice, Aquinas argues that justice is the virtue that directs humans in their relations with one another and "denotes a kind of equality."[23] From Aristotle, Aquinas further defines justice to be "the perpetual and constant will to render to each one his right."[24]

Four particular characteristics of justice are given by Aquinas in II.II.58. First, justice is a general virtue.[25] By general virtue, Aquinas denotes that justice is directed toward the common (or general) good. Justice is always exercised within a community for the common good. Second, justice is concerned with observing the mean in external action.[26] The other cardinal

[20] James Keenan, SJ, *Goodness and Rightness in Thomas Aquinas's Summa Theologiae* (Washington DC: Georgetown University Press, 1992), 124.
[21] II.II.27.4.
[22] II.II.23.7.
[23] II.II.57.1.
[24] II.II.58.1.
[25] II.II.58.5.
[26] II.II.58.10.

virtues (temperance, fortitude, and prudence) observe the mean internally with respect to the agent possessing these virtues. "The matter of justice is external operation," writes Aquinas, ". . . wherefore the mean of justice consists in a certain proportion of equality between the external thing and the external person."[27] Third, just action is the action of giving each person his or her due.[28] Finally, justice stands above the other moral virtues.[29] The primary reason for this claim is that justice concerns the common good rather than the individual good.

The precepts of justice are identified, according to Aquinas, by the Ten Commandments. "Whereas in matters that refer to another it appears manifestly that a man is under obligation to render to another that which is his due," Aquinas contends, "Hence the precepts of the decalogue must needs pertain to justice."[30]

9.2.1.3 Kant on Respect for Persons

Moving now to an exploration of Kant's view on respect for persons, the concept is a shorthand expression for Kant of the doctrine of the second formula of the categorical imperative found in the *Groundwork for the Metaphysics of Morals*: "Act in such a way that you treat humanity, whether in your own person or in the person of another, always at the same time as an end and never simply as a means."[31] This formula is, according to Kant, merely a different expression of the supreme principle of morality. Though the claim is a disputed one among Kant scholars, Kant asserts that these various formulas of the categorical imperative are, "At bottom only so many formulas of the very same law."[32] Furthermore, the formula of the end in itself provides material content to moral maxims in contrast to the merely formal requirement of the principle of morality.[33]

The basis for this second formula of the categorical imperative is in Kant's concept of an autonomous will. Only a will that legislated autonomously (apart from external coercion or heteronomy) is of absolute moral worth and fitting to the rational nature of a person. "Autonomy is the ground of the dignity

27 II.II.58.10.
28 II.II.58.11.
29 II.II.58.12.
30 II.II.122.1.
31 Immanuel Kant, *Groundwork for the Metaphysics of Morals*, trans. James Ellington (Indianapolis: Hackett, 1981), 429. References to Kant will include a citation of the translation used and the Berlin Academy pagination.
32 Ibid., 436.
33 See Kant, *Groundwork*, 436, and Immanuel Kant, *Metaphysics of Morals*, trans. Mary Gregor (Cambridge: Cambridge University Press, 1991), 380.

of human nature and of every rational nature."[34] This claim of dignity is a deliverance of practical reason and is not derived empirically. Kant offers two arguments for this claim. First, the formula holds universally, and experience is incapable of comprehending anything of universal human nature. Second, Kant remarks that, in experience, humanity is not thought of as an end.

The term "respect" designates a moral feeling elicited by reason and pertaining both to the moral law and to persons. It derives solely from within the moral agent and cannot be externally constrained. "It is to be understood as the *maxim* of limiting our self-esteem by the dignity of humanity in another person," Kant writes in the *Metaphysics of Morals*.[35] Independent of feeling, attraction, or repulsion, even the vicious person is an object of respect: "I cannot deny all respect even to a vicious man as a man; I cannot withdraw at least the respect that belongs to him in his quality as a man, even though by his deeds he makes himself unworthy of it."[36]

9.2.1.4 Beneficence

Having dealt with Kantian respect for persons, we are now able to compare and contrast beneficence – doing well to others – in Aquinas and Kant. It is through this consideration of beneficence that we can begin to see ways in which the theological and philosophical traditions we have been discussing might bear on a particular manifestation of beneficence in, for example, the duties of care imposed by the law of torts.

After considering charity in itself, Aquinas continues the treatise on charity by examining the inward and outward effects of charity. Beneficence is considered as the first of the outward acts or effects of charity, the others being almsgiving and fraternal correction (recall that charity is the love of friendship with God and extending out to other persons in relation to God).

Beneficence is defined simply as "doing good to someone" (as distinct from benevolence, which is wishing good to someone).[37] As will be seen also in Kant, Aquinas argues that goodwill to others, "if possible," issues in action. Thus, "beneficence in its general acceptation is an act of friendship or charity."

Aquinas and Kant are similar in their common refusal to provide a carefully delimited set of rules as to the proper acts of beneficence. Despite the standard view that Kant's ethic is rigorist or excessively dependent on rules, Kant provides very little in the way of normative guidance for what would

[34] Kant, *Groundwork*, 436.
[35] Kant, *Metaphysics of Morals*, 449.
[36] Ibid., 463.
[37] II.II.31.1.

seem to be a central subject for ethics, the positive acts of assistance between moral agents. Aquinas similarly leaves the exercise of beneficence to prudential judgment. "Beneficence should extend to all, but according as time and place require," Aquinas writes, "because all acts of virtue must be modified with a view to their due circumstances."[38] So also in the law of torts, the duties of care imposed generally are a working out in practical reasoning based on judgments made in particular cases.

The changing notion of those to whom beneficence should be extended constitutes another manner in which Aquinas and Kant share similar views. Each recognizes both a universal and a specific (or exclusive) aspect to beneficence. For Aquinas, the specificity of the order of charity is spelled out in a way Kant mentions only briefly, while Kant's universalizing tendency is tempered considerably in Aquinas's account. It is to this question of similar and differing emphases that we now turn.

9.2.1.5 Universal Moral Concern

Charles Taylor notes that one hallmark of modernity is the universalization of moral personality. Citing Kant as the earliest formulation of the notion, Taylor writes:

> What is picked out as of worth here is a *universal human potential*, a capacity that all humans share. This potential, rather than anything a person may have made of it, is what ensures that each person deserves respect. Indeed, our sense of the importance of potentiality reaches so far that we extend this protection even to people who through some circumstance that has befallen them are incapable of realizing their potential in the normal way – handicapped people or those in a coma, for instance.[39]

For our purposes in this essay, we are interested in the basis for this ascription of moral dignity and how it pertains to duties of care owed to others, most especially where such duties of care are imposed by the positive law.

Aquinas addresses the question whether one ought to do good to all in II.II.31.2. He concludes that ideally beneficence does extend to all, though he acknowledges the impracticability of this. The first objection in the article takes up Augustine's position in *On Christian Doctrine* that, "We cannot be

[38] II.II.31.2.

[39] Charles Taylor, "The Politics of Recognition," in *Philosophical Arguments* (Cambridge, MA: Harvard University Press, 1995), 235. This essay was originally published in *Multiculturalism and "The Politics of Recognition,"* Amy Gutmann, ed. (Princeton: Princeton University Press, 1992). The idea runs through much of Taylor's writing. See also Charles Taylor, *Sources of the Self* (Cambridge, MA: Harvard University Press, 1989), 515.

of assistance to everyone."[40] Aquinas makes two clarifications and corrections to the statement in the objection. First, we must be "prepared in mind to do good to anyone if we have time to spare."[41] Second, Aquinas argues that there is "a good that we can do to all, if not to each individual, at least to all in general, as when we pray for all, for unbelievers as well as for the faithful."[42]

By virtue of what are we obligated, even if in an idealized sense, to do good to all? This notion of universal moral personality has several different, though related, bases in Aquinas, two of which will be mentioned here. In his treatment of creation, Aquinas asks whether the image of God is found in every person (*homine*).[43] He responds affirmatively, for all have a "natural aptitude for understanding and loving God." This aptitude is "found in all humans" ("*invenitur in omnibus hominibus*").

A second foundation for universal concern occurs in the treatise on charity itself. The first article of the treatise asks whether charity is friendship.[44] As mentioned earlier, Aquinas's affirmative answer runs throughout the remainder of the treatise. In II.II.23.1 ad 2, Aquinas draws an important distinction between ways in which friendship extends to a person. By one way, friendship is reserved to one's friends (meaning those who reciprocate love). In another way, friendship is extended to "someone in respect of another," where it is on account not of the person himself or herself (in reciprocity) but another (third, as it were) person. Accordingly, just as all have capacity for blessedness and "belong to God," so one ought to extend the love of charity even to those who do not reciprocate our love (our enemies). Even those who hate us are "not . . . contrary to us, as men and capable of happiness: and it is as such that we are bound to love them."[45]

Aquinas goes so far as to echo (even if not prominently) a theme that finds its strongest formulation in Kierkegaard: Christian love admits of no distinctions among neighbors (with an important Thomist qualification). "Love is not differentiated specifically on account of the various degrees of goodness in various persons, so long as it is referred to one good common to all," Aquinas writes, "consequently we love all our neighbors with the same love of charity, in so far as they are referred to one good common to them all, which is God."[46] Of course, this text should not be read in isolation from the larger context

40 Augustine, *On Christian Doctrine*, trans. D. W. Robertson, Jr. (New York: Macmillan, 1958), I. 28.
41 II.II.31.2.ad 1.
42 Ibid.
43 I.93.4.
44 II.II.23.1.
45 II.II.25.8.
46 II.II.25.1.

of the treatise on charity, particularly the following question (II.II.26) on the order of charity. There, Aquinas asks whether we ought to love one neighbor more than another, and he responds that, properly understood, we should.

The key to grasping Aquinas's argument here is his strong endorsement of an ordering principle to the inclination of grace that perfects and elevates, but does not obliterate, the natural inclinations, "[f]or both inclinations flow from Divine wisdom."[47] This ordering among the objects of love is in relation to the principle of love, which is twofold: God and the lover. Thus, Aquinas concludes, "It must needs be that the affection of love increases in proportion to the nearness to one or the other of those principles." This does not abrogate the duty to be equally loving out of charity with respect to benevolence, for we wish that all share in everlasting happiness.

It might be surprising, then, to learn that Aquinas expressly denied that we are obliged to love all neighbors equally. In fact, Aquinas held that we are *required* to love some neighbors more than others, and Aquinas is forced to explain away Augustine's insistence in *De Doctrina Christiana* that "[o]ne ought to love all persons equally." For Aquinas, charity (*caritas*) is simply the love of friendship of human beings and God. The order of charity, according to Aquinas, is based on the *natural* order of love and is not a replacement of the natural order of love, such as we might see in a more Lutheran account of love. According to Aquinas, God is to be loved out of charity before all others, followed by the self, and then the neighbor. Furthermore, some are loved more by God than others, and those neighbors are due greater love.

As with Aquinas's order of charity, Kant admits the impossibility of actually doing good to all and the need to direct beneficence to some at the expense of others. "For in wishing I can be *equally* benevolent to everyone, whereas in acting I can, without violating the universality of the maxim, vary the degree greatly in accordance with the different objects of my love (one of whom concerns me more closely than another)."[48] While granting that Kant perceives the need to restrict and order beneficence, he never provides a means by which one could judge proper or improper beneficence. One is left with the conclusion that those among Kant's readers in the Protestant tradition who give even shorter shrift to specialized spheres of beneficence (such as Kierkegaard and Gene Outka) are carrying Kant's thought through to its logical conclusion.

[47] II.II.26.6. Note that "nearness" is a fluid term here. It can mean nearness to God (holiness), geographic proximity, or familial relations.

[48] Kant, *Metaphysics of Morals*, 452.

9.2.2 *Charity and Equal Regard*

9.2.2.1 Outka on Equal Regard

Gene Outka's 1972 book *Agape: An Ethical Analysis* is an attempt by a Protestant Christian theologian steeped in Anglo-American analytic philosophy to synthesize the various interpretations of Christian love. While drawing primarily on Protestant sources, Outka is well aware of the Thomistic alternatives to his view, and he frequently cites a book by the Thomist moral theologian Gerard Gilleman, *The Primacy of Charity in Moral Theology*. Nevertheless, Outka's main interest is to draw together the writings on love by Soren Kierkegaard, Reinhold Niebuhr, and Anders Nygren. The result of this impressive project is the hallmark of Outka's work over many decades: "Agape is a regard for the neighbor which in crucial respects is independent and unalterable. To these features there is a corollary: the regard is for every person qua human existent, to be distinguished from those special traits, actions, etc., which distinguish particular personalities from each other."[49]

"Regard" entails that "one ought to be committed to the other's well-being independently and unalterably; and to view the other as irreducibly valuable prior to his doing anything in particular."[50] The agent is enjoined to love with "permanent stability," holding the other as "irreducibly valuable." Equal regard is "the regard which is independent and unalterable; and which applies to each neighbor qua human existent."[51]

Clearly, Outka's conception of agape is sharply distinct from Aquinas's notion of charity.

Recall that, for Aquinas, some neighbors were to be loved more than others according to the order of charity. By contrast, Outka argues, "Comparisons at the most basic level are also ruled out. One ought not, strictly speaking, to talk of superior and inferior neighbors, or of preferring one neighbor to another."[52] From Kierkegaard, Outka adopts a strong suspicion, if not exclusion, of distinctions among one's neighbors. Outka quotes Kierkegaard, from *Works of Love,* in the epigraph to the first chapter of Outka's book: "Since one's neighbour is every man, unconditionally every man, all distinctions are indeed removed from the object."[53]

In the decades since the publication of his book, Outka's theory of agape as equal regard has come under scrutiny and criticism. Some begin by arguing

[49] Outka, *Agape: An Ethical Analysis*, 9.
[50] Ibid., 10.
[51] Ibid., 13.
[52] Ibid., 13.
[53] Ibid., 7.

against Outka's reliance on Kierkegaard theologically and Kant philosophically for the underpinnings of his account. These critics contend that Outka presupposes a self–other dichotomy, a goal of moral autonomy, and an individualistic ethic that sits uncomfortably with traditional Christian commitments. "The kind of life Christians describe as faithful is substantively at odds with any account of morality that makes autonomy the necessary condition and/or goal of moral behavior," writes Stanley Hauerwas.[54]

Outka himself raises many questions for his theory in the final chapter of his book. One problem is how special relations, such as particular friendships and family, can be justified in an equal regard ethic. Philosophically, Bernard Williams makes a convincing case for the legitimacy of special projects and the impossibility of an impartial and universal morality, whether Kantian or utilitarian, in *Ethics and the Limits of Philosophy*.[55] Theologically, Stephen Pope argues that Christian love derives from the sphere of special relations, not the impersonalist stance of equal regard.[56]

Outka refines his position somewhat but continues to defend the main elements of his thesis in an article refining the claims of agape, "Universal Love and Impartiality."[57] There he changes his language from "equal regard" to "universal love." Outka places the universal love argument within an expressly theocentric context.[58] Impartiality toward all is derived from this universal love.[59] Finally, he gives some communitarian elements attention: "We ... have good reason to make strong sociality claims and to resist any ghostly individualism."[60]

9.2.2.2 Equal Regard and Aquinas's Order of Charity

The sharp differences between Aquinas's conception of charity and Outka's account of equal regard are most clearly seen in Aquinas's proposed order of charity, discussed briefly earlier. Rather than demanding equal and impartial treatment for all, Aquinas argues that charity entails different treatment for different people. This so-called "order of charity" is the subject of II.II.26. The primary object of charity is, of course, God. The second object of charity

54 Stanley Hauerwas, *A Community of Character* (Notre Dame: University of Notre Dame Press, 1981), 130.

55 Bernard Williams, *Ethics and the Limits of Philosophy* (London: Routledge, 1985).

56 Stephen J. Pope, *The Evolution of Altruism and the Ordering of Love* (Washington DC: Georgetown University Press, 1995).

57 Gene Outka, "Universal Love and Impartiality," in *The Love Commandments: Essays in Christian Ethics and Moral Philosophy*, eds. Edmund N. Santurri and William Werpehowski (Eugene: Wipf and Stock Publishers, 1992).

58 Ibid., 6–10.

59 Ibid., 10–17.

60 Ibid., 63.

is the self, for the self directly partakes of the divine good, but a neighbor is loved for his or her fellowship in pursuit of that good.[61] While privileging self-love over neighbor-love is at odds with one aspect of equal regard, it is in Aquinas's answer to the question of whether one neighbor ought to be loved more (i.e. unequally) than another that he contradicts most squarely Outka's argument for equal regard. Not only is the self to be loved above the neighbor, but some neighbors are to be loved more than others. In II.II.26.6, Aquinas states, "Since the principle of love is God, and the person who loves, it must needs be that the affection of love increases in proportion to the nearness to one or the other of those principles." Those closer to the first principle of love, God, are those who possess greater goodness: "Our neighbors are not all equally related to God; some are nearer to Him, by reason of their greater goodness, and those we ought, out of charity, to love more than those who are not so near him."[62] Members of one's family and other special relations are proximate to the second principle, the person who loves.[63]

The remainder of the treatise on charity primarily deals with those acts that manifest charity or those vices that are opposed to charity. For instance, Aquinas discusses fraternal correction (II.II.33) as an act of charity (because it is directly concerned with the neighbor's relationship to God). One of the most famous questions in the *Summa Theologiae*, concerning the possibility of fighting a just war and whether doing so is inconsistent with charity, is II.II.40 (Aquinas, following Augustine, famously holds that it is possible to wage a just war under certain conditions).[64] Finally, in II.II.44.1, Aquinas asks whether there should be precepts given about charity. He answers affirmatively, and in II.II.44.4 and II.II.44.5, he identifies these precepts as the dual love command: love of God and love of neighbor.

Outka spends an entire chapter of his book examining the relationship between agape and justice. He contends that three relations are possible: agape and justice opposed, distinguished (but related), and identical to one another. The argument that agape and justice are opposed is heavily reliant upon Anders Nygren's formulation in Agape and Eros. Nygren draws from the parable of the laborers in the vineyard (Matt. 20: 1–16) the lesson that God's love violates the principle of justice. "It is futile to try to eliminate from this parable that which is offensive in it from a juridical point of view," Nygren

61 II.II.26.4.
62 II.II.26.6 ad 2.
63 II.II.26.7.
64 II.II.40.1 ad 3 ("Those who wage war justly aim at peace, and so they are not opposed to peace.").

contends. "The offence only ceases when the principle of justice itself is eliminated as inapplicable to the religious relationship."[65]

Reinhold Niebuhr is the central advocate cited by Outka to defend the position that agape and justice are distinctive but overlapping concepts. Outka quotes extensively from Niebuhr's book *Love and Justice*, in which Niebuhr wrote, "The final law in which all other law is fulfilled is the law of love. But this law does not abrogate the laws of justice, except as love rises above justice to exceed its demands."[66] Of course, much is left to be said about Niebuhr's formulation. What is meant by the demands of justice? How does love rise above justice without abrogating it?

The third possibility is agape and justice identified or completely overlapping. "Love and justice are the same, for justice is love distributed, nothing else," Joseph Fletcher argues.[67] Additionally, for Fletcher, agape is identical with utilitarianism. It is primarily through this equation of agape and utilitarianism that Fletcher is able to argue for the identity of agape and justice. As Outka points out, however, Fletcher and all other authors considering this question of how agape and justice relate presuppose a particular conception of justice that stands against or among various other conceptions of justice.[68]

According to Outka, there are four ways of understanding justice: (1) "similar treatment for similar cases," (2) "to each according to his merit or works," (3) "to each the same thing," and (4) "to each according to his needs."[69] The strongest relation to agape, according to Outka, is found in the last two formulations of justice. Justice as "to each the same thing" is tantamount to a strictly egalitarian ethic. Justice as "to each according to his needs" is thought by Outka to be the best approximation of agape. It allows for equality of treatment for equal cases, though cases will differ because the needs of one person will differ from the needs of another. "This conception is also close to agape in that what is often sought above all is to lessen suffering, and usually without reference to desert," Outka writes.[70] Certain needs are properly basic, leading to a fundamental equal regard for all people based upon the attainment of these basic needs. The primary element linking agape to this notion of justice is its egalitarianism. Outka's conclusion seems to be that insofar as a notion of justice stresses equality and egalitarianism, to that extent will it coincide with agape.

65 Outka, *Agape: An Ethical Analysis*, 77.
66 Ibid., 80.
67 Ibid., 85.
68 Ibid., 88.
69 Ibid., 89–91.
70 Ibid., 91.

While not holding that agape and egalitarian justice are interchangeable, Outka sees significant material overlap: "The point of crucial overlap is that in the case of agape and these notions of justice, one reasons solely from equalitarian premises."[71] The lack of interchangeability leaves little room for special relations in Outka. In certain circumstances (especially family) agape will be more "inclusive" than justice, though Outka is careful to avoid saying agape violates justice in these cases.[72] Equality, then, becomes the common denominator and the crucial concept underlying both agape and justice.

While it would be anachronistic to assimilate Outka's equal regard to Thomistic justice, some similarities do exist. Thomistic justice, by its insistence on equality, performs the function of constraining possibly abusive misinterpretations of Aquinas's order of charity, just as equal regard constrains the abuses of special relations. Both Jean Porter and Stephen Pope have suggested a link between Aquinas's virtue of justice and Outka's portrayal of agape as equal regard. "Aquinas' interpretation of the fundamental norm of neighbor love, insofar as it serves as the foundation for justice toward the neighbor, is very similar to Outka's account of agape as equal regard," contends Porter.[73] "Impartiality and the duty to regard all persons as equals play an important role in Thomas's account of justice, particularly in ruling out considerations that distort the proportions of justice," Pope writes, "but these are not, in his view, the primary or constitutive characteristics of Christian love per se."[74]

One question deserving careful attention is how Aquinas's order of charity in the treatise on charity compares with his conception of justice. As Porter argues: "There is at least a prima facie incongruity between the egalitarian thrust of Thomas' analysis of justice, and the sharply inegalitarian delineation of the order of charity."[75] To hold that charity and justice are simply opposed, however, is implausible. Aquinas insists that charity is the form of all the virtues, including justice. In II.II.44.8, Aquinas ascribes injustice to those who violate the order of charity. Porter finds a way out of this problem by returning to the distinction between acquired and infused virtue. Only the person possessing the infused virtue of charity (who would also then possess infused justice) lives

[71] Ibid., 309.

[72] See Stephen J. Pope, "'Equal Regard' or 'Special Relations?' The Inclusiveness of Agape," *Journal of Religion* 77 (1997): 354 ("Agape, in other words, is inclusive – it encompasses both universal respect and particular affections.").

[73] Jean Porter, *The Recovery of Virtue: The Relevance of Aquinas for Christian Ethics* (Louisville: Westminster John Knox Press, 1990), 135.

[74] Stephen J. Pope, "The Moral Centrality of Natural Priorities: A Thomistic Alternative to 'Equal Regard,'" *The Annual of the Society of Christian Ethics* 10 (St. Cloud: Society of Christian Ethics, 1990), 125.

[75] Porter, "*De Ordine Caritatis*," 209.

according to the order of charity, Porter contends. Therefore, merely acquired justice may be opposed to charity, but infused justice is not: "The precepts of Christian love that are specifically associated with charity include far more in the way of obligations of positive promotion of others' well-being than do the precepts of bare justice."[76] (A distinct but related question for later is how these precepts of love and justice pertain to the positive law.)

There is, however, a common denominator between Outka and Aquinas on these subjects. Equality is invoked by Aquinas when writing on justice, and it is the cornerstone, as shown above, of "equal" regard. Since equality is prevalent in both accounts, justice for Aquinas is in those key (if limited) respects similar to Outka's equal regard. Indeed, egalitarianism is raised from the level of justice, where it sits for Aquinas, to the level of Christian love for Outka.[77]

Furthermore, these themes of universality and equality in love are occasionally reflected in modern papal teaching on love and justice. In the writings of both John Paul II and Benedict XVI one finds a recurring theme that evangelical love is *universal*. John Paul II, for example, writes in *Redemptoris Missio* that missionary love is "a sign of God's love in the world – a love without exclusion or partiality." Similarly, Benedict XVI's *Deus Caritas Est* summarizes the New Testament view as "the concept of 'neighbor' is now universalized." In these papal statements, one hears echoes of the dominant interpretation of Christian love in contemporary theological ethics with which we have been concerned, love as "equal regard," from the classic formulation of this view in Kierkegaard ("Since one's neighbor is every person, unconditionally every person, all distinctions are indeed removed from the object") through its most influential proponent in Gene Outka ("[O]ne person's well-being is as valuable as another's; no one of us objectively matters more than anyone else"). Benedict states in *Deus Caritas Est* that this universal love is "concrete," and, though "extended to all mankind," "it is not reduced to a generic, abstract, and undemanding expression of love." But Aquinas reminds us that an adequate account of Christian love must account for particularity, for the ties of marriage, blood, family, and friendship amid the roles and practices that shape the moral life. On the Thomist view of love and its accompanying doctrines of grace and creation, we love in and through the particular.

76 Ibid., 212.

77 For a discussion of equality as applied to different areas of law, including torts, see Arthur Ripstein, *Equality, Responsibility, and the Law* (Cambridge: Cambridge University Press, 1999).

9.3 LOVE, DUTY, AND TORT LAW

In the long-running debate about duties of care in torts, the law has tended to oscillate between views (sometimes associated with more formalist accounts) of limited duty and views (sometimes associated with more realist accounts) of broad duty. The former is most famously expressed in the contractual privity limitation on duty in *Winterbottom* v. *Wright*,[78] which was (or so the conventional story goes) overturned or significantly modified by *MacPherson v. Buick Motor Company*,[79] cases that are still read by almost every first-year torts student.

In *Winterbottom*, the driver (Winterbottom) of a coach delivering the mail sued a contractor (Wright) for the postal service, who was charged with maintaining the coaches. The court held that because there was no contractual privity between Winterbottom and Wright (Wright's contractual duties extended only to the postal service), Winterbottom could not sue in tort for his injuries. In *MacPherson v. Buick*, the driver of a car sued the manufacturer after the wheel broke and led to an accident. Under the privity limitation on duty of *Winterbottom*, though, the lack of a contract between the manufacturer and the injured plaintiff (who had purchased the car from an intermediary dealer) seemed to bar recovery. But in a famous opinion by Judge Benjamin Cardozo, the New York Court of Appeals held that privity did not limit the duty of care owed by a manufacturer defendant such as Buick toward a plaintiff such as MacPherson.

The standard story about duties of care in tort law runs from MacPherson to a series of cases that expanded duties of care owed by defendants to a wider range of potential plaintiffs, notwithstanding a set of doctrines (contractual privity, categories of entrants upon land, and the fellow-servant rule, to cite familiar examples) that had historically led to dismissal of cases for lack of a duty of care. In *Rowland* v. *Christian*,[80] for example, the California Supreme Court held that occupiers of land owed all entrants to their property a duty of reasonable care, not a lesser duty based on the common law's traditional three-part distinction among invitees, licensees, and trespassers. In another notable California Supreme Court case from the same era, *Tarasoff* v. *Regents of the University of California*,[81] therapists were held to owe a duty of care to warn those who might foreseeably be injured by their patients.

This decades-long expansion of duties of care during the twentieth century was widely interpreted to be part of a move from more "formalist" or

[78] 152 Eng. Rep. 402 (Ex. 1842).

[79] 111 N.E. 1050 (N.Y. 1916).

[80] 69 Cal. 2d 108 (1968).

[81] 17 Cal. 3d 425 (1976).

"conservative" limitations to more "realist" or "progressive" expansions of duty. This expansion was based on all-things-considered judgments of "policy" by judges, so that almost nothing remained of doctrinal limitations based on common law principles – except insofar as they served ends of policy. And so while limitations on duty were left in place in particular circumstances (social host liability, for example), these were mere policy determinations.[82]

Even if this essay cannot purport to resolve every aspect of this drive toward "duty skepticism" over the past century, my hope is that it does illustrate how an exploration of traditions that have long grappled with universalism, particularism, and duties of beneficence might perhaps cabin such wholesale skepticism about duties of care in tort law. Rather than unmoored judgments of policy (or judgments moored to economic efficiency or some inchoately expressed socially desirable value), determinations of duties of care can be better understood as a working out in practical reason of judgments based in love and justice. Of course, the law of torts – like all positive law, as Aquinas argued – will not seek to require all acts of virtue (including charity and justice) or prohibit all acts of vice. But the virtues of charity and justice in their elaborate and differentiated considerations (through the various traditions we have discussed) of equality and special relations help inform a richer treatment of duties of care than the skepticism that has marked the modern view.

As an example, take a particular problem in the literature on duties of care – what should be the scope of a duty of rescue? In tort law, duties of rescue generally (absent a special relationship, such as parent–child or where one has been the cause of the plaintiff's peril) have been rejected. Supererogation (going beyond what moral duty requires) is a much-debated concept in contemporary moral philosophy and Christian ethics. Attention to supererogation may shed light on the question of whether the demands of Christian love exceed the demands of justice. The traditional account is that justice requires certain duties with regard to others (to give each person his or her due) that are inviolable. Through love, one may surpass these duties to perform acts that are not required but are praiseworthy. The task for Christian ethics is to give an account of supererogation from a Christian perspective, including an examination of how and why love may elicit acts that surpass justice. A perspective informed by this discussion of agape may lead to a reexamination of the wholesale rejection of duties of rescue (or might emphasize more

[82] See Goldberg, "The Moral of MacPherson," 1733 (describing duty-skepticism as the view that "'[d]uty' . . . is nothing more than a conclusory label for judicial assessments of prudent policy").

the broad range of special relationships that give rise to duties of rescue).[83] Where the prevailing duty skepticism of modern tort law sees only policy judgments based on, say, libertarian reluctance to impose an affirmative duty of rescue, a more robust account would delineate cases where duties of rescue should be imposed as a requirement based on special relations and cases where the law should not demand universalized supererogation.

This opens up to a range of provocative questions in tort law. Should duties of care in general be viewed as universal in scope, without limitation to special relationships? Corrective justice and civil recourse views in tort law have begun to recover a basis for rejecting realist skepticism about duties in tort law, including assessments of where duties of care are broad in scope and where they are limited by special relationships. Attending to moral concepts such as beneficence and the interplay between universal and particular moral concern provides a much-needed foundation for thinking about duties of care in tort law.

Indeed, one manifestation of such particular moral concern is in the everyday transactions that occur in the law of torts, where the law seeks to discern duties of care and beneficence among equal persons. As John Gardner notes in a recent contribution to the debate about justice in tort law, those who have focused on the importance of justice have left unresolved the question of what a norm of justice is *for*:

> The real question, with which economic analysts grapple heroically, but their "corrective justice" opponents seem curiously reluctant even to mention, is: What is tort law's norm of corrective justice for? What does it have going for it? The answer [efficiency] espoused by Posner himself may be asinine, the typical answer of one who knows the price of everything and the value of nothing. But at least it is an answer. Whereas "corrective justice," as it stands, is no answer at all.[84]

The beginning of an answer to that question would be to understand the place of justice in a larger moral framework, one informed by a richer set of concepts than merely "corrective justice" but including love and beneficence. By doing so, we could begin to understand why we have obligations and duties in tort law in the first place, when and why those duties are owed to all equally, and how tort law helps us understand better (in a way anticipated in the essay by Bernard Williams with which I began) our moral concepts such as justice and love.

83 See Ernest J. Weinrib, "The Case for a Duty to Rescue," *Yale Law Journal*, 90 (1980): 247.

84 John Gardner, "What Is Tort Law For? Part I. The Place of Corrective Justice," *Law and Philosophy* 30 (2011):20.

10

The When and the Where of Love: Subsidiarity as a Framework for Care of the Elderly

Lucia A. Silecchia

10.1 INTRODUCTION

What would law be like if we organized it around the value of Christian love . . .?[1] is a provocative question. It invites reflection on "love" as an organizing principle for individuals, family members, citizens of a nation governed by law, and participants in many other groups and communities. The reflections in this essay are on care for the elderly and the way in which the principle of "subsidiarity" presents both a significant politico-legal challenge and a moral lens through which to study the when and the where of the obligation to love in this vitally important area.

Subsidiarity requires that human needs be met at the proper level – the lowest capable of offering an effective response and the highest necessary to do so. Because this principle has obvious implications for the role and reach of government, subsidiarity's legal, economic, diplomatic, and practical consequences garner much attention.

Less obviously, this doctrine also has important moral implications for the obligation of love.[2] The way one views the obligations of individuals,

[1] This question was raised by Jeffrie G. Murphy in "Christian Love and Criminal Punishment," in *Christianity and the Law: An Introduction*, eds. John Witte and Frank S. Alexander (New York: Cambridge University Press, 2008), reprinted in this volume. The question was the subtitle of the "Love and Law" conference at Pepperdine University School of Law, 7–8 February 2014, at which I presented the forerunner to this essay.

[2] Beyond love, subsidiarity raises other fundamental moral questions. See, e.g., Richard M. Esenberg, "Never Let a Good Crisis Lead You Astray: The Lessons of Christian Realism and Subsidiarity for Public Policy," *University of St. Thomas Law Journal* 7 (2010): 371 ("Subsidiarity is, . . . a moral judgment about human empowerment."); and John F. Coverdale, "The Legacy of John Paul II to Lawyers," *Seton Hall Law Review* 36 (2005): 1 ("[S]ubsidiarity . . . reflects the larger vision of human beings as free and responsible persons created by God 'for their own sake' and yet called to live in relation with others and to achieve their fulfillment precisely in making a free gift of themselves to others").

intermediary institutions, and government to care for critical needs shapes the answer to the important questions of "when" and "where" love of neighbor can best be manifested. It requires asking complex questions such as:

- Can anything replace the personal love of one individual for another?
- Are there ways to organize intermediary institutions to better manifest the loving intent of those who participate in those institutions?
- Does a substantial role for government diminish individual incentives to love? Conversely, can an expanded government role be a public expression of the value of love in a society? Could both be true?

These questions are particularly urgent in the context of providing care to the elderly. As changing demographics reflect a steadily aging population, and as costs of care rise rapidly, the often hidden conversations about elder care are complex and, often, heart-breaking. Subsidiarity can be a critically important part of these conversations.

10.2 SUBSIDIARITY AS AN ORGANIZING PRINCIPLE FOR LOVE

The subsidiarity doctrine is practical in a worldly way,[3] but it also reflects a vision of the human person and the web of relationships that bind us to each other in ways both mundane and profound. Perhaps the most famous formulation of subsidiarity is from *Quadragesimo Anno*, where Pope Pius XI explained:

> Just as it is gravely wrong to take from individuals what they can accomplish by their own initiative and industry and give it to the community, so also it is an injustice and at the same time a grave evil and disturbance of right order to assign to a greater and higher association what lesser and subordinate organizations can do. For every social activity ought of its very nature

[3] Many have commented on these practicalities. In addition to sources referenced throughout this essay, see generally Michelle Evans and Augusto Zimmerman, eds., *Global Perspectives on Subsidiarity* 37 (Springer: the Netherlands, 2014); Edmund Aku, *Subsidiarity and Common Good: Fundamental Principles for Community and Social Cohesion* (Bloomington: Xlibris, 2011); Robert K. Vischer, "Subsidiarity and Suffering: The View from New Orleans," *Catholic Studies* 45 (2006): 183; Michael Warner, "From Subsidiarity to Subsidies: America's Catholic Bishops Re-Orient Their Teaching on Society and Entitlements, 1966–1986," *Notre Dame Law Journal, Ethics & Public Policy* 11 (1997): 581; David H. Mcilroy, "Subsidiarity and Sphere Sovereignty: Christian Reflections on the Size, Shape, and Scope of Government," *Journal of Church and State* 45 (2003): 739; Robert K. Vischer, "Subsidiarity as a Principle of Governance: Beyond Devolution," *Indiana Law Review* 35 (2001): 103; and Pontifical Academy of the Social Sciences, "Pursuing the Common Good: How Solidarity and Subsidiarity Can Work Together," *14th Plenary Session* (2–6 May 2008).

to furnish help to the members of the body social, and never destroy and absorb them.[4]

This appears to be a commentary on social organization. It begins with the supposition that individual initiative and industry can accomplish much, and that this ability should not be seized by larger structures – even benevolent ones. Put differently, "[t]he successful outcome of human life depends largely on the readiness and capacity of the individual person to take initiatives, to accept challenges, to entertain risks, and to deliver performances."[5] This should change only when a greater and higher association is needed to accomplish what the lower association cannot.[6] The simple, profound challenge is discerning what is required when.

Although subsidiarity is a doctrine of prudential judgment on societal structure, it is more. Its salutary benefits also lie in its guidance about the reality of human love as "a fundamental principle that stands alongside the dignity of the human person and the social nature of human life."[7] It demands discerning how to answer the call to love.

4 Pope Pius XI, *Quadragesimo Anno*, ¶ 79 (15 May 1931). *See also* Pope John XXIII, *Mater et Magistra*, ¶ 66 (15 May 1961) and Pope John XXIII, *Pacem in Terris*, ¶ 141 (11 April 1963) (2 April 2004). See also Pontifical Council for Justice and Peace, *Compendium of the Social Doctrine of the Church*, ¶ 187 (2005):

> [S]ubsidiarity protects people from abuses by higher-level social authority and calls on these same authorities to help individuals and intermediate groups to fulfill their duties. . . . [D]enial of subsidiarity, or its limitation in the name of an alleged democratization or equality of all members of society limits and sometimes even destroys the spirit of freedom and initiative. . . . [S]ubsidiarity is opposed to certain forms of centralization, bureaucratization, and welfare assistance and to the unjustified and excessive presence of the State. . . .

5 Manfred Spieker, "The State and the Family in a Subsidiary Society: Guidelines for a Subsidiary Family Policy," *Pontifical Academy of the Social Sciences*, Fourteenth Plenary Session (1–6 May 2008), 314; Margaret S. Archer and Pierpaolo Donati (eds.), *Acta 14* (Vatican City, 2008), 708. See also *Mater et Magistra*, ¶ 51 ("[I]n the economic order first place must be given to the personal initiative of private citizens working either as individuals or in association with each other in various ways for the furtherance of common interests.") and ibid., ¶ 57 ("[W]here personal initiative is lacking, political tyranny ensues.").

6 See, e.g., Andrew Murray, "The Principle of Subsidiarity and the Church," *The Australasian Catholic Record* 72 (April 1995): 164; and Margaret S. Archer, "Caritas in Veritate and Social Love," *International Journal of Public Theology* 5 (2011): 278–79. Interestingly, however, while many papal documents and classic Catholic teachings extol the importance of subsidiarity, in practice there are many circumstances in which American bishops have erred on the side of greater state involvement in social welfare matters. See Warner, "From Subsidiarity to Subsidies."

7 Sirico, *Understanding and Application*, 549. See also Robert K. Vischer, "Subsidiarity as Subversion: Local Power, Legal Norms, and the Liberal State," *Journal of Catholic Social Thought* 2 (2005): 279.

The first and primary call to love is the search for the Creator, and the invitation to love the unseen God within human limitations. This is a call individual to each, yet common to all. Subsidiarity does not address this call, although for many their love of God is the source, strength, inspiration, and impetus for the call to love others. As Pope Benedict XVI reflected, "[s]eeing with the eyes of Christ, I can give to others much more than their outward necessities; I can give them the look of love which they crave. Here we see the necessary interplay between love of God and love of neighbor."[8]

The second call to love, deep and profound, is the natural vocation to love those who, through bonds of blood, marriage, or adoption, form our families – families Pope Francis described as "the fundamental cell of society, where we learn to live with others despite our differences and to belong to one another."[9] This most intimate, "subordinate" level calls is to love deeply, sacrificially, and, sometimes, simply heroically. Subsidiarity demands that familial love receive the support it needs to be productive and fruitful, having as its root the word "*subsidium*," or "help."[10]

What does this tell us of the when and the where of love? It suggests that the primary obligation to love lies where we are most intimately acquainted with those who need our love, and where "those closest to the problem . . . are the most competent to understand and deal with the issue."[11] Reflection on subsidiarity should ask, first and foremost, whether the ways in which we structure government and society correctly respect the centrality of the individual as a member of a family – the place where love beckons us to meet the needs of those entrusted to our care and to accept with gratitude care from those to whom we have been entrusted.[12] Indeed:

8 Pope Benedict XVI, *Deus Caritas Est*, ¶ 18 (25 December 2005).

9 Pope Francis, *Apostolic Exhortation Evangelii Gaudium*, ¶ 66 (24 November 2013).

10 See *Compendium*, 186. See also Patrick McKinley Brennan, "Subsidiarity in the Tradition of Catholic Social Doctrine," *Global Perspectives on Subsidiarity*, 35:

> [S]ubsidiarity enjoys both positive and negative aspects. Negatively, it is a principle of non-absorption of lower societies by higher societies, above all by the state. . . . Positively, it is also the principle that when aid is given to a particular society . . . it be for . . . encouraging and strengthening that society; correlatively, flourishing societies contribute to the flourishing of the greater societies of which they are so many irreducible parts.

11 Robert A. Sirico, "Subsidiarity and the Reform of the Welfare of the Nation State," *Global Perspectives on Subsidiarity*, 108.

12 See, e.g., *Mater et Magistra*, ¶ 55:

> [H]owever extensive and far-reaching the influence of the State on the economy may be, it must never be exerted to the extent of depriving the individual citizen of his

> [H]uman beings are "gifted servants": people with gifts or talents, willing to serve others in need, out of fellowship with them. In this service, they should be encouraged by higher authorities rather than being regulated or incorporated into the state apparatus. . . . When governmental bureaucracy dominates voluntary agencies, it also cuts the motor of free giving that is the foundation of social love.[13]

Recently, families in the West have generally grown smaller. Their members are further flung, and the marriages on which families are built are too frequently fragile and short-lived. This might tempt us to view the family's role in love and caregiving as less practical than it used to be – or than it is imagined to have been. Yet, if we are to envision a society organized around Christian love, subsidiarity asks whether we, as individuals and as members of our families, do enough to ensure that in these sacred capacities we provide help and *subsidium* to the first providers of care. We must also ask the harder and more uncomfortable question whether we are tempted to ask others to provide the love that can come only from our own hearts. That is, while medical necessity and lack of personal resources may mandate that those outside the family and in places other than the family home provide physical and medical care to those who are elderly or ill, the family has an indispensable and irreplaceable role in providing the intangible but irreplaceable gift of human love.

Realistically, there are limitations to what we can do, as individuals or in families, even with the greatest love of which we are capable. Thus, the next question is whether and how other intermediate communities larger than the family might assist in the task of love, and whether the organization of our legal and political frameworks can contribute to this in a helpful way, or will detract from it.

Subsidiarity describes the important role of individual and family, and recognizes an irreplaceable role for the state. However, it also acknowledges the other intermediate communities beyond the family to which we frequently belong and asks us to consider how these communities that lie between family and state are, in themselves, a way to aid in the task of love. For consideration of subsidiarity "is not necessarily limited to intra-governmental

freedom of action. It must rather augment his freedom while effectively guaranteeing the protection of his essential personal rights. Among these is a man's right and duty to be primarily responsible for his own upkeep and that of his family.

[13] Archer, "*Caritas in Veritate* and Social Love," 279.

relationships. . . . [I]t is equally applicable to relationships between government and other social institutions."[14] Indeed:

> It is impossible to promote the dignity of the person without showing concern for the family, groups, associations, local territorial realities; . . . for that aggregate of economic, social, cultural, sports-oriented, recreational, professional and political expressions to which people spontaneously give life and which make it possible for them to achieve effective social growth.
>
> . . . This is the realm of *civil society*, understood as the sum of the relationships between individuals and intermediate social groupings, which are the first relationships to arise. . . . This network of relationships strengthens the social fabric and constitutes the basis of a true community of persons, making possible the recognition of higher forms of social activity.[15]

We may belong to many intermediate groups – neighborhoods, congregations, academic communities, workplaces, clubs, teams, civic groups, friendships, philanthropic organizations, alumni associations, and, in an increasingly important way, online communities.[16] While many may think of these as communities merely for pleasure, entertainment, or advancement, they also have an underappreciated role in the task of love. Subsidiarity acknowledges the irreplaceable role of these communities and the complex way in which they relate to each other:

> [T]he human being needs the web of relations that he establishes with other people. He thus places himself at the centre of a web formed by concentric circles that are the family, his home, his workplace, his neighbours, his nation and, finally, the whole of humanity. A person draws from each of these circles the necessary elements for his growth, at the same time he contributes to their improvement, what a person cannot obtain by himself, but receives thanks to his quality as a social being, is the common good.[17]

Pope John XXIII described this network of intermediary organizations as both "partly result, partly the expression of a natural, well-nigh irresistible urge in man to combine with his fellows for the attainment of aims and objectives which are beyond the means or the capabilities of single individuals."[18]

[14] Mcilroy, "Subsidiarity and Sphere Sovereignty," 762.

[15] *Compendium*, 185.

[16] See also United States Conference of Catholic Bishops, *Economic Justice for All* ¶ 98 (November 1986), enumerating diverse intermediate institutions.

[17] See generally Roland Minnerath, "The Fundamental Principles of Social Doctrine: The Issue of Their Interpretation," *Pontifical Academy of the Social Sciences*, 48.

[18] *Mater et Magistra*, ¶ 60.

Intermediate associations draw together people who have something in common, but who also have strengths and weaknesses of such great variety that they may be an enormous source of mutual help. It is easy to ignore these intermediate associations and the ways they can help organize society to become more fully and effectively loving. As individuals, we each have limitations, despite our best intentions. Governments and large institutions also have limitations. Their ability to help with love is largely impossible because of the impersonal nature of large-scale assistance and their inability to know, with precision, what a particular person's needs may be at any given time. But, in the middle, lies a broad panoply of intermediate organizations to assist with the task of love.

Supportive workplaces, caring congregations, neighborhoods of helpful friends, social clubs that meet members' material needs, or organizations assisting those burdened by illness or adversity can contribute enormously to the great task of love and assist the family. It is worth asking whether these organizations are still appreciated for their vital roles. Fraternal, benevolent, ethnic, and religious organizations that historically assisted in the giving of loving care now often struggle to attract members. It may be that we turn, or have incentives to turn to our own independence alone. Conversely, it might be that we become dependent on larger entities because the nature of modern problems seems overwhelming. Given this, it is time to consider the ways in which there might be greater room for intermediate organizations in the great task of love and to ensure that laws do not undermine the efficacy of intermediate organizations.[19] It is also time to consider restructuring these intermediary communities so they can effectively respond to the changes that have come to modern society. Increased mobility, scattered families, and electronic communication suggest that we need different types of intermediate communities.

Subsidiarity does not preclude the intervention of local, state, national, and international governments in response to human needs. When needs exist that truly cannot be met at a lower level, then the call to *subsidium* rises to higher levels. In such cases, "[h]igher and larger groups may sometimes need to intervene in the activities of smaller and lower groups; but that

[19] The importance of these entities and their freedom has long been noted. See, e.g., *Mater et Magistra*, ¶ 65 ("[W]e consider it altogether vital that the numerous intermediary bodies and corporate enterprises . . . be really autonomous, and loyally collaborate in pursuit of their own specific interests and those of the common good.") and *Compendium*, ¶ 187 ("In order for the principle of subsidiarity to be put into practice there is a *corresponding need* for . . . ever greater appreciation of associations and intermediate organizations in their fundamental choices and in those that cannot be delegated to or exercised by others.").

intervention should seek to help the smaller group better pursue those goods appropriate to it."[20]

Catholic teaching expresses caution about this, but simultaneously recognizes it as a legitimate need:

> *Various circumstances may make it advisable that the State step in to supply certain functions.* One may think, for example, of situations in which it is necessary for the State itself to stimulate the economy . . . One may also envision the reality of serious social imbalance or injustice where only the intervention of the public authority can create conditions of greater equality, justice and peace. . . . [H]owever, this institutional substitution must not continue any longer than is absolutely necessary, since justification for such intervention is found only in the *exceptional nature* of the situation.[21]

With the caveat that intervention should be "exceptional," there is a proper, important role for larger entities.[22] Obviously, impersonal governmental institutions are incapable of feeling love. States cannot be a meaningful substitute for intimate human relationships. Yet, there is a role for love even here. What we set as local, state, or national policy and the priorities we collectively articulate say much about our common values, what we care for, and, yes, what we love. As we create legal frameworks and decide what law should advance and support, we have a sacred opportunity to consider what we love and how best to protect it. Law is not a neutral construct, but is a reflection of values. It can structure public priorities in a way that lovingly responds to needs. Our laws can declare to ourselves, to others, to those in need, and those unloved what we truly value. Ideally, the state's role in the task of love – at any level – is not

[20] Gregory R. Beabout, "Challenges to Using the Principle of Subsidiarity for Environmental Policy," *University of St. Thomas Law Journal* 5 (2008): 223. See Stabile, "Subsidiarity and the Use of Faith-Based Organizations," 316 ("[S]ubsidiarity emphasizes action at the level most suited to address a problem, not merely action at the lowest level. It is thus important that subsidiarity not be used as an excuse to merely devolve responsibility downward . . .").

[21] *Compendium*, ¶ 188.

[22] See also *Quadragesimo Anno*, ¶ 80:

> The supreme authority of the State ought, therefore, to let subordinate groups handle matters and concerns of lesser importance, which would otherwise dissipate its efforts greatly. Thereby the State will more freely, powerfully, and effectively do all those things that belong to it alone because it alone can do them.

and *Centesimus Annus*, ¶ 48: "A community of a higher order . . . should support a community of a lower order in case of need and help to coordinate its activities with the activities of the rest of society, always with a view to the common good."

merely symbolic. It is a way to love with a public statement backed by practical help, or *subsidium*.

10.3 SUBSIDIARITY AND CARE FOR THE ELDERLY

Many have studied subsidiarity in contexts as diverse as environmental regulation,[23] torts,[24] education,[25] entitlement programs,[26] criminal enforcement,[27] human rights,[28] labor,[29] the economic organization of the European Union,[30] ecclesiastical structures,[31] and health care,[32] to name but a few. Elder care makes a particularly good case study for exploring the link between subsidiarity and love. It is a complex field gaining ever-greater attention due to

[23] See, e.g., Jerome M. Organ, "Subsidiarity and Solidarity: Lenses for Assessing the Appropriate Locus for Environmental Regulation and Enforcement," *University of St. Thomas Law Journal* 5 (2008): 262 and Beabout, "Challenges to Using the Principle of Subsidiarity for Environmental Policy."

[24] See, e.g., Robert F. Cochran, Jr., "Tort Law and Intermediate Communities: Calvinist and Catholic Insights," in McConnell, Cochran, and Carmella, eds., *Christian Perspectives on Legal Thought* (New Haven: Yale University Press, 2001).

[25] See, e.g., Patrick McKinley Brennan, "Harmonizing Plural Societies: The Case of Lasallians, Families, Schools – and the Poor," *Catholic Legal Studies* 45 (2006): 131; and Michael P. Moreland, "Subsidiarity, Localism, and School Finance," *Journal of Catholic Social Thought* 2 (2005): 369.

[26] See, e.g., Sirico, *Understanding and Application*; Lew Daly, "European Dream: The Political Theology of George W. Bush's Faith-Based Initiative," *Theoria* (April 2008): 32–63; Susan J. Stabile, "Subsidiarity and the Use of Faith-Based Organizations in the Fight Against Poverty," *Journal of Catholic Social Thought* 2 (2005): 313; and Don Fier, *The Principle of Subsidiarity and the Welfare State*, available at www.catholicculture.org/culture/library/view.cfm?recnum=9533

[27] See, e.g., John F. Stinneford, "Subsidiarity, Federalism, and Federal Prosecution of Street Crime," *Journal of Catholic Social Thought* 2 (2005): 495.

[28] See, e.g., Paolo Carozza, "Subsidiarity as a Structural Principle of International Human Rights Law," *American Journal of International Law* 97 (2003).

[29] See, e.g., Michael Lower, "Subsidiarity and Employee Participation in Corporate Governance," *Journal of Catholic Social Thought* 2 (2005): 431.

[30] See, e.g., Beabout, "Challenges to Using the Principle of Subsidiarity for Environmental Policy," 216 ("Subsidiarity is mentioned explicitly in the European Union's founding treaty of 1992, and there has been ongoing debate in Europe about the meaning and application of subsidiarity to a range of issues.").

[31] *Deus Caritas Est*, ¶ 20 ("Love of neighbor, grounded in the love of God, is first and foremost a responsibility for each individual member of the faithful, but it is also a responsibility for the entire ecclesial community at every level; from the local community to the particular Church to the Church universal in its entirety.").

[32] J. Peter Nixon, "When Bigger Is Better: How Not to Argue Against Health-Care Reform," *Commonwealth* 12–13 (2009) and Patrick McKinley Brennan, "Religious Freedom, the Individual Mandate, and Gifts: On Why the Church is not a Bomb Shelter," *Villanova Law Review* 58 (2013): 437.

changing national[33] and international[34] demographics – changes that require rethinking how best to offer not merely care, but love and companionship to an increasingly aging population. More importantly for purposes of studying subsidiarity, this field offers models of care on many different levels, offering the opportunity to assess what is best done where. Elder care is replete with examples of care provided by individuals, by family members, by religious groups, by nonprofit organizations, by for-profit organizations, by city, state and federal programs, and by myriad other entities. Most importantly, elder care is a field in which the presence of true love makes a difference that cannot be underestimated.

It is timely to consider whether we properly respect subsidiarity in caring for those whose age and vulnerability place them in particularly great need of love.[35] In this context, the family should be assisted in its sacred task of love; intermediate organizations of various kinds should be involved in an effective way; and the government should play a proper but limited role of help or *subsidium*. In asking whether these entities properly assist each other in the task of love, there are many issues to consider.

Home Care v. *Institutional Care*: Government social programs tend to favor institutional provison[36] of elder care rather than home care, even when the

[33] For comprehensive demographic analysis, see generally Loraine West *et al.*, *Current Population Reports: 65+ in the United States: 2010* (United States Census Bureau, June 2014). This report notes, "[a]s the large Baby Boom cohort ages, the United States will experience rapid growth in both the number aged 65 and older and their share of the total population." Ibid., 1. See also ibid., 3 ("In 2010, there were 40.3 million people aged 65 and older, 12 times the number in 1990."); ibid. ("By 2050, the percentage of the population aged 65 and over is projected to reach 20.9 percent, with the steepest increase occurring between 2010 and 2030."); and ibid., 6 ("Population aging has been remarkable in the oldest-old population, those aged 85 and older.").

[34] West *et al.*, 19 ("In 2050, it is projected that 100 countries will have an older population comprising at least a 20 percent share of the total population.") and ibid., 20 ("An unprecedented shift will occur between 2015 and 2020, when the percentage of older people (aged 65 and over) in the global population will surpass the percentage of the very young (aged 0 – 4) for the first time".).

[35] See, e.g., Sirico, *Understanding and Application*, 561: "[E]very society includes a large and ever-changing group of people who are not in a position to be completely independent, whether physically, economically, mentally, or spiritually.").

[36] See Spieker, "The State and the Family in a Subsidiary Society," 320–21 ("In relation to providing for elderly citizens who need care and attention, subsidiarity family policy demands that priority be given to measures which strengthen the readiness and capacity of families to undertake such care."). In recent years, the nature of institutional care has changed and there appears to be a corresponding trend in expenditures, which may reverse the current situation. See West, *et al.*, 3 ("Medicaid funds for long-term care have been shifting away from nursing homes with funding for home-and community-based services increasing from 13 percent of total funding in 1990 to 43 percent in 2007.") and ibid. ("The share of the older population residing in skilled nursing facilities declined from 4.5 percent in 2000 to 3.1 percent in 2010. The share in other long-term care facilities, such as assisted living, has been growing.").

latter is far more common,[37] economical,[38] and overwhelmingly favored by both the elderly and their loved ones if it is medically, financially, and practically feasible. In a world of limited resources, Medicaid funds are slowly being reorganized in a way that may offer support for in-home long term rather than institutional care. However, programs providing such resources are not easy to navigate, and funding is not sufficient. It is important to consider how to support trained compassionate home care providers as well as family members who still play an irreplaceable role in the material, physical, and emotional well-being of elderly loved ones. While situations in which the elderly have no one to care for them are tragic, it is also heartrending to see situations in which there is a loved one ready to assume in-home care but cannot do so for want of a relatively small amount of financial or other support.

Intergenerational Conflicts: Child care has become a vitally important political issue – particularly as a so-called "women's issue." Yet, we often neglect to discuss the critical need for assistance to families caring for elderly loved ones, a task often performed by women and often provided to women who outlive their male counterparts.[39] Both require thinking of ways to assist families in the task of offering loving service to those in need of care, but elder care does not seem to have the priority it should in the public discourse.[40] Many of the issues that

[37] See Kim Parker and Eileen Patten, "Caregiving for Older Family Members," *Pew Research Social and Demographic Trends* (30 January 2013), available at www.pewsocialtrends.org/2013/01/30/caregiving-for-older-family-members/ ("Among all adults with an aging parent who say their parent or parents need care, 31% say they provide most of the help, 39% say someone else in the family does it, and 14% say most of the care is managed by paid help or assisted living facilities."); Id. at 5 ("[A]bout a quarter (23%) of all adults in their 40s or 50s who have at least one parent age 65 or older . . . are providing at least some day-to-day assistance to a parent."); and West *et al.*, above note, at 50 ("Most of the care provided to older people comes from family members, friends, and others who are unpaid, and most of the care is provided in the recipient's home.").

[38] See West *et al.*, 51 ("The average cost of a private room in a nursing home was $229 per day or $83,585 annually in 2010. . . . Average assisted living rates were $3,293 per month or $39,516 annually. For in-home care, rates averaged $21 per hour for home health aides and $19 per hour for homemakers."); and ibid. ("Less than one-fifth of older people have enough personal resources to live in a nursing home for more than 3 years, and almost two-thirds cannot even afford even 1 year.").

[39] See Parker, "Caregiving for Older Family Members," 3–5 and West, *et al.*, 50. Because of the greater longevity generally enjoyed by women, women are also more likely to need care themselves. See West *et al.*, 11 ("There were 89 men per 100 women among those aged 65 to 69, and 38 men per 100 women among those aged 90 and over."). Furthermore, elderly women are more likely to experience poverty. See West *et al.*, 80 ("Poverty rates differ between men and women. Higher percentages of older women lived in or near poverty in 2010 than men. . . . 10.7 percent of older women were living below the poverty line, compared with 6.7 percent of older men.").

[40] The scale of elder care provided by family members is significant. See Parker, "Caregiving for Older Family Members" ("14% of adults in their 40s and 50s have already cared for an aging

involve the provision of supportive care to children are very similar to those that arise in elder care. Yet child care tends to garner more attention, possibly because it is filled with hope and a daily movement toward independence on the part of the person being cared for. However, elder care often involves those subject to progressively diminishing strength and independence. This is an opportunity for those with an interest in elder care and child care to learn from each other about what has worked and what has failed. The options for child care – care by relatives, in-home nannies, baby-sitting co-ops, flexible workplace arrangements for employees, day care centers in homes or schools, and short-term camps, to name a few – have generated successes and failures as well. These experiences can be instructive for the provision of loving elder care. It may also be time to be more creative about developing methods for providing intergenerational care – that is, creating situations in which the elderly and the young can be cared for in the same place. This is not always practical. However, it is frequently reported that the elderly benefit from contact with young children, and vice versa. Yet, rarely are there good models for caring for both together in a way that benefits both. The shortage of care for both groups might be precisely the impetus for new ways of care that embrace both ends of life's spectrum.

The Role of Entitlements: A politically powerful elder care bureaucracy has arisen in which permanent entitlements are often seen as preferable to temporary assistance. However, if "[h]igher orders can intervene in the affairs of the lower ones only as auxiliary aids, and even then only under certain well-defined circumstances,"[41] then we need to narrow the scope of bureaucracies so they assist only when necessary or beneficial[42]

Well over a century ago, Pope Leo XIII, in a different context, considered the task of balancing aid to a family with state intervention, warning:

parent or other elderly family member, and nearly seven-in-ten say that it is 'very' (48%) or 'somewhat' (20%) likely that they will have to do this in the future.") and Id. at 3 ("According to data from the Bureau of Labor Statistics, 16% of all Americans ages 15 and older (including 23% of Americans ages 45 to 64) provided some level of unpaid care to an adult aged 65 or older in 2011. More than four-in-ten eldercare providers (42%) were caring for a parent.").

41 Sirico, *Understanding and Application*, 551.

42 See Sorondo, "Solidarity and Subsidiarity as Parts of Justice and Agape/Charity," 63 ("[H]elp, to remain such, must not entail the absorption, elimination or subjugation of the persons or societies that are helped. This means that the society that helps limit its actions, forcing itself to act so as not to invade the space of the responsibilities of others or at least invading that space solely in exceptional cases of need where substitution is required.") and Sirico, *Understanding and Application*, 564 ("[T]he notion of an 'entitlement' is directly contradictory to the subsidiarity principle. In this case, the state is not intervening when other lower orders have failed, but assuming that failure is a constant pattern of the lower orders, and robbing them of the opportunity to provide better care for those who need.").

> To desire, therefore, that the civil power should enter arbitrarily into the privacy of homes is a great and pernicious error. If a family perchance is in such extreme difficulty and is so completely without plans that it is entirely unable to help itself, it is right that the distress be remedied by public aid, for each individual family is a part of the community. Similarly, if anywhere there is a grave violation of mutual rights within the family walls, public authority shall restore to each his right; for this is not usurping the rights of citizens, but protecting and confirming them . . . Those in charge of public affairs, however, must stop here; nature does not permit them to go beyond these limits.[43]

Unfortunately, there is no shortage of situations in which the elderly are vulnerable. When there is a lack of love in the most intimate communities, there is an irreplaceable role for local, state, and federal assistance to ameliorate this.[44] These situations are, sadly, more common than one would hope. Likewise, there is an irreplaceable role for higher-order communities where a family's poverty may leave material resources in short supply.[45] Subsidiarity respects the benefits of higher-order problem-solving in cases of such great need.[46] Yet, great caution is required to prevent these situations from driving large-scale decision-making about elder care rather than a more finely tuned approach.

There is a danger that the entitlements created by large government bureaucracies will create disincentive for individuals, families, and intermediate communities to offer more personalized, lovingly active care.[47] Overreliance on

[43] *Rerum Novarum*, ¶ 21.

[44] Aku, *Subsidiarity and Common Good*, 54 ("Such assistance is not simply a moral, but a legitimate juridical function of the state. It is a question of justice and not charity. By endorsing legitimate intervention, he shows that the highest human value is not liberty but the dignity of the person.").

[45] There has been some reduction in poverty among older Americans. *See* West *et al.*, 78 ("The proportion of the older population living in poverty generally declined during the 1960s and early 1970s due to the expansion of Social Security and the expansion of Medicare. Since 1975, the older population's poverty rate has continued a slower downward trend, with fluctuations."). Yet, poverty among the elderly remains a challenge. See ibid., 78 ("9.0 percent of the population aged 65 and over lived in poverty in 2010. . . . [A]n additional 5.7 percent lived 'near poverty.'").

[46] See, e.g., *Mater et Magistra*, ¶ 61.

[47] This problem is explored more fully in Pier Paolo Donati, "The States and the Family in a Subsidiary Society," in *Pontifical Academy for the Social Sciences*, 266–310, at 276 ("Entrusting a good number of family functions to services which are outside the family leads to an over-burdening of the welfare state. The state fails to meet the expectations which are thus aroused."); ibid., 277 ("The state's attitude and actions towards the family should turn away from the idea of making the family more passive. This does not mean that there should be fewer services rather, it means the complete opposite, that there should be more services for the family."); and Spieker, "The State and the Family in a Subsidiary Society," 314–15 ("When subordinate entities prove unable to live up to their tasks on their own, the principle of subsidiarity further

government assistance may mean that families will no longer have incentives to make the loving sacrifices that bind them to care for each other throughout life. This is a complex question in the context of elder care – particularly as entitlement programs grow in scope, as the population benefitting from them grows in size, and as political pressures deter meaningful efforts to shrink these programs. Certainly, the allocation of resources to assist those in need is one way of directing large-scale government institutions to reflect an ideal of love. But, absent restraint, what was originally designed as a loving response to a temporary, acute need, can become a permanent reliance on the government to provide what individuals, families, or intermediary groups can more locally and more lovingly provide.

In a compassionate society, providing necessary assistance to those who cannot provide for themselves is a necessary and important function for the larger community. However, it is critically important to delineate clear standards for who needs help, for how long, and under what conditions that assistance should end. Of course, for those whose situations become progressively worse, this assistance may never end. But, for those who are capable or greater independence, expiration dates, sunset provisions, or continued evaluation of need should be implemented to ensure both that individuals are not harmed by unnecessary dependence and that scarce public resources are devoted to those in the most acute need.

Neglect of Spiritual and Emotional Needs of the Elderly: Public policies often focus exclusively or primarily on providing financial and material assistance to the exclusion of spiritual and emotional needs.[48] In the rush to make sure vulnerable people are healthy and safe, it can be easy to overlook the need for companionship, spiritual care, and emotional support during an often difficult season of life. Smaller entities are uniquely capable of doing this well. In past years, religious groups often played an essential role in this

obliges the State to not simply assume these tasks but rather search for ways to increase self-help capacities of the lesser units. The long-term strengthening of self-help capacities has a clear priority over any short-term gains in effectiveness."). See also *Mater et Magistra*, ¶ 62:

> [M]ultiplication and daily extension of forms of association brings with it a multiplicity of restrictive laws and regulations in many departments of human life. As a consequence, it narrows the sphere of a person's freedom of action. The means often used, the methods followed, the atmosphere created, all conspire to make it difficult for a person to think independently of outside influences, to act on his own initiative, exercise his responsibility and express and fulfill his own personality.

[48] Pope Benedict XVI cautioned, "[l]ove does not simply offer people material help, but refreshment and care for their souls, something which often is even more necessary. . . . [T]he claim that just social structures would make works of charity superfluous masks a materialistic conception of man: the mistaken notion that man can live 'by bread alone.'" *Deus Caritas Est*, ¶ 28.

aspect of elder care by operating homes and health care facilities for those in need. However, as religious communities have declined in number and have had to surrender many of their institutions, these intermediary institutions are becoming rarer. Thus, without conscious effort to address them, spiritual and emotional needs can be neglected.

An increasing body of literature touts the importance of the spiritual life and emotional support in the difficult seasons of life. Thus, in the training of elder care professionals, this should be a part of the curriculum. As religious institutions become rarer, religious institutions and faith communities might have a new role to play not in the direct provision of faith-based services but, perhaps, in sponsoring training sessions and support programs for caregivers – both professional and unpaid – so that the importance of spiritual and emotional well-being can be emphasized. Likewise, in circumstances where faith-based care for the elderly is still an option, it is becoming ever more important that laws recognize and protect the conscience of those caregivers so that they and the institutions in which they work need not betray their religious convictions in the provision of care.

Regulation of Caregivers: The state has an important role in ensuring the safety and well-being of vulnerable elderly people. However, there is a danger that the over-professionalization of such care may discourage family members from offering care if they come to believe that these tasks are too difficult or that they can be liable for neglect if they do not provide the same level of care that professionals do. It is important to be creative in ensuring that elder care is regulated while, at the same time, preserving space for the loving care provided by non-professional relatives, friends, neighbors, and religious communities.[49] It is also important to ensure that well-publicized incidents of elder abuse and neglect by relatives do not lead to an exaggerated, negative view of human nature that breeds suspicion about family care. Thus, providing training to family care providers and initiatives to grapple with caregiver stress may

[49] Put differently:

> the standardization involved in meeting centrally defined performance indicators deters or distorts provisions – in . . . care for the aged – which independent, voluntary or mutual providers attempt to supply. . . . [S]ocial relationships lose both their spontaneous and civil character and cease to have human content. . . . Instead, we are assumed to be and can hardly avoid becoming passive rule followers, occupants of closely prescribed roles, policed by annual reviews, with no gifts to bring unless acquired through in-service training . . . rather than human beings capable of free giving and of service one another through organizations based upon subsidiarity.

Archer, "*Caritas in Veritate* and Social Love," 287.

go a long way in assuring that the care provided by family members is not only loving but also competent and effective.

Elder Care Employees: As the need for elder care workers increases, it is also vitally important to consider how those employees who provide professional elder care to strangers may be assisted in extending love as a part of a sacred vocation of service, rather than as a mere job. Those who work in the demanding field of elder care are paid very little and work under stressful physical and emotional conditions. Yet, it is critically important to attract and retain loving, generous caregivers for this task. As the elderly population increases, the current shortage of such caregivers will be exacerbated and more keenly felt in the years ahead. This is becoming more true as serious illnesses increasingly generate chronic conditions rather than sudden death,[50] requiring support and love for the elderly and their families through the challenges of prolonged serious illness.[51] With burn-out of those already in the field combined with a disinclination of young professionals to enter the field, it is important to consider how to inspire loving service in this profession. Better pay, more secure benefits, and greater respect in the workplace are, of course, ways of acknowledging the importance of this loving service. However, there is a need for greater creativity – considering such measures as scholarships for those entering the field of elder care or programs of long-term service in elder care that mimic successful programs in education.

Decline in Family Support: With decline in the rates of and endurance of marriage, the availability of spouses to care for each other in old age has declined.[52] Traditionally, this has been the most common sphere in which

[50] See West *et al.* ("Over the past several hundred years, the United States, along with other parts of the world, has experienced an 'epidemiological transition' during which the main causes of death have shifted from infectious diseases . . . to chronic diseases.").

[51] This need for loving care may be nowhere more necessary than for those who live with Alzheimer's disease, a devastating illness increasing at a rapid rate. See, e.g., West *et al.*, 33 ("Between 1999 and 2007, . . . the death rate for Alzheimer's disease rose more than 50%, from 127 to 195 per 100,000 people"); ibid. ("In 2009, death rates due to Alzheimer's among those 85 and over were 901 per 100,000 people, 45 times the death rate due to Alzheimer's among those aged 65 to 74 – no other leading cause of death exhibits such a steep increase in death rates among the older population."); and ibid. ("Above age 85, Alzheimer's is now the fourth leading cause of death.").

[52] See West *et al.*, 127:

> [T]he divorce rate among the population aged 65 and over rose from 1.8 in 1990 to 4.8 in 2010. . . . Divorce rates have also increased among the population aged 50 to 64, rising from 6.9 in 1990 to 13.1 in 2010. One in 4 persons who divorced in 2010 was aged 50 or over compared with just 1 in 10 in 1990. The divorce rate may continue to rise among the older population as remarriages, which are more likely than first marriages to end through divorce, become a larger share of all marriages.

care has been provided. Given that fewer people age with the care of a lifelong spouse to depend on, it is even more important to examine how children, grandchildren, siblings, other relatives, neighbors, friends, faith communities, and other institutions can be supported in their tasks of love. More fundamentally, it is important to ask whether there is anything the law can do to encourage and strengthen marriage so that, among all its other well-documented benefits, long-standing marriages will provide sources of loving, intimate elder care. It is also critical to ensure that our tax structure and allocation of social security and other retirement benefits do not provide financial incentives for the elderly to remain unmarried. Likewise, in the event of divorce – in particular, in the event of divorce after many years of marriage – the financial arrangements after the marriage should be designed to ensure that neither side is left financially destitute in his or her elder years.

It is also important to consider ways in which care for the young might be lovingly supported. Many factors can certainly contribute to declining family size. However, if policies enacted today discourage child raising, the implications of this will be felt in several decades as the elderly of tomorrow will have a smaller generation to care for them both within their own families and in society as a whole.

In addition, a number of states have passed limited "filial responsibility" laws that, in discrete circumstances, may hold children financially responsible for essentials provided to their parents.[53] These have been largely unpopular since they clash with competing views on the child's responsibilities to support his or her own children – and they can create conflicts among siblings as to how this filial responsibility should be allocated among them. Nevertheless, this is an area that demands reconsideration and requires, at the least, greater attention to accommodating parents in the task of raising children who can, in turn, offer tangible or intangible support for their parents.

10.4 CONCLUSION

More recently, and with great urgency, Pope Francis spoke of the need for elder care at different levels. Without using the word "subsidiarity," he recognized the urgent need for love and the challenge of providing this love in family settings and in larger communities. While he spoke first of the blessings

[53] See generally, U.S. Congress, Office of Technology, *Losing a Million Minds: Confronting the Tragedy of Alzheimer's Disease and other Dementias* (Washington DC: U.S. Government Printing Office, 1987).

of family as a place in which the elderly find love, he recognized the love that should also be provided by subsidiary communities:

> [T]he elderly person . . . does not always have a family that can receive them. And so homes for the elderly are established. . . . but they must be truly homes and not prisons! They must be for the elderly and not for the interests of someone else! There must not be institutes where the elderly live forgotten, as hidden, neglected.
>
> . . . I think with gratitude of all those who go to visit them and take care of them. Homes for the elderly should be "lungs" of humanity in a country, in a neighbourhood, in a parish; they should be "shrines" of humanity where one who is old and weak is taken care of and protected as an older brother or sister. . . . However, the reality also exists of abandonment of the elderly. How many times the elderly are discarded with attitudes that are a true and proper hidden euthanasia.[54]

In this, Pope Francis captures the challenge of subsidiarity in the care of the elderly – creating and supporting opportunities for love within the family, but also recognizing that myriad other institutions have an important role to play in that task of love. Our sacred task is, in his words, "to design, with imagination and wisdom, the ways to address this challenge."[55]

What, then, does subsidiarity mean for the great task of love – in care for the elderly and elsewhere? It means that we have opportunities to love on many social levels that we may not yet have considered. It means that law can shape these opportunities in more effective ways, and it means that love, or charity can infuse institutions at all levels with a greater sense of the love that beckons us all.[56]

[54] Pope Francis, *Address of His Holiness Pope Francis at the Meeting with the Elderly*, 28 September 2014, available at www.zenit.org/en/articles/pope-s-meeting-with-the-elderly-in-st-peter-s-square.

[55] Ibid.

[56] A well-known passage from *Quadragesimo Anno* offers another perspective emphasizing love's irreplaceable role:

> Charity cannot take the place of justice unfairly withheld, but even though a state of things be pictured in which every man receives at last all that is his due, a wide field will nevertheless remain open for charity. . . . [J]ustice alone, even though most faithfully observed, can remove indeed the cause of social strife, but can never bring about a union of hearts and minds. Yet, this union, binding men together, is the main principle of stability in all institutions, no matter how perfect they may seem, which aim at establishing social peace and promoting mutual aid. In its absence, as repeated experience proves, the wisest regulations come to nothing.

Quadragesimo Anno, ¶ 137.

In his great encyclical on love, Pope Benedict XVI eloquently sums up the relationship of subsidiarity to love in words that capture the complex beauty of subsidiarity as a guide to the when and the where of love:

> Love – *caritas* – will always prove necessary, even in the most just society. There is no ordering of the State so just that it can eliminate the need for a service of love. . . . There will always be suffering which cries out for consolation and help. There will always be loneliness. There will always be situations of material need where help in the form of concrete love of neighbor is indispensable. The State which would provide everything, absorbing everything into itself, would ultimately become a mere bureaucracy incapable of guaranteeing the very thing which the suffering person – every person – needs: namely loving personal concern.[57]

57 *Deus Caritas Est*, ¶ 28(b).

11

Agape, Grace, and Immigration Law: An Evangelical Perspective

Jennifer Lee Koh

Christianity has increasingly influenced public discourse surrounding US immigration law and policy. On 20 November 2014, during a nationally televised speech in which President Barack Obama outlined his administration's plans to extend temporary safety from deportation to certain parents of US citizens and lawful residents, the President invoked the Bible: "Scripture tells us that we shall not oppress a stranger, for we know the heart of a stranger – we were strangers once."[1] In late June 2014, some Evangelical Christians participated, along with a diverse spectrum of Christian leaders, in a call for the federal government to extend compassion to thousands of Central American child migrants seeking entry to the United States.[2] By contrast, around the same time, one Texas megachurch pastor asserted on national television that Jesus Christ would have wanted a border fence and that border security should constitute the federal government's primary focus.[3]

Like the rest of America, Evangelical Christian communities reflect little consensus on immigration. A pro-immigrant Christian view advocates the rights of noncitizens and has emphasized biblical directives to love the stranger and the alien, extend hospitality to those outside of one's immediate community, and to value the inherent worth of all human beings. An enforcement-oriented view, which emphasizes biblical passages on the

1 The White House, Remarks by the President in Address to the Nation on Immigration, 20 Nov. 2014, available at www.whitehouse.gov/the-press-office/2014/11/20/remarks-president-address-nation-immigration.

2 See Michael Paulson, "U.S. Religious Leaders Embrace Cause of Immigrant Children," *New York Times*, 23 July 2014 (describing religious leaders' opposition to political backlash against Central American migrant children, and noting participation of broad range of Christians, including Evangelical Protestants).

3 David Edwards, "Pastor Robert Jeffries tells Fox: Jesus Would Have Wanted a Border Fence," *The Raw Story*, 10 July 2014, available at www.rawstory.com/rs/2014/07/10/pastor-robert-jeffress-tells-fox-jesus-would-have-wanted-a-border-fence/

rule of law and individual responsibilities toward one's immediate family and community, also holds strong influence among some Evangelical Christians.

This essay explores the disconnect among Evangelical Christian communities over immigration, and suggests that the fundamental faith commitments associated with Christianity – the gospel, grace, and agapic love – should lead to a shift in favor of the noncitizen. With respect to agapic love, the essay treats agape as inseparable from the Christian's experience of receiving grace through the gospel of Jesus Christ, and argues for a vision of immigration laws that arises out of agape and grace. The essay articulates several principles that might guide a grace-based approach and distinguishes a grace-centered analysis from both sides of the prevailing conversation about immigration taking place in Christian communities. Finally, the essay explores aspects of the legal framework governing noncitizens with criminal convictions, an area of immigration law in which agape and grace are particularly absent. The essay focuses on the Evangelical strand of the Christian faith, but, given the central roles that grace and agape play in all variations of Christianity, this essay also addresses all Christians regardless of denominational affiliation.

11.1 CONTEMPORARY CHRISTIAN DISCOURSE ON IMMIGRATION

Although the Christian Bible does not provide an exact blueprint for how to structure US immigration policy, it contains direct and indirect guidance that might shape Christian thinking about immigration. Evangelical Christians generally believe that the Bible constitutes the divine word of God. Thus, understanding how Evangelicals have understood what the Bible says about immigration provides a critical backdrop for this essay.

The current discourse on immigration within Christian communities to some degree resembles the secular conversation over immigration: deeply divided (though not necessarily evenly split), and unable to forge a healthy dialogue with the other side. The pro-immigrant Christian narrative emphasizes biblical teaching specifically related to foreigners, broader scriptural directives regarding love for one's neighbor, and the presence of migration stories throughout the Bible. The enforcement-oriented view takes issue with scriptural interpretation that supports the rights of undocumented immigrants, and emphasizes biblical passages regarding the rule of law. This section briefly describes these two positions and provides contemporary examples of each.

11.1.1 *Welcoming the Stranger: Christian Perspectives Favoring the Immigrant*

A Christian perspective that adopts the side of all noncitizens contains several scriptural themes,[4] the most prominent being the assertion that God has through scripture commanded his people to protect foreigners in their midst. The Bible emphasizes that God created all human beings in His image. In the Old Testament, God repeatedly exhorts the nation of Israel to show compassion to "aliens," or what the Hebrew text refers to as the *ger*.[5] Indeed, the Old Testament recognized immigrants as belonging to a group of particularly vulnerable populations, also including widows and orphans – referred to by biblical scholars as the vulnerable[6] – whom God would affirmatively "defend," "love," and "watch over."[7] In addition, Christian voices have emphasized biblical teaching on hospitality[8] and the presence of migration stories throughout the Bible.[9]

Jesus' teachings on agapic *love* have also informed the position of Christians who adopt pro-immigrant views. Jesus Christ's teaching on agapic *love* was neither sentimental nor convenient; it defied prevailing social norms and hierarchies. He told the parable of the Good Samaritan after discussing God's command that his people love their neighbors, in direct response to a lawyer who asked Jesus to define the term "neighbor."[10] Samaritans at the time were socially reviled by most Jewish people. Yet Jesus invoked the example of a Samaritan – an outsider – showing generosity to a Jewish man as an example of obedience to the command to love the neighbor. Jesus taught that the term "neighbor" encompassed all persons irrespective of ethnic group or social status and that God desired for his people to love social outsiders. Jesus repeatedly aligned himself with the poor and the marginalized. Throughout Jesus'

4 Two books written for popular audiences expand upon biblical perspectives that emphasize welcoming noncitizens. See Matthew Soerens and Jenny Hwang Yang, *Welcoming the Stranger: Justice, Compassion, & Truth in the Immigration Debate* (Downers Grove: IVP Books, 2009), and M. Daniel Carroll, *Christians at the Border: Immigration, the Church, and the Bible*, 2nd ed. (Grand Rapids: Baker Academic, 2013).

5 See Carroll, *Christians at the Border*, 100–102.

6 See Elizabeth McCormick and Patrick McCormick, "Hospitality: How a Biblical Virtue Could Transform United States Immigration Policy," *University of Detroit Mercy Law Review* 83 (2006): 857, 866 ("[L]ike the widow and the orphan, the alien is part of a protected class, the *anawim*, or 'little ones' who are especially beloved and protected by God.").

7 Deut. 10:8; Ps. 146:9.

8 See McCormick, "Hospitality."

9 See Carroll, *Christians at the Border*, 75 (describing migrations due to hunger, forced exile, and deportation in Old Testament, as well as quality of life for Israelites as foreigners).

10 Luke 10:25–37.

life he frequently resisted traditional social conventions, maintaining close associations with lepers, prostitutes, tax collectors, and women. As Jesus told those who failed to care for the needy, "[w]hatever you did not do for one of the least of these, you did not do for me."[11]

Inspired by the Bible's teaching on foreigners and love, broad sectors of the Evangelical Christian community have engaged in concrete advocacy of comprehensive immigration reform.[12] Since its founding in mid-2012, the Evangelical Immigration Table has worked within Christian communities to raise awareness of the biblical teachings on immigration that ultimately align with proposals to provide a pathway to citizenship for undocumented immigrants. The Evangelical Immigration Table has hosted prayer initiatives, produced a Bible study on immigration and the Bible, organized press calls, and released a documentary film, "The Stranger," which uses Christian teaching to encourage churches to support immigration reform. Evangelical Christian leaders have testified before Congress, lobbied members of Congress for immigration reform, and spoken to their churches about the scriptural basis for a more compassionate immigration policy.

Several factors explain the emergence of a pro-immigrant view of the Bible. Growing numbers of Asian and Latino young people have been drawn to the Evangelical Christian faith, and Christian churches often serve as rich sources of community and identity within immigrant communities. Moreover, churches have witnessed the human costs of immigration enforcement, such as raids and family separation, and the everyday challenges faced by immigrants. The Evangelical Christian church, especially among its younger generations has increasingly supported social justice.[13] Despite the perception of Evangelicals as politically conservative, more young Evangelicals are active in a range of social issues, such as human rights, the death penalty, the global

[11] Matt. 25:45.

[12] See Trip Gabriel, "Christians on Right Urge Reform on Migrants," *New York Times*, A16 (13 June 2012); Julia Preston, "For Evangelicals, a Shift in Views on Immigration," *New York Times*, A14 (13 April 2013). Although biblical teachings have long animated many immigration activists, such as humanitarian aid workers seeking to supply water in the US–Mexico desert or churches providing sanctuary to immigrants facing deportation, participation from Evangelical Christians in such efforts has not been visible.

[13] See David P. Gushee, "Evangelicals and Politics: A Rethinking," *Journal of Law & Religion* 23, no. 1 (2007–2008) (describing increased disillusionment with the Christian right among Evangelicals); Nicholas D. Kristof, "Evangelicals a Liberal Can Love," *New York Times* (3 February 2008) (noting that Christian Evangelicals "constitute one of the few minorities that . . . it remains fashionable to mock," and yet observing that "conservative Christian churches [today] do superb work on poverty, AIDS, sex trafficking, climate change, prison abuses, malaria and genocide in Darfur").

AIDS epidemic, poverty, and the environment, and are motivated to engage in such activism because of their faith. The work and theological commitments of entities like the human rights organization International Justice Mission, the annual gathering of social justice-minded Christians known as the Justice Conference, and the Red Letter Christian movement suggest that more Christians today refuse to treat a disposition for conservative politics as a litmus test for devotion to Jesus Christ. Today's Evangelical Christians thus appear more engaged in social justice issues than prior generations, leading to greater support for immigrants and immigration reform.

11.1.2 *Enforcing the Rule of Law and Distinguishing the Biblical "Alien:" Christian Perspectives Rejecting the Undocumented Immigrant*

In contrast to a view of the Bible that emphasizes a particularized divine concern for immigrants, a counter-Christian narrative has long existed and continues to hold sway for a significant number of believers. This view is grounded in biblical passages concerning the rule of law, takes issue with the Hebrew meaning of the word *ger* (alien) in the Old Testament, and prioritizes the Christian's responsibility to one's immediate community and family. The enforcement-oriented view of Scripture emphasizes rules and law, but does so at the expense of the doctrines of grace and agapic *love* that lie at the heart of the Christian faith.

Chapter 13 of the Book of Romans emphasizes the rule of law, and this passage serves as a critical source of biblical authority for Evangelical Christian voices who adopt an enforcement-oriented approach to immigration laws. In that passage, the Apostle Paul asserts that God has given authority to the existing secular government, and characterizes the secular leaders as "God's servants."[14] As a result, Paul directs the early Christians to submit themselves to the authorities,[15] and instructs them to give "respect" and "honor" to the legal authorities in place.[16] Romans 13 goes so far as to warn that "whoever rebels against the authority is rebelling against what God has instituted."[17] With respect to undocumented migration, then, the biblical directive to honor the earthly authorities presents a problem. Individuals who have entered or

[14] Rom. 13:4.

[15] Rom. 13:5 ("Therefore, it is necessary to submit to the authorities . . .").

[16] Rom. 13:6–7 ("This is also why you pay taxes, for the authorities are God's servants, who give their full time to governing. Give to everyone what you owe them: If you owe taxes, pay taxes; if revenue, then revenue; if respect, then respect; if honor, then honor.").

[17] Rom. 13:2. See also Rom. 13:4 ("But if you do wrong, be afraid, for rulers do not bear the sword for no reason.").

remained in the United States in violation of the immigration laws have not obeyed the legal authorities put into power by God and have failed to adhere to the rule-of-law principles embedded in Romans 13. An extension of this view is that civil government has a God-given right and duty to safeguard its own borders, including from migrants who have not followed the secular laws.[18] Another strand of the Evangelical Christian rule-of-law perspective on immigration asserts that a Christian's highest duties are to one's immediate family, community and nation, and that these duties take priority over the well-being of foreigners.[19]

Furthermore, some commentators have argued that the Old Testament passages directing believers to extend special welcome or protection to the alien should be interpreted to exclude persons who do not have a legal right to reside in the national territory. According to this view, the Hebrew word for an alien or immigrant used in the Bible – *ger* – refers only to resident aliens or permanent residents. Thus, when God commanded the nation of Israel to welcome immigrants, God intended the command to apply exclusively to individuals who had received some permission to reside in the land even though they owed their ultimate allegiance to a different nation.[20] By contrast, when the Old Testament refers to true foreigners in the Israelite's land, the scriptures use different words – either "nekhar" or "zar."[21] Under this perspective, special biblical duties do not apply to the "zar" or "nekhar" and thus have limited relevance in the contemporary American context to noncitizens who lack authorization to reside in the United States.[22] Moreover, some Christians view biblical instructions given to the nation of Israel – including directives to love the noncitizen – as not directly relevant to Christians today because the bulk of the Old Testament commands were intended for the nation of Israel alone.[23]

One need not go far to identify practical examples of Evangelical Christians treating the enforcement of existing law as the appropriate Christian response to immigration. One political science study concluded that Evangelical

18 See James R. Edwards, Jr., "A Biblical Perspective on Immigration Policy," in *Debating Immigration*, ed. Carol M. Swain (New York: Cambridge University Press, 2008), 59 (arguing that the "rightful power of the sword includes policing the nation's borders, as well as the arrest and deportation of immigrant lawbreakers, even when their only violation is of immigration status.").

19 Ibid., 46.

20 James K. Hoffmeier, *The Immigration Crisis: Immigrants, Aliens and the Bible* (Carol Stream: Crossway 2009), 51–55.

21 Ibid.

22 See ibid., 52, 156–57.

23 See Edwards, "A Biblical Perspective on Immigration Policy," 49.

Christians are "particularly hostile" to immigrants.[24] In 2006, when Congress considered but did not vote in favor of several comprehensive immigration reform bills, a number of Evangelical Christian groups opposed proposals that would have legalized those without legal immigration status.[25] Shortly after the creation of the pro-immigrant coalition the Evangelical Immigration Table, a counter organization that also purported to speak from an evangelical Christian perspective, Evangelicals for Biblical Immigration, emerged. Evangelicals for Biblical Immigration has actively opposed congressional proposals to create a path to citizenship for many undocumented immigrants.[26] In November 2013, the Heritage Foundation sponsored a panel discussion in which most participants alleged that the Evangelical Immigration Table and other pro-immigrant Christian groups had misinterpreted the Bible.[27]

The enforcement-oriented Christian response to immigration may also flow from Evangelical Christians' relationship with the political right in the United States. A 2011 Pew Research report found, for instance, that white Evangelical Christians were five times more likely to agree with the Tea Party than disagree with it, and found a strong nexus between Americans who support the conservative Christian movement and the Tea Party.[28] The Tea Party, in turn, has joined sectors of the Republican Party in opposing legal or policy changes that would limit deportation or provide a pathway to citizenship.[29] And 2016 presidential candidate Donald Trump's vitriolic anti-immigrant rhetoric discouraged only some evangelical voters from supporting him.

[24] See Eric Leon McDaniel, Irfan Noorudding, and Allyson Faith Shortle, "Divine Boundaries: How Religion Shapes Citizens' Attitudes Toward Immigrants," *American Politics Research* 39(2011): 205.

[25] See Alan Cooperman, "Letter on Immigration Deepens Split among Evangelicals," *The Washington Post*, A04 (5 April 2006).

[26] Evangelicals for Biblical Immigration, "Open Letter to Congress," available at http://Evangelicalsforbiblicalimmigration.com/read-the-letter/.

[27] Napp Nazworth, "Evangelical Immigration Table Misuses Scripture, Critics Say," *Christian Post* (21 November 2013), available at www.christianpost.com/news/evangelical-immigration-table-misuses-scripture-critics-say-109190/. Similarly, a panel on Christianity and immigration, organized by the Center for Immigration Studies in October 2009, featured one speaker accusing pro-immigrant Christians of being "opponents" who "cherry-pick and dumb down sacred texts." Center for Immigration Studies, "Remarks of Stephen Steinleight" (2009), available at www.cis.org/Transcripts/ReligousPerspectivesonImmigration.

[28] Pew Research Report, *The Tea Party and Religion*, 23 February 2011, available at www.pewforum.org/2011/02/23/tea-party-and-religion/.

[29] See Jeremy W. Peters, "After Obama's Immigration Action, a Blast of Energy for the Tea Party," *New York Times* (25 November 2014) (describing shift within Tea Party toward "stopping any changes that would legitimize people who are here illegally, through granting them either citizenship or legal status").

For some, a Christian worldview gives rise to a pro-enforcement sentiment with respect to immigration law.

To some degree, the two opposing positions that have emerged over immigration in Evangelical Christian communities resemble dueling legal positions, but with no court in which to adjudicate their positions and to provide resolution. Each side prioritizes different texts, with one side emphasizing the biblical directives to love the noncitizen and the other emphasizing the biblical instructions to respect civil authorities. Canons of statutory interpretation shape and help resolve the meaning of ambivalent terms in secular law. But in the Bible, the scope of the biblical command to "love the stranger" and the precise meaning of the Hebrew word for "stranger," remain unresolved. Does Christianity provide nothing more for the immigration debate than biblical authority that Christians can pick and choose at their convenience?

This essay argues that the fundamental spiritual teachings of Christianity can and should influence how Evangelical Christians approach immigration law. It suggests that agape can serve as a foundational principle for framing the immigration debate within Christian communities, but that agape must be understood as an outgrowth of the gospel of Jesus Christ and the doctrine of grace. On balance, a Christian worldview that places primacy on grace and the gospel should ultimately favor a pro-immigrant approach to the immigration laws. One might ask whether or how a grace-based Christian approach to immigration differs from the pro-immigrant Christian discourse described earlier.[30] At first glance, one might think the difference is minor. Yet, upon closer examination, the difference is quite profound. In much of the prevailing Christian discourse that takes the side of the immigrant, the emphasis rests on specific biblical passages and directives from God to treat immigrants in a welcoming manner – to love the alien, to welcome the stranger, and to value the inherent worth of all human beings. The underlying assumption is that secular laws should conform to biblical authority drawn from discrete biblical commands. The same practice is characteristic of the opposing, pro-enforcement vision. Taking different biblical passages, the message of organizations like Evangelicals for Biblical Immigration and others who ascribe an enforcement-oriented approach to immigration as more consistent with Christianity, is that the immigration laws should conform to select verses of scripture. The two sides are prone to cherry-picking, and attempts at resolution are destined to fail given the lack of an earthly adjudicator.

[30] See Part I.

The problem is that both approaches to immigration within Evangelical Christian communities treat the central message of Christianity – the notion that the world is broken (the bad news of the gospel), but redeemed (the good news of the gospel), not through our own good work but because of the sacrificial love of God through Jesus Christ (grace) – as peripheral to the biblical passages that support each position. A grace-based framework requires Christians on both sides of the immigration debate to speak from a common starting point, and to engage the core commitments of their faith. A grace-centered perspective on immigration does not ignore the weight of biblical authority related to immigration. However, it shifts the focus toward the fact that Christians have been recipients of grace – a radical, costly grace – and then asks how Christians' personal and collective responses to the existing immigration laws might be shaped, first and foremost, by their need for and receipt of such grace.

11.2 AGAPE, GRACE, AND THE LAW

Evangelical Christianity's emphasis on grace is shared among Christians, but has received particular emphasis within Evangelical communities. Christians believe that God became a human being through Jesus Christ. As C. S. Lewis put it, the Christian belief in God being born into the world as a human might be analogized to his readers "becom[ing] a slug or a crab."[31] Although many throughout human history have praised Jesus Christ as a good teacher, Christians do not believe he was simply a source of good advice. Returning to the words of Lewis, "A man who was merely a man and said the sort of things Jesus said would not be a great moral teacher," but either a "lunatic" or "the Devil."[32] Rather, Christians believe that Jesus Christ's trial, execution, death, and subsequent resurrection constitute the ultimate work of God, in that God sacrificed Himself in order to reconcile humanity's broken state with His holiness. The belief that "on the cross Jesus actually saved us by standing in our place and paying our debt to the law of God"[33] reflects the doctrine of grace. God's motivation for extending grace to the world lies in His intense, surprising, and unbounded love – a love that

[31] C. S. Lewis, *Mere Christianity* (New York: HarperCollins, 1943), 133.

[32] Ibid., 52. Lewis went on to state, "Either this man was, and is, the Son of God: or else a madman or something worse. You can shut Him up for a fool, you can spit at Him and kill Him as a demon; or you can fall at His feet and call Him Lord and God. But let us not come with any patronising nonsense about His being a Great human teacher." Ibid.

[33] Timothy Keller, *Generous Justice: How God's Grace Makes Us Just* (London: Penguin Books, 2012), 101.

serves as the basis for Christians' agapic duties toward their fellow humans.[34] Christians believe that the more one reflects on, experiences, and understands the extent of God's love, the more the Christian's life and behavior will come to resemble that of His Son.

Late legal scholar William Stuntz's work serves as a rich source for reflecting on the implications of agape, grace, and the law. Stuntz notes that "[a]t its core, Christianity is a radical faith – not necessarily in traditional left–right terms, but radical nonetheless,"[35] and that Christianity might thus have some radical – even unexpected – impact on the law. After all, the One Christians worship "is not a tame lion."[36] Stuntz's efforts to generate a series of principles for viewing the law through Christian eyes involve more than simply applying a select number of biblical passages to a particular policy issue or area of law. Indeed, Stuntz (along with law professor David Skeel) warns against the tendency, common among politically active Christians, to expect US law to mirror biblical law: "Conflating God's law and man's law thus does violence to both. It makes far too much of man's law, and far too little of God's."[37]

Stuntz's work suggests that belief in Christianity might lead to meaningful critiques of the legal status quo, as well as of Christians' role in the creation and continuation of existing legal frameworks. As a renowned criminal law scholar, Stuntz expresses deep criticism of the punitive nature of the American criminal justice system. He is particularly critical of Evangelical Protestant political support for those policies,[38] observing that "America's justice system is more punitive in large part because voters in church communities like mine supported policies and politicians who made it so." Yet Stuntz's writing also reflects deep hope for the transforming power of the gospel, noting that the relationship between Christian voters and excessively harsh criminal justice policies "should seem strange, because my faith – and the faith of the large majority of evangelical Protestants . . . – emphasizes grace and mercy, not rules and punishments."[39] Indeed, Christianity states that obedience to God's rules does not earn an individual the approval of God. The approval and love of God exists, fully, because of the *Christ's* obedience to the Cross.

[34] See John 13:34 ("A new command I give you: Love one another. As I have loved you, so you must love one another.").

[35] William J. Stuntz, "Christian Legal Theory," *Harvard Law Review* 116 (2003): 1709.

[36] Ibid. (quoting C. S. Lewis, *The Lion, the Witch, and the Wardrobe* (New York: HarperCollins, 1950)).

[37] David A. Skeel and William J. Stuntz, "Christianity and the (Modest) Rule of Law," *University of Pennsylvania Journal of Constitutional Law* 8 (2006): 809, 838.

[38] William J. Stuntz, "Law and Grace," *Virginia Law Review* 98 (2012): 367.

[39] Ibid., 369.

Stuntz's critique of the American church's support for punitive criminal justice policies also suggests hope in the possibility that alternative visions of the legal system could arise out of the Christian belief in grace. Reluctant to conflate the behavior of the American church at the current political moment with the time-transcending beliefs of Christianity, Stuntz looks to history for an example of the gospel leading to a different approach to the law. In contrast to Americans today, Christians developing the early British criminal justice system were reluctant to impose punishment at all, to the point of near-dysfunction, because "Christian judges and jurors worshipped a Savior who was Himself the victim of wrongful criminal punishment, and they feared damnation if they convicted defendants notwithstanding doubts about their guilt."[40] The belief in a God whose Son chose wrongful punishment so that humanity might be spared of its rightful punishment thus led the British church to take whatever steps it could to avoid excessive punishment in its country's legal system.

According to Stuntz, Christians' belief in Christ as the ultimate lawyer/advocate before God as the divine judge should also shape Christians' perception of the work of lawyers, especially lawyers working on behalf of the unpopular and the guilty. For example, Stuntz praises the work of criminal defense lawyers who choose to devote their careers to defending the poor. He acknowledges, however, that some Christians might assess the value of such work as contingent upon the actual innocence or guilt of the defendants since in the minds of some Christians, guilty defendants might not deserve talented lawyers or legal rules that favor them. But in Stuntz's view, such a response "should cause Christians to wince."[41] The Christian belief in grace grounds Stuntz's explanation:

> For if the Christian story is true, each of us is a guilty defendant, without hope save for a divine advocate. That is precisely Christ's role in this supernatural litigation: the accuser becomes the advocate, and the client is acquitted not by his own merit, but by the merit of his lawyer. In our justice system, the advocate's merit occasionally secures the guilty client's acquittal, but that happens mostly to wealthy clients, who have the resources to buy the best lawyers. . . . The Christian story turns that story upside down: the lawyer buys – redeems – the client.[42]

The grace that lies at the heart of Christianity might thus cause Christians to share a deep love for criminal defendants and value the work of their advocates,

[40] Ibid., 373 (discussing James Q. Whitman, *The Origins of Reasonable Doubt: Theological Roots of the Criminal Trial* (New Haven: Yale University Press, 2008)).

[41] Stuntz, "Christian Legal Theory," 1732.

[42] Ibid.

not out of politeness, but out of solidarity, because Christians once occupied nearly the same position as all defendants. Indeed, Christianity says that one who shapes her life around the fact that God loved her to the point of the Cross will extend agapic *love* to others and engage in sacrificial acts of love, even if the recipient does not appear worthy or to have earned that love. In other words, awareness of God's love leads to actions showing love for others. The gospel also teaches that God's sacrificial love is available to all who accept it, leading to the conclusion that all persons are deeply valued and loved by the Lord. As C. S. Lewis stated, "There are no *ordinary* people. You have never talked to a mere mortal. Nations, cultures, arts, civilization – these are mortal, and their life is to ours as the life of a gnat. But it is immortals whom we joke with, work with, marry, snub, and exploit – immortal horrors or everlasting splendors."[43]

Finally, Stuntz discourages scholars from seeing the relationship between law and Christianity as a one-way street. The general tendency among Christian legal scholars is to ask how *Christianity* could shape the *law*. But Stuntz suggests that the *law* might actually contain lessons – "delightful hints, buried in the law itself" – for *Christianity*.[44] One example, grounded in bankruptcy law in particular, is the legal phenomenon of "amnesty – the canceling of a conceded legal obligation, not because of any special virtue of the obligor, but because . . . well therein lies the story."[45] Modern-day bankruptcy laws recognize that someone in a great deal of debt can have the debt cancelled. The history of bankruptcy laws shows that the law can effect two radically different outcomes. One option is for the law to "wipe out the debt, as it does" today.[46] But the other, reflected in American bankruptcy laws until the early and mid-1830s that required the imprisonment of those with excessive debt is law's punitive effect: "it can wipe out the debtor."[47] As Stuntz notes, the analogy between the basic functioning of modern secular bankruptcy law and the primacy of grace in Christianity is clear:

> Before the Father we are all quite literally bankrupts, with debts far higher than we can pay, without the courage to confront the consequences save in response to the Father's undeserved and complete mercy. We need redemption – a financial term, not just a theological one – that is, we need to have our creditors bought off.[48]

[43] C. S. Lewis, *The Weight of Glory* (New York: HarperCollins, 1965).
[44] William J. Stuntz, "Law and the Christian Story," *First Things* (December 1997), available at www.firstthings.com/article/1997/12/002-law-and-the-christian-story.
[45] Ibid.
[46] Ibid.
[47] Ibid. (emphasis in original).
[48] Ibid.

Thus, the Christian's experience of having been in the position of the bankrupt might change how she views the secular bankruptcy laws, and vice versa. To be clear, Stuntz did not argue that Christianity offers a moral imperative on how to structure the law. However, a Christian's identification with the law's subject, whether a debtor or a criminal defendant, might shape their thinking about the law.

11.3 AGAPE, GRACE, AND IMMIGRATION LAWS

This section examines how a grace-based view of the law might cause Christians to think about the immigration regime. Drawing from Stuntz's work on Christian legal theory, it first articulates a series of grace-centered Christian principles, which could apply to immigration law. Next, it applies a grace-based approach to a dimension of the immigration laws in which grace and agape seem most absent: the legal framework governing the detention and deportation of noncitizens with criminal convictions.

11.3.1 *Principles and Distinctions*

Immigration law scholars have suggested that the immigration laws reflect who America is as a nation.[49] The immigration laws arguably reflect America's soul. Christians committed to the gospel message of grace and to the manifestation of agape in the law might find that at least six principles have particularly strong resonance in the immigration realm.

First, Christians might critique areas of law in which grace is *severely deficient*, such as legal rules that refuse to permit the possibility of forgiveness, no matter the circumstances. Relatedly, Christians might embrace and actively look for examples of grace in the law. Where grace in the law exists, Christians might conclude that the secular law more clearly reflects a divine truth. The challenge, of course, is to determine the optimal amount of grace that should exist. A precise formula is not proffered in this essay, but a sensitivity to the absence of grace should be particularly pronounced in the areas of life that have the most profound effect on matters of human dignity and relationship, such as family, community, and personal liberty. Immigration clearly is such a category.

[49] See, e.g., Mae M. Ngai, *Impossible Subjects: Illegal Aliens and the Making of Modern America* (Princeton: Princeton University Press, 2004) ("Immigration policy is constitutive of Americans' understanding of national membership and citizenship, drawing lines of inclusion and exclusion that articulate a desired composition – imagined if not necessarily realized – of the nation.").

However, structuring the law around moments of grace – situations in which the law provides exemptions to the law's demand for judgment and punishment – should not serve as the exclusive ordering principle. Focusing exclusively on exceptions to the legal order can obscure the need to develop reasonable and fair rules to begin with, as scholars exploring the relationship between mercy and the law have noted.[50] Furthermore, secular attempts to mirror divine grace will inevitably be imperfect and incomplete. However, Christians might express skepticism and discomfort when the law reflects severe grace deficiencies, as is arguably the case with immigration law.

Second, and relatedly, the severe absence of grace-based exceptions to the law might lead Christians to question and seek to change the fairness of the legal system from a broader perspective. To say that evaluating the justice of an overall legal system is a complex and difficult task is an understatement. Nonetheless, Christians might be deeply cognizant of the potential for the law to destroy lives, relationships, and communities. In fact, Christians might be even more sensitive to the law's potentially destructive effect than non-Christians. After all, Christians believe that their lives without Christ's intervention could have been crushed by the judgments required by God's law. Instead of punishment, Christians have received the loving embrace of the Father and a promise that God will treat Christians as his own adopted children, even though Christians have done nothing to deserve such a divine welcome.

The immigration laws, which have been characterized as "broken" a countless number of times, offer a wealth of examples in which fundamental rethinking of the status quo might take place. For the broad immigration questions, such as whether to provide a legal mechanism for undocumented immigrants to regularize their status, a grace-based response might recognize that each Christian was once without lawful status in the Kingdom of God. Rather than treat "amnesty" for undocumented immigrants as a pejorative proposal, Christians might find loveliness in the prospect of the law providing for amnesty. After all, the gospel promises not only that Christians will be relieved of a divine judgment, but that Christ's work on the Cross leads to full adoption – not second-class status – as sons and daughters into a heavenly kingdom.[51] Grace might also have obvious implications for state laws that promote enforcement by attrition by causing the increased suffering of the undocumented and laws that criminalize the provision of aid to immigrants.

[50] See, e.g., Allison Brownell Tirres, "Mercy in Immigration Law," *Brigham Young University Law Review* 6 (2013): 1567 (exploring limits of mercy in the law).

[51] See Gal. 3: 26–4:7 ("God sent his Son . . . to redeem those under law, that we might receive the full rights of sons.").

Grace might lead Christians to welcome opportunities to soften the harsh realities and fear experienced by those without status by extending temporary reprieve from deportation to certain undocumented immigrants. Grace might support immigration laws that protect vulnerable populations such as asylum-seekers, children, and trafficking or domestic violence victims.

Third, Christians might treat respect for the rule of law as something different from ensuring that other people exercise blind obedience to every rule issued by a governmental authority, and seeing that punishment is swiftly meted out for every legal violation. Christians should not emphasize strict compliance with the law to the point that they forget to ask how agape and grace might shape what the laws *should* be, particularly if the existing laws are unjust. The gospel teaches Christians that even obedience to God's law does not lead to eternal life; rather, entry into the heavenly kingdom is given because of Christ's work on the Cross. After all, the Pharisees and legal experts – the "religious" authorities of the day – tirelessly criticized Jesus for not adhering to every part of the Jewish code.[52] Jesus' response was that rigid and blind obedience to the law would not gain one entry to the Kingdom of Heaven, and that the Pharisees' lack of love for God and other people reflected their spiritual alienation from God.[53] To be sure, Romans 13 does command respect for the secular laws, but nothing in Romans 13 calls for the government to enforce every single law on the books or to disengage from the process of improving, reforming, and even reimagining the laws.[54]

Fourth, Christians might support laws that reflect gospel values even if those laws impose a cost on them. Many on the enforcement-oriented side of the immigration debate have a concern that lax immigration enforcement leads to a host of societal problems that US citizens bear, such as wage depression, increased crime, and fiscal burdens on the government. The empirical validity of such concerns is open to contestation. But even if migration does impose a burden on Americans, whether in the form of fiscal costs or social discomfort, Evangelical Christians might recall the cost of their own redemption in the torture, execution, and punishment of Christ. Given that the love Christians received involved a high cost, the agapic *love* they extend to others might also involve a cost.

Fifth, Christians might place special value on the role of advocates in the legal system, particularly those who speak on behalf of the vulnerable. The

[52] See, e.g., Mark 3:1–6 (Jesus healing on the Sabbath); Matt. 15:1–2 (Pharisees' criticism of disciples' failure to follow handwashing rituals).

[53] See, e.g., Matt. 15:3–20 (Jesus' response to Pharisees' criticism of disciples' handwashing habits). See also Matt. 23:1–36 (Jesus' condemnation of Pharisees); Luke 11:37–54 (same).

[54] See Rom. 13.

Christian's experience of having received grace because of Christ's role as our advocate, and our deep need for His advocacy, might lead to a sustained concern for the availability of lawyers for the vulnerable. The concern might intensify in areas of the law – like immigration – in which legal and practical obstacles make securing counsel extremely difficult, where the ability to obtain a quality defense hinges on one's ability to pay, and where the dangers of proceeding without a lawyer are high.[55]

Finally, Christians might find inspiration from advocates within the immigrants' rights movement. In the early part of the twenty-first century, some immigration advocates acted at significant risk to themselves. Scores of immigrant youth who themselves lacked immigration status were at the forefront of efforts to seek immigration relief for themselves and their communities. Christians might disagree on the propriety of civil disobedience. But Christians might also see a movement of young people who have been willing to incur a direct cost in order to revise laws they view as unjust, and be challenged by their courage and love.

11.3.2 *Grace and the Immigration Laws, Applied to "Criminal Aliens"*

A grace-centered Christianity might also have something to say about portions of immigration law that have typically garnered less attention from Christians. I next examine the legal framework governing noncitizens with past criminal convictions, an aspect of the contemporary immigration regime that has been relatively marginal in the Christian discourse on immigration.

"Criminal aliens" have long been one of the least politically popular groups in the United States; since their genesis the immigration laws have imposed adverse consequences on noncitizens who engage in criminal activity. Over the past twenty years, the legal framework governing noncitizens with criminal convictions has become particularly harsh, leaving those individuals with few opportunities to contest deportation, even for old or minor convictions. The expansion of legal provisions that bar noncitizens from immigration relief or subject them to detention and deportation has led to the separation of families, to fear of law enforcement and other authorities in immigrant communities, and to the deportation of long-term residents including former refugees, veterans, and individuals who have lived in the United States since they were small children.[56]

55 See below, discussion accompanying notes 67–70.

56 See Jennifer Lee Koh, "The Whole Better than the Sum: A Case for the Categorical Approach for Determining the Immigration Consequences of Crime," *Georgetown Immigration Law Journal* 26 (2012): 269–71.

The availability of discretionary relief from deportation for noncitizens, especially those with prior criminal convictions, has long been a component of the immigration laws. Several courts have characterized discretionary relief in the immigration context as an "act of grace" in order to clarify that noncitizens have no right or entitlement to such relief.[57] Discretionary relief from deportation approximates grace, albeit roughly, in the sense that it offers legal redemption for past wrongdoing. Indeed, the immigration laws – or adjudicators interpreting the reach of those laws – have articulated a connection between spiritual grace and the secular immigration law. As Second Circuit Judge Denny Chin recognized in determining that a Vietnam veteran with 51 years of residence in the country had met the requirements for citizenship, "no man is beyond redemption,"[58] and Congress did not "enact[] a legislative doctrine of predestination of eternal damnation."[59]

But to vast numbers of immigrants who have past convictions, the immigration laws proclaim a resounding message: you are wholly irredeemable. In 1996, Congress drastically reduced the range of circumstances in which an individual could have an opportunity to request discretionary relief, while simultaneously expanding the types of activity that could subject a person to deportation. Some Christians might applaud this state of affairs, pointing to the need for immigrants to experience the consequences of sin and for the state to carry out the rule of law. But the immigration laws stand in sharp contrast to other areas of the law that incorporate limitations on punishment, such as bankruptcy law, statutes of limitation or the availability of pardons. When one views the law through the lens of Christian grace, the immigration laws tell a radically different story in comparison to the bankruptcy example discussed by Stuntz,[60] and not only in the sense that discretionary relief is highly restricted. In the immigration law, statutes of limitation rarely exist.[61] With the exception of a few narrowly tailored removal provisions that provide for temporal limits,[62] the immigration laws permit the government to deport individuals for convictions received or immigration violations committed decades in the past. The broad scope of the restrictions on discretionary relief means

[57] *See Jay* v. *Boyd*, 351 U.S. 345, 354 (1956).

[58] *Lawson* v. *U.S. Citizenship & Immigr. Services*, 795 F. Supp. 2d 283 (S.D.N.Y. 2011) (quoting *Yuen Jung* v. *Barber*, 184 F.2d 491, 395 (9th Cir. 1950)).

[59] *Lawson*, 795 F. Supp. at 299.

[60] See Part II.

[61] See Juliet P. Stumpf, "Doing Time: Crimmigration and the Perils of Haste," *UCLA Law Review* 58 (2011): 1743–46 (exploring the costs and benefits of enacting statutes of limitation in immigration law).

[62] See, e.g., 8 U.S.C. § 1259 (registry provision for persons who have resided in the United States since 1 January 1972).

that in many of these cases, individuals facing deportation from a long-past crime or immigration law transgression simply have no option other than to accept removal.[63] The immigration laws can operate retroactively, meaning that actions that did not lead to deportation at the time of commission can later subject a person to deportation.[64] In other words, for noncitizens facing the immigration consequences of convictions, the immigration laws are the opposite of grace and agape.

Compounding the lack of discretionary relief for noncitizens with criminal convictions is the legal reality that immigrants often operate in a punitive environment that centuries-old immigration law jurisprudence has nonetheless characterized as *not* punishment.[65] A number of practical consequences flow from the fact that deportation for any noncitizen is classified as a civil sanction rather than criminal punishment, namely that the constitutional rights that typically apply in the criminal context are not required in immigration proceedings. What rights that do exist generally attach through the immigration statute. Thus, a noncitizen's right to a lawyer must come "at no expense to the government."[66]

The immigration detention framework in place today, which subjects many noncitizens with prior criminal convictions to physical incarceration in immigration detention, makes it even more difficult as a practical matter for many noncitizens to obtain a lawyer. Mandatory detention provisions in the immigration statute foreclose the opportunity for many noncitizens with prior convictions to seek release on bond before an immigration judge.[67] The use of immigration detention is classified legally as a form of civil administrative detention, meaning that the types of limitations and standards associated with criminal incarceration do not apply with full force. Once an individual is detained, Immigration and Customs Enforcement can transfer the individual to any immigration detention facility around the country at will. Immigration detention facilities are often located in remote areas of the country where few lawyers have access to the facilities. Unrepresented immigrant detainees have also become highly susceptible to giving up their legal rights and agreeing to deportations owing to the inherently coercive nature of detention, language

[63] Individuals facing removal might also contest removability, which can amount to a complicated and resource-intensive inquiry, as I have discussed elsewhere. See generally Jennifer Lee Koh, "Rethinking Removability," *Florida Law Review* 65 (2013): 1803.

[64] See *Harisiades* v. *Shaughnessy*, 342 U.S. 580, 594–6 (1951); *INS* v. *St Cyr*, 533 U.S. 289, 316–17 (2001).

[65] *Fong Yue Ting* v. *the United States*, 149 U.S. 698 (1893).

[66] 8 U.S.C. § 1362.

[67] See 8 U.S.C. § 1226(c) (describing categories of aliens whom the Attorney General "shall take into custody").

barriers, and the complexity of the immigration laws.[68] Thus, the absence of counsel together with the realities of immigration detention arguably have as much, if not more, impact on a noncitizen's ability to legally contest the charge of deportation as the substance of the laws themselves. Lawyers working with immigrant detainees acutely live out the biblical command to "speak up for those who cannot speak for themselves, for the rights of all who are destitute."[69]

Without prescribing the practical details of what a Christian response to criminal-based dimensions of the immigration laws should look like, Christians who allow their faith to shape their normative visions of the law should have a reaction that ranges somewhere between discomfort and outrage. Christians, and theologically conservative evangelical Christians in particular, believe that they were once both outsiders and aliens.[70] Yet through no good work, Christians were brought into the heavenly community and given full citizenship, with full benefits. Christians' citizenship in God's community was not free. It was extremely costly, but Christ's followers did not bear the cost, Christ did. According to the Christian story, any wrongdoing can be undone. But according to the immigration story, certain kinds of wrongdoing can almost never be undone.

A grace-based immigration framework does not mean that Christians ought to embrace a vision of law that amounts to nonenforcement. Nor does the availability of discretionary relief in the immigration laws mirror the Christian doctrine of grace perfectly. After all, convincing an adjudicator to exercise favorable discretion generally entails putting on a convincing case that the immigrant's actions merit such a disposition. The Christian story, by contrast, teaches that we cannot earn God's grace through good behavior; Christ has done the work for us. Nonetheless, to the extent Christians look for inflections of grace in the law, the immigration laws instead reflect a severe absence of grace. Followers of Christ might seek to inject those laws with a grounding in agapic *love*.

The lack of access noncitizens facing possible deportation have to lawyers might also resonate with Christianity's focus on the role of Jesus Christ as a divine advocate. Without Christ as the ultimate lawyer, Christians have no hope of avoiding the ultimate judgment. A Christian response to this state of affairs might thus include a critique of the inability of immigrants facing the penalty of deportation to access lawyers. Christians exercising agapic *love*

68 See, e.g., Jennifer Lee Koh, "Waiving Due Process (Goodbye): Stipulated Orders of Removal and the Crisis in Immigration Detention," *North Carolina Law Review* 91 (2013): 475.

69 Prov. 31:8.

70 See, e.g., Eph. 2:19 ("Consequently, you are no longer foreigners and strangers, but fellow citizens with God's people and also members of his household . . .").

might support efforts to develop panels of local lawyers for noncitizens facing removal, and more Christian lawyers might devote their careers to the defense of immigrants facing removal. My point is not to advocate a specific policy platform around which evangelical Christians need coalesce, but to suggest that Christians might first find dissonance between the current laws and the ideas of agape and grace, and then identify appropriate steps that follow from that dissonance.

11.4 CONCLUSION

This essay has sought to move the Christian discourse on immigration beyond individual Bible passages, and instead tether it to evangelical Christianity's core spiritual faith commitment: belief in the saving grace of Jesus Christ and humanity's dependence on the message of the Cross. I argue that extending agape to the law first requires placing it in context of grace and the gospel, and that prioritizing the value of grace should shape evangelical Christians' response to the immigration laws. I have also identified general principles that might guide evangelical Christians seeking to engage the immigration laws. Finally, I have applied a grace-based Christian analysis of the law to aspects of the legal regime governing noncitizens facing removal due to prior criminal convictions. The hope underlying this essay is that, as Christians are motivated to extend grace to others as a result of the grace they have already received, they will be compelled to bring deeper consensus and agape to the immigration debates that tend to cripple the country.

12

Law, Agape, and the Corporation

Lyman Johnson

The purpose of a business firm is to be a community of persons endeavoring to satisfy basic needs at the service of the whole of society.

— Pope John Paul II[1]

12.1 INTRODUCTION

The sacrificial love of others – agape – has been among the most captivating, powerful, and enduring ideas in Western society for millennia, while the business corporation, of more recent origins, is today the most economically potent institution in the Western world. Each being central to our lives together, what have agape and the corporation to do with each other? Their very vocabularies seem incommensurate; the one is spiritual in nature and speaks of altruism, compassion, and gift, while the other seems devoted to mammon and to revolve around self-interest, bargain, and acquiring.

In part this apparent incongruity may stem from what Frederick Buechner once observed: "The world speaks of holy things in the only language it knows, which is a worldly language."[2] Thus, even if love inhabits the

[1] Pope John Paul II, *Centesimus Annus* (Vatican City: Ignatius Press, 1991).

[2] Frederick Buechner, *Secrets in the Dark – A Life in Sermons* (New York: HarperCollins, 2006), 94. Different modes of discourse in the spiritual and secular-business realms may also contribute to what John Witte has described, in another context, as the "hidden sacrality of the secular." John Witte, Jr., "God Is Hidden in the Earthly Kingdom: The Lutheran Two-Kingdoms Theory as Foundation of Scandinavian Secularity," in José Casanova *et al.*, *Secular and Sacred? The Scandinavian Case of Religion in Human Rights, Law, and Public Space* (Bristol CT: Vandenhoeck & Ruprecht, 2013), 56. Professor Witte's assessment is pertinent to this essay, where it is argued that agape is and can be at work in the business corporation, even if not easily seen.

corporation, it might go unrecognized because it is not acknowledged in its own terms, but may instead be couched in a business vernacular.[3] If true, then agape and corporateness may well co-exist, but our conceptual and linguistic powers of observation simply are not strong enough to fully capture them. Although impeded by the lack of a bi-vocal language combining secular and religious grammar, the effort to more fruitfully explore love and the corporation together can be advanced by appreciating the quite liberating nature of corporate arrangements and by understanding how law can and does open the corporate domain of "mine" to agape's emphasis on "thine."

With the corporation's arrival as a significant socioeconomic actor in the early twentieth century, the corporation itself, like human actors, became subject to a growing number of legal regimes designed to regulate its effect on employees, consumers, investors, competitors, and the environment. With the exception of investor protection laws, most of these initiatives, building on a growing if begrudging acceptance of the corporation as a distinct legal "person," regulate the "external" conduct of the corporation toward others.[4] Law has been less successful – notwithstanding certain promising developments – at reforming the "internal" governance mechanisms to better achieve agapic goals from the very center of corporate decision-making. This latter area of law – corporate law – continues largely to be preoccupied with the so-called "agency problem" between managers and shareholders – and to have primarily a monetary focus – but not to be concerned with other considerations.

Nonetheless, although modern corporate law may not affirmatively encode or mandate agape, it assuredly does not prohibit it, and it readily enables it. Moreover, the growing influence of federal securities laws on corporate governance and the widespread enactment of benefit corporation statutes signify disenchantment with unbridled profit maximization by corporations, especially as these latter laws encourage a broadened focus on stakeholder well-being. Thus, not only is the business corporation already regulated to reduce various

3 In the business culture even acts of generosity frequently are described in terms of self-interest, the predominant norm. Dale T. Miller, "The Norm of Self Interest," *American Psychologist* 54, no. 12 (1999).

4 As the *Hobby Lobby* decision shows, a sincere faith-based corporate purpose grounded on Christian love can sometimes *exempt* corporate endeavor from certain demands of generally applicable law. *Burwell* v. *Hobby Lobby Stores, Inc.*, 134 S. Ct. 2751 (2014) (business corporations are distinct legal persons that may exercise religion and be exempt from providing government-mandated contraceptive coverage).

harms, those who control corporations can govern in affirmatively benevolent ways because corporate law does not strongly constrain such actions.

Part II of this essay examines key features of contemporary corporate law and various regulatory efforts to require or encourage corporate decision-makers to broaden their focus beyond profit making at all costs. These efforts include ongoing initiatives from the Securities and Exchange Commission ("SEC") and, at the state level, multi-constituency statutes and the new benefit corporation statutes. All these efforts respond to the pervasive if faulty belief that corporate law itself mandates profit maximization, a belief that deeply influences modern corporate norms and practices.

Part III examines corporate theory, another significant obstacle to expanding agape's influence in the modern corporation. Certain theoretical premises – such as the assumption that humans pervasively pursue self-interest – seem starkly at odds with the notion of sacrificial love.[5] On the other hand, the remarkable permissiveness of the corporate structure and corporate law can readily accommodate a company governed with greater compassion if key decision-makers choose to conduct business in that manner. Even if the corporate institution itself is not governed benevolently, however, individuals within it can routinely relate lovingly to those they encounter. Thus, it is not the corporate structure as such or even corporate *law* that hinders constructive thinking about agape and corporateness together; it is misunderstandings within corporate *theory*. Modern theory lacks a compelling ontology of the corporate institution as being capable of combining monetary and social goals. Moreover, theory rests on an impoverished account of the very individuals so central to its analysis, an account that leaves out the deep human capacity and yearning to give sacrificially. In terms used by James Boyd White in his essay for this collection, modern corporate theory may wrongly "frame" issues so as to seemingly preclude agape *a priori*. Yet if theory's dubious premises about people and institutions are rethought, then corporate discourse can be enlarged to permit agape's refreshing influence. Part IV suggests several ways in which agape can play a more meaningful role in the business corporation, and the benefits to be gained from that.

[5] This essay will not elaborate on the idea of agape itself as other essays in this book do that fully and very helpfully. For the author's purposes, Robert Vischer's succinct phrasing will do: agape is "love in which the individual seeks not his own good, but the good of his neighbor." Robert K. Vischer, *Martin Luther King Jr. and the Morality of Legal Practice: Lessons in Love and Justice* (New York: Cambridge University Press, 2013), 84.

12.2 AGAPE IN CORPORATE LAW

12.2.1 *Permissive Statutes*

Corporations are formed pursuant to law, their inner relations are governed by law, and, like humans they must comply with law. The field of corporate law largely focuses on governance and relationships within the corporation, and a key attribute of modern corporate law is its essential enabling quality. Although there are several mandatory features, such as the requirement for a board of directors and voting rights for at least some stockholders, many of these features simply construct the inner decision-making apparatus of the corporation, but have no particular substantive thrust. They establish only the essential governance scaffolding, specifying who makes decisions and, loosely, how, but not decreeing *what* must be done. Corporate statutes thus do not strictly "regulate" corporations in the way we frequently think of law as being "regulatory" by prohibiting or requiring specified conduct.

In addition, many statutory provisions can easily be modified. This core trait of modifiability and the overall permissive thrust of many corporate law provisions is a necessary precondition for compassion. Corporate law thus accords broad latitude for benevolence in corporate capacity, and is no obstacle to it, even if law does not require it. This opens the corporate context to the possibility of agape, but without statist mandates. Persons in responsible positions within a corporation may choose to act caringly or not, just as humans do outside the corporate context.

Pervasively in the United States, moreover, a corporation is considered to be a distinct legal "person," separate in identity from any of its participants, and it has many (but not all) of the rights and privileges of individuals. This outcome – recognized by the Supreme Court – remains politically controversial as seen in the aftermath of the 2010 *Citizens United* decision recognizing a corporate free speech right,[6] and more recently in reaction to the 2014 *Hobby Lobby* decision upholding a business corporation's right to exercise religion.

The notion of separate corporate personhood, beyond being clear legally, imparts a distinctive institutional quality to corporate purpose, as well as a moral dimension to corporate conduct. Both of these features are helpful to appreciating how agape can influence corporations as powerful actors in their own right, and not just as an aggregation of diverse humans. As to purpose, corporate law is agnostic about, and broadly permissive of, various corporate goals. Surprisingly to many, no statute in the United States requires

6 *Citizens United* v. *Fed. Election Comm.*, 130 S. Ct. 876 (2010).

the pursuit of either profit maximization or shareholder wealth maximization. The corporation's purpose, moreover, need not be the same as the goals of its various associated persons. At the same time, being a distinctive person that can act to advance its own particular purpose, there is an inescapable moral quality to the corporation's conduct, both internally and externally. For this reason, and given corporate law's own remarkable laxness, various legal initiatives have sought to require, not simply permit, corporate decision-makers to take socially laudable actions.

12.2.2 *Federal Securities Law and Corporate Governance*

Unlike state corporate law, federal securities law extensively regulates corporate conduct, largely through a disclosure philosophy requiring companies to fully and accurately explain how they operate. In addition, however, federal law sometimes penetrates into the inner workings of corporate governance, both to broaden corporate focus and to prohibit harmful conduct by corporate officials.

A key legal tool for attempted governance reform is SEC Rule 14a-8, which permits qualified shareholders of public companies to place proposals for the annual shareholder meeting in the company's own proxy statement. Beginning around 1970, this tool of shareholder democracy has been used not just to advocate that managers pay greater heed to shareholder well-being, but to advocate for a broadened focus on corporate responsibility in the larger society. Today, numerous shareholder proposals are sponsored every year by religious, environmental, consumer, and labor groups to address such subjects as corporate political contributions, discriminatory employment practices, the treatment of animals, environmental and climate issues, supply chain concerns, and many others. Generally, these "social" proposals do not succeed, with one study finding they are favored by only about 11 percent of the votes cast and with none receiving more than 50 percent.[7] Frequently, the aim is simply to publicize a corporation's conduct and to induce voluntary change.

The two most extensive federal regulatory initiatives centering on corporate governance were not enacted until the first decade of the twenty-first century. These were the Sarbanes–Oxley Act of 2002,[8] and the Dodd–Frank

7 Randall S. Thomas and James F. Cotter, "Shareholder Proposals in the New Millennium: Shareholder Support, Board Response, and Market Reaction," *Journal of Corporate Finance* 13 (2007): 368, 373–78.

8 Sarbanes–Oxley Act of 2002, PL 107-204, 116 Stat. 745. Codified in Sections 11, 15, 18, 28, and 29 of USC, July 2002.

Wall Street Reform and Consumer Protection Act of 2010 ("Dodd–Frank").[9] The Sarbanes–Oxley Act ("SOX") grew out of the widespread corporate frauds at such brand name companies as Enron, Tyco, WorldCom, HealthSouth, and many others.[10] Importantly, SOX addressed in unprecedented fashion certain subjects associated with internal corporate governance, which historically had been left to state corporate law. For example, SOX imposed new responsibilities on the audit committee and required greater independence of committee members, prohibited corporate loans to officers, enhanced requirements for officer certifications of periodic reports, provided for forfeiture of certain executive bonuses and profits in connection with restatements of financial statements, and required management to assess and report on the quality of internal controls.[11]

The Dodd–Frank Act, enacted in 2010, arose out of congressional concerns about the near collapse of US financial markets in the autumn of 2008, the greatest economic crisis since the Great Depression. Like SOX, the Dodd–Frank Act extended federal law into what was traditionally considered the province of state corporate law. For example, under that Act public companies must give shareholders a periodic nonbinding advisory vote on executive compensation ("say on pay");[12] all the directors who serve on a company's compensation committee must be independent;[13] disclosure of the relationship between executive compensation and financial performance ("pay for performance") must be made;[14] and disclosure is required as to whether, and why if so, a company has selected the same person to serve as chair of the board of directors and chief executive officer.[15] Also, in an effort to encourage the reporting of corporate wrongdoing, Dodd–Frank strengthens whistleblower incentives, permitting 10–30 percent of a monetary recovery to be paid to someone who provides "original information" leading to successful prosecution of an SEC enforcement action.[16] In rules proposed in April 2016 to reduce risk taking, the nation's largest financial firms must defer payment of at least half of an executive's bonus for four years, and such firms must have seven years to "claw back" bonuses if an executive's actions harmed the firm

[9] Dodd–Frank Wall Street Reform and Consumer Protection Act of 2010, 124 Stat. 1376 (codified as amended at 12 U.S.C. §§ 5301–641) (2010).

[10] See Lyman Johnson and Mark A. Sides, "The Sarbanes–Oxley Act and Fiduciary Duties," *William Mitchell Law Review* 30, no. 4 (2004) (describing background and overview of Act).

[11] See ibid., 1155–85.

[12] 12 U.S.C. §§ 5301–5641.

[13] Ibid., § 952.

[14] Ibid., § 953.

[15] Ibid., § 972.

[16] Ibid., § 922.

or if a company restates financial results. This would represent unprecedented substantive regulation of officer pay.

These federal regulatory efforts undoubtedly evince profound frustration with state corporate law's narrow focus and its ongoing resistance to meaningful corporate reform from within. Nonetheless, certain modest regulatory reforms also have taken place at the state level.

12.2.3 *State Constituency Statutes and Benefit Corporations*

Beginning in the 1980s, in what are known as "constituency statutes," a majority of states began expressly permitting boards of directors to consider the interests of numerous stakeholders such as employees, consumers, and others when making corporate decisions, not just shareholder interests.[17] These statutes were the result of an emergent "stakeholder" theory of corporate relations in which directors are considered to be fiduciaries for an array of investor and noninvestor interests.[18]

Stakeholder accounts of corporate relationships, although seemingly more benevolent, simply broaden beyond shareholders the groups of people whose interests are to be considered in some fashion when corporate decisions are made, including employees, consumers, suppliers, and so on. This is not truly a rival theory of the corporation, however, because, like shareholder primacy accounts – those that require corporate managers to singularly benefit shareholder interests[19] – stakeholderism fails to attend to and deeply value the overarching common *corporate* good. Instead, stakeholderism simply expands beyond shareholders the various interests to be balanced and mediated.[20] Besides the troubling "two masters" problem of accountability that stakeholder-centric theory presents for decision-makers who are given no guidance as to how they are to reconcile competing interests, like shareholder-centric theory (itself just a single-interest version of stakeholder theory), a stakeholder account still conceives of the corporation as a mere association of aggregated individual interests.

[17] See James D. Cox and Thomas L. Hazen, *The Law of Corporations* (St. Paul: Thomson, 2010), 245.

[18] For an explanation of stakeholder theory, see Ronald E. Freeman, *Strategic Management: A Stakeholder Approach* (Boston: Pitman, 1984), 31–42.

[19] For a description of "shareholder primacy" and a genealogy of its use in corporate law, see David Millon, "Radical Shareholder Primacy," *University of St. Thomas Law Journal* 10, no. 4 (2013): 1013. Professor Millon defines traditional "shareholder primacy" as the idea that "management's broad discretion with respect to conduct of corporate affairs must be exercised solely for the benefit of the shareholders." Ibid., 1015.

[20] This point is developed in Lyman Johnson *et al.*, "Rethinking How Business Purpose Is Taught in Catholic Business Education," *Journal of Catholic Higher Education* 32, no. 1 (2013): 70–72.

Thus, while superficially there may appear to be a more humane aspect to stakeholder theories, they struggle to truly fortify community and the indispensable other-directed virtues that bind people together. Stakeholderism neither fundamentally reconceives the self-interested nature of the individuals within the company nor the make-up of the company itself; it simply brings more people to the table looking for, and expecting, their piece of the corporate pie. Another drawback of constituency statutes is that the various noninvestor groups have no voting rights in the corporation, unlike shareholders. Thus, stakeholders are dependent on directors to consider their interests, which directors need not do because such consideration is permitted but not required.

Between 2010 and 2016, a majority of states enacted statutes that, if a company opts into coverage, *require* directors to consider various stakeholder interests. These "benefit corporations," a new type of business corporation, expressly can combine the corporate purposes of profit making with advancing other general or specific social or environmental purposes.[21] Those social goals can, of course, be motivated by concern for others. In Delaware, the leading corporate law state, the new benefit corporation statute specifically defines "public benefit" to include, among many other effects, having an "effect" of a "charitable," "environmental," "cultural," or "religious" nature, among others. Still, these statutes, like constituency statutes, provide little guidance to directors as to how they should balance an array of interests and the various noninvestor groups have no voting rights. Moreover, no person except shareholders may enforce director duties. The statutes would be better if they obligated directors to advance the specified public benefit/purpose of the company itself, subordinating stockholder and stakeholder interests to the pursuit of the *corporate* common good, with the latter being defined as equivalent to advancing the company's identified public benefit(s).

For all their failings, these statutes recognize business corporations as legally able to combine the spiritual and business domains. Broadly liberating as these new types of statutes are – and thus highly conducive to business strategies animated by agape – they should not be construed to alter the continuing freedom of *traditional* business corporations to pursue mixed purposes or to pursue profits in a compassionate manner, lest such agapic efforts become "ghettoized" in benefit corporations only. To be sure, in the United States profit-maximizing behavior is a strong norm and a common

[21] See Benefit Corp Information Center, available at http://benefitcorp.net/state-by-state-legislative-status. For a discussion of these statutes, see J. Haskell Murray, "Social Enterprise Innovation: Delaware's Public Benefit Corporation Law," *Harvard Business Law Review* 4 (2014): 345.

practice – particularly in the public corporation setting – but, as noted earlier, it is not a binding legal rule. An important 2014 Supreme Court decision served to correct considerable misunderstanding on this point.

12.2.4 *Hobby Lobby*

In *Hobby Lobby*, three business corporations sought a partial exemption from the Affordable Care Act's mandate to provide specified contraceptive coverage for employees. Invoking the Religious Freedom Restoration Act, the three companies objected to the mandate because it impermissibly burdened their exercise of religion in the business setting. Agreeing with those corporations, the Court rejected the federal government's position that the three companies lacked the legal power to exercise religion "because the purpose of such corporations is simply to make money."[22] The Court began by stating that the government's contention "flies in the face of modern corporate law."[23] Acknowledging that although "a" central objective of business corporations is to "make" money,[24] the Court did not regard that as the only legally permissible goal. Instead, the Court noted that "modern corporate law does not require business corporations to pursue profit at the expense of everything else, and many do not do so."[25] The Court observed that many business corporations support charitable causes, and pursue humanitarian and altruistic objectives. Notably, the Court did not say that corporations may advance those objectives only as a pragmatic means to maximize profits; nor did the Court say that doing so had to be consistent in some way with the overarching aim of making profits. The language was far stronger. When the pursuit of profits comes "at the expense of everything else," the Court stated the corporation may forgo profits. If, then, business corporations can lawfully pursue such worthy nonmonetary objectives as those cited, the Court reasoned, there is no reason they do not have the legal power to further religious objectives as well. Here too, the Court did not attempt to rationalize the religious dimension of the three companies as somehow consistent with profit maximization on instrumentalist grounds because the record clearly indicated that the religious emphasis reduced corporate profits.

In addition, the Court recognized that many business corporations simply are not organized "in order to maximize profit." Many companies regard

[22] *Burwell*, 134 S. Ct. at 2770. The *Hobby Lobby* decision and its implications for corporate law are thoroughly discussed in Lyman Johnson and David Millon, "Corporate Law after Hobby Lobby," *The Business Lawyer* 70 (2014).

[23] *Burwell*, 134 S. Ct. at 2771.

[24] Ibid.

[25] Ibid.

the corporate form of organization as beneficial for other reasons, the Court pointed out, such as the freedom to lobby or campaign for political candidates. Here, the Court is clearly rejecting as overly simplistic the supposed stark and binary taxonomy of corporations, to the effect that one type, nonprofits, cannot and do not distribute any profits they may generate, while the other type, so-called "for-profits," must and do singularly seek to maximize profits for the benefit of their shareholders. Instead, the Court recognized that companies fall along a spectrum, with some maximizing profits, others coupling the pursuit of profits with other nonmonetary objectives, and yet others (nonprofits) not distributing profits to owners/members at all.

In reaching that conclusion, grounded as it is on the Court's understanding of state corporate law, the opinion extends far beyond the specific contraception context of the *Hobby Lobby* case itself. The Court's view of corporate law's permissive ambit means that such avowed goals as social justice, environmental concerns, and employee welfare, as well as various charitable, humanitarian, and other socially responsible pursuits emerge as legally possible for business corporations and as valid corporate ends in themselves. The Court thus effectively addressed a core trait of the business corporation's legal ontology, not just by saying what it is – a "person" – but also by expansively interpreting what it can *do*, that is, pursue a host of objectives besides just making money. Consequently, those who control traditional business corporations violate no legal requirements when they operate them according to mixed commercial and religious or moral purposes. Commercial ambitions therefore may be tempered by religious and moral commitments motivated by agape, not simply as to the means of acting, but also in establishing the very goals of a business.

This represents the legal triumph of a view many might acknowledge to be normatively desirable but not legally possible. The importance of this legal ground-clearing for both richer thinking about corporate objectives and actual corporate practice was anticipated in the papal encyclical *Caritas in Veritate* (*Charity in Truth*). Pope Benedict XVI observed that:

> What is needed, therefore, is a market that permits the free operation, in conditions of equal opportunity, of enterprises in pursuit of different institutional ends. Alongside profit-oriented private enterprise and the various types of public enterprise, there must be room for commercial entities based on mutualist principles and pursuing social ends to take root and express themselves. It is from their reciprocal encounter in the marketplace that one may expect hybrid forms of commercial behavior to emerge and, hence, an attentiveness to ways of *civilizing the economy*. Charity in truth, in this case, requires that shape and structure be given to those types of economic

initiative which, without rejecting profit, aim at a higher goal than the mere logic of the exchange of equivalents, of profit as an end in itself.[26]

Without the openness of corporate law to a broad range of corporate objectives as seen in *Hobby Lobby* and as called for by Pope Benedict XVI, we run the risk of an unhealthy monoculture in which a fanatical devotion to profit-making crowds out other goals, not because of law, but because of custom and habit. The result in our corporate sector would then be what business ethicist Kenneth Goodpaster aptly described as "teleopathy" – goal sickness.[27] Put another way, all businesses necessarily have some moral vision, recognized or not, healthy or infirm; there simply is no moral-free zone in the corporate world when the law permits such broad choices. Corporate theory, however, lags behind law and practice in addressing this range of action.

12.3 CORPORATE THEORY

The field of corporate law was not especially theoretical until the 1970s when the law and economics movement swept into what had been an area almost entirely doctrinal in nature. Since then, corporate law has been examined from a variety of disciplinary vantage points, including sociology, psychology, history, critical race theory, and others, but only infrequently from a moral or religious perspective. The predominant theoretical influence stems from economics and finance, particularly the neoclassical school but, more recently, also behavioral economics.[28] Economics and finance exert such a powerful paradigmatic grip on modern thinking about corporations that its core features must be briefly sketched to pave the way for understanding how agape can influence corporate law, theory, and praxis.

12.3.1 *The Missing Corporation*

Although the corporation is unquestionably a legal person distinct from its participants, and although the hallmark of "corporate" endeavor is collaborative

[26] Pope Benedict XVI, *Caritas in Veritate (Charity in Truth)* (Vatican City: Ignatius Press, 2009), 76.

[27] Kenneth E. Goodpaster, *Conscience and Corporate Culture* (Indianapolis: Wiley, 2007), 28.

[28] Much of the seminal work introducing the insights of new-classical economics into corporate law was done by Frank Easterbrook and Daniel Fischel. See Frank H. Easterbrook and Daniel R. Fischel, *The Economic Structure of Corporate Law* (Cambridge: Harvard University Press, 1991). For a collection of essays describing how behavior, beliefs, values, and emotions influence market interactions, see Paul J. Zak, *Moral Markets: The Critical Role of Values in the Economy* (Princeton: Princeton University Press, 2008).

productive effort, neoclassical economics has trivialized the group by its excessive emphasis on the individual actors within the corporation. This is especially true in the mainstream nexus of contracts conception of the corporation prioritizing shareholders,[29] but it is also true in so-called "stakeholder" theory described earlier.

Ironically, a truly robust, organic, *corporate* account of the corporation is lacking in contemporary theory, notwithstanding undoubted corporate personhood. Nonetheless, compassion can deeply influence the corporation, whether it continues to be theorized as a mere network of individual actors (encompassing shareholders only or also a broader set of stakeholders) or is more helpfully and accurately seen as the institution embodying the larger missioncentric common good of the company itself. Doing so, however, requires identifying those constitutive features of modern corporate theory that stand as impediments to more fully realizing benevolence within and beyond the corporation.

Mainstream corporate theory disaggregates (and thus disregards) the corporation itself through the use of two powerful, reductive metaphors.[30] These are the "principal–agent" account of the shareholder–manager relationship and the "nexus of contracts" conception of the firm as simply a network of individuals making bargains. Normatively, in each of these metaphors the shareholder remains preeminent, and the corporation itself, notwithstanding its distinctive legal personhood and institutional heft, is reduced to a mere cipher or semantic stand-in for the body of shareholders. Metaphors, of course, can be sufficiently illuminating and vivid that they excite the mind into novel ways of thinking. Here, regrettably, metaphor has led to a prolonged stalling of thought. As a result, today the theoretical landscape, although more densely filled in, remains largely unchanged from the late 1970s and early 1980s when these provocative but descriptively flawed accounts were transplanted wholesale into corporate law from financial economics.[31] It is highly unlikely that financial economists of that era, untrained in law, ever intended their work to be understood as accurately depicting legal reality. For example, the fact that organizational representatives such as directors can and frequently do misbehave in relation to investors does not mean that they are "agents" of shareholders or that shareholders are "principals," or that maximizing investor wealth

[29] See Easterbrook and Fischel, *Economic Structure*, 15 (corporate law is a "standard-form contract").

[30] Easterbrook and Fischel acknowledge, for example, that their contract terminology, as extended into corporate law, is "no more than a rhetorical device." Ibid.

[31] The story is well told in Millon, *Radical Shareholder Primacy*.

is or should be the sole purpose of the corporation. The terminology used by financial economists to analyze vexing structural issues in the management of complex companies simply does not seamlessly map onto established legal categories such as agency law.

In corporate law the shareholders are not "principals" who control the directors and officers, and the latter groups certainly are not "agents" who are obligated to act as shareholders may desire. Control of the company lies squarely with the board of directors and executive officers. To be sure, shareholders have voting rights and they can initiate lawsuits and obtain limited information. Shareholders, therefore, certainly have greater legal power within the corporation than do other noninvestor stakeholders, but they do not control the day-to-day business and affairs of the corporation, nor do they navigate its larger strategic path. To realize agape within the corporation on a reasonably wide-scale basis means that, at a minimum, a majority of shareholders must not sufficiently object to a course of benevolent action that they vote to remove directors. In this way shareholders can choose to absorb a lower return by permitting directors to engage in some range of benevolence. Subject to this shareholder constraint, however, the key actors will always be directors and senior executives, given their vast discretion. Thus, while some see managerial discretion as a necessary but chronically worrisome attribute of corporateness, for compassionate action to be possible it is absolutely indispensable. In this respect, agape may be easier in the corporate context than in the attorney–client setting recently explored by Robert Vischer.[32] This is because directors and executive officers really do control corporate affairs, unlike lawyers who, respecting client autonomy, should (but may not) submit important questions to their clients for resolution.

By adopting the principal–agent imagery of financial economics, corporate law theory also implies that shareholders, like principals to which they are analogized, *should* exert greater control over corporate affairs. In this way theory not only fails to reflect the true allocation of decision-making power within the corporation as codified by positive law, it continually seeks techniques to tighten managerial allegiance to shareholder financial interests, the assumed normative goal. Of course, in companies with relatively few participants, the directors and shareholders will likely be the same persons, so corporate policies deviating from strict shareholder primacy will be less problematic because investor and manager interests will frequently align.

By disaggregating the corporation, the nexus of contracts metaphor also fails to satisfactorily reckon with the role of the corporation itself in the larger

[32] See Vischer, *Morality of Legal Practice*.

society, with attendant concern being given to its proper social responsibilities and moral possibilities. Furthermore, this contractarian theory does not seriously grapple with the political significance of this powerful "person" that stands between the individual citizens participating in it and the state itself. Positive law, however, does vindicate politically potent corporate rights, the signal importance of which is evidenced by the *Citizens United* and *Hobby Lobby* decisions, each of which freed corporations qua corporations from governmental constraint. Corporate law theory struggles with the issues of corporate responsibility and corporate political influence because it struggles, due to disaggregation, to advance a theory that explains rather than ignores the reality of corporate existence and influence. Serious as those social and political influence failings are, however, more important for this essay is the fact that corporate theory's ongoing neglect of the corporation itself means that the key unit of analysis remains the individual actor, not a shared overarching *corporate* mission to which the various participants' self-interests might sacrificially yield.

Although legal theory struggles to explain the topology of those various groups – that is, corporations, schools, unions, churches, and myriad other organizations – that populate modern law and culture, Christian thought, by way of contrast, provides a powerful, cohesive metaphor – the body. The Apostle Paul explains about the corporate church that "we, though many, form one body, and each member belongs to all the others."[33] This bracing image of corporateness radically reorients our thought because it emphasizes both the unity of the many and the rightful place of each to all others; both unity and belonging are underscored. One does not simply relate to the corporate body itself in a sort of bilateral contract; one has a rightful place, a just ordering, in relationship to all others as well. At the same time, Paul preserves unity while fully acknowledging difference in role. He does this by likening the corporate church body to the human body that, while having various parts such as eyes, ears, and feet, is still "but one body."[34] This also opens a moral dimension to relationships within the group because, being connected to a larger whole, its various parts, however different their function, "should have equal concern for each other."[35] In this way, a truly *corporate* moral vision and an overarching organic unity can be achieved through the participants' shared commitment to a common purpose of service to others.

This constitutive linkage of individual person to the group is wholly apt for theorizing about the business corporation. The etymology of the word

[33] Rom. 12:5, New International Version (NIV).

[34] 1 Cor. 12:20, NIV.

[35] 1 Cor. 12:25, NIV.

"company" comes from "companions" – *cum*, meaning "with" and *panis*, meaning "bread," or breaking bread together.[36] The etymology of the word "corporation" derives from the Latin corpus, which means "body," a *corps*, a group of people united in one body.[37] These etymologies clue us into a deeper understanding of the corporate institution and the relationships within it, and how agape can play a vital role under modern law. The corporation, so understood, is not simply an "association of individuals," but instead can be a "community of persons" who join together to serve an interest outside themselves.[38] This alters not only how we think and talk about corporateness, it can transform how persons involved in corporations conceive of themselves, as elaborated below. It may also yield a payoff for society at large. As Alfred North Whitehead observed, a social dividend can be realized where business persons have a broad understanding of their social significance: "[A] great society is a society in which its men of business think greatly of their function."[39] Before elaborating on possible avenues for implementing an expanded corporate vision in the fourth section of this essay, however, another central assumption and stumbling block in modern corporate theory must be examined: the thin anthropological account of human make-up.

12.3.2 *Key Premises: Individual or Person?*

As noted, in modern corporate theory the individual is regarded as the key focal point of analysis, not the company itself. But corporate theory suffers from an impoverished understanding of the very human persons that stand at its center, an understanding that could be overcome by looking outside its narrow neoclassical economic premises. Humans, in conventional corporate thinking, are conceived to be atomistic, continually seeking their own individual well-being in business dealings and connected to others largely through a series of voluntary negotiations with other self-serving individuals. There are no posited *a priori* limits or principles – beyond illegality – to constrain the design of these self-seeking choices. This general anthropological portrayal of humans is specifically extended to interactions within the corporation, which for that reason, is considered to be merely an aggregation or "nexus" of these bargained-for exchanges. Thus, for such "nexus" theorists, humans

[36] Johnson, *Rethinking How Business Purpose Is Taught*, 73.

[37] Ibid.

[38] Pope John Paul II used the insightful phrase "community of persons" in the encyclical *Centesimus Annus*.

[39] Daniel Yankelovich, *Profit with Honor: The New Stage of Market Capitalism* (New Haven: Yale University Press, 2006), 2 (quoting Whitehead).

are – remembering this is metaphor – said to be joined in the corporate context by contractual relationships that will endure only as long as the arrangements are personally beneficial;[40] the presumed human aim is to exercise shrewd choices so as to acquire goods and services for one's self, thereby maximizing one's own material welfare. That this may lead to a corporate sector characterized by fleeting, money-based interactions rather than to sturdier relationships that endure through thick and thin is of no evident theoretical concern.

Although such a dreary and highly deterministic view of human behavior in the business setting might be defended theologically as realistic in a fallen world,[41] it suggests an incorrigibility that holds out little hope for a regenerative generosity in business dealings. Fortunately, this stark depiction does not accurately reflect social reality. Evidence, along with simple observation, reveals that vast numbers of people behave in sacrificial ways, some habitually and others at least on occasion.[42] Many of these people, moreover, do so because of moral or religious beliefs. This suggests that people's moral convictions not only give inner meaning and purpose to their lives, they also shape actual behavior in an other-directed manner.

Yet, in corporate theory, little attention is given to the role of altruism or to other admirable human traits such as virtue, temperance, character, compassion, honesty, benevolence, and trust, which precede and permit (and might be damaged by) an ethos of unfettered self-interest. None of these traits or qualities originates in bargain or law. Thus, at the theory level, people are simplistically regarded as "individuals," who although, individuated from others, are not conceived of as fully formed "persons" who sometimes behave sacrificially as well as selfishly. In contrast, much religious thinking fully acknowledges human shortcomings, such as an inclination toward self-centeredness, but regards these as hindrances to be overcome, not qualities to be passively accepted. In corporate theory, however, the workings of markets and competition, fueled by human self-interest, supposedly serve as a sufficient impersonal (and ironic) substitute for empathy and compassion. This facilitates a hands-off policy prescription because markets are said to be self-correcting, thereby obviating the need for the protective guardrails of personal moral virtue and state regulatory intervention.[43]

[40] Easterbrook and Fischel, *Economic Structure*, 12.

[41] See Stephen Bainbridge, "The Bishops and the Corporate Stakeholder Debate," *Villanova Journal of Law and Investment Management* (2002): 21–23 (arguing against stakeholderism on the ground that social policy must be realistic and acknowledge that directors may use their discretion to prefer themselves, not just stakeholders).

[42] See Lynn A. Stout, "Taking Conscience Seriously," in *Zak, Moral Markets*, 158–72.

[43] See Easterbrook and Fischel, *Economic Structure*, 15.

As a result, altruism, sacrifice, and gift – impulses in abundance throughout human society – are not part of the heavily monetized lexicon or calculative conceptual framework of mainstream corporate thought. If agape is about the "give" in human dealings, business emphasizes the "get," creating for many a profound dissonance between what is valued in life generally and what is demanded in business. Corporate theory's descriptive account, faulty as it is, then magnifies the problem because it can take on an insidious prescriptive force with many businesspersons believing they *should* be self-serving. This creates a gnawing sense of alienation from one's deeper set of beliefs, leading to a "divided life" where matters of spirit ("thine") and finance ("mine") are said to occupy wholly separate spheres.[44] As Pope John Paul II noted, a company's financial accounts may be in good order and yet people within the business may be humiliated and have their dignity offended.[45] Equally bad from a pragmatic standpoint, business actors who perceive that senior management is self-interested and motivated by personal financial gain will themselves be more likely to misbehave.[46] This outcome flows from social identity dynamics whereby an individual conforms to group norms and internalizes the values and behaviors that are institutionally lauded. The result can be entire corporate cultures characterized by, because they prominently reward, rampant self-aggrandizement.

This quality of human selfishness and the absence of agape in corporate interactions is, in corporate theory, assumed *a priori*. Yet, as elaborated in the second section above, there is no legal rule requiring such behavior, and the empirical reality of self-sacrifice abounds.[47] Corporate theory gives little attention to the many counter-examples in the corporate sector where neither individual nor corporate monetary goals are paramount, including those companies where religious faith has played a formative role in business strategy, such as Chick-fil-A, Reell Precision Manufacturing, Service Master,

[44] The concept of the "divided life" is elaborated in Helen J. Alford and Michael J. Naughton, *Managing as if Faith Mattered: Christian Social Principles in the Modern Organization* (Notre Dame: University of Notre Dame Press, 2001), 10.

[45] Pope John Paul II, *Centesimus Annus*.

[46] Gary R. Weaver, "Encouraging Ethics in Organizations: A Review of Some Key Research Findings," *American Criminal Law Review* 51 (2014): 293.

[47] See Stout, *Taking Conscience Seriously*. Hobby Lobby Stores, Inc. contributes one-third of its annual profits to charity, will contribute ninety percent of profits to charity if the company is ever sold, pays employees no less than $14 per hour (well above minimum wage), and is closed on Sundays, an action the founder calculated costs several million dollars a year in lost business. Janet Adamy, "Are Firms Entitled to Religious Protections?," *Wall Street Journal* (21 March 2014), available at http://goo.glVCLScW; *Burwell*, 134 S. Ct. at 2766.

Cummins Engine, Hobby Lobby, and many other successful businesses.[48] These flourishing companies with distinctive and other-serving corporate missions confound the mainstream theoretical view that religiously influenced businesses aren't "tough" enough to compete effectively in developed markets.

This description of modern corporate theory and its foundational premises may dishearten those interested in exploring what corporate law and life as organized around agape could look like. It suggests that corporate life must unalterably be "disenchanted," to use Max Weber's term.[49] But law is not the problem. As noted above, corporate law, somewhat refined by stakeholder and the new benefit corporation statutes, remains remarkably permissive and flexible, mandating very little. Much thinking about the corporation and corporate relationships today is therefore driven not by law, but by faulty understandings of law, by corporate theory, simplistic preconceptions about human motivation, and by business lore, norms, and practices, all of which can change without relying only on positive law reform. Given that for many people of faith, the whole point of work means to be called into the everyday world to serve

[48] The corporate purpose at Chick-fil-A is as follows: "To glorify God by being a faithful steward of all that is entrusted to us. To have a positive influence on all who come in contact with Chick-fil-A." Corporate Information, available at www.chick-fil-a.com/FAQ#?category=2.

The Reell Precision Manufacturing Declaration of Belief includes the following: "We believe the dignity of every individual to be sacred . . . We believe the highest purpose for the Corporation is to make worthy contributions to the common good . . ." Declaration of Belief, available at http://reell.com/about/philosophy.

Hobby Lobby Stores, Inc.'s statement of corporate purpose expresses a commitment to "[h] onoring the Lord in all we do by operating the company in a manner consistent with Biblical principles," while offering customers exceptional value and service, serving employees and their families while sharing blessings with them, investing in the community, and providing a return on the owners' investment. Statement of Purpose, Hobby Lobby, available at www.hobbylobby.com/our_company/purpose.cfm.

A secular company, Whole Foods Market, also is an example of a corporation that has several purposes, as described by CEO John Mackey. These include a commitment to supporting a much higher level of livestock animal welfare, seafood sustainability, raising the public's awareness about the principles of healthy eating, ending poverty by micro-credit working loans to impoverished people, and other purposes. John Mackey and Raj Sisodia, *Conscious Capitalism: Liberating the Heroic Spirit of Business* (Boston: Harvard Business Review Press, 2013), 64.

Other examples are cited in Lewis D. Solomon, *Evangelical Christian Executives: A New Model for Business Corporations* (London: Transaction Publishers, 2004).

[49] Weber himself was pessimistic about the influence of religious ethics on a capitalist economy: "The more the world of the modern capitalist economy follows its own immanent laws, the less accessible it is to any imaginable relationship with a religious ethic of brotherliness." Max Weber, "Religious Rejections of the World and Their Directions," in *From Max Weber: Essays in Sociology* (Abingdon: Routledge, 1948), 323, 331.

God in his creation,[50] with imagination and resolve corporate law and corporate practices are highly susceptible to the redemptive influence of agape.

12.4 AGAPE IN THE CORPORATION

Linking the discourse of corporate law and theory to agape is a daunting task, even after understanding that the flawed human and anti-institutional premises in modern corporate theory need not be an insurmountable impediment.[51] The challenge is especially great for publicly traded corporations compared to the more numerous – and economically more significant[52] – close corporations. Shareholders in public corporations number in the thousands, are widely dispersed, are not "owners" of the corporation (they only own stock), may feel quite detached from activities in and by the corporation itself, and typically exercise little real control over corporate strategy or operations. Conceding that managers of publicly traded corporations are going to be primarily concerned with making money for investors, agape in the public corporation thus is more likely to influence the means of corporate endeavor rather than the end, whereas both may be influenced in close corporations. There are several avenues by which benevolence can shape relationships within the corporation and also the corporation's own conduct in the larger society.

12.4.1 *Permitted Corporate Objectives*

Those who govern business corporations can pursue a variety of goals. Many companies will seek to pursue, but not necessarily maximize, profits because they wish to advance nonpecuniary objectives as well. Other companies no doubt will avidly seek to maximize profits to the exclusion of all other goals. Even profit-maximizing companies do much good in providing products and

[50] See Alister McGrath, "Calvin and the Christian Calling," in *The Second One Thousand Years: Ten People who Defined a Millennium*, ed. Richard J. Neuhous (Grand Rapids: Wm. B. Eerdmans Publishing Co., 2001), 66, 71–73.

[51] As observed by Robert Vischer in advocating agape in the lawyer–client relationship, "practicing agape in the context of a face-to-face relationship with a real human being is challenging enough; practicing agape in the context of representing a corporate entity made up of far-flung and often anonymous stakeholders seems more difficult by an order of magnitude." Vischer, *Morality of Legal Practice*, 101.

[52] For example, the Small Business Administration reports that "small businesses" make up more than 99 percent of all employers, create more than 50 percent of nonfarm private Gross Domestic Product, employ about 50 percent of all private sector employees, and create 75 percent of net new jobs. Robert Longley, *Top Ten Reasons to Love U.S. Small Business*, available at usgovinfo.about.com/cs/businessfinance/a/sbatopten.htm.

services for consumers and jobs for employees. Also, profit-maximizing companies can decide to pursue that objective only within certain constraints, besides those imposed by positive law and market forces. These self-imposed constraints may include, for example, providing employees a certain measure of job security and higher-than-market compensation, affording them "flex" time to coordinate work with family demands, or insisting that co-workers and customers be treated with dignity and respect. Certain goods and services may be priced so as to make them more affordable to lower-income consumers. Profit-maximizing companies may not consider the advancement of employee or consumer welfare to be a distinct business goal, but they can still adopt limitations on how the profit-making goal will be sought. Within those self-chosen constraints, however, a company may be entirely profits-focused.

Decision-makers at many business corporations in our society may thus believe that the *manner* in which the *goal* of profit maximization is pursued matters. This is a hard issue to get at empirically because observation of daily interactions in the corporate setting is difficult, and such businesses might be thought by observers to act in certain ways simply as an instrumentalist means of enhancing the profit objective. At the same time, given the business orthodoxy that corporations are supposed to maximize profits, many business leaders may not articulate,[53] or even conceive of, their consideration of employee or consumer welfare as an explicit goal. Yet the possible role of agape in the *conducting* of such businesses cannot be dismissed. Although hard to ascertain, in the countless large and small decisions made in the workaday corporate culture, many people may in fact be acting in kind and giving ways toward others without saying so or drawing much attention. An improved understanding, therefore, that law does not require profit maximizing may not only increase the frequency of agapic behavior, but it may make such conduct easier to talk about and more visible, thereby possibly altering business norms and practices.

Other companies, by way of contrast, might explicitly seek to pursue (but not necessarily *maximize*) profits as well as one or more other nonpecuniary objectives. The founders and directors of these businesses might decide that the very goals of the business – not simply the means by which the goals are advanced – should be broadly shaped by compassion. They might avowedly seek to provide a service or product that meets an unmet need, but do so for the purpose of filling that need, not to maximize profits by doing so. This might be done by addressing a social problem of some kind that also represents a business opportunity, such as upgrading poor sanitation practices, water quality, or providing

[53] This is the point of the opening paragraphs of this essay. See Miller, *Norm of Self-Interest*.

access to reliable power sources. Or it might target chronic unemployment among youths in urban centers and remote rural areas, or by offering services to the elderly on a favorable basis, or providing locally grown, wholesome food at affordable prices. Many entrepreneurial endeavors are springing up today to advance social aims through business corporations. The twin aims of profit and social mission, unlike pure profit seekers or pure nonprofit endeavors, are to make profits (and thereby provide returns to investors) while also seeking to achieve one or more nonmonetary goals.

The result of these approaches is a richer, more pluralistic business ecology in which corporate founders and managers can position a business corporation at any point along a continuum that runs from, at one end, zealous, single-minded profit maximizing (think here of hedge funds and other investment pools) up to, at the opposite end, purely nonprofit religious, charitable or humanitarian activities, and, critically, at any point *in between* those extremes, where mixed purposes are pursued. In a diverse business society we need not have an unhealthy either/or bi-culture in which all companies that are not expressly nonprofit in orientation must singularly maximize profits to the exclusion of all other considerations. A range of business visions is possible because different moral visions for business are possible under the loose constraints of corporate law.

12.4.2 *Actual Influence on Corporate Conduct*

One can make the case for love influencing corporate conduct on deontological grounds, because, after all, Jesus commands us to love our neighbor in all settings, not just some. Yet, in recent years, a literature is beginning to develop that takes a consequentialist look at how religious piety may influence corporate behavior. For example, studies employing different methodologies have linked religious belief to managerial honesty and risk aversion, a reduced likelihood to engage in misleading "earnings management," fewer financial reporting irregularities, and higher levels of corporate social responsibility.[54] The last observation, however, is true only when religious piety is sufficiently strong. This suggests that a lukewarm or half-hearted religious influence, perhaps done for "branding" or public relations reasons, is not correlated with higher levels of corporate social responsibility. Ironically then – and this is a danger to guard against – if religious identification does enhance profits owing

54 The literature is summarized in Pornsit Jiraporn *et al.*, "Does Religious Piety Inspire Corporate Social Responsibility (CSR)? Evidence from Historical Religious Identification," *Applied Economics Letters* 21, no. 16 (2014).

to consumer perceptions of quality or integrity, unscrupulous businesses may hypocritically promote themselves as religious to drive profits, not to serve larger goals.

This area is beginning to receive the careful study it deserves. Particularly in light of the high-profile *Hobby Lobby* decision, more business people who have been reticent about whether and how their religious and moral beliefs can influence corporate practices may be more outspoken. But to have an actual impact on corporate behavior may require a certain level of commitment, not simply a change in rhetoric or mindset. Actual practice must change as well. This is a problem that in a parallel way has plagued various empirical studies on secular corporate responsibility because they rely on surveys of directors or published corporate documents as to business objectives. Although such studies frequently reveal that interests other than just shareholders are stated to be considered, whether those *expressions* are carried out in corporate *action* is not known. This too should be empirically ascertained with specific respect to religious and moral influence on the corporation: how exactly do religious and moral convictions shape corporate conduct?

12.4.3 *Agape in Corporate Management*

As fiduciaries, all business leaders must be faithful to and serve the company's purposes, not their own. This ethic of stewardship applies as well to leaders who want their companies to express agape in identifying institutional goals or in deciding how those goals are achieved.

Faithfulness is central to the legal duties of corporate directors and officers, subsuming the concepts of loyalty, care, and good faith. As expressed by the former Delaware Court of Chancery Chancellor William Chandler, "[T]he duties traditionally analyzed as belonging to corporate fiduciaries, loyalty and care, are but constituent elements of the overarching concepts of allegiance, devotion, and faithfulness. . ."[55] Faithfulness in law thus retains a core moral and sacrificial element even in an age of legal positivism. Moreover, this moral principle may be traced back to biblical roots, as even the Supreme Court recognized in cautioning corporate managers not to "violate the ancient precept against serving two masters."[56] The dishonest manager in the Gospel of Luke embodied the faithless serving of his own interests, not those of his master.

[55] *In re Walt Disney Co. Derivative Litig.*, 907 A.2d 693, 756 (Del. Ch. 2005), *aff'd* 906 A.2d 27 (Del. 2006).

[56] *Pepper* v. *Litton*, 308 U.S. 295, 311 (1939).

Later he was called to give an account, leading to Jesus' enduring proscription against serving two masters, especially when one "master" is one's own self.[57]

More positive examples are the two faithful servants in Matthew's Gospel recounting Christ's Parable of the Talents.[58] Those servants did far more than simply refrain from serving their own self-interest; they affirmatively advanced their master's affairs by adding to his resources. That positive aspect of the faithfulness precept still resonates in modern fiduciary jurisprudence as corporate managers must not simply renounce self-interest, they must act in the best interests of the corporations they serve. This obligation, moreover, is not contractual in origin, it may not be waived in the corporate context, and it is not rooted solely in economic efficiency – although it is in fact highly efficient. And it is not designed simply to serve as an *ex post* remedial doctrine, but also as an *ex ante* normative standard to guide all business decision-making.

Importantly, Jesus expresses the stricture of managerial faithfulness as a broad standard,[59] not a narrow rule. This captures the need for managers to retain broad discretion in how they act, while according them the opportunity for critical reflection as they decide which actions best serve overarching corporate interests. Two points flow from this: first, the legal fiduciary obligation of managers is to faithfully advance the *corporation's* distinctive objectives and best interests, not those of a single stakeholder (such as shareholders) or group of stakeholders. The corporation, as noted in Part III, is not just a nexus of individual bargain-makers, but has its own distinctive institutional identity and seeks to advance a specific overarching mission/objective. Each stakeholder-member of the corporate body serves the common good as represented by the larger corporate purpose. Whole Foods CEO John Mackey and Raj Sisodia nicely phrased the issue, in a secular setting, this way: "When all stakeholders are aligned around a common higher purpose, they are less likely to care only about their immediate, narrowly defined self-interest."[60] The common corporate good in turn serves as the appropriate touchstone for managerial decision-making, giving a sharper missioncentric focus to it than a diffuse stakeholderism, while also ordering the relationship of the various participants to the larger corporate body. This imbues the corporation with a more meaningful social and institutional reality, rather than being a sort of fictitious avatar of various competing interests as is the case with modern

57 Luke 16:1–14, NIV. This point is nicely made by Joseph Johnston. Joseph F. Johnston, Jr., "Natural Law and the Fiduciary Duties of Business Managers," in *Business and Religion: A Clash of Civilizations?*, ed. Nicholas Capaldi (Salem MA: M & M Scrivener Press, 2005), 279, 281.

58 Matt. 25:14–28, NIV.

59 See *Chen* v. *Howard-Anderson*, 87 A.3d 648, 666–67 (Del. Ch. 2014) (explaining standards).

60 Mackey and Sisodia, *Conscious Capitalism*, 42.

theory. Such higher corporate purpose can be agapically aimed toward enhancing the welfare of others touched by corporate activity. It can also be motivated *by* agape on the part of individuals acting within the corporation.

This refocusing carries an important benefit for the human participants as well. They are understood as whole "persons," not as mere individuated, one-dimensional input providers exchanging a resource solely for financial gain. This permits people of faith to ground their work lives on something enduring, transcendent, and spiritual, rather than on something precarious, fleeting, and material. It permits people in all kinds of organizational settings to inhabit their workspace and workday with a fuller portion of their defining humanity, which for many includes religious faith and a desire to give, not just get.

The second point is that managerial discretion, to some significant degree, must be preserved. Managerial discretion in the corporate context is doctrinally housed in the business judgment rule under which courts accord directors and officers broad latitude in decision-making. Such discretion, that is, legal freedom, while always being guided by faithfulness to the corporate common good, should also be tempered by key touchstones of agape, compassion, and charity. We expect the Good Samaritan to take pity on and attend to the wounded stranger even when journeying on business as a faithful fiduciary for his master's affairs.[61] And the vineyard owner in the Gospel of Matthew honored his bargains with the early workers while also doing what he thought was right to those hired later.[62] Of course, he did so from his own resources, not those of another to whom he owed a duty. But we must ask whether, as a condition of faithfulness to others, we wish to eliminate entirely the capacity to be generous. The good corporate servant is commanded to be faithful, not unmerciful.

12.5 CONCLUSION

Corporate law may not demand agapic conduct, but it also does not forbid it. Agape is possible within the corporation whether business leaders pursue distinctive corporate objectives motivated by compassion or simply pursue profits to varying degrees in a more benevolent manner. Agape is also possible within a corporation that itself is not governed benevolently because each individual within it can routinely relate lovingly to those they encounter, even if only in small ways. As the corporation navigates its way in the larger economy and society, business leaders, drawing from the wellspring of a personal and

[61] Luke 10:25–37, NIV.

[62] Matt. 20:1–16, NIV.

institutional commitment to agapic action, can do more good than is legally required and refrain from doing the bad that is legally permitted.

This is far easier if we do what corporate theory currently does not do: take the corporation seriously, as a distinct social-legal actor with institutional goals that transcend those of various stakeholders. Hobbled by an effort to understand corporateness by in fact ignoring it and instead focusing on its individual participants – but then advancing an impoverished understanding of those very individuals – modern corporate theory is an obstacle to love. But law itself is not.

13

Agape, Gift, and Intellectual Property

Thomas C. Berg

13.1 INTRODUCTION

We live in "the age of intellectual property."[1] Patent law and copyright law protect, respectively, the high technology and creative works that have become increasingly crucial to the US economy. And intellectual property (IP) is hotly debated today. The scope of US patent and copyright protections, as well as the duration of copyright protection, have greatly expanded, prompting much criticism. And in the international arena, developed nations have used trade agreements to push developing nations to strengthen their IP laws because, it is asserted, this will attract innovation and investment. Critics say this harms people in the poorer nations, for example by blocking affordable generic versions of AIDS and malaria drugs, and affordable versions of educational materials.[2] IP has become a social-justice as well as business issue.

Christians have only begun to respond to these questions. The one significant Christian institutional voice has been the Catholic Church, which has supported limits on patents over essential medicines and over genetically modified crops.[3] Pope Benedict's encyclical *Caritas in Veritate*, in surveying the obstacles to "authentic human development," complained that "[o]n the part of rich countries there is excessive zeal for protecting knowledge through an unduly rigid assertion of the right to intellectual property, especially in the

1 See, e.g., Gaelle Krikorian and Amy Kapczynski, *Access to Knowledge in the Age of Intellectual Property* (Cambridge: Zone Books, MIT Press, 2010).

2 See, e.g., Lawrence R. Helfer and Graeme W. Austin, *Human Rights and Intellectual Property: Mapping the Global Interface* (Cambridge: Cambridge University Press, 2011); Margaret Chon, "Intellectual Property and the Development Divide," *Cardozo Law Review* 27 (2006): 2821.

3 Thomas C. Berg, "Intellectual Property and the Preferential Option for the Poor," *Journal of Catholic Social Thought* 5 (2008): 193, 197–98 (summarizing statements by Vatican officials).

field of health care."[4] Meanwhile, a growing body of scholarship has addressed IP-related issues in the light of Christian themes such as creation, stewardship, and solidarity with the poor.[5] This chapter explores the implications that the theme of agapic love might have for intellectual property. In particular, it argues that the related theme of "gift," central to Christian theology and social ethics, can be fruitfully applied to IP law. Creativity is a fundamental gift from God, and IP law should encourage the dissemination of that gift to others to benefit them, and empower them to realize their own creative gifts.

13.2 THE IP BACKGROUND

To have property is to have a bundle of rights in a thing, including the right to exclude others. IP gives exclusive rights for set times in the intangible intellectual components of products: 20 years for a novel, useful invention under patent; 70 years from the author's death for a creative work under copyright. These laws rest on Congress's constitutional power "to promote the progress of science and the useful arts, by securing for limited times to authors and inventors the exclusive rights to their respective writings and discoveries."[6] As already noted, IP has also become a contested international issue because of instruments, such as the 1994 Trade Related Aspects of Intellectual Property agreement (TRIPs), that have pushed all nations to increase their protection of IP.

Debates in both domestic and international arenas involve arguments between those favoring maximal IP protection and those favoring minimal protection, and positions in between. Each side uses both economic-instrumental and moral arguments. IP maximalists first make the instrumentalist claim that IP protections provide necessary incentives to innovation and creation by preventing free-riding that would undercut the creator's return on investment. Some maximalists add that property rights must be strong not just to provide a minimum incentive for creation, but also to facilitate market

4 Pope Benedict XVI, *Caritas in Veritate*, ¶ 22 (2009), available at www.vatican.va/holy_father/benedict_xvi/encyclicals/documents/hf_ben-xvi_enc_20090629_caritas-in-veritate_en.html (accessed 10 March 2014).

5 See, e.g., David Carey, *The Social Mortgage of Intellectual Property* (Acton Institute, 2012); Berg, "Intellectual Property and Preferential Option"; Roman Cholij, "IP in Christian Law," *Intellectual Property Quarterly* 3 (2012): 137; Gabriel J. Michael, "Catholic Thought and Intellectual Property: Learning from the Ethics of Obligation," *Journal of Law and Religion* 25 (2009–10): 415, 418; and several articles in the symposium "Intellectual Property and Religious Thought," *University of St. Thomas Law Journal* 10, no. 3 (2013) (articles by Margo Bagley, Marco Fioretti, Paul Griffiths, Alina Ng, and David Opderbeck), available at http://ir.stthomas.edu/ustlj/vol10/iss3/.

6 U.S. Const., art. I, § 8, cl. 8.

exchanges that most efficiently commercialize inventions and creations. As to moral and philosophical arguments, IP maximalists may proceed from natural rights premises epitomized by John Locke: that the content creator is entitled to full reward for the talents and labor she has applied to preexisting materials. Or they may proceed from Hegelian arguments that intellectual creations are important to, and inseparable from, the creator's personality.[7]

From the side favoring IP law minimalism, one set of critiques is instrumentalist. The minimalists argue that broad IP protection laws actually impede innovation and creation by raising the costs to users engaging in downstream creation.[8] But as the next section discusses, another set of critiques extends more broadly.

13.3 THE "GIFT ECONOMY" CRITIQUE OF IP

Some critics of IP laws offer a broad account of human creativity, how it is motivated and disseminated, and the social relationships and obligations that accompany it – an account that competes with the pro-IP narrative of creativity. These critics of IP appeal to the virtues of sharing and invoke the concept of the "gift economy," in which valuables are not sold in markets but rather conferred in circles of giving with no explicit agreement for immediate or future rewards.[9] The term "gift economy" originated with anthropologists and sociologists, such as Marcel Mauss, studying the practices of traditional societies.[10] But the framework has been adopted by critics of market capitalism, particularly critics of IP rights, who point to examples where significant knowledge has been generated and refined through sharing. Open-source software, such as the Linux/GNU operating system, is free to all other persons to use and improve as long as they in turn allow free use of their improvements. Programmers participate in open-source projects to enhance their

7 Such arguments, in particular, ground the "moral rights" that are prominent in Continental legal system IP rules. See, e.g., Edward J. Damich, "The Right of Personality: A Common-Law Basis for the Protection of the Moral Rights of Authors," *Georgia Law Review* 23, no. 1 (1988); Justin Hughes, "The Philosophy of Intellectual Property," *Georgetown Law Journal* 77 (1988): 287.

8 See, e.g., James Bessen and Michael J. Meurer, *Patent Failure: How Judges, Bureaucrats and Lawyers Put Innovators at Risk* (Princeton: Princeton University Press, 2008) (describing costs of patent litigation in various industries).

9 See, e.g., Lewis Hyde, *The Gift: Creativity and the Artist in the Modern World*, 2nd ed. (Vintage Books, 2007).

10 Marcel Mauss, *The Gift: Forms and Function of Exchange in Archaic Societies* (1925; Engl. trans. 1954), available at https://archive.org/details/giftformsfunctiooomaus.

reputation within the group, and simply to make the software better.[11] Then there is Wikipedia, which has generated a staggering amount of content from dispersed, anonymous, unpaid contributors.

For the gift-oriented critics of IP, the expansion of property control over information not only cuts off sharing-based avenues of generating knowledge (an instrumentalist concern); it also encourages selfishness and breaks human connections (a problem of intrinsic morality). For example, novelist and essayist Jonathan Lethem argues that "[a] gift economy may be superior when it comes to maintaining a group's commitment to certain extra-market values":

> [A] gift establishes a feeling-bond between two people, whereas the sale of a commodity leaves no necessary connection. I go into a hardware store, pay the man for a hacksaw blade, and walk out. I may never see him again. . . . But a gift makes a connection, [as with] the candy or cigarette offered to a stranger who shares a seat on the plane.[12]

Whether or not one is convinced by the general idea of a gift economy, it finds support in the area of IP from a couple of distinctive arguments. First, some critics argue that creative goods in particular contain an element of gift that ought to be preserved. This was the attitude of most pre-modern civilizations, ancient Greek, Chinese, Islamic, Jewish, and Christian: they viewed knowledge and art as gifts of God that could not be owned by any human being.[13] That outlook has been muted by modern IP, but it has echoes in many current critics of copyright law. For example, Lethem writes, "Art that matters to us – which moves the heart, or revives the soul, or delights the senses, or offers courage for living – is received as a gift is received. Even if we've paid a fee at the door of the museum or concert hall, . . . something comes to us that has nothing to do with the price."[14] If it is true "that where there is no gift there is no art," he worries, "it may be possible to destroy a work of art by converting it into a pure commodity."[15]

[11] See, e.g., David Zeitlyn, "Gift Economies in the Development of Open Source Software: Anthropological Reflections," *Research Policy* 32, no. 7 (2003): 1287.

[12] Jonathan Lethem, "The Ecstasy of Influence," *Harper's Magazine* (February 2007), available at http://harpers.org/archive/2007/02/the-ecstasy-of-influence/.

[13] See, e.g., Carla Hesse, "The Rise of Intellectual Property, 700 B.C.–A.D. 2000: An Idea in the Balance," *Daedalus* 26, 27 (Spring 2002) ("A tour of [these] great civilizations of the pre-modern world – Chinese, Islamic, Jewish, and Christian – reveals a striking absence of any notion of human ownership of ideas or their expressions."); Paul Griffiths, "The Natural Right to Property and the Impossibility of Owning the Intangible: A Tension in Catholic Thought," *University of St. Thomas Law Journal* 10 (2013): 590.

[14] Lethem, "The Ecstasy of Influence."

[15] Ibid.

Concern about artistic commodification may apply only to goods like music or paintings, but a second argument for the relevance of the gift economy may apply to all information goods, scientific as well as artistic. All are generally "nonrivalrous" in nature. If I give you my bicycle, I lose its use as long as you have it. But if I give you an idea, we can use it simultaneously and, indeed, derive greater value from the shared use than the sum of our solitary uses. In Thomas Jefferson's well-known image, "He who receives an idea from me, receives instruction himself without lessening mine; as he who lites his taper at mine, receives light without darkening me." For this reason Jefferson thought that ideas were "less susceptible than all other [things] of [being] exclusive property": "that ideas should freely spread from one to another over the globe," he said, "for the . . . improvement of [man's] condition, seems to have been . . . designed by nature."[16] If ideas can be shared freely without interfering with anyone's use of them, why not share?

The gift economy thus has several attractive features, especially as applied to information. But it also has significant drawbacks, even as applied to information. First, in many cases there must be relatively sure rewards to induce and support sharing. True, rewards can be non-monetary or indirect: open-source programmers reap reputational benefits from their work, as do academics, who also receive salaries and grants. Wikipedia contributors receive none of these; but writing Wikipedia content is relatively low-cost. For contributions to knowledge that require much more investment, we may need more substantial monetary rewards, for which some property rights are an important component.

A second problem is that gift-giving often is effective only within distinct communities such as traditional societies, academics in a discipline, or software programmers. Economists tell us that people may be unwilling to share knowledge freely outside a group of familiar, repeat players: the ongoing relationship inspires greater sharing and creates reputational incentives that reduce free-riding. Even major forms of free software themselves depend on copyright protection. The GNU software license, created by the Free Software Foundation, recognizes that simply putting software in the public domain "allows uncooperative people to convert the program into proprietary software"; therefore GNU's "copyleft" strategy, and that of other organizations, uses the power of copyright to make its permission for free use contingent on the user's in turn offering free licenses to others for any

[16] Thomas Jefferson to Isaac McPherson (13 August 1813), in *The Writings of Thomas Jefferson*, 13 (Washington, Thomas Jefferson Memorial Association, 1905): 33–35, available online at http://press-pubs.uchicago.edu/founders/documents/a1_8_8s12.html.

improvements it makes.[17] Only that way can users far downstream be compelled to distribute their own improvements for free.

Finally, gifting practices limited to personal contexts can reinforce hierarchies and cronyism. The traditional societies Marcel Mauss studied were hierarchical, as is one of the most familiar examples of a gift economy in popular culture: the way Mafia don Vito Corleone rules in *The Godfather* by personal favors that bind the recipients to give him their loyalty. Writing on "the dark side of gratitude" throughout human history, Peter Leithart notes that "gifts impose obligations that can be used to dominate the recipient."[18]

Impersonal markets have freed people from many such restrictions. But markets can also destroy feelings of connection to, and responsibility for, others. How, for example, do officials of a US multinational drug or software manufacturer feel responsibility to people they are affecting in distant, far poorer nations? Markets, including global IP laws, are here to stay. But is it possible to preserve both (1) the freedom and global reach they provide and (2) some sense of being in relationship with others, even on a global scale?

13.4 AGAPE: UNIVERSALIZING THE GIFT ECONOMY

I have focused on the "gift economy" because it has important connections with the Christian theme of agapic *love*. As theologian Peter Leithart observes, for Christians "'gift' is a basic element of human life." He cites Martin Luther's *Large Catechism*, which "sums up the entire history of creation and redemption under the rubric of gift": the Father gives at creation, the Son "give[s] himself to reconcile us to the Father"; and the Spirit gives himself so we can receive and retain the gift.[19]

Leithart adds: "Since all is gift, Luther taught, we are bound to be grateful, to 'thank and praise, serve and obey.'" As this suggests, the sense of gift and gratitude in turn connects directly to our love of God and neighbor. "We love because He first loved us," 1 John says; "if God loved us so much, we also ought to love one another."[20] As Pope Benedict writes in *Deus Caritas Est*,[21]

[17] Free Software Foundation, "What Is Copyleft?," available at www.gnu.org/copyleft/; see also Creative Commons, "About the Licenses: What Our Licenses Do," available at http://creativecommons.org/licenses/.

[18] Peter J. Leithart, "The Dark Side of Gratitude," *First Things* (31 August 2012), available at www.firstthings.com/web-exclusives/2012/08/the-dark-side-of-gratitude.

[19] Ibid.; see generally Peter J. Leithart, *Gratitude: An Intellectual History* (Waco: Baylor University Press, 2014).

[20] I John 4:19, 4:11 (New Revised Standard Version).

[21] *Deus Caritas Est (God Is Love)*, #18, available at www.vatican.va/holy_father/benedict_xvi/encyclicals/documents/hf_ben-xvi_enc_20051225_deus-caritas-est_en.html.

this changes love from an externally imposed (and impossible) "commandment" into "a freely-bestowed experience of love from within, . . . which by its very nature must then be shared with others." Think of the two kinds of love in Anders Nygren's *Agape and Eros*,[22] and what motivates each. If the motivation we experience in eros is desire for the beloved, the motivation in *agape* is joyful gratitude.

A number of Christian theologians have been attracted by the gift economy because it preserves an echo of God's gifts to us and can also (as mentioned above) sustain a sense of human connectedness. For example, John Milbank discusses Christian social ethics as a set of connections between God's gifts to human beings and our gifts and obligations to each other. He commends the gift, as opposed to the commodity, because it "is not *alienated* from the giver but expresses his personality, so that the giver is *in* the gift"; "our historical tragedy," he adds, "is that replacement of the gift with contract . . . means the treating of all and everyone as a stranger."[23] In Peter Leithart's words, the appeal of the gift economy reflects a yearning for a time "when interpersonal generosity rather than money made the world go 'round.'"[24]

But these theologians also recognize the limitations of gift economies noted above. Milbank, for example, observes that gift-giving as systematic mode of exchange "was possible only within tight communities possessing strong familiarities of blood and tight expectations of what would be appropriate gifts"; thus in order to trade with strangers, societies had to shift to modes of contractual exchange, beginning with barter and moving on to commodities.[25] And the theologians acknowledge what Leithart calls the "dark side" of gift relationships: their tendency to reinforce personal indebtedness and social hierarchies.[26]

The Christian theologians thus pose the same question noted above: can we maintain some of the advantages of gift economies while avoiding their dark side? Leithart restates those problems:

> Is it possible to retain the gains of modern freedom while restoring the goods of personal ties of gratitude? . . . Does the freedom of the market *necessarily* corrode social bonds? . . . [I]s there a way to extricate myself from the nexus

22 Anders Nygren, *Agape and Eros* (1932; trans. Philip S. Watson, Harper & Row ppb. ed. 1969).

23 John Milbank, *Being Reconciled: Ontology and Pardon* (London: Routledge, 2003), 167.

24 Leithart, "The Dark Side of Gratitude."

25 Milbank, *Being Reconciled*, 167.

26 Leithart, "The Dark Side of Gratitude"; Milbank, *Being Reconciled*, 168 (recognizing "the many ways in which gift-giving was used (as hierarchy tended to increase) to secure arbitrary power within the clan itself").

> of exchange and [still] remain a being-in-relationship? . . . Can gratitude function as a political virtue without justifying corruption and cronyism?[27]

These Christian theologians also identify an answer to the question: namely, a sense, as Milbank puts it, of "universal gift."[28] It is possible to conceive the circle of giving in an economy as universal rather than personal: as encompassing all human beings rather than merely those within kinship or other personal relationships of beneficence and gratitude. The gift relationship can be universalized if we maintain, or recover, the sense that the human talents that produce goods are themselves gifts from some universal source – in the Jewish and Christian understanding, from the God who gives all gifts in the first place.

Thus, for example, Leithart contrasts traditional gift economies with the Christian view that "[b]ehind every gift is a transcendent giver, the generous Father, and his gifts create an all-encompassing bond that relativizes all human loyalties and obligations."[29] The circle of gift-giving becomes "infinite," Leithart says, "because God is the source of *every* gift, even gifts mediated through human beings." Therefore "[t]hanks is due, but it is due to the ultimate Giver, the Father. Human givers give, but recipients owe thanks and grateful service not to the giver but to God."[30]

Universalizing the gift-experience has two implications. First, it redirects the proper reciprocation so that it goes not (or not solely) to the original human giver, but toward other human beings. The command of the God who is the ultimate source of gifts is that we respond in gratitude by giving to others. In David Opderbeck's words,

> "[w]hile [ancient] Greek theology emphasized the city and the gift and the reciprocity of virtues among people whose varying social stations defined their ends, Christianity stresses [reciprocity] still more by seeing justice as fulfilled in charity – an unlimited concern to fulfill the real potential of all, and of all in harmony with all."[31]

It's not (or not only) "pay it back," but rather, as the recently popular phrase puts it, "Pay it forward": to others.

27 Leithart, *Gratitude*, 14–15.

28 Milbank, *Being Reconciled*, 169.

29 Leithart, "The Dark Side of Gratitude."

30 Leithart, *Gratitude*, 7 (emphasis in original). In a similar vein, Milbank argues that the idea of gift-giving can only be made coherent by participation, through a commitment of faith, in the universal "abundant life" that God gives. Milbank acknowledges Jacques Derrida's critique that the idea of a "unilateral, purely sacrificial gift" is an impossibility, since "short of death one always does cancel one's giving in receiving something back," and thus no person in a human relationship could actually give a unilateral gift to the other. *Being Reconciled*, 156. Milbank responds that "a mutual and unending gift-exchange" is possible, and only possible, if "construed as . . . absolute faith in the arrival of the divine gift, which is grace." Ibid., 154.

31 David W. Opderbeck, "Beyond Bits, Memes, and Utility Machines," *University of St. Thomas Law Journal* 10 (2013): 738, 764, available at http://ir.stthomas.edu/ustlj/vol10/iss3/8/.

Jennifer Morse further explains how the universality of divine gift motivates giving out of gratitude:

> There is a level at which no one really has reasonable bragging rights. I didn't create my intellect, my health or my family background, any more than I created my own life. The gift perspective helps us to see that each of these talents and endowments was entrusted to us, and is not of our own creation.[32]

Note also how the transcendent origin of gifts frees the gift recipient from servility to the human benefactor. The fundamental obligation is not to the human patron but to God.[33]

The second implication of universal gift is that the obligations to others are universal, at least at the level of principle. We do not reach the boundaries of charity by showing concern for others in our own group(s). As has already been said, we are also being called, stretched, by "an unlimited concern to fulfill the real potential of all"; the divine gift creates "an all-encompassing bond that relativizes all human loyalties and obligations."[34] Universality is a fundamental feature of *agape*, indeed perhaps the feature that most distinguishes it from other forms of love such as eros (the attraction to beauty in the other) or philia (the attraction of shared features or interests between friends). Gene Outka, in his detailed analysis of agape, begins with what he describes as the "most common" formulation of its principle, "equal regard":

> Agape is a regard for the neighbor which in crucial respects is independent and unalterable. . . . The regard is for every person qua human existent, to be distinguished from those special traits, actions, etc., which distinguish particular personalities from each other. . . . [E]veryone alike [has] an irreducible worth and dignity.[35]

The parable of the Good Samaritan, of course, epitomizes this universality. Pope Benedict wrote that before the parable,

> the concept of "neighbor" was understood as referring essentially to one's countrymen and to foreigners who had settled in the land of Israel; in other words, to the closely-knit community of a single country or people. This limit is now abolished. Anyone who needs me, and whom I can help, is my neighbor.[36]

32 Jennifer Morse, "Why the World Needs the Needy," in *Wealth, Poverty, and Human Destiny*, eds. Doug Bandow and David L. Schindler (Wilmington: ISI Books, 2002), 179, 202.

33 Leithart, *Gratitude*, 7 ("Christianity freed people from onerous personal bonds by defining gratitude as *right use* of the gift rather than gratitude as *return*") (emphasis in original).

34 Opderbeck, "Beyond Bits," 764; Leithart, *Gratitude*, 7.

35 Gene Outka, *Agape: An Ethical Analysis* (New Haven: Yale University Press, 1972), 9, 260.

36 *Deus Caritas Est*, #15.

No doubt we have a variety of special obligations to those who are in varying degrees close to us; conditions of finitude, if nothing else, make it impossible to show love to all in precisely the same way. Outka, in particular, discusses this complication in the logic of equal regard, recognizes that varying obligations must exist, and concludes that not every special relationship can be founded in some application of *agape*. But even he emphasizes that special relationships must not "become the effective center of gravity, so urgent and really ultimate that they swamp human dignity as such"; agape must "se[t] the boundaries within which [other attachments] may be allowed distinctive expression."[37] No one is so distant that we might not be called to give to him. *Agape* constrains and directs not just personal gift relationships, but commodity transactions in the global economy. Globalization means that the activity of American producers, including producers of inventions and creative works, affects people in distant places. Thus, by the logic of the Samaritan parable, those people are neighbors we must not harm, and neighbors we are called to help.

Indeed, the universality of gifts – that we all have received them and that we must share them, in principle, with all – provides an undergirding, arguably a crucial one, for moral limits on global market structures. By it we might preserve the freedom and extended reach of layers of markets while infusing them with some sense of human relationship to replace that of the community whose members are closely connected by location or other shared feature. But if any sense of community is to be maintained outside of these bounded groups, John Milbank argues, it must be by "an appeal to transcendence," which "alone can mythically and rationally sustain the 'universal gift.'" Or as Peter Leithart puts it, "only the infinite Christian circle" – the sense that gifts are given to all and should, in principle, be shared with all – "is capable of preserving the political, scientific, economic, and social advances of modernity, while restoring a personal and human world."[38]

These notions apply fully to the gifts of inventiveness and creativity that are the subject of IP law. They surely count among the most fundamental of God's gifts, for they constitute perhaps the chief way in which we bear God's image: we share in some tiny measure God's power to conceive and create. In the first Genesis creation narratives, God "create[s] humans in his image"; in the second, among Adam's first acts is to conceive ideas, creating knowledge, by giving names to all the animals.[39]

[37] Outka, *Agape*, 272, 274.

[38] Milbank, *Being Reconciled*, 170; Leithart, *Gratitude*, 15.

[39] Gen. 1:27, 2:19–20 (NRSV).

Copyright scholar Roberta Kwall, in her book *The Soul of Creativity*, begins with the Rabbinic interpretation of these scriptures, the teaching "that the human ability to engage in expression, including artistic skill, [was] endowed by" God at the creation of humanity.[40] Lewis Hyde, in his book *The Gift*, quotes numerous creators who describe "inspiration as emanating from an external source beyond that of the author herself" – frequently, though not always, a spiritual source. For example, the environmentalist and poet Gary Snyder says, "You get a good poem and you don't know where it came from. 'Did I say that?' And so . . . you feel humility and you feel gratitude."[41] Hyde adds that the gift "isn't fully realized until it is given away," and he quotes the Christian mystic Meister Eckhart that the true form of gratitude for a gift is to be fruitful in it.[42]

Thus, the first thing Christian love might add to the subject of IP is an additional, and distinctive, motivation to create and share. Intellectual creation may reflect eros, the pursuit of the beautiful or true; but it is also *agape*, the sharing of a gift. And if gift and gratitude issue in love, this inspires one not simply to create – which might still be consistent with restricting access solely to maximize profit. Love should also inspire the creator to share in ways such that all can benefit. In short, love has the potential to unite the motivation for creation *and* the obligation to benefit others through it.

The universality of *agape* also means that these obligations may extend to others far distant in the national, even global economy. Protections for producers of IP must not harm those in need, and in fact should help them.

40 Robert Rosenthal Kwall, *The Soul of Creativity: Forging a Moral Rights Law for the United States* (Stanford: Stanford University Press, 2010), 15.

41 Hyde, *The Gift*, 193 (quoting Gary Snyder, *The Real Work: Interviews and Talks 1964–1979* (New York: New Directions, 1980), 79).

42 Hyde, *The Gift*, 69 (quoting Meister Eckhart, "Jesus Entered" (Sermon), in Reinhard Schürmann, trans., *Wandering Joy: Meister Eckhart's Mystical Philosophy* (Herndon: Lindisfarne Books, 2001), 18 ("[T]he fruitfulness of a gift is the only gratitude for the gift.")).

As the Snyder quote in text indicates, the sense that creativity is a gift from some transcendent, universal source is not limited to Christians, or traditional theists. Quoting numerous authors and artists, Roberta Kwall traces their reported experience of a transcendent source of creative insight, one that is also present within themselves, that might be called "quasi-divine." Kwall, *The Soul of Creativity*, 14–16; see ibid., 15 ("Although the classical Jewish tradition, as would be expected, views God as the external source of expression and creativity, the more generalized idea is that creative expression is gifted in that it comes from a source beyond the author's control."). The sense of obligation to share the creative gift can be felt by authors with many different spiritual views.

13.5 AGAPE AND JUSTICE

Before turning to the concrete implications of *agape* for the law of IP, I briefly discuss my conception of how agape relates in general to civil law and justice. I offer only a sketch; others in this collection of essays will address the question in far greater detail. My view, influenced by theologians from Paul Ramsey and Reinhold Niebuhr to Nicholas Wolterstorff, is that justice is not the same as love, but neither is it divorced from it. From Ramsey and Niebuhr we can draw a number of insights. First, principles of justice must be shaped by, and must always stand under the judgment of, the basic affirmations of *agape*, such as human dignity and equality. Justice should also be shaped by the recognition, discussed above, that there is a pervasive element of gift in the very fact of human life, and a pervasive need for gift-giving in human relations. But justice also must take into account the human conditions of finitude and sin, particularly the conditions that apply among people not bound by family ties, geographic proximity, or religious or other share cultural commitments. These limiting conditions include imperfect knowledge, limited sympathy for others, and outright self-centeredness, as well as the conflicts among the interests of multiple other people all of whom we are called to love. Commands of love are always relevant to – but will not always translate directly into – principles of justice.[43]

From Wolterstorff we can draw the insight that treating people justly is a necessary aspect of treating them with love. Jesus both commanded love and said he was bringing (and God's reign would bring) justice; thus, Wolterstorff argues, love must incorporate justice, and love that perpetuates injustice is malformed. In particular, Wolterstorff argues, justice emphasizes not only advancing people's well-being but also treating them as having worth and deserving respect.[44]

13.6 *Agape* AND IP LAWS

What are the concrete implications of *agape*, universal gift-giving, for IP law? Admittedly, the general relationship of love and justice sketched above can give only general guidance; moreover, any concrete judgments about the content of laws turn significantly on empirical judgments, not only on theological

[43] Reinhold Niebuhr, "The Relation of Justice to Love" and "Laws and Principles of Justice," in *The Nature and Destiny of Man, Vol. II: Human Destiny* (New York: Scribner, 1943), 246–56; Paul Ramsey, *Basic Christian Ethics* (New York: Scribner, 1950), 74–90, 166–72.

[44] Nicholas Wolterstorff, *Justice in Love* (Grand Rapids: Wm. B. Eerdmans Publishing Co., 2011), 71–72, 90; Nicholas P. Wolterstorff, *Journey toward Justice: Personal Encounters in the Global South* (Grand Rapids: Baker Academic, 2013), 109.

principles. But some general observations are possible. Indeed, it is entirely proper that IP should serve a social purpose, one directed, like *agape*, at promoting the common good. As David Opderbeck has pointed out, "Already in Western intellectual property law there is encoded a broader social purpose – 'to encourage the progress of science and the useful arts'" – and that purpose may be informed by ideals of productivity and generosity.[45]

A first proposition informed by love and justice is that IP laws are proper and necessary. In an imperfect world, they incentivize people to create. In particular, they institute some incentive to create things that other people need, as measured – admittedly very imperfectly – by their willingness to pay for them. Beyond that, as Opderbeck puts it, "For a creator to receive recognition and material substance from the community is a fitting response. A system of intellectual property that expresses gratitude for the generativity of its creators can therefore be virtuous."[46] And if the circle of gift-giving is (in principle) universal, then markets and IP rights play an important role in making possible that global reach across distances and cultural differences. Markets, structured and enforced by basic rights of private property, enable transfers across vast distances, to those connected only indirectly – in a way that gift-giving relationships cannot do alone.

At the same time, Opderbeck emphasizes, we must remember that what is given is first a *gift*, what is exchanged is *gratitude*, and the result is continual *generativity*. In contrast, a system built on *greed* will distort these values. It will not "incentivize" true invention and creativity; it will turn the creators of culture away from common flourishing and in on themselves.[47]

Limits on IP rights are necessary to reflect and enforce the obligation to use the gift rightly to benefit, and not harm, others. And just as with other products, the price of intellectual creations cannot be allowed to define their value. As Pope John Paul II put it, "[T]here are many human needs which find no place on the market," and "[i]t is a strict duty of justice and truth not to allow fundamental human needs to remain unsatisfied, and not to allow those burdened by such needs to perish," regardless of their ability to pay.[48]

45 Opderbeck, "Beyond Bits," 766–67. Gabriel Michael argues that determining the scope of IP rights calls for social-ethical analysis, not merely empirical economic analysis, "because economics comprises only one of several justifications for the institution." Michael, "Catholic Thought and Intellectual Property," 418–19 (citing Lockean rights theory and Hegel's philosophy of the self, and adding that "[w]hen these justifications are invoked in debates about intellectual property policy and law, we need . . . a mode of analysis capable of handling philosophical questions of individual and common good: we need an ethical analysis.").

46 Opderbeck, "Beyond Bits," 766–67.

47 Ibid., 767 (emphasis in original).

48 Pope John Paul II, *Centesimus Annus*, #34, available at http://w2.vatican.va/content/john-paul-ii/en/encyclicals/documents/hf_jp-ii_enc_01051991_centesimus-annus.html.

Universalizing the concept of gift-giving can therefore justify a system of global IP rights – but one that also places important limits on those rights so as to protect and empower those most in need.

Any focus on loving others and including them in the expanding circle of gift, productivity, and exchange will almost inevitably focus on two key concepts: ensuring basic needs and empowering others to become creators.

13.6.1 *Ensuring Basic Needs*

First, sharing must occur – and IP rights must give way if necessary – when basic human needs are at stake, for example, when people face death or serious harm from disease or starvation. Gene Outka concludes that "to each according to his needs" is the distributive principle closest to *agape*. It "includes those things essential to the life and welfare of humans, considered simply as humans" – capturing *agape*'s egalitarianism – while still allowing for differential treatment when, because of individuality, those basic needs differ. Outka adds that "[m]any of Jesus' teachings [and actions] emphasize the urgent importance of meeting mundane needs (apart from merit): food, drink, shelter, clothing, health, and liberty." In the gospels, Christ "does not dismiss his hearers without feeding them first."[49]

Thus the obligations of *agape* were, and are, implicated by the crisis over the affordability of essential medicines and the uses of patents to block far cheaper generics. In the early 2000s a year's supply of AIDS drugs cost more than $10,000 in the United States under patent, but less than $400 in generic batches from Indian manufacturers, yet patent holders tried to block the least developed countries (LDCs) from importing generics. Even prominent pro-globalization economists, such as Columbia's Jagdish Bhagwati, concluded that patent enforcement was "[c]learly . . . unnecessarily harmful to the poor countries" because it inflated drug prices while failing to incentivize research and development directed at epidemics in LDCs.[50] The concepts of love and giving imply a preference for voluntary solutions, which means Christians should be happy that drug companies are increasingly providing subsidized cheap supplies. But the poorer nations were quite warranted when, in the early 2000s, their governments declared public health emergencies and

[49] Outka, *Agape*, 264.

[50] Jagdish Bhagwati, *In Defense of Globalization* (Oxford: Oxford University Press, 2004), 184–85 (concluding that diseases limited to poor countries, like malaria, generated minimal R&D, and that for diseases present in both rich and poor countries, like AIDS, drug patents simply forced relief organizations "to give money to the poor countries to buy the drugs at [the higher] prices").

resorted to law: compelling licenses at reduced costs, importing generics from India and elsewhere (legally produced in those countries), and convincing the World Trade Organization to validate these steps in the Doha Declaration of 2001. People were dying; few voluntary agreements were then in place; companies were not developing new drugs but instead were enforcing patents based on an unwarranted claim that cheap drugs might be diverted to the rich-nation markets.[51]

But massive challenges remain. The solutions may include prizes for essential medicines when demand in LDCs will not support the necessary investment in R&D.[52] Prizes have the advantage of compensating the creator while leaving the creation in the public domain and thus likely reducing the cost to those ultimately receiving it. But it is far from clear that all diseases in poorer nations could be handled in this way. Given that the patent system will remain with us, LDCs should have flexibility to legislate and put immediate needs above the speculative promises of long-term benefits from full patent enforcement.

13.6.2 *Empowerment*

In addition to meeting basic needs, IP law should be shaped to help empower people in need to become gift-givers themselves – producers and creators, that is, participants and agents in economic life. *Agape* emphasizes empowerment because – as Wolterstorff has shown – *agape* seeks not only to improve the other person's well-being, but to respect his or her value as a moral agent.[53] To quote Gene Outka again, "it is of the essence of proper respect that we encourage others to be co-agents, and accept and welcome them as such, as co-operating

[51] As Nobel Prize recipient Joseph Stiglitz observed in response to drug company claims that generic drugs provided to developing countries "will eventually come into United States and spoil the market there": "But there are already huge disparities in prices (for instance between prices in Europe and the United States), and the problem, while present, is limited. The pharmaceuticals industry is one of the most regulated in the world. . . ." It is even less likely that Americans (or Europeans) will get their drugs from South Africa or Botswana. Joseph E. Stiglitz, *Making Globalization Work* (New York: W.W. Norton, 2006), 122.

[52] James Love and Tim Hubbard, "Prizes for Innovation of New Medicines and Vaccines," *Annals of Health Law* 18, no. 2 (2009): 155, 157 *et seq.*, available at http://lawecommons.luc.edu/cgi/viewcontent.cgi?article=1111&context=annals (summarizing and defending system of "mega cash prizes [for medicines] that are linked to the impact of the product on health care outcomes").

[53] Wolterstorff, *Journey Toward Justice*, 109 ("Love attends to both dimensions [well-being and respect] – not just to the former. . . . Love does not promote the well-being of someone at the cost of treating that person or anyone else in a way that does not befit his or her worth or dignity. . . . What makes paternalistic benevolence wrong is that the agent seeks to advance the good of the recipient while failing to pay due respect to his or her worth.").

with ourselves in a common enterprise."[54] The model again is God's love, which theologian Thomas Oord emphasizes is a "freedom-giving love [that] creates essentially free creatures." A corollary is that "God empowers rather than overpowers. We might call God's love . . . 'cooperation-empowering grace.'"[55]

Here again, the relationship between *agape* and gift-giving is informative. As David Opderbeck emphasizes, "A 'gift' produces good for its recipients. The receipt of a gift allows the receiver to flourish and, in turn, to become a giver."[56] Gifts are thus "generative."

Treating *agape* as empowerment avoids the charge sometimes leveled that Christian love, by seeking the betterment of all people, would become too paternalistic, even tyrannical, if it had any influence on civil law. Empowerment seeks to enable people to create what they want, not what the government thinks is best for them. On the other hand, empowerment affirms that being creative is a good. In that sense it seeks to move people to a better state.

How should IP law be shaped to promote empowerment?[57] Again, on the one hand IP protections can be of value. Poor people can use their own IP rights to protect and to benefit from their own creativity, both in generating innovations and creations (patent and copyright) and in marketing them (trademark). Ensuring these benefits may require adjustments in IP laws to recognize the communal cultural processes that are more common in traditional societies as contrasted with the generally individualistic premises of Western IP law.[58]

But empowerment also requires significant limits on IP, or obligations that accompany and balance IP rights. Because developing countries often lack the capacity to absorb and benefit from new technology, strong IP rights may act primarily to "retard diffusion of new products (because of high prices)" while doing little to promote "access by local firms to foreign technologies."[59]

[54] Outka, *Agape*, 267 (quoting W. G. Maclagan, "Respect for Persons as a Moral Principle – II," *Philosophy* 35 (October 1960): 289, 294).

[55] Thomas Jay Oord, *The Nature of Love: A Theology* (St. Louis: Chalice Press, 2010), 126.

[56] Opderbeck, "Beyond Bits," 766.

[57] For more detailed discussion of means of empowerment, see Berg, "Intellectual Property and Preferential Option," 215–21, 225–28.

[58] On the use of IP laws to protect poor people's creativity, see, e.g., ibid., 216 (describing organizations aiming to "mak[e] IP laws work for the poor"); on protection of traditional knowledge, see, e.g., Paul Kuruk, "Protecting Folklore under Modern Intellectual Property Regimes: A Reappraisal of the Tensions between Individual and Communal Rights in Africa and the United States," *American University Law Review* 48 (1999): 769.

[59] Carlos M. Correa, "Pro-Competitive Measures under TRIPS to Promote Technology Diffusion in Developing Countries," in *Global Intellectual Property Rights*, ed. Peter Drahos and Ruth Mayne (London: Palgrave, 2002), 40, 42.

Thus, empowering the poor requires preserving and solidifying certain limits on IP rights that encourage new creativity by lowering the costs to users of building on existing works, as well as by encouraging education. The fair-use defense in American copyright law already favors "transformative uses," those that build upon the copyrighted work to add "new meaning, expression, or message," as well as uses for "teaching, scholarship, or research." Other provisions promote empowerment through education by explicitly protecting certain copying by libraries and archives and performances and displays of works in classroom teaching or distance education.[60] The Copyright Act also exempts multiple nonprofit uses – by religious groups, agricultural organizations, veterans' and fraternal organizations, and groups transmitting information to the blind or deaf – which as a class are not particularly remunerative even though they "serve important social purposes."[61]

Reasonable limitations of this sort, reducing the costs of education and of charitable assistance, should be encouraged. Indeed, they should be focused even more on empowering vulnerable populations, as does the recent international Marrakesh Treaty on copyright exceptions to assist the visually impaired.[62] Such provisions may be particularly beneficial for developing countries to enact; the United States and the rest of the developed world should not seek to discourage them through trade agreements. Beyond that, the limitations in US law itself should also be preserved and strengthened. Patent law should make more room for fair-use and analogous exceptions.[63] And while copyright law's fair-use doctrine is stronger, it is under pressure from copyright owners who argue that the defense should be inapplicable whenever a use might cause even the most speculative harm to license fees or other sources of revenue.[64] Such erosion should be resisted.

Finally, if IP is to empower the poor to create and innovate, there must be enforceable obligations on developed nations to transfer technology and

[60] On fair use, see *Campbell* v. *Acuff-Rose Music*, 510 U.S. 569, 579 (1994), and 17 U.S.C. § 107; on library exemptions, see 17 U.S.C. §§ 108, 110(1), (2).

[61] 17 U.S.C. § 110(3), (4), (6), (8)–(10); Molly Shaffer Van Houweling, "Distributive Values in Copyright," *Texas Law Review* 83 (2005): 1535, 1545.

[62] World Intellectual Property Organization (WIPO), Marrakesh Treaty to Facilitate Access to Published Works for Persons Who Are Blind, Visually Impaired, or Otherwise Print Disabled (27 June 2013), available at www.wipo.int/treaties/en/ip/marrakesh/.

[63] See Berg, "Intellectual Property and Preferential Option," 226, 227–28 (citing sources) (discussing arguments for adding a general fair-use defense to US Patent Act and for strengthening the "experimental use" defense).

[64] See ibid., 226–27 (discussing "anti-circumvention" laws that threaten to undermine fair use, and arguments that more and more uses of copyrighted works can be metered and thus produce licensing fees that all users must pay).

training to developing nations. In the 1990s, the United States assured developing nations that strengthening their IP laws would not only encourage their citizens' innovation but "attract foreign investment and spur technology transfer."[65] But while TRIPs created mechanisms to force developing nations to increase IP protections, it created no mechanism to force developed nations to reciprocate with technology transfers and training. As a result, "the grand bargain has been ephemeral" or even "a major disappointment" for developing nations; "most studies show that there is no direct influence of [IP] protection on the promotion of transfer of technology [to] LDCs."[66] Effective enforcement mechanisms are necessary "because the private sector does not have automatic incentives to transfer technology."[67]

Without such limits on IP rights, and concerted efforts to transfer technology, IP will be – as it too often has been – a great immediate deal for the wealthy nations and a bad one for the poor. That result is contrary to love and justice.

13.7 CONCLUSION

Creative and inventive works, so central to the functioning of the modern economy, also provide a rich field for the application of principles of *agape* to law. Crucial to that application is the concept of gift. Creativity is a gift from God, and that realization should motivate us to shape IP law, along with other institutions, so as to encourage generosity – to return the gift to the Giver by distributing it to and empowering others.

65 E. Anthony Wayne, "Why Protecting Intellectual Property Rights Matters," *Focus on Intellectual Property Rights* (US Department of State, Bureau of International Information Programs, January 2006), 10 (article by Assistant Secretary of State for Economic and Business Affairs).

66 Gehl Sampath and Pedro Roffe, *Unpacking the International Technology Transfer Debate: Fifty Years and Beyond*, ICTSD Issue Paper 36 (ICTSD, 22 November 2012), at 26, 25, available at http://papers.ssrn.com/sol3/papers.cfm? abstract_id=2268529.

67 Ibid., 33.

14

"That Vast External Realm": The Limits of Love and Law in International Politics

Alberto R. Coll

In his celebrated opinion in the 1936 US Supreme Court landmark decision, *Curtiss- Wright Corp.* v. *United States*, Justice Robert Sutherland drew a sharp distinction between the powers of the president in domestic affairs and those in foreign affairs.[1] Referring to the world outside the United States as "that vast external realm . . . with its numerous complications and special circumstances," Sutherland argued that, whereas the powers of Congress and the president in domestic matters were limited to those specifically enumerated in the Constitution, a much different logic prevailed with regard to foreign policy. In the latter, the president's powers were far broader; he could do whatever he considered necessary in defense of the national interest unless the Constitution specifically prohibited it or delegated it to another branch. It was an acknowledgment by the Court of the essential distinctiveness of the realm of international relations and politics as an area with far more extensive complexities, risks, dangers, and uncertainties, and one in which established norms and expectations found within a society may not be as easily or as broadly applicable. This distinction, long recognized also by historians, political theorists, and Christian theologians, is of continuing relevance.[2]

This essay presents a three-part argument. First, the distinction between international and domestic politics is real, and presents formidable obstacles for any kind of application of the Christian ethic of love to the problems of international politics. The dilemmas posed by the power–security dilemma, nuclear deterrence, and large-scale, mass international migrations illustrate such obstacles. Second, even law, including the substantial body of international legal norms shaped over centuries by the Christian tradition and its

[1] *United States* v. *Curtiss-Wright Export Corp.*, 299 U.S. 304 (1936).

[2] Kenneth Waltz, *Man, the State, and War* (New York: Columbia University Press, 1962).

secular offshoots, has faced profound obstacles in its attempts to attenuate the chaotic and inhumane course of international relations. Third, there remain distinct though limited possibilities open to the Christian faith to influence, however indirectly, the conduct of foreign policy through its emphasis on, and cultivation of, the intellectual and moral virtues of justice, moderation, realism, prudence, existential humility, and much more indirectly the ideal of agape or selfless, disinterested love.

It has been difficult enough for human beings over the course of millennia to construct a few reasonably orderly societies within which minimal justice is administered, a measure of domestic order is maintained, and the power of the sovereign is sufficiently bounded and regulated to permit a limited degree of liberty and social welfare. Even more demanding, and notably less successful, has been the quest to keep different societies from engaging in destructive international conflict.[3] In the twentieth century alone, such conflicts cost over 100 million lives and trillions of dollars.[4] The difference between domestic and international politics is not simply one of degree; it is also one of substance. The issues at stake in the latter include the very survival of entire communities in the face of culturally and politically alien adversaries. Legal and moral restraints, present in however attenuated a form in domestic political life, are much weaker at the international level. In the absence of a world government, there is no sovereign capable of maintaining effective order and law. The result is far greater anarchy, chaos, and violence than might be the case otherwise.

Throughout history, the pleadings of philosophers, saints, and moral and religious leaders, including Christian leaders, seem to have had limited impact on deterring or preventing human conflict. Also, however genuine a political leader's Christian faith may be, it does not translate necessarily into a consistent attachment to peace and non-violent means of dispute resolution. Although President Jimmy Carter's evangelical faith seems to have had an impact on his efforts to avoid military confrontations with the United States' adversaries, President George W. Bush's equally sincere Christian faith did not stop him from rushing to war against Iraq in the spring of 2003 even in the face of the pleadings by America's closest allies to give the United Nations inspectors more time to corroborate the true extent of Saddam Hussein's

[3] An especially insightful and ambitious account, covering the entire spread of known human history, by a contemporary historian and anthropologist can be found in Ian Morris, *Why the West Rules, for Now: The Patterns of History and What They Reveal About the Future* (New York: Farrar, Straus, and Giroux, 2011).

[4] Available at http://warchronicle.com/numbers/WWII/deaths.htm; http://encyclopedia.1914-1918-online.net/article/war_losses_germany

weapons of mass destruction programs. President Woodrow Wilson's serious commitment to Christian faith served as an impulse to promote international law and organizations as means to deter conflicts, while President William McKinley's equally devout Christian faith seems to have motivated him to push the United States into an unnecessary war with Spain in 1898 that eventually extended into a bloody campaign of occupation and subjugation of the Philippine Islands.[5]

These considerations lead to the equally compelling question, far beyond the scope of this essay, of whether Christianity has made the world a better, more humane and more peaceful place. Herbert Butterfield, the leading Christian historian of the twentieth century and Master of Peterhouse College, Cambridge, famously argued that Christianity indeed had made the world a better place, often despite the behavior of Christians themselves. Butterfield was well aware of the great evils for which Christian zeal had been responsible, from the burnings of heretics, the Crusades, and the Inquisition to the Protestant–Catholic Wars of the seventeenth century. But, he argued that the great creeds of what we might call humane liberalism, including the abolition of slavery and the core contemporary beliefs in equality, liberty, freedom of conscience, and human dignity were all rooted in the gospel.[6] In spite of the sin and zeal of many Christians, the gospel had exerted a leavening influence on Western civilization by generating these beliefs. Meanwhile, the enemies of Christianity – the secularists – wielded these very same Christian beliefs against the church itself as they claimed the higher moral ground in their struggle for a more just, egalitarian society rooted in the dignity and preciousness of every human being. In doing so, the secularists helped to weave Christian notions of human dignity, equality, and the worthiness of life into the fabric of modernity, thereby affirming and strengthening these values even if in a secular variant. But even as he laid out his case, Butterfield was quick to recognize that, in the "vast external realm" of international relations, personal piety or evangelical zeal was likely to be less helpful in resolving the dilemmas of international politics than a dose of hard-headed political realism combined with an awareness of the catastrophic and often futile consequences of major war.[7]

With regard to the application of Christian norms in international relations, the proper question is not necessarily whether love can replace law as

5 Richard Pierard, "Nation on a Mission," *Christianity Today*, available at www.christianitytoday.com/history/issues/issue-99/nation-on-mission.html

6 Herbert Butterfield, *Christianity and History* (New York: Charles Scribner's, 1950).

7 Herbert Butterfield, *Christianity, Diplomacy and War* (Nashville: Abingdon Press, 1953); Alberto R. Coll, *The Wisdom of Statecraft: Sir Herbert Butterfield and the Philosophy of International Politics* (Durham: Duke University Press, 1985).

the guiding logic for foreign policy. Often the question is, rather, how far law itself can have an impact on the international realm with its chaos, unpredictability, and vast moral dilemmas. If legal norms are difficult to agree on and implement in "that vast external realm," the dictates of love are even more so. The limitations of love and law in international politics are best understood by looking at several issues: the problem of war, the problem of nuclear deterrence, and the dilemmas posed by large-scale transnational migrations.

14.1 THE PROBLEM OF WAR

Early in the history of the Church, Christian thinkers such as St. Augustine developed the just war doctrine to address the large gap between love and international politics, especially the problems of maintaining peace, the ubiquity of the power–security dilemma, and the prevalence of war.[8] The power–security dilemma is the fundamental condition of political communities in an anarchic international system. Every state seeks to guarantee its security by increasing its military, political, and economic power, in the process making every other state more insecure than before, and triggering a similar response on their part in the form of efforts to increase their own power. As the process unfolds, every state in the system is increasing its political and military power, while levels of insecurity rise for everyone.[9] The only way to stop this self-defeating process would be for some "insurer" to guarantee everyone's security in exchange for everyone agreeing to reduce rather than increase their military and other forms of power. This concept of an overall "guarantor" is behind the creation of the League of Nations and the United Nations Security Council. In both cases, we know empirically how things have turned out, and it is not well. Related to the power–security dilemma is the problem of war, the endemic nature of military conflict throughout all periods of history. Societies resort to war frequently and for multiple reasons, including religious, ideological, political, economic, and strategic ones.

The essence of the gospel is the Love commandment. Possibly the most revolutionary aspect of Jesus' teaching is the Sermon on the Mount and his insistence on the logic of love as the ultimate guide to individual human

[8] Herbert A. Deane, *The Political and Social Ideas of St. Augustine* (New York: Columbia University Press, 1966); Michael J.S. Bruno, *Political Augustinianism: Modern Interpretations of Augustine's Political Thought* (Minneapolis: Fortress Press, 2014).

[9] The best presentation of the power–security dilemma remains Hans Morgenthau, *Politics among Nations*, 5th ed. (New York: McGraw-Hill Education, 1978).

action. Faced with the dichotomy between this logic and the prevailing logic of international politics, Christian theorists developed several ways around the resulting Gordian Knot. One was the idea of the two cities, adumbrated by Jesus' imperative "to give unto Caesar the things that are Caesar's, and give unto God the things that are God's." For St. Augustine, human beings live simultaneously in two cities, the City of God and the City of Man. The City of God is ruled by God's love, the City of Man by human passions, foremost among them the lust for power. To deal with the deleterious consequences for human order and justice of the unceasing struggle for power among human beings, God has ordained the institutions of government and law, and the whole coercive apparatus of state power, to insure that evildoers are deterred and punished and the worst consequences of human sin are held at bay. The universe of international relations, along with the power–security dilemma and war, are part and parcel of the City of Man and its disorders, and require the same instruments of coercion, deterrence, and skilled political and diplomatic statecraft to preserve basic order and justice from being overwhelmed by grasping and violent outside enemies, some of them barbarians and bereft of even common cultural ties with their presumptive victims.

Although there has always been a formidable body of pacifism in the church that has sought to apply Jesus' Love commandment directly to international politics, it has remained a minority view.[10] St. Augustine won the debate by placing in a Christian framework the key elements of just war doctrine. Force and the resort to war are appropriate in response to aggression, and as part of the natural right of self-defense.[11] Force also may be used in what today we would call "humanitarian interventions," to address massive violations of human rights, to protect the victims and stop and punish the perpetrators. Although we tend to think of "humanitarian intervention" as a modern, late-twentieth-century concept, it is actually quite old. St. Augustine adumbrated it in his argument that wars against heretics were justifiable, among other reasons, to assist the victims and subjects of the heretics. In the early sixteenth century,[12] Vitoria carried the argument further by openly stating that wars were justifiable to save people from great harms and evils committed by their own princes or by others.[13] According to the just war tradition, the use

[10] The classic account remains John Howard Yoder, *The Politics of Jesus* (Grand Rapids: Wm. B. Eerdmans Publishing Co., 1994).

[11] Harold Palmer, *Christian Pacifism and Just War Theory: Discipleship and the Ethics of War, Violence and the Use of Force* (Chicago: TellerBooks, 2016).

[12] Deane, *The Political and Social Ideas of St. Augustine*.

[13] Francisco de Vitoria, *Vitoria: Political Writings*, eds. Anthony Padgen and Jeremy Lawrence (Cambridge: Cambridge University Press, 1992).

of force also should be regulated by the principle of proportionality: the evils and harms caused by the resort to force must be proportional to the evils and harms sought to be remedied, or the aggression to which it is a response. In his own lifetime, St. Augustine saw the Vandals sack Rome, as the Western Roman Empire tottered under the combined assaults of barbarian hordes and domestic incompetence, corruption, and military feebleness. Here was clear evidence, if any was required, of the need for magistrates to wield the sword effectively, both within the state and outside of it, to keep barbarism and its concomitant violence at bay.

For St. Augustine, as for many Christian thinkers after him, the political sphere, including that dimension of it involving relations among different political communities, was perpetually vulnerable to disorder and the depredations of human beings seized with what he described as "the lust for power and dominion." Hence, peace and justice required that force be used to maintain a minimum of order and tranquility.

The fundamental problem with applying the Love commandment directly in the realm of international politics is the torrent of immorality that is often unleashed by well-intentioned human beings who are unable or unwilling to counter the depredations of those willing to stop at nothing to achieve their goal of domination. History is sadly littered with countless examples of entire communities, from the Melians of Thucydides' *History* to the sixteenth-century Incas to the Jews of twentieth-century Europe, who were murdered, enslaved, and exterminated because of their inability to resist successfully through force their militarily more powerful conquerors.[14] These are historical facts that Christian pacifists and moral idealists sometimes have difficulty taking seriously. Long periods of relative peace and happiness have rested, more often than not, on a balance or a preponderance of military power that has deterred, restrained, and if necessary defeated potential adversaries. Alternately, unspeakable evils have flourished as a consequence of weakness on the part of peoples who underestimated the ruthlessness and lust for power of their challengers.

Broadly speaking, there are three different ways most Christians tend to look at the maintenance of a strong military. One group, which we can call the "optimists" or "just warriors" argue that a strong national defense is a form of agape, an act of love, through which a community protects itself and the

[14] Robert B. Strassler, ed., *The Landmark Thucydides: A Comprehensive Guide to the Peloponnesian War* (New York: Free Press, 1998); Peter O. Koch, *The Spanish Conquest of the Inca Empire* (Jefferson: McFarland, 2007); Martin Gilbert, *The Holocaust: A History of the Jews of Europe During the Second World War* (New York: Rosetta Books, 1987).

lives and welfare of the millions of persons that are part of it. For just war thinkers such as Paul Ramsey, agape is the positive virtue that drives the maintenance of justice, order, and peace in a society through means of coercion.[15] As part of our love for God's created world, we build mechanisms to restrain and punish the anarchy and sinful chaos that is always just below the surface, threatening to erupt. The second group, which we might call the Christian "pessimists" or "realists," agree with the "just warriors" that, in a world that remains broken and fallen, political leaders have basic responsibilities to use power in order to check the power and ambition of potential enemies and evildoers. But these "realists," such as Reinhold Niebuhr,[16] were quite critical of the just war tradition for attempting to sanctify or portray as manifestations of agape certain institutions such as a strong national defense, that are essentially the lesser of evils. Moreover, the realists believe that sometimes Christian statesmen may have to get their hands "dirty" – they may have to resort to less than good means, and do in the political realm things that we never would do in our personal lives. The third group, the "pacifists,"[17] recoils from the pessimism and what they would describe as the resulting accommodation with the world exhibited by the realists. And they are equally critical of the just warriors, whom they see as self-deluded at best in their attempts to put a positive spin on what they see as the Church's two-thousand-year sellout to capital punishment and the sanctification of military force.

Just warriors might see a strong military and even the willingness to go to war in defense of one's allies as an act of agape. Realists would tend to see both of these things more as a sad necessity, and they would be skeptical of claims to attribute righteousness to necessary acts that are simple requirements of justice and political responsibility in a chaotic world. Pacifists tend to consider a strong, expensive military and resort to war as obscene and incompatible with Jesus' ethics, the proverbial road that leads to hell through a thousand rationalizations and betrayals of one's faith.

14.2 THE PROBLEM OF NUCLEAR DETERRENCE

One of the starkest forms of the problem of reconciling agape with the realities of international politics is posed by nuclear deterrence. The issue generated a great deal of political controversy as well as philosophical commentary and

[15] Paul Ramsey, *War and the Christian Conscience: How Shall Modern War Be Conducted Justly?* (Durham: Duke University Press, 1961).

[16] See Niebuhr, *Moral Man and Immoral Society*.

[17] See Yoder, *The Politics of Jesus*.

pastoral focus in the early 1980s, at a time of worsening Cold War tensions between the Soviet Union and the Western Alliance. Although the debate reached particular public salience then, it had been carried out in a more muted form since the late 1940s and gradually lost its bitter edge only as the two superpowers ended the Cold War and shrank their nuclear arsenals in the early 1990s. In reality, though, the dilemmas that gave rise to the debate have never gone away, even if people do not pay as much attention to them as they once did. The essential immorality of nuclear deterrence, as articulated by some of its most sophisticated Catholic critics, is this: the security of the United States to this day depends, not only on its government's possession of weapons of mass destruction, but also on its threat to use them in response to a first strike by the enemy, under circumstances in which their use would entail the deaths of hundreds of millions of innocent people on the other side.[18] China or Russia never will be tempted to launch a preemptive first strike against the United States if they know that the response to such a first strike would be certain annihilation of hundreds of millions of their people. For deterrence to work, the threat to respond to a first strike must be credible. In other words, political and military leaders must give every indication that they intend to follow through on their threat and actually carry out the horribly immoral deed of killing hundreds of millions of innocent people in response to the first strike. It is difficult to conceive of a more immoral or hideous deed than that which must be credibly threatened, in order for deterrence to work. The threat leaves in tatters the two concepts at the heart of just war theory: the concept of discrimination between non-combatants and combatants (between the innocent and the not-so-innocent), and the concept of proportionality – what could possibly justify, or be proportional to, the incineration of several hundred million human beings?

Faced with this awful dilemma, Christians, understandably hesitant to abandon the possibility of connecting the commands of love with the realities of international politics, have tried one of two approaches. The first, favored by many politically conservative "just warriors," whether Catholic or Protestant, is to attempt to separate the threat from the deed; to argue that the two are not the same thing; and to suggest that, although the actual launching of the weapons would be highly immoral, the mere threat to do so is not immoral, and is in fact a morally justifiable course of action because it keeps an adversary from engaging in the horrible deed of using the weapons first. Although this proposed solution is understandable and seems sensible, it amounts to a

[18] John Finnis, Joseph Boyle, and Germain Grisez, *Nuclear Deterrence, Morality and Realism* (Oxford: Clarendon Press, 1987).

surrender to consequentialism by people who often have taken great pride in opposing consequentialist ethics. Although perhaps ultimately unsatisfying theologically, this is the rationale that has enabled Christian policy-makers to sleep at night since 1945.[19]

The second approach, favored by a number of classical just war philosophers and many American Catholic bishops who have become *de facto* pacifists, is to argue that the threat is highly immoral to the point of being unacceptable from the viewpoint of Christian ethics, and therefore there is a religious and moral imperative to move as urgently as possible away from reliance on nuclear weapons and nuclear deterrence. One of the earliest expressions of this position was taken by the Christian historian Herbert Butterfield in the 1950s,[20] who called on the West to renounce nuclear weapons altogether and live with whatever risks that might entail. The noted American *realpolitik* theorist and diplomat George Kennan[21] came close to advocating a similar position later in his life. The bishops and the philosophers traditionally have been short on the details of how a unilateral renunciation of nuclear weapons would be worked out in a world in which the proverbial genie is out of the bottle, and where it would be therefore extremely risky for a state to give up all of it nuclear weapons while its adversaries retain theirs. Both approaches to the problem obviously have severe limitations, practical and moral.

14.3 THE PROBLEM OF LARGE-SCALE MIGRATIONS AND THE SYRIAN CIVIL WAR

An equally stark dilemma is posed by the large flows of migrants and refugees in today's world, particularly those from the Middle East and Africa into Europe. It is worth spending some time analyzing in detail the migration crisis afflicting Europe because it crystallizes the complex difficulties of applying the ethic of Love directly to the messy problems of international relations. The counsels of agape seem straightforward enough: wealthier societies should open their doors to migrants from poorer countries. We are called to offer our cloak to our needy brothers and sisters, a Gospel injunction that most Christian saints from St. Francis of Assisi to Mother (now St.) Theresa of Calcutta have interpreted to apply not just to our fellow Christians but to all

[19] For the outlines of the often-fierce debate, see James E. Dougherty, *The Bishops and Nuclear Weapons: The Catholic Pastoral Letter on War and Peace* (Glasgow: Harper Voyager, 1984).

[20] C. T. McIntire, "Modern Pioneers: Herbert Butterfield," *Christianity Today*, available at http://www.christianitytoday.com/history/issues/issue-72/modern-pioneers-herbert-butterfield.html

[21] See generally, John Lewis Gaddis, *George F. Kennan: An American Life* (London: Penguin, 2011).

our fellow human beings on God's created earth. In several highly publicized visits to the thousands of Syrian refugees huddled on the Greek islands of Chios and Lesbos in April of 2016, Pope Francis called for compassion toward them, implicitly calling on European nations to welcome them. In one of his trips, he took the highly symbolic step of taking twelve Muslim families with him to the Vatican. Beyond the millions of Syrian refugees seeking asylum in Europe, there were millions more Iraqis, Afghans, and Africans from Morocco, Algiers, Somalia, and West Africa trying to move to Europe for economic reasons. Unlike the Syrians claiming asylum to escape persecution in their native country, the latter were generally economic migrants from societies where they were not persecuted but their lives were poor and bereft of meaningful economic opportunities. Should the European Union, with a population of 500 million people and the world's second largest economy, take in all these millions? What would it mean to apply the Love commandment?[22]

This is a situation in which the Love commandment could be applied, not absolutely, but prudentially and with still significant consequences. There is clearly no political will on anyone's part in Europe to apply the Love commandment absolutely. No European society, government or political party would support such a policy. Nor would an absolute application be a wholly positive step. An absolute application would imply an open-door policy to all who want to come, including all economic migrants in search of a better life for themselves and their families. Europe would be overwhelmed by the resulting mass migration, facing gigantic economic, social, and religious tensions that would damage its relatively orderly democratic societies beyond repair. Africa is the world's poorest continent, and as of 2015 had a population of 1.166 billion people. Most of its governments are corrupt, ineffective, and prone to violence. Iraq and Afghanistan, both of them poor and torn by endless civil strife, had a combined population of some 70 million persons as of 2015. It is no exaggeration to predict that tens of millions, perhaps as many as 100 million people, would attempt to migrate in the face of an open-door policy, with tens of millions more to follow over the years.

As I write, a prudential application of the Love commandment would require countries, first, to give strict priority to refugees over economic migrants, so as to consider for admission only persons who are in danger of being persecuted if they are returned to their country of origin.

This would leave mostly the Syrian refugees. Secondly, a prudential application would require countries to raise the question of who should be

[22] For a discussion of agape and transnational migration, in the American context, see the chapter by Jennifer Koh in this volume.

responsible for offering asylum to several million Syrian refugees. A reasonable answer would be that many countries in addition to the European Union bear such responsibility, including some of Syria's wealthy neighboring states that have fanned the flames of the Syrian war by providing financial and military assistance to some of the leading factions in that conflict, thereby prolonging it and raising its levels of destructiveness. Saudi Arabia and Qatar particularly come to mind. Other countries, not part of the European Union, that bear responsibility for prolonging the conflict as a consequence of their economic, military, and political involvement in it include the United States, Russia, Iran, and Turkey. In the case of Turkey, it was already housing 2.5 million refugees by mid-2016, and therefore could be said to be carrying more than its fair share of responsibility for the refugees.[23]

The Syrian civil war itself provides an illustration of the moral complexities at the heart of international politics. It is far from the clear-cut, black-and-white case that partisans on either side of it make it out to be, especially in the United States, where there has been a particularly vocal lobby in favor of intervention on the side of overthrowing Syrian president Bashar al-Assad. Like his father Hafez, Bashar has run his country with a strong fist, crushing his political opponents, but providing economic and political stability, keeping radical Sunni Islamists at bay, and maintaining a safe space for the Christian minority. Surrounded by large, hostile Sunni states, Assad has cultivated strong ties with Iran and Russia, making him undesirable among the large portions of the Washington establishment that see Iran as a deadly threat to Israel and the United States. For the sake of trimming Iranian influence in the region, they have been prepared to facilitate Assad's overthrow since the beginning of a major uprising against Assad in 2011. Five years into the rebellion, however, it became evident that most of the factions battling Assad were not the democratic, religiously tolerant freedom-fighters imagined by anti-Assad advocates of 'regime change." Most of them represent various strands of viciously intolerant, anti-democratic, radical Sunni fundamentalism. And they would pose an even greater threat to Israel than Assad. This is true not only of the Islamic State (ISIS) but of other anti-Assad factions to varying degrees. If Assad was overthrown and these factions gained power, some of their first victims would be the Christian minority in Syria. Although Assad indisputably has committed gross violations of human rights throughout the conflict, including the use of chemical weapons against innocent people, his enemies have been guilty of

[23] Matt Broomfield, "Pictures of Life for Turkey's 2.5 Million Syrian Refugees" (5 April 2016), available at www.independent.co.uk/news/world/europe/pictures-of-life-for-turkeys-25-million-syrian-refugees-crisis-migrant-a6969551.html.

numerous atrocities as well.[24] Thus, the Syrian civil war has not been a contest of good versus evil to which the tidy logic of a "just war" might apply, but a messy cauldron of political, religious and ideological passions undergirding a ruthless struggle for power by all parties, such as have littered the pages of human history. Any conceivable outcome will carry significant costs for human rights, peace, and economic and political order.

This observation leads to another one: the outside powers that have intervened in the conflict have not done so for humanitarian or moral reasons, but out of *realpolitik* dressed up in humanitarian motives. The United States has sought to weaken Iran's influence in the region. Russia has wanted to preserve its old and valuable alliance with an Assad-dominated Syria.

Russia's only Mediterranean naval base is located in Tartus, Syria, and it has been Syria's main arms supplier for the past sixty years.[25] In addition, the Syrian connection gives Russia a much-wanted status in the Middle East as a great power that cannot be ignored, a position that was reinforced in 2015 when President Putin decided to send Russian forces to Syria. Sunni Turkey has decided that, as a matter of its national interest and future power projection in the region, it is better off supporting the anti-Assad Sunni rebels. Saudi Arabia and Qatar see Iran as an implacable enemy and rival, and Assad's overthrow would deprive Iran of a valuable ally, while also reducing Iranian influence in Lebanon. It is undeniable that outside intervention by all these powers has prolonged the conflict, raised the levels of violence, pushed the Assad regime into ever more desperate measures to insure its survival, and increased exponentially the numbers of refugees triggered by the war. No one can deny either that these same outside powers bear major moral responsibility for the fate of the refugees, their future resettlement, and their adequate care. Had there been no outside intervention in the Syrian civil war, the established Assad government most likely would have won, the conflict would have ended much sooner, and the scale of material destruction and human suffering would have been considerably more limited. The number of displaced persons also would have been much smaller. The ensuing peace would have been harsh to the losers. But so would any peace than can be imagined in any of the different alternative scenarios involving a victory by Assad's enemies, the

[24] "World Report 2015: Syria," Human Rights Watch, available at www.hrw.org/world-report/2015/country-chapters/syria.

[25] "How Putin's Russia Props Up Assad's Military," Channel 4 News, available at www.channel4.com/news/syria-russia-weapons-arms-chemical-fighters-missiles; Matthew Bodner, "Why Russia Is Expanding Its Naval Base in Syria," *The Moscow Times* (21 September 2015), available at www.themoscowtimes.com/business/article/why-russia-is-expanding-its-syrian-naval-base/531986.html.

main difference being that the country would have emerged far less damaged had the conflict ended much sooner.

Supporters of foreign intervention in the Syrian conflict have difficulty proving that intervention has been a positive step in any form, strategic, material, or moral.

It is not difficult to posit a basic principle of moral responsibility in international politics, supported by Christian reason, according to which states that involve themselves in the internal conflicts of other states bear a significant share of moral and material responsibility for the human and material damages generated by such a conflict and its prolongation. This does not mean that intervention is always wrong or undesirable. It only means that the decision to intervene must take into its calculation the intervening power's responsibility for the consequences of that intervention, including whatever new instabilities and fresh damages result from the intervention itself. At the level of common sense, the idea was put forth colorfully by Gen. Colin Powell, then Secretary of State, when he advised President George W. Bush against invading Iraq, referring famously to the "Pottery Barn rule": "if you break it, you own it."[26] As Powell was to put it later in 2015, warning against American intervention in Syria, "if you get yourself involved – if you break a government, if you cause it to come down, by invading or other means, remember that you are now the government. You have a responsibility to take care of the people of that country."[27]

This is a sound moral and political principle, even though sadly it is widely disregarded. President Obama's exceedingly modest proposal to welcome to the United States (with 320 million people and the world's wealthiest economy) 10,000 carefully vetted Syrian refugees (out of the 4.5 million outside of Syria) was fiercely resisted by the opposition party, with a Gallup poll indicating that 60 percent of Americans sided with the Republicans on this issue.[28] Nor did the United States offer any significant financial support to help Turkey and the European Union manage the significant costs of coping with the refugee exodus. The gap between the vast scale of American resources and the absence of any willingness to provide assistance inevitably brings to mind one of the most venerated passages in the gospels:[29]

> "For I was hungry and you gave me nothing to eat; I was thirsty and you gave me nothing to drink; I was a stranger and you did not invite me in; naked and

[26] Kathy Gilsinan, "The Pottery Barn Rule: Syria Edition," *The Atlantic* (2015), available at www.theatlantic.com/international/archive/2015/09/the-pottery-barn-rule-syria-edition/408193/.

[27] Ibid.

[28] Jeffery M. Jones, "Americans Again Opposed to Taking in Refugees," Gallup (2015), available at www.gallup.com/poll/186866/americans-again-opposed-taking-refugees.aspx.

[29] Matt. 25:42–45.

> you did not clothe me; sick and in prison, and you did not visit me." Then they themselves also will answer, "Lord, when did we see you hungry, or thirsty, or a stranger, or naked, or sick, or in prison, and did not take care of you?" Then he will answer them, "Truly I say to you, to the extent that you did not do it to one of the least of these, you did not do it to me."

An equally appalling lack of moral and political responsibility has been shown by Saudi Arabia and Qatar, states that bear a major share of the blame for lengthening the conflict, and which have substantial economic resources. One of the world's largest exporters of liquefied natural gas, Qatar has a sovereign wealth fund, the Qatar Investment Authority, which in 2015 had $256 billion of assets. As of 2015, Saudi Arabia's sovereign wealth fund, SAMA Foreign Holdings, had over $750 billion in assets.[30] As of the end of 2015, Qatar also had $42 billion in foreign exchange reserves, while Saudi Arabia had $660 billion.[31] According to the IMF, the World Bank, and the CIA, in 2015 Qatar was the world's wealthiest country, as measured by GDP (PPP or purchasing power parity) per capita of $102,000–$132,000. Saudi Arabia ranked between 10th and 13th on the list, with GDP (PPP) per capita of $53,000.[32] Even though they are unwilling to accept the refugees, and most of the refugees would prefer to go to other countries, Saudi Arabia and Qatar easily could extend economic support to states willing to receive the refugees. This is not even a matter of Christian ethics. It is an issue of natural justice and basic moral responsibility for millions of people whose lives have been made more miserable by policies pursued by these two states. Puzzlingly, hardly any public commentator, or for that matter, any European political leader, has put these two wealthy Sunni states on the spot, challenging them to assist with the refugee crisis.

Another issue that needs to be addressed is the potential difficulties of assimilating large numbers of mostly Muslim refugees into Western, liberal, secular societies, at a time when there are wide divergences between the more liberal cultural and social values of the West (some of which are rooted in the Christian faith, others in the Enlightenment), especially regarding women's rights, sexuality, and notions of personal autonomy, and the prevailing values in large swaths of the Middle East, where highly conservative, traditionalist strands of Islam, Shiite and Sunni, prevail. It is reasonable to expect

30 "The World's Biggest Sovereign Wealth Funds," CNBC (2015) available at www.cnbc.com/2015/07/17/the-worlds-biggest-sovereign-wealth-funds.html?slide=3.

31 "The World Factbook," available at www.cia.gov/library/publications/the-world-factbook/rankorder/2188rank.html.

32 World Economic Outlook Database, April 2016, International Monetary Fund; "GDP per capita, PPP (current international $)," World Development Indicators Database, World Bank; GDP – per capita (PPP), The World Factbook, Central Intelligence Agency.

that anyone coming into a society, including a refugee, is under the strictest obligation to obey and respect that society's laws. Societies also have the right to expect that newcomers learn the language of the country that is welcoming them; that they understand and respect the prevailing cultural ethos even when they disagree with it; and that they seek to become active participants in its social and political life instead of isolated or hostile bystanders. Essentially, migrants as well as refugees should not be allowed into a society unless they are prepared to sign up to a social compact in which they agree to all the above conditions. It would not be appropriate to require these conditions after they have entered the country. Instead, it would make most sense to educate the would-be refugees or migrants about the social compact required of them before they enter. This could be done through special programs at holding facilities while they are in transit. The programs would make very clear to the potential newcomers the expectations of the society they are about to enter regarding its laws, customs, and ethos. The clear message would be, "you may only come if you are prepared to accept our social compact and respect our essence as a society and a culture. We require you to learn who we are, and what our values are. Your human rights will be respected, including your freedom to worship, but we expect you to be respectful of our customs and seek to make positive contributions to our society." Refugees unwilling beforehand to understand and agree to the social compact should not be allowed to enter a Western, liberal democratic society.

14.3.1 *Christianity and International Law*

As we have seen with regard to the power–security dilemma, nuclear deterrence, and transnational migration, the counsels of agape face enormous constraints in the everyday conduct of foreign policy. If love is so severely limited, could law be of help in smoothing out some of the rougher edges of international politics? In Western civilization, international law owes a large debt to Christianity for its origins and development. Francisco de Vitoria drew from Roman notions of the *ius gentium* (the law of nations), as well as Aquinas's synthesis of Aristotle and Christian faith, to sketch out the idea that the Spaniards had a legal and moral obligation to respect certain basic human rights of the indigenous peoples of the New World. Such norms transcended time, space, and even Christendom itself. Even though the indigenous peoples were not Christian or European, they could not be enslaved.[33] Building on Vitoria, and inspired by his own Christian

[33] Francisco de Vitoria, *Relecciones Teologicas Sobre los Indios y el Derecho de la Guerra* (1537–1539).

faith, Hugo Grotius developed the foundations of modern international law in his *De Iure Belli ac Pacis* (1625). Grotius is particularly relevant because he lived in the midst of Europe's vicious religious wars of the first half of the seventeenth century. The focus of his celebrated treatise was to develop commonly acceptable rules for the conduct of relations between states, both in peacetime and during military conflict, even when the warring states did not share a common religion. In his section on war, Grotius wound up developing the core of what we know as modern humanitarian law – that part of international law that attempts to regulate the conduct of military conflicts so as to reduce their inhumanity. The rules he drew up pushed hard for the distinction between what we might call today combatants and non-combatants; against excessive violence and destruction; against wanton outrages against human dignity such as rape, pillage, and the murder of civilians. His work was truly foundational, and led to the gradual building of a sturdy body of international law – the laws of war – that came to be codified in the United States' Lieber Code (1863), the Hague Conventions of 1904, and the Geneva Conventions of 1925. How successful has international law been at moderating human conflict? Even if law has failed to prevent conflicts, has it made them less inhumane?

Perhaps the clearest answer to those questions can be found in the devastating experience of World War II. All major belligerents – Germany, Japan, the United States, Great Britain, the Soviet Union – ran roughshod over the key distinction between combatants and non-combatants, and deployed military power against cities in highly indiscriminate ways that caused the destruction of millions of innocent lives. Some 28 million civilians died in the war as a consequence of military action, war crimes, and crimes against humanity.[34] The cruelty and sheer savagery against civilians displayed by Germany's campaigns in Poland and Russia are well known, as are those of Japan in its invasion and occupation of eastern China, the Philippines and Southeast Asia.[35] For their part, the Western Allies deliberately bombed German and Japanese cities with the avowed goal of "breaking the enemy's will." The idea behind strategic bombing was not simply to destroy military facilities or factories, but to cause sufficient pain and dislocation to the civilian population as to lower its morale and weaken the war effort.[36] The result was millions of German

34 "Estimated War Dead World War II," available at http://warchronicle.com/numbers/WWII/deaths.htm.

35 Gerhard Weinberg, *A World at Arms: A Global History of World War II* (New York: Cambridge University Press, 1994), 299–305, 322.

36 See Mark Selden, "A Forgotten Holocaust: US Bombing Strategy, the Destruction of Japanese Cities, and the American Way of War from World War II to Iraq," *The Asia-Pacific Journal* 5 (2 May 2007) available at http://apjjf.org/-Mark-Selden/2414/article.html.

and Japanese civilian casualties. On two different nights, Allied conventional bombing of Tokyo and Dresden respectively killed over 100,000 innocent people in each city. It is true that all belligerents abstained from resorting to the dreaded poison gas and chemical warfare, which they had agreed to ban after their use in World War I. But they observed no limits on the use of new technologies that had developed since, such as the greatly expanded air power capabilities. And at the very end of the war the United States did not hesitate to drop atomic bombs on two Japanese cities. What is significant about World War II – the most recent global conflict in which modern technology was dominant – is that the massive violations of the laws of war that took place were not isolated incidents but part and parcel of deliberate policies and military strategies approved by the wartime leaders. This amounted to the near absolute triumph of military necessity over the Christian-inspired counsels of humanity and morality laboriously threaded through the norms of international law from Vitoria and Grotius onwards.

International law's failure in the last hundred years to ameliorate war's cruelty and inhumanity has been matched by its failure to prevent wars of aggression and conflicts in which there were ample opportunities to eschew the use of force in favor of less violent means. The brutal inter-state conflicts and civil wars of the twentieth and early twenty-first centuries bear witness to this epic failure. The League of Nations (1919–39), the Kellogg–Briand Pact for the Renunciation of War (1923), the Permanent Court of International Justice (1921–49), its successor the International Court of Justice (1949–), the United Nations (1945–), and the numerous attempts since 1945 to define aggression and effectively ban it constitute a massive failure of law to prevent war. None of this is to deny the important, and exceedingly valuable, contributions that international law has made, and continues to make, to international order. It is simply to underline its colossal impotence in restraining the outbreak of numerous catastrophic conflicts over the past century.

14.4 WHAT POSSIBILITIES ARE OPEN TO CHRISTIAN FAITH IN INTERNATIONAL POLITICS?

Reinhold Niebuhr argued that the Christian ethic of love is extremely difficult to apply directly to the conduct of statecraft.[37] The best that could be expected to happen was that the Christian Love commandment might serve as inspiration to deal justly with one's adversaries and allies alike. In the realm

[37] Reinhold Niebuhr, *The Children of Light and the Children of Darkness* (Chicago: University of Chicago Press, 1953).

of politics, justice, itself quite difficult to achieve, could serve as a transmuted and more feasible version of love. Indeed, taking Niebuhr's insight as a point of departure, one could posit a series of earthly political virtues, including but not limited to justice, for which Christian love can serve as a source of inspiration and support in a broken world riddled with perpetual conflict and injustice. Some of these virtues, in fact, can be found in Aristotle's *Nicomachean Ethics*. While they fall short of Jesus' Love commandment, they do not contradict it, and represent an impressive approximation in a fallen world.

Justice. Many, though not all, international conflicts are rooted in injustice. One thinks of states that have abused their military and political strength to subject neighboring states or peoples under their rule to an unjust distribution of territory and economic resources. Justice involves giving everyone their due. The ancients believed that some people were innately superior and had the right to rule others, while some individuals were naturally inferior and deserved to be slaves. This, in turn, provided a ready-made justification for slavery and for substantial inequalities in rights. There is, of course, a different way of looking at things. One can argue that, although human beings have widely divergent levels of intellectual and other abilities, they are fundamentally equal in their claim to our common dignity and humanity. A Christian understanding of reality can enrich definitions of justice by reminding us of the essential dignity and equality of every human being and every political community on the basis of their identity as children of God sharing a common Creator. If one takes seriously the equal dignity and basic human rights of all persons, it then becomes more feasible, albeit still tremendously challenging, to grant them "their due." The logic of exploitation and domination can give way to the logic of basic fairness and equity.

Moderation. Although the Christian faith often has been the source of horrific zeal, fanaticism, and self-righteousness that have fueled bitter hatreds and international conflicts, it also can be the foundation for an existential humility that recognizes the limits to our knowledge, our fallibility, and our propensity for sin. That humility, in turn, can be the basis for, and a strong source of inspiration for, the virtue of moderation in politics. It is difficult to overrate the value of moderation. In fact, one properly can describe moderation as the indispensable political virtue. It holds us back from the common tendency to overreach and to claim for ourselves and our country more than is our due. It softens the tendency of our egos and our biased understanding to push us toward policies that overlook the legitimate interests and moral claims of others. It can put brakes on our struggle for unilateral power and security, and help us to craft political and security arrangements that satisfy both the needs of our country and those of others for power and security. It is unfortunate that in recent times moderation has lost its ancient connotation as an undisputed positive moral and political virtue. In modern-day America, as well as in many parts of Islam, moderation is often seen as supposed lack of moral clarity, as "wishy-washiness," capitulation, or weakness. Nothing could be further from the truth or more dangerous to the future of humanity than the ongoing disparagement of the virtue of moderation in politics. In an age of growing pressures on the earth's resources and environmental capacity, clashing cultures and religions, and the spread of nuclear weapons and other lethal technologies, we need more rather than less emphasis on the value of moderation.

14.4.1 *Realism*

As Reinhold Niebuhr liked to point out, of all people Christians should be freest to be realists; to have the courage to acknowledge how difficult and intractable the world's problems are, and the hope not to be overwhelmed by the ensuing natural despair.[38] Realism need not lead to nihilism, cynicism, or the shrinkage of expectations. But in a world in which sin and evil play out their political implications persistently across the span of millennia regardless of cultural, ideological, and religious differences, one must be alert to the reality of sin and evil. Human beings are capable of unfathomable depths of greed, evil, and inhumanity, and much harm has been done by well-intentioned people in positions of political power and responsibility who have overlooked or minimized this. Untold millions of lives would have been saved and unspeakable human sorrow averted had their adversaries early on taken the true measure of Adolf Hitler, Josef Stalin, Tamerlane, and Genghis Khan. Had the unsuspecting Incas surrounded, and promptly disabled and executed Pizarro and his handful of invaders in the summer of 1525 as they trekked from the Peruvian coast to Cajamarca, the subsequent holocaust and horrific enslavement of their nation never would have happened.

In international politics, it is of the foremost importance to be able to take the true measure of one's potential rivals or adversaries, even though this is an extremely difficult thing to do. It matters whether one is dealing with Otto von Bismarck or Gustav Stresemann instead of Adolf Hitler, with Marco Polo as opposed to Francisco Pizarro, with Mikhail Gorbachev rather than Joseph Stalin. The German theorist of war, Carl von Clausewitz, taught about the importance of correctly estimating the full range of the weaknesses, strengths, capabilities, and true aims of the adversary.[39] Military strategists and planners call this process "net assessment."

38 Niebuhr, *The Children of Light and the Children of Darkness.*
39 Carl von Clausewitz, *On War* (1831).

It is not a process of simply adding up the other side's forces and material advantages. It includes the far more demanding task of estimating their psychology, objectives, and something even more difficult to ascertain, their essential dependability or trustworthiness. There are no scientific formulae for doing a correct net assessment. It is easy to miscalculate or be badly off the mark. But the analysis needs to be as thorough and comprehensive, as inclusive of divergent viewpoints, and as deliberative as possible.[40] Underlying it all must be the assumption that in a sinful, broken world, anything is possible, anything can go wrong, and there are no depths of deceit and evil to which an adversary may not sink. This awareness is part of Christian realism.

14.4.2 *Prudence*

Medieval Christian writers such as Thomas Aquinas wrote of prudence as the highest political virtue. Borrowing from Aristotle, who distinguished prudence or "practical wisdom" from "theoretical" or abstract wisdom,[41] Aquinas, like Aristotle, pointed out that in the world of politics, rulers cannot translate moral ideals or visions of the good directly into reality. A series of skills or moral virtues is needed in order to achieve the best possible approximation of the ideal to the fractured world in which we live. These moral virtues or skills constitute prudence.[42]

The skills at the core of prudence are deliberation, which includes careful reflection in making a decision; the capacity to see things not as we wish to see them but as they really are; a sense of limits to human action and to one's wisdom and knowledge; foresight or the capacity to imagine and conceive of different ways in which the future may play out; caution and a serious concern for possible dangers; and a capacity for calculating the consequences of one's

[40] Michael I. Handel, *Masters of War: Classical Strategic Thought* (London: Routledge, 2000).

[41] Aristotle, *Nicomachean Ethics*, Book VI.

[42] As Aquinas stated,

> The wicked can indeed deliberate well with regard to a wrong end or to some particular benefit, yet with regard to the final good of the whole of life they are not perfectly well-advised, for they fail to carry good counsel into effect. And so they lack the prudence which is only for good . . . that is a sort of native shrewdness, which lends itself to right or wrong, or a sort of cunning which lends itself only to wrong, and this we have already referred to as false prudence, or prudence of the flesh.

Thomas Aquinas, *Summa Theologiae*, trans. Thomas Gilby, O.P. (London: Blackfriars, 1964), vol. 36, II.II.47.13. The noted Catholic philosopher Josef Pieper also expounded on this point. See Joseph Pieper, *The Four Cardinal Virtues* (Notre Dame: University of Notre Dame Press, 1966), 21.

actions. Aristotle went as far as to say that without prudence or practical wisdom a person could not be good, no matter how intellectually wise of morally well-intentioned she might be. Aquinas referred to prudence as the virtue necessary to complete and perfect morality and goodness in the political realm.[43] Although the cultivation and exercise of prudence is no guarantee against catastrophic errors in foreign policy, it can make a vital contribution toward a statecraft that connects moral ends with practical means in a sustained, creative, morally responsible way.

In earlier ages, prudence was celebrated not only as a classical virtue, but also as a Christian virtue essential to accomplishing morally positive ends in the turbulent world of self-interest, passionate attachments, and blinding ideologies characteristic of political life. In the realm of international relations and the conduct of foreign policy, prudence was considered equally essential since the issues at stake revolved around the security and even the survival of an entire political community in a world of highly competitive, often hostile adversaries.[44] A long line of statesmen, many of them self-described Christians, consciously admired and cultivated the intellectual and moral skills, habits, and traits of temperament associated with prudence. They included such diverse figures as Cardinal Richelieu, Edmund Burke, Otto von Bismarck, the Viscount Salisbury, and in the twentieth-century Konrad Adenauer, one of the key builders of postwar democratic Germany.

14.4.3 *Humility*

Following Herbert Butterfield's salutary reminder that Christianity's positive influence on the world has come in spite of the behavior of most Christians,[45] one can argue that, in an age of weapons of mass destruction, terrorism, potentially catastrophic climate change, and a population of seven billion persons, one of the most vital contributions the Christian faith can make to international politics is its emphasis on existential humility as one of the highest virtues. Like prudence, humility encompasses a strong sense of limits to our nation's power, and our own knowledge and wisdom. The very opposite of the more popular brands of exceptionalism dominant in much of American

[43] Aquinas, *Summa Theologiae*, I.II.57.4.

[44] Pierre J. Payer, "Prudence and the Principles of Natural Law: A Medieval Development," *Speculum* 54 (January 1979): 55, 68 (noting that Aristotle and Aquinas both believed that prudent leadership could establish a successful society); see also (stating that Burke promoted "moral prudence" as a method of protecting societal rights) Bruce Miroff, John Adams' Classical Conceptions of the Executive, 17 *Pres. Stud.* Q 365 (Spring 1987).

[45] See generally, Butterfield, *Christianity and History*.

foreign policy discourse today, humility embodies an awareness that, in a world created by God, it is truly blasphemous to argue that our nation and our people are inherently superior to all others. In the conduct of foreign policy, humility need not equal weakness or surrender. It is possible, as a patriot, to love one's country and consider it quite special, without also believing it to be superior to the rest. It is possible to recognize our limitations, and even our flaws, while also recognizing that, in a fallen world, we must be ready to defend ourselves vigorously against potential adversaries that otherwise might be tempted by our weakness. Humility is the radical recognition that others, including those who may see things differently than we do, may have something valuable and insightful to contribute to the ongoing conversations about the meaning of international security and peace. From the core of classical philosophy, with its Socratic understanding about the limits of human knowledge, to the Old and New Testament affirmations about human fallibility and the universality of God's judgment on all nations, humility emerges as a central political virtue essential to the Christian understanding of reality.

In closing, we come to the point at which our discussion initially began. First, it is exceedingly difficult for Christian love to influence the actual course of foreign policy in a direct way. Second, it has been equally difficult for international law – including those major norms of international law directly shaped by the Christian tradition including its counsels to moderation and humanity – to restrain the incidence and brutality of international conflict. Third, one of the ways in which the Christian faith may influence the conduct of foreign policy may be through a series of reminders it persistently issues, all of them involving the importance of cultivating some particular intellectual and moral skills, certain modes of perceiving reality, and some specific habits of conduct in the political world: justice, moderation, realism, prudence, and humility. It is far from clear that these various Christian virtues can serve as a guarantee against any and all of the egregious evils to which all peoples and their leaders are prone at different crisis points in their history. But these virtues do run against the grain, not only of American exceptionalism, but also of the obsessive and self-defeating worship of technology characteristic of our world.

Reinhold Niebuhr and some of his fellow Christian realists such as Herbert Butterfield liked to remind their contemporaries of the stark differences between the realms of politics and personal morality.[46] Although Niebuhr warned against the dangers of moral dualism, he emphasized that there were

[46] Reinhold Niebuhr, *Moral Man and Immoral Society* (Louisville: Westminster John Knox Press, 1932).

sharp differences between the two realms. In foreign policy, in particular, it is not enough for someone to be personally virtuous to be a good statesman. As Aristotle had pointed out much earlier, "theoretical wisdom" has to be translated into "practical wisdom"; good ends require practical means for their realization; and all of this calls for the cultivation of certain intellectual and moral skills and habits that are not necessarily the province of the proverbial "man of principle." In fact, for Niebuhr the "man of principle" could be dangerous and downright harmful in international politics. He much preferred policy-makers who understood that, most of the time, in the realm of foreign policy many different principles come together, competing and clashing in a cacophony of multiple, conflicting moral dilemmas and highly uncomfortable trade-offs. Niebuhr juxtaposed the moral confidence and certainty of the "man of principle" with the agony, doubt, and guarded skepticism more often seen in statesmen associated with the tradition of prudence. Filled with the ultimate hope of the Christian faith, Niebuhr nevertheless thought that the "optimists" and "just warriors" made things seem too easy.

In the end, Christian realists such as Niebuhr take us to this essay's paradoxical conclusion. In foreign policy, contemporary Christians will do best not only by reading the gospels. They also need to return to the tragic canon in the Old Testament, especially Ecclesiastes and the great prophets. And then, mindful of the sweeping scope of God's universal grace and revelation, they need to engage with the ancients and rediscover some of the classical virtues. Finally, they can do worse than acknowledge that in our current times, one of the most authentic expressions of Christian faith and humility is Christian skepticism. As Niebuhr would remind us, skepticism about our own intentions, our own rightness, and our own exceptionalism may be one of the highest forms of faithfulness as we grapple with the tragic limits of agape in international politics.

Afterword: Agape and Reframing

James Boyd White

The essays in this volume deal with the relation between agape and law from a wide range of perspectives and in the service of a variety of concerns. That is as it should be. One of the great strengths of this book is the fact that the authors represent different Christian traditions, different disciplinary predilections, different social and political concerns, and different personal styles.

The main question I address here is why it is so difficult to talk about agape and law in our world, and how that difficulty might be addressed. I shall speak, as you will see, from a generally Christian point of view, but I hope what I say will be intelligible to everyone, including people from different religious traditions

1

One reason for the difficulty I refer to is linguistic, having to do with the history and nature of the word agape itself. Agape is after all a term from another language, which, like other such words, cannot be translated into English without distortion. Even in Greek it is a term with deep and shifting meanings. Like almost all important words, in any language, it has somewhat different meanings to different speakers, and to the same speakers in different situations.In some contexts this kind of difficulty can be addressed by agreed-upon definitions, that is, by stipulating a set of words that can substitute for the problematic term, in this way creating what we might call a specialized or technical language. This is not possible with agape, in part because the

Like many of the essays in this book, this afterword was first presented as a talk at the conference on "Love and Law" that was held at Pepperdine University in 2014. This is not a scholarly essay so much as an invitation to attend to certain themes. I have accordingly retained the oral and familiar style of the original talk.

English words we would use – "love," for example – are themselves full of rich and conflicting significance, but even more importantly because what agape points toward in the world of experience is not an object or concept of some kind, but the transformation of the whole self from the marrow outward.

Even if we try, that is, we cannot just decide that from now on we will act out of agape. What the word calls for is a change in ourselves and souls, a change that cannot really be described or predicted, though it may be perceived. It is a center of mystery.

This means that as we speak about agape, in any context, each of us will be giving it definitions of our own, for better or worse, not only in the connections we establish with other terms but more substantively and performatively: in who we become as we use it, in who we ask one another to become, and in the way we talk to each other too. Whenever we talk about agape we are constantly performing and reperforming its meaning.

2

There are two other reasons for our difficulty in thinking about agape, the first of which I will not address, except indirectly. This reason has to do not with language, but with our own selfishness as human beings – those defective aspects of our own nature that resist the love of God and neighbor to which Jesus is calling us when he uses the word agape. This is a topic for another occasion.

The other source of difficulty, which has to do not with our nature but with our culture, is my main subject here. I am thinking of those active forces in our world, and therefore within each of us, that resist and hobble our efforts to think and talk about agape, let alone realize it in our lives. We might think of this problem as a set of cultural mind-sets we cannot escape.

I don't mean to suggest that our culture is uniquely or especially bad, but simply that it has its own characteristic qualities, its ways of focusing and rewarding attention, and that in our case many of these work powerfully against the possibility both of understanding agape and of acting on it in a real way. It was always so, for as agape was used in the early Christian texts it was a way of working against the premises of the culture it was intended to transform – a function it still has, or should have, in our own.

In a well-known story in the Gospel of Luke (12:13–21) a man asks Jesus to make his brother give him his inheritance. Jesus refuses to do that, then uses the man as an example in talking to the crowd around him: "Beware of all sorts of greed." Then he tells a story about a rich farmer who plans to build a new barn for his bumper crop, only to learn that his soul is demanded of him that very night.

In this parable we can see that the whole side of the imaginary farmer's self that makes plans, seeks acquisitions, and hopes to maintain and increase his property – that acts out the cultural imperatives of his time – is in a single moment rendered empty and futile by the immediacy of his death. This is meant as a lesson to the original questioner, to the crowd, and to us, urging us all to focus upon the first and most important things in life, not matters of ultimate indifference.

It is important to see that Jesus's questioner is not a bad person, but caught up in the motives and values that define his society, which are so widespread and deeply rooted that they seem to him utterly natural. Of course he wants his inheritance. We would too.

What Jesus does in telling this parable and talking directly to the crowd is to reframe the moment to include what is normally left out of their, and our, ways of thinking – above all, here, the reality of death. The idea is that this reframing may make it possible for us to recognize and accept what Jesus repeatedly tells us matters most in life, which is not possessions or successes, but agape: love of God and neighbor.

In this case what is brought into the circle of attention – the fact that we will surely die, and may do so at any moment – is something that the questioner, the crowd, the farmer, and all of us in some sense "know." It is not brand-new information. What the reframing does is to make it, for the moment, not an unfelt thought but an inescapable reality. This experience in turn asks us to imagine how our lives would be different if we could keep that reality always before us.

It is true that after such reframings we slide back into normalcy, over and over; this means that our search should be not only for the experience of reframings themselves, but for ways of keeping the shifts of consciousness they produce more fully and permanently alive within us.

3

How about us? Are we culturally situated like the farmer and the man who wants his inheritance? We can certainly imagine how shocking such a reframing would be if it came to us suddenly while we were drafting a cost/benefit analysis, working on a brief, preparing a class, or feeling anxious about promotion. The force of this kind of reframing will I think always be disturbing – which is also why it is potentially transforming.

What are the particular forces at work in our culture that might be seen to call for and to resist such a reframing? There are many possible responses to such a question. My own sense is that we live in a culture that is distinctively and dominantly quantitative, competitive, and ranked, often monetized, and this fact subjects us to pressures on our minds and imaginations which it is very hard indeed to resist. Another way to put this is to say that we know something dimly in our hearts that we cannot express or even see – something that is not at all quantitative, competitive, or ranked – but we have great difficulty acting out of that knowledge.

The knowledge I mean is itself a kind of agape. We are born with a form of it, for every healthy baby comes into the world ready to give and receive love. This is the center of our affective lives, the center out of which everything is built. In babies this love is individual and particular; in grown-ups it can expand to include the love of our neighbor, based on the recognition that every human soul is of equal and infinite value.

4

In thinking of the pressures at work against agape in our own culture, we might start with the places most of us work every day. In my own case that is, or was until my retirement, a university and a law school. The question for me and my colleagues has been how our university or law school is to be imagined, thought about, and evaluated. Today it is almost impossible for academics and university leaders not to think in terms of the idiotic rankings of the *U.S. News and World Report*, not only as they give us satisfaction or dissatisfaction, but also as they shape our efforts to make our college or school "better" – not better in substantive ways, relating to a real education, but better in the sense of making us more highly ranked. "How do we rank? How do we compare with others, our peers? Are we going up or down?" These are the questions we are driven to ask, questions that all too often dominate and shape our thinking and our desires. In my experience, it is a disturbing fact that we often find ourselves actually wanting to *be* the kind of school that this news magazine ranks highly!

The real questions we should be asking are very different: "Are we doing a good job at what we are called to do, as teachers of future lawyers? Are we good teachers? Is our writing of real and permanent value? How could we be a better school with respect to our students' real education?" These are crucial questions in the definition of a law school, but in my experience it is almost impossible to think about them collectively. As soon as that conversation gets started it is drawn away by the powerful magnet of the rankings to another subject entirely. When we spend our time concerned with what others think of us we stop being concerned about what we think of ourselves.

Or think of good teaching, important to all of us: how much of what we mean by such a phrase could possibly be captured by the multiple-choice evaluations of teaching that are now such a part of university life?

If you are a teacher, think about your hopes and desires when you first began to teach. You had at one time an idea of teaching, which made teaching a worthy aim for a life – an idea of a good class, a good teacher, a good school. What has happened to those ideas and ideals? With whom do you talk about these things?

What we need is a way of talking about teaching, that is based on agape, that is on love both for our students, and for what we do as teachers: a way of talking in which we recognize our students as complex and complete human beings, with souls as well as minds; in which we respect the difficulties of their ethical and professional choices; and in which we ourselves believe in the value, to them and to the world, of the activities in which we are educating them.

We need, that is, a reframing, like the one Jesus offered the people in his parable: one that will work a transformation in the way we imagine our work, freeing us from the motives and patterns that now clutter our minds so that we can stand firmly on another kind of ground, the transformation of the self that is implied in the term agape.

5

But legal education, and education more generally – both of which seem today to be beset by practices of mechanical evaluation – are only small instances of a much larger problem. Other professions and institutions have their own versions of the "rankings" I refer to. I think much of what I have said here about the university and the law school has application throughout our culture.

Ask yourself this: based on what you hear, and what you say, what is the purpose of the nation to which many of us belong, the United States of America? What are the aims and values by which its performance is to be evaluated?

As I remember my childhood, I would have thought that the common response would have been framed in terms of democracy, self-government, the rule of law, and fundamental equality. Today I think we could be forgiven if we thought this country existed mainly to do two things: to increase something called economic "prosperity," and to dominate the world.

Putting aside the second of these, perhaps for another day, what is this thing called "prosperity"? For most of us, most of the time, it is measured quantitatively in the form of the gross national product, a process that works on certain fundamental assumptions of economic science.

One such assumption is that wealth and hence prosperity can be measured in dollars of constant or uniform value. The richest country is the one with the greatest total wealth. But we know that this assumption is simply not true. We know that the value of $10 or $100 to a poor person is vastly greater than the same amount to a rich person. We know this in part from our own experience, and in part from the story of the widow's mite, where Jesus makes plain that the widow's gift of a penny is greater than the most magnificent gift imaginable from a rich person – so long as it is less than all he has.

Here Jesus reframes the custom of treating money in the arithmetic way we normally do, and instead sees it as a human and moral reality. He recognizes that a dollar – or a copper penny – in the hands of someone who really needs it is worth much, much, more than a dollar in the hands of one who has lots of them.

For us as individuals this means something troubling, that we should look at our own bank accounts in a different way, recognizing that they misstate value: as the accounts get bigger the dollars get less valuable; as the dollars are put in the hands of people poorer than we are, they become more valuable. Jesus is telling us something of immense importance: that to distribute wealth to those who do not have it is actually to create wealth. This is part of what it means to know that every human being is of equal and infinite value.

In a sense we know these things, but can we make that knowledge real, a basis on which we can function and work? Can we reframe our understanding of the economy and find a new way to evaluate it, to shape it? Can we, that is, imagine an economics based upon what we know is true but do not allow ourselves to think about?

6

Here is a related question: what activities should be thought of as contributing to our prosperity? The kind of economic thinking that dominates our world and our minds measures only exchanges for gain. Gifts, like that of the widow, or other gifts of oneself or of time, do not count in computing economic activity. They are said to be transfers of wealth, not productions of wealth.

On the other hand, the sale of anything that is not criminal – from soft drinks loaded with corn syrup to jet-skis that pollute the water to drugs that make us dependent upon them to pornographic pictures to violent and sadistic war games to machine guns – is said to enhance our wealth.

We know this is not right. We know that in any real estimate of our prosperity we should value activities that are good in themselves but do not involve exchanges – walks in the woods, playing with children, loving our spouses, listening to music, talking with friends. These are things we value not for what we can obtain by them, but for their own sake, as aspects of a healthy and good life. We should certainly not trivialize them with labels "entertainment" or "consumption." Similarly, we should give negative value to some activities that do involve exchanges but are worth little or nothing, or do real harm.

Here too we need a reframing, a way of bringing into the center of our consciousness what we know in our hearts to be true about the nature of wealth and the value of human activities, including both those that involve exchange and those that do not. To do this, if we could, would be a form of agape, a love of our neighbor.

The treatment of the natural world – for some of us, the Creation – is another matter on which our language, our habits of thought and speech, twist and deform our imaginations. To the person who thinks in terms of the GNP the natural world really has no value at all until it is commodified in some way: a piece of it is broken off and made an article of commerce, like iron ore or salmon. Our system of thought seems often to speak as if the most successful community, the most "prosperous one," were the one that made the largest impact on the natural world, converting it as much as possible into the material of exchange.

But this would be silly. Nothing could be more plain than the fact that we depend upon the world of nature, the world we have been given, for everything in our lives, from air and water and food to shelter to the activities of the highest cultural value. A violin after all must be made of wood. An injury to the world of life that is our planet is an injury to all of us, present and future.

We need to find a way of talking about that world, the world of nature, not as a limit on economic activity as that is now envisaged, but rather as the center of economic thought of a new kind.

Would it be possible for us to reframe this situation so that we could treat the whole of the Creation as a holy organism, of which we are all parts, upon which we depend for everything? This would be a form of agape, but in another sense: a love of God as well as love of neighbor.

Notice that when we face these and similar questions, the idea of prosperity itself begins to undergo a change. Instead of a purely "economic" idea it becomes an idea of social health, of attunement, of respect for others, of an interest in meaning in life. In his talk about agape, after all, Jesus is telling us that what matters is not wealth, but who we are, as individuals and as a community – what kind of relation we have to each other and to the God from whom all good things come.

7

A final brief story: in the 1970s The Third London Airport Commission was given the task of determining where the third London airport should be located. They tried to do this by an almost unimaginably elaborate analysis of costs and benefits. They were aware that this process had limits but were confident that it would lead to the best result.

But their Report ended up a comic mess. They tried to use actual market exchanges to measure the value of costs and benefits – for example, they tried to discover how much people would pay to get to the airport more quickly, per minute – but this did not work in its own terms and could certainly not begin to take account of all the consequences. How could this method possibly determine the value of a Norman church that was to be destroyed so that a runway could be built?

In the end, the majority of the Commission wanted to locate the airport in the only green space between London and Birmingham, ostensibly basing their judgment on the cost–benefit analysis, but I think revealing in their opinion that they were really functioning out a shapeless fear – fear of what American travel agents would do if the airport were located any further from London. The dissent favored a location east of London largely on the sensible ground, utterly disregarded in the cost–benefit analysis, that this would have a hugely positive social and economic effect in rehabilitating East London. In fact the airport was never built at all.

In my view all this made a mockery of the attempt to resolve a complex social issue by a mechanistic invocation of "cost–benefit analysis."

In fact, the Report of the Commission unwittingly demonstrated the need for something else, for which perhaps the best word is judgment – judgment of the kind that lawyers in particular have to make every day, whenever they are confronted with a real situation that cannot be reduced to the formulas of a rule or system, judgments for which actual individuals are responsible, and which they should be prepared to justify in statements that do not pretend it is easy but reflect the limits of their own minds and imaginations. Here the dissent's recognition of the plight of the constantly overlooked East Londoners was such a judgment, one that reframed the whole situation and exposed the empty way in which the majority was thinking about it. This dissent was itself an act of agape.

8

So in all these ways we are subject to pressures from our culture, and from within ourselves, that keep us from thinking and talking in ways that will reflect what we know in our hearts about law school and other forms of education and all that they involve; about the marginal utility of money; about the positive value of gifts and other activities that do not involve exchanges; about the negative value of certain actual exchanges; and about the problem of complex social judgments. I could go on and on with more examples, and so could you, but I think these will do.

In all these cases I think we experience a fundamental tension: between something we dimly know or feel in our hearts to be true – something that teaches us the equal and infinite value of all human beings – and the ways in which we have learned to think and talk about the topic in question, ways that are false or incomplete or deceptive or destructive. We are thus situated very much like the man who wanted his inheritance, like the rich farmer, and like the rich men making large gifts to the temple.

How can we resist these pressures? Can we reframe our own perceptions and thoughts and feelings to recognize what it would mean to truly love our neighbor, as the word agape asks us to do? Suppose we actually thought, all the time, of every human being on the earth as of equal and infinite value?

Resisting is of course not just a matter of deciding to do it. We can certainly be mistaken when we listen to our hearts. We may find there not agape but yet another form of selfishness.

The question is rather one of orientation: do we direct our minds and attentions toward acting out the patterns of thought and feeling and action that we absorb from our culture? Or do we direct ourselves toward what we hope will be a more profound and central kind of truth – to seeing with God's eyes, not human eyes? If we could do this, what I have been calling the knowledge within our hearts could be heard as a summons or a call.

We can at least try. And we do not have to do it alone: we can do it together, listening to each other, responding, and criticizing, all in an effort to be open to the kind of basic reframing that is so clearly needed, founded on love of God and neighbor.

Part of it is just trying, keeping our energies focused on expanding the frame so that we can see and hear more clearly what emerges, and respond more deeply to it. Part of it is learning to trust our own deepest impulses, the lessons we have learned in our hearts. Part of it is learning to pay attention to the gospels, especially to the ways they show Jesus reframing the world for his interlocutors – and, I should add, to pay attention as well to the sacred texts of other traditions that work in much the same way. Part of it is learning that we cannot do it perfectly, that we will always fail, at least in part, and that we need each other. Where this would lead us we cannot say. But it is surely worth trying.

A final word of warning, specifically to university and college teachers, namely a reminder that in our profession we are subject to another set of cultural forces that need to be faced and resisted. I have in mind the cluster of conventions that define academic discourse itself – abstract, conceptual, insistently rational, ostensibly neutral. This is the discourse that is second nature to us. Good things can be done in that language, but it tends to erase or leave out much of human reality, often by reducing it to a label. The burden of what I have been saying is our task is to see to it, so far as we can, that it does not erase the reality of agape.

We need a new place to stand from which we can see ourselves and our world more truly. Let us take Jesus seriously when he locates that place in agape, that is, in love of God and our neighbor.

General Index
(for biblical citations, see Scriptural Index)

Scriptural Index

CPSIA information can be obtained
at www.ICGtesting.com
Printed in the USA
LVOW13*1837280817
546691LV00009B/151/P

9 781107 175280